The NIXON-KISSINGER YEARS

The Washington Institute for Values in Public Policy

The Washington Institute sponsors research that helps provide the information and fresh insights necessary for formulating policy in a democratic society. Founded in 1982, the Institute is an independent, non-profit educational and research organization which examines current and upcoming issues with particular attention to ethical implications.

ADDITIONAL TITLES

Vietnam: Strategy for a Stalemate
By F. Charles Parker (1989)

Stability and Strategic Defenses
Edited by Jack N. Barkenbus and Alvin M. Weinberg (1989)

Soviet Nomenklatura: A Comprehensive Roster of Soviet Civilian and Military Officials (Second edition, revised and updated)
Compiled by Albert L. Weeks (1989)

The Politics of Latin American Liberation Theology: Challenges to U.S. Public Policy
Edited by Richard L. Rubenstein and John K. Roth (1988)

Arms Control: The American Dilemma
Edited by William R. Kintner (1987)

The East Wind Subsides: Chinese Foreign Policy and the Origins of the Cultural Revolution
By Andrew Hall Wedeman (1987)

Rebuilding A Nation: Philippine Challenges and American Policy
Edited by Carl H. Landé (1987)

Human Rights in East Asia
Edited by James C. Hsiung (1986)

The
NIXON-KISSINGER YEARS

Reshaping America's Foreign Policy

RICHARD C. THORNTON

A Washington Institute Press Book

PARAGON HOUSE * NEW YORK

First edition, 1989
Published in the United States by
Paragon House Publishers
90 Fifth Avenue
New York, NY 10011
Copyright © 1989 by Richard C. Thornton

A Washington Institute Book

Library of Congress Cataloging-in-Publication Data

Thornton, Richard C.
The Nixon-Kissinger years.

"A Washington Institute Press book."
Includes bibliographical references.
1. United States—Foreign relations—1969-1974.
2. United States—Foreign relations—1974-1977.
3. Kissinger, Henry, 1923-   . 4. Nixon, Richard M.
(Richard Milhous), 1913-   . I. Title.
E855.T52   1989   327.73′009′047   89-23166
ISBN 0-88702-051-8

The paper used in this publication meets the minimum
requirements of American National Standard for Information
Sciences—Permanence of Paper for Printed Library Materials,
ANSI Z39.48-1984.

Printed and Bound in Canada

This book is dedicated to my wife Joanne and my sons Douglas and James, who make it all worthwhile.

It is not enough to remember the past. It is necessary to understand it.

Table of Contents

PART II. Detente And Transition: The Kissinger Shogunate, 1973–1976

Preface

This volume is the first of three analyzing American strategy and foreign policy during the period 1968–1988. Those to follow will treat the Carter and Reagan presidencies. My purpose is to offer an integrated, strategic approach for the analysis of one of the most complex twenty-year periods in American history. The approach includes consideration of arms control and strategic weapons, conventional power and geopolitics, and questions of oil, trade, and monetary policy. During this period the United States moved away from its traditional containment strategy and sought, as it still seeks, to construct a new global order.

By the late sixties fundamental changes in key global relationships generated by the war in Vietnam — militarily between the United States and the Soviet Union and economically between the United States and its principal allies, West Germany and Japan — had compromised containment. The growth of Soviet strategic power gradually neutralized the United States security guarantee to the Western alliance, while the shifts of Germany and Japan threatened to destroy the international order which the United States had done so much to construct after World War II.

These global changes produced a prolonged, but carefully veiled, internal debate within the American leadership which spanned four administrations and transcended party labels. A new strategy eventually emerged, incrementally but erratically, over the course of two decades as American leaders sought to maintain as favorable a position as possible in a rapidly evolving political-military-economic environment.

The debate within the United States leadership centered on the advisability of continuing but modifying containment or moving toward a new global order. Containment in this context means the forward American position on the Eurasian landmass around the periphery of the Soviet bloc — in which American power provides the essential security shield — and includes the political-military-economic relationships which sustain it.

The new global order, on the other hand, involved a gradual reshaping of America's international relationships and responsibilities to permit, and indeed to require, Germany and Japan to play greater security roles to match their expanding economic capabilities and thus to enable the United States to shift from forward and exposed containing positions to more secure ones. This, too, includes changes in political-military-economic relationships to support the new strategy.

Although the new strategy calls for the reconfiguration, and in some cases the withdrawal, of American military power from forward positions in Europe and Asia, it is by no means a retreat, nor does it represent the decline of the United States. Indeed, politically and economically, the United States is playing, and will continue to play, a greater role than ever before. Military disengagement in order to facilitate economic reengagement would more accurately describe the dynamics of the new strategy. The focus of containment was the American-Soviet adversary relationship; the focus of the new strategy is American economic competition with Germany and Japan.

Two key but much misunderstood terms require definition — strategy and policy. Strategy is the selection of both means and ends; strategic choice requires determination in the abstract of both objectives and ways to achieve them. Strategy's essence is structure — whether it is the structure of the strategic or conventional weapons balance, global or regional geopolitical balances, the trade balance, or the international monetary balance. The essence of policy, on the other hand, is a consistent, specific course of action. Thus the essential relationship is between strategy and policy, not strategy and tactics. Policy is the consistent application of specific means to achieve larger, structural ends. All diplomacy, the execution of policy, is tactics.

In each of the administrations treated in this trilogy, key issues arose containing clear and umambiguous strategic implications as to whether the specific policy under consideration would reinforce the structure of containment or move away from it toward the new order. Of course, not every policy issue would carry the same strategic implications, but a few salient examples will illustrate the point.

During the Nixon administration the central issue was the outcome in Vietnam. Would the United States maintain the fragmented structure of Indochina, supporting South Vietnam in the manner it supported South Korea, or would we withdraw from the region? The principal protagonists were President Nixon, who sought to maintain a modified containment position, and his national security adviser, Henry Kissinger, who pressed for movement toward a new order. The decision, as will be shown in this volume, was to withdraw; and withdrawal, in turn, was the first step in a larger scheme to construct a new international order. Other issues, such as arms control, exchange rate realignment, and the structure of world oil, carried similar implications.

The Carter administration pursued a very active foreign policy agenda in which the containment–new order dichotomy was marked. SALT II with the Soviet Union, normalization of relations with China, deployment of the neutron bomb and Pershing II missile in Germany, withdrawal of troops from South Korea, greater military expenditures for Japan, policy toward Iran and the Middle East—all contained the same strategic implications. Would the policy decided upon move the nation toward containment or toward a new order? The principals here were national security advisor Zbigniew Brzezinski, who argued the case for containment, and Secretary of State Cyrus Vance, who pressed for adjustment. The strategic continuity between Kissinger and Vance is apparent.

In the Reagan administration, arms control, the deployment and removal of intermediate-range nuclear weapons in Europe, divisive trade issues with Japan and Germany (including the gas pipeline crisis), and the opening to Iran, to name only a few, contained the same strategic implications. The president himself initially espoused containment against the views of his secretary of state, George Shultz, who pressed forward with the Kissinger-Vance line. The collapse of the Iran initiative seems to have brought efforts at containment to an end and settled the two–decade-long debate.

But the problem of building a new international order was complicated by more than the internal opposition of the proponents of containment. For movement toward a new order to be feasible, there was an external precondition—detente with the Soviet Union. The new order involved reconstruction of collective security structures around the Soviet periphery in connection with the repositioning of American power, but such movement in a context of unfriendly relations with Moscow would simply open the door to a Soviet advance. Detente was a necessary precondition to disengagement and the construction of a new global order.

Thus, as we shall see, much of the disagreement in each administration between the advocates of containment and those arguing for movement toward a new order centered on the question of the timing of detente and arms control with Moscow. In essence, containment advocates argued that consolidation of geopolitical positions around the Soviet periphery should occur prior to any offer of detente with the Soviet Union. Advocates of the new order, on the other hand, argued the reverse, that detente should precede the disposition of geopolitical positions around the Soviet periphery. And in each administration proponents of the new order offered Soviet leaders the same quid pro quo—trade and technology in exchange for strategic weapons and geopolitical restraint.

For most of the period under study, Soviet leaders, judging by their actions, appeared not to have understood the positive implications for the Soviet Union in the new order. Soviet strategy demonstrated a straightforward geopolitical approach based upon growing strategic and conventional weapons power. Thus, in each administration, Moscow took initial steps toward detente only to draw back and attempt to exploit what appeared to be a geopolitical opportunity arising in the context of a perceived American disengagement from containment. Most recently, under Mikhail Gorbachev, the Soviet approach appears to be changing, but only time will tell if that is in fact the case.

I would like to thank Neil Salonen, Director of the Washington Institute, for support to undertake this extensive study. I would also like to give credit to Jonathan Slevin for his careful and insightful handling of this project and to Rebecca Salonen, whose brilliant editorial skills have transformed a scholarly tome into a very readable book. Thanks also go to the students, faculty, and staff of George Washington University's Elliot School of International Affairs and Institute for Sino-Soviet Studies, where the author teaches.

Introduction

The legacy of President Lyndon B. Johnson to the administration of Richard M. Nixon was a gravely weakened American position in the four fundamental categories of global power: wealth (a severely weakened international economic position); power (the loss of strategic weapons superiority); geopolitical position (the evisceration of containment); and national will (erosion of popular consensus). In each category during the Johnson presidency the strategic indicators had turned from positive to sharply negative.

In strategic weapons, the United States fell from clear-cut superiority over the Soviet Union when President Johnson assumed office to virtual parity with Moscow as he was leaving it. Johnson's dogged effort to exhaust Hanoi in a war of attrition led instead to the weakening of the containment structure around the Soviet Union. The increasing cost of the war in Vietnam led to adoption of an expansionary monetary policy in hopes of paying for the war without affecting prosperity at home. Johnson refused to increase taxes (until 1968), cut back on "Great Society" expenditures, or call up military reserves.

The unfortunate effect of attempting to prosecute a major war without either sufficient financial resources or necessary manpower was to weaken the United States vis-à-vis its principal adversary, the Soviet Union, and to create the conditions for the rapid rise in economic power of America's two key allies—the former Axis powers, West Germany and Japan. The combined effect of war, inflation, and domestic disaffection sapped the national will and undermined the very foundations of American global preeminence.

Failure to Maintain Strategic Weapons Superiority

In a brief four years, between 1965 and 1968, President Johnson allowed the once superior United States ICBM advantage to slip badly in the face of an extensive and clearly visible Soviet missile construction program. High administration officials, especially Secretary of Defense Robert S. McNamara, argued not only that the Soviet missile buildup presented no foreseeable threat to United States missile superiority but also that the United States actually had mistakenly built too large a nuclear force.[1] In failing to maintain the United States ICBM lead President Johnson moved the nation closer toward an already predictable, even though not yet existent, counterforce inferiority and land-based missile vulnerability.

The counterforce issue centered on the evolution of the land-based ICBM into a highly accurate offensive weapons system. From its earliest stages the developmental progression of the ICBM was scientifically well understood. Improvements in range, reliability, accuracy, numbers of warheads, launchers, warhead yield, and silo survivability were all key factors which, when compared to the development of the same characteristics in Soviet systems, allowed projections of relative system strengths and vulnerabilities into the future. Together, they constituted a measuring rod by which to gauge Soviet progress.

President Johnson had allowed the launcher-to-launcher ratio to narrow through 1968 without recommencing new American launcher construction, on the grounds that the United States could always maintain its advantage through technological superiority, by improving the accuracy of its ICBMs and by MIRVing them — that is, mounting several warheads on each missile. But the problem, which could already be anticipated in the mid-sixties, was that technological superiority could only temporarily compensate for launcher parity because it was only a matter of time before the Soviet Union would develop and deploy MIRVs, and make them accurate, too.

Improvements in range, reliability, and warhead yield simply refined the offensive threat for both sides, permitting destruction of even the hardest missile silos then possible to construct. Deployment of an anti-ballistic missile defense (ABM) offered a degree of survivability for the ICBM, for Moscow lagged well behind the United States in this fledgling technology, but missile defense was deemed destabilizing in the Johnson administration's strategic weapons concepts.

The Johnson administration's theorists, under the lead of Secretary of Defense McNamara, had contrived a strategic doctrine sanctifying the decision not to maintain missile launcher superiority. This concept was known as "mutual assured destruction," or MAD. The theory postulated that once each side had sufficient power to destroy the other in a retaliatory second strike, stability would be achieved. Since the United States already possessed that capability, according to MAD, there was no need to add to the ICBM force. The theory assumed that the Soviet Union sought the same objective the United States did — a stable nuclear balance, not superiority — and that therefore once the Soviet Union reached strategic weapons parity with the United States further missile construction would be curtailed.

The trouble with the theory was that the Soviets never subscribed to it. They continued to build far more missiles than were necessary for the establishment of a stable nuclear balance. Although MAD presumed similarity of objective for the two superpowers, the problems each faced were quite different. For Washington, strategic weapons superiority was the essential undergirding of the forward American global position on and around the Eurasian landmass, commonly called "containment."

For Moscow, reduction if not elimination of the United States nuclear advantage was its principal objective, for before Soviet strategy could succeed, American strategy would have to be defeated. Improvement of Soviet strategic weapons capability to the point where it neutralized American strategic weapons power therefore dictated continued growth of missile systems beyond the level of a retaliatory second strike. Termination of the United States ICBM program simply provided added incentive for the Soviet Union to accelerate its own programs to catch up. A position of strategic weapons strength, in turn, would enable the Soviet Union to embark upon more active efforts to destroy containment and to alter the geopolitical balance according to its own design.

A second, more important factor invalidating the theory of mutual assured destruction was the evolution of missile technology itself. By the time the Soviet Union had reached essential launcher parity with the United States (in the 1968–1969 timeframe), the first of several significant changes had occurred in strategic weapons technology. When President Johnson made the decision to terminate new missile launcher construction in 1965, the state of the art of strategic weaponry was such that the manned nuclear bomber was a far more accurate weapons system than the ICBM.

At that time both land- and sea-launched ballistic missiles were "city-busters" or, in the jargon, countervalue weapons of low accuracy. Ballistic missiles still did not possess the precision guidance necessary to destroy enemy missile launchers. By 1968, however, the ICBM began to approach, and then excel, the manned nuclear bomber in delivery accuracy (while its sea-borne counterpart, the SLBM, remained a countervalue weapon until the late eighties). Indeed, accuracy combined with speed of delivery introduced a new factor into the calculation of the strategic weapons balance — the time-urgent, hard-target kill probability, or what may simply be called the "counterforce factor."

The United States was first to deploy a highly accurate ICBM, Minuteman, raising however briefly the possibility of victory in a ballistic missile exchange by means of a disarming counterforce strike. Since the Soviet Union was well over a decade behind the United States in ABM technology, with no hope of protecting its forces against such a strike, the only feasible course for Moscow was to construct more launchers than the United States had warheads. The Soviets were thus driven by the very less developed state of their ballistic missile program to seek a larger number of missile launchers than the United States possessed. This was, moreover, now a feasible goal, since the Johnson administration had placed a self-imposed limitation on the United States land-based force, and thus on its counterforce threat.

Construction of a large number of missile launchers, particularly the heavier types, contained within itself the clear possibility of not only ensuring that a fraction of the missile force would survive an American first strike, but also of providing the basis of a Soviet first-strike capability — *once problems of accuracy and MIRVing were solved in the future.* Since the Soviet Union had chosen to deploy the bulk of its strategic rocket force on land, while the United States had allocated its forces in a land, sea, and airborne "triad," the emerging danger for the United States lay in the increasing vulnerability of its relatively smaller land-based force as the Soviet Union's relatively larger time-urgent, hard-target kill capability improved.

In other words, while initially defensive, the Soviet construction of a large ICBM force held the future possibility of fairly rapidly turning the tables on the United States and allowing Moscow to gain strategic weapons superiority, because only the land-based ICBM would possess a counterforce capability for many years. The reverse, however, was not true.

For the United States, increasing ICBM accuracy (without also increasing the number of launchers) would not present a similar threat to the Soviet Union's ICBM force because the Soviet force was so large. Even MIRVing the United States launchers, which was begun in 1970, could not neutralize the Soviet threat. It increased the United States threat to the Soviet Union, but did nothing to decrease the Soviet threat to the United States, since the number of United States launchers remained the same and they were unprotected. Simply put, the theory of mutual assured destruction, based originally upon countervalue capability — the mutual destruction of cities — began to fail in the face of the growing counterforce threat — the ability to destroy the enemy's missiles.

Whether or not one assumed that the Soviet Union sought strategic weapons superiority over the United States, there was every reason to expect Moscow to develop its missile systems to the limits of their technological potential, as the United States was doing. Even a cursory analysis of Soviet missile research, development, testing, and deployment in the sixties conveyed the impression of a large, carefully thought-out program. For example, by 1968, the Soviet Union was well along in the deployment of the SS-9, a very large, "heavy" missile, which could in the future be fitted to carry multiple warheads, and the Soviets were hard at work to develop a capability to MIRV their missiles.

In 1966 the Soviets deployed 30 SS-9 missiles, tripling that figure the following year. In 1968 Moscow increased SS-9 deployment from 90 to 156 and had 72 more under construction, for a total of 228. (By 1971 they would have 308 in the heavy missile category.) The Soviets had developed and deployed a promising hard-target launcher and were well along in research and development of MIRV technology. To assume as the Johnson administration publicly did that the Soviet Union would *not* seek to perfect the technology to which it was committing extensive resources, and to believe that Moscow would ignore whatever advantages accrued to that weapons technology, was particularly short-sighted, if not politically irresponsible.

Outgoing Secretary of Defense Clark Clifford admitted what his predecessor Robert McNamara had refused to acknowledge regarding the Soviet Union's growing counterforce capability. On January

15, 1969, he said, "It is quite evident that if the Soviets achieve greater accuracy with their ICBMs, together with a MIRV capability, our land-based strategic missiles will become increasingly vulnerable to a first strike."[2] It would not be too strong to say that the Johnson administration's failure to maintain the United States strategic advantage in ICBMs, particularly in counterforce development, would be a critical factor affecting the policies of all subsequent administrations.

The Evisceration of Containment

President Johnson also presided over the disintegration of the containment structure around the periphery of the Soviet Union. This was the case in East, South, and Southeast Asia; in the Middle East, and in Europe. The central factor determining the collapse of the American position was the decision to pursue a full-scale war effort in Southeast Asia, without arranging to meet its domestic and international costs.

The cost of the Vietnam War exceeded $100 billion during the Johnson administration alone ($200 billion overall), and drove the president to select relatively low-cost and ad hoc foreign policy options in other areas to divert resources to the war effort. The need to acquire funds to sustain the military effort led to his strategic weapons decision and to such diverse foreign policy choices as the complete withdrawal of United States influence from South Asia, the abandonment of an even-handed approach in the Middle East, and the weakening of NATO through the drawdown of United States weapons stocks in Europe for use in Vietnam.

In four years of fighting, the United States had done enough in Vietnam to prevent South Vietnam's defeat but not enough to bring victory.[3] Despite the presence of over half a million troops in Vietnam (though at any one time no more than 70,000 were combat forces), when President Johnson left office no satisfactory solution was in sight. American forces never lost a major engagement with the enemy—not even during the Tet offensive of 1968, which initially and erroneously was believed to have been a serious defeat. Victory was ruled out by the decision to prosecute the war without seeking the military defeat of North Vietnam itself, or without separating North Vietnam from its suppliers. The only possible outcomes were an American defeat or a stalemate — and a stalemate would occur only if Hanoi or its suppliers became exhausted.

A long war of attrition for a democracy has a dubious prospect, at best. North Vietnam could continue to wage the war in the South at its own pace and at varying levels of combat indefinitely, before launching a major offensive, taking in some cases years to build up the necessary stocks of weapons and supplies, all of which came from outside the country, from Soviet, East European, and Chinese sources. In the meantime, Hanoi retained the initiative, keeping American and South Vietnamese forces off balance with widespread guerrilla and small-unit operations. Perhaps more important, American soldiers in the field were depicted as an alien occupation force instead of as an ally; and the longer the United States remained bogged down in what seemed to be a pointless conflict with no end in sight, the more difficult it became to stay in Vietnam because of growing and virulent anti-war sentiment at home.

In South Asia, the same cost-saving impulse led to the extraordinary policy decision to withdraw American power from the region, providing the Soviet Union with an unparalleled opportunity to manipulate the geopolitical balance on the subcontinent to its advantage.[4] Earlier, as Sino-Soviet and Sino-Indian relations had deteriorated in the late fifties, Soviet relations with India had improved markedly. In late 1960 the Soviets began to ship arms to India, spurring Delhi's military modernization program and a more aggressive border policy toward Beijing.

When sporadic border clashes between India and China erupted into full-scale conflict in October 1962, the Soviet Union, after some hesitation, took a pro-Indian position. India's humiliating defeat in the Himalayas led to a fundamental decision to accelerate the buildup of Indian military power, which under the circumstances meant an increased reliance on the Soviet Union. Although the United States had extended emergency aid to India during that crisis, Washington declined to support a major Indian military buildup in view of the United States-Pakistani relationship. The improvement of Sino-Pakistani ties that also evolved in the aftermath of the conflict left India with only the Soviet Union as a sure source of military aid.

War between India and Pakistan in 1965, just as the United States was entering the conflict in Vietnam in force, was the proximate cause for the withdrawal of American influence from the region. At the same time the conflicts — first in May over the Hindu Kush and later in September over Kashmir—presented the Soviet Union with both a problem and an opportunity to improve its geopolitical position at United States expense. As a result of the conflicts, Beijing moved to support Pakistan as a counterbalance to India, while the United States imposed an embargo on arms aid to both India and Pakistan.

Thus, Moscow's problem was how to forestall the increase in Beijing's influence in Pakistan, and its opportunity was the freedom to maneuver in Washington's absence. In the fall of 1965, as the United States was becoming heavily involved in its initial Vietnam buildup, the Soviet Union temporarily backed off from unequivocal support for India to assume the role of mediator in the Indian-Pakistani conflict, a role which became clear at the Tashkent summit later in December.

In early 1966 it appeared that the Soviet Union sought to develop a more balanced approach to the subcontinent as it offered supplies to both India and Pakistan. But appearances were deceiving. A visit to Moscow that summer by newly elected Indira Gandhi marked a major departure in the evolution of Soviet-Indian relations. Moscow agreed to undertake a billion-dollar aid program for India over the next five years, through 1971. Indira Gandhi immediately and continuously demonstrated her gratitude by assuming an increasingly hostile and antagonistic posture toward American involvement in Vietnam. Soviet promises to provide arms to Pakistan dragged on until 1968, when it was agreed to supply some $30 million in military aid. However, only a small fraction of that amount was ever delivered.

In retrospect, it is clear that the power balance between Pakistan and India began to tip in India's favor following the 1965 conflict and Washington's decision to withdraw. Between 1965 and 1970, India devoted roughly four times the amount of resources to its defense budget that Pakistan did. Combined with the Soviet billion-dollar aid program and the United States embargo, the emergence of Indian military superiority over Pakistan was a foregone conclusion.

Since the establishment of India and Pakistan as independent states in the late forties, American strategy had been to maintain an equilibrium between the two countries. In 1965 the Johnson administration, in an effort to seek economies in anticipation of the high costs of war, jettisoned that strategy, opening the door to Soviet manipulation of the region and the ascendancy of India to preeminence in South Asia, a development which would occur in the Indo-Pakistani war of 1971.

The Johnson administration's policy in the Middle East had similar adverse consequences. Perhaps more than elsewhere, American policy in the Middle East must be appreciated in both regional and global contexts. The implications of several trends were apparent within the region by early 1967. The Soviet decision of 1963 to improve Arab (primarily Egyptian, Syrian, and Iraqi) military capability versus Israel was beginning to show results, tipping the quantitative military balance against Tel Aviv.

The Soviet program, centering on the supply of late-model T54/55 tanks, artillery, interceptor aircraft, and surface-to-air missiles, came at a time when Israel's main suppliers, France and to a lesser degree West Germany, had begun to turn away from Tel Aviv in an effort to develop reliable bilateral relations with Arab oil-producing states. Britain, too, under increasing economic stress, had decided to withdraw its protective naval presence from Aden—a redeployment which was substantially completed by November 1967. The growing vacuum in the region, accentuated by the imbalance against Israel, led the Johnson administration to attempt to counterbalance Israel's growing vulnerability, initially by supplying tanks and air defense missiles to Tel Aviv and, from mid-1966 onward, taking a more active role as a supplier of military goods.

In a broader context, the Suez Canal had become increasingly important to Moscow as a supply route to Vietnam. Early in the Vietnam conflict, Soviet supplies went to North Vietnam primarily across Chinese territory by rail, and from Vladivostok by sea. But in China growing domestic strife (which would soon engulf the nation as the Great Proletarian Cultural Revolution) prompted Moscow in early 1966 to commence a buildup of its military forces on the Chinese border.[5] Both events forced a shift in the primary supply route to Hanoi.

The Cultural Revolution made shipment of supplies across Chinese territory a high-risk venture, while the buildup of Soviet forces on the Chinese border received priority over Vietnam-end goods on the Trans-Siberian railway, which at several points was still single-tracked. Supplies to North Vietnam were therefore increasingly rerouted by sea via the Odessa-Dardanelles-Suez-Indian Ocean-Malacca Straits route to Haiphong. By the spring of 1967 some two-thirds of all Soviet supplies to Hanoi were transiting the Suez Canal.

Events in Asia and the Middle East thus evolved to bring about an unusual coincidence of interests between Israel and the United States. Israel's need was to counterbalance the growing strength of the Arabs, while the Johnson administration perceived an opportunity to achieve multiple objectives. The Israeli attack on Egypt, Syria, and Jordan in the Six Day War and the closure of the Suez Canal satisfied both Tel Aviv's need to redress the military balance in the region and Washington's need to interdict the Soviet flow of arms and supplies to Vietnam. In the immediate aftermath of the conflict, the United States moved rapidly to strengthen its position in the region, compensating for Great Britain's withdrawal as well as becoming Israel's main supplier of military goods, a relationship which continues to the present.

While the United States may have satisfied some short-term deficiencies in position in the region, however, the long-term consequences of shifting from the previous policy of attempting to deal evenhandedly with Israel and the Arabs to adoption of a more one-sided policy opened the door to Moscow here, too, to consolidate a position among the radical Arabs and attempt to further polarize Middle East politics.

In Europe, the Johnson administration encouraged Bonn's *Ostpolitik* in an effort to destabilize the Warsaw Pact. Termed "building bridges" to Eastern Europe, the policy may have succeeded too well. In the summer of 1968, Moscow moved to stamp out the growing unrest among its East European satellites by striking at the state where unrest was most advanced—Czechoslovakia. The Soviet invasion of Czechoslovakia, however, brought an unanticipated reward to Washington. While the Soviet move defeated any effort to undermine the Soviet hold on the Warsaw Pact—at least at that time—it also dashed efforts in Western Europe spearheaded by Charles de Gaulle to draw closer to Moscow as a means of achieving greater independence from Washington.

The French challenge, personally led by de Gaulle, roughly coincided with the entry into office of Lyndon Johnson and ended a short time after his departure. De Gaulle's concept, expressed most clearly in early 1965, was to revitalize and unify Europe from the Atlantic to the Urals. The approach was designed to help unify Europe, on the one hand. On the other hand, detente with the Soviet Union was to emancipate the continent from perceived American domination. It was, of course, a transparent effort to undermine the global position of what de Gaulle disparagingly referred to as the hegemony of the Anglo-Saxons.

De Gaulle also objected to the Santo Domingo intervention, opposed British entry into the European Community, urged independence for Quebec, recognized the People's Republic of China, attempted to become spokesman for the third world, and took the lead in opposing American involvement in Vietnam. Central to de Gaulle's efforts to weaken the American position were the withdrawal of France from NATO's military organization and the attack on the dollar.

De Gaulle took French forces out of the NATO military command and required the removal of all allied forces from French soil, including NATO headquarters, which was shifted from Paris to Brussels. The French attack on the dollar came as confidence in United States currency began to wane with the inflationary impact of the Vietnam War. As confidence fell, several European countries, egged on demonstratively by de Gaulle, sought to convert dollars into gold as allowed under the Bretton Woods system. The "gold rush" of early 1968 caused a severe drain on United States gold reserves, for which de Gaulle took credit, even though in fact it was not caused by French policy.

Actually, the primary cause of pressure on American gold reserves at this time was the collapse of the Sterling area the year before beginning with the devaluation of the British pound in November.[6] The result was a large movement of former sterling area countries away from the pound and into dollars and gold—in most cases, first into the former and then into the latter. The pressure on the dollar, in other words, would have occurred whether or not France had attempted to play a destabilizing role. At best, de Gaulle's policy exacerbated an existing condition. A more significant challenge to American economic hegemony came not from Paris, but from Bonn and Tokyo.

The Failure to Maintain International Economic Hegemony

From the establishment of the postwar international monetary system at Bretton Woods in 1944 until 1958, the dollar played the dominant role in satisfying the demand for financing and credit for the Western world. The Bretton Woods dollar system was the cornerstone of the United States global position as it evolved after the war, helping to govern the growth of the world economy and shaping the distribution of wealth and power within it.

Throughout this period the United States played the role of the world's central banker, creating international money (credit) by increasing its liquid liabilities to the rest of the world. This enabled allied economies first to recover from the ravages of the war and then to prosper. The strong American economy seemed to allow for perennial deficits without unduly harming the nation. The fact of the matter was that the Western world was dependent upon dollar deficits for the growth of credit and for overall economic growth in general.

The creation of the European Economic Community (EEC) in 1958 was a watershed in the economic history of Western Europe. The United States welcomed the formation of the EEC because it came at a time when it appeared that the Soviet Union might be successful in undermining West European-United States ties. In the mid-fifties, Moscow had combined a brief period of missile assertiveness with an extensive economic campaign in the West, built around the export of petroleum. First Sweden and then NATO members West Germany, France, Italy, and Belgium began to contract for the purchase of Soviet oil in substantial quantities, much to the consternation of American leaders.[7]

Welcoming the integrative effects of the EEC on West European unity, the United States acted to counter the Soviet drive and to improve its position within the alliance. To counter the Soviet petroleum offensive, the United States placed a quota on its own oil imports—first voluntary in 1957, then mandatory in 1959 (until 1973)—opening up an alternative source of highly competitive, inexpensive oil. The huge quantities of petroleum which thus became available to Western Europe and Japan inaugurated a period of cheap energy that greatly assisted the economic take-off the Western allies experienced in the sixties.

From the perspective of the strategy of containment, however, the formation of the EEC was not an unmixed blessing. While it allayed anxiety regarding the immediate external Soviet threat, the EEC raised other long-term concerns. It would be only a matter of time before economic integration led to political resurgence and created a major, increasingly independent, power bloc within the Western world. That bloc would also increasingly come under the sway of a revitalized West Germany, already easily the most economically powerful state in Europe.

To shape if not to delay that evolution, the United States moved to establish as close an economic relationship as the European allies would permit. The diversion of energy sources was of course one step; another occurred in the wake of the currency convertibility decision of December 1958, which saw the dismantling of many foreign exchange controls in effect up to that time. Convertibility, of course, facilitated not only European integration, but also opened the door to heavy American investment in European industry and commerce. The idea was to bring about a high degree of monetary integration under the dollar — what de Gaulle would call "le défi américain" — and in the process bind Europe and America closer together.

Expansion of the dollar area, in turn, saw the emergence of the multinational corporation and Eurocurrency market. The growth of the multinational corporation was a convenient American means of leapfrogging the market barriers erected by the EEC to bar or restrict outside competition. The Eurocurrency market enabled the United States to run even larger payments deficits, acquire European enterprises, and finance the increased expenditures made necessary by the war in Vietnam.

Indeed, it would be the main economic thrust of the Johnson administration to finance United States deficits by expanding the international role of the dollar and attempting to draw additional countries further into the dollar area. During the sixties, Canada, the United Kingdom, West Germany, and Italy moved significantly into the dollar area.[8] Those countries were then prevailed upon to switch their dollar holdings from short-term to long-term assets, such as bonds and time deposits — or, as in the case of West Germany, to agree not to convert dollars into gold at all — to assist in the United States balance of payments position.

By 1968, the high costs of financing the war had strained the system to the point of collapse. The dollar was approaching the limits of its utility as a reserve asset. The previous year, as a result of the devaluation of the pound, sterling had merged into the dollar area, ending its reserve role. Then, in the spring of 1968, the resultant run on the dollar led to the establishment of the two-tiered system of free market and official prices for gold, effectively eliminating gold as an asset for reserve growth as well.

To provide for greater liquidity, the United States agreed to establish a scheme of Special Drawing Rights (SDRs) within the International Monetary Fund to augment gold, the dollar, and sterling as a means of providing for reserve growth and credit. In other words, it was apparent by 1968 that the disequilibria in the international monetary system reflected deeper shifts in economic power within the Western alliance, of which the foreign exchange problem was only one manifestation.

By the late sixties, West Germany and Japan in particular among the Western allies had entered into a period of rapid economic growth, while the United States economy was moving toward recession, deeply affected by the inflationary policies pursued by the Johnson administration. President Johnson had succeeded to an extent in spreading the cost of the war throughout the system. Inflation at home was inevitably translated into inflation abroad because of the central role played by the dollar in the international monetary system. Yet, even though it was ultimately debilitating, in its early stages an inflationary dollar was advantageous to the allies because it stimulated exports and generated growth.

In fact, an overvalued dollar was the basis for the economic upsurges of West Germany and Japan as well as for several other free-world countries during this period. The important point, however, is that regardless of how United States deficits and West German and Japanese surpluses were being accumulated, the result was the distention of the entire system and the weakening of the American global position, even as individual allies within that system paradoxically became wealthier. By the end of 1968 the nature of the problem had changed. It was no longer simply a question of financing Washington's deficits; now the need was to restore the United States global economic position.

Strategic Failure of the Johnson Administration

In strategic terms, the Johnson administration was badly outmaneuvered by both the Soviet Union and America's own allies. The central problem driving the selection of policies was clearly the need to meet the financial exigencies of the war in Vietnam. Its end result was the failure to maintain American superiority in strategic weapons, erosion of the integrity of the containment structure versus the Soviet Union, and the loss of cohesion of the international economic system, the bedrock of American hegemony in the post–World War II era.

Indeed, while the United States was mired in Vietnam, as great a shift occurred between the United States and its allies—Germany and Japan—in the economic sphere as occurred between the United

States and the Soviet Union in the strategic weapons realm. The only positive development of this period for the United States was one which the Johnson administration did little or nothing to bring about. This was the Sino-Soviet split. By the late sixties, as the Sino-Soviet conflict deepened beyond any immediate possibility of repair, the prospects for a positive turn in United States-China relations began to emerge. This is the point of departure for the study which follows.

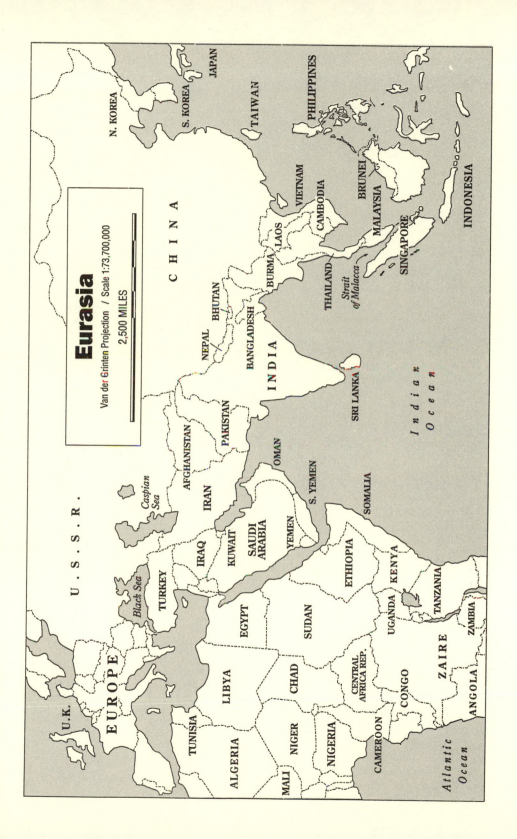

Eurasia

Van der Grinten Projection / Scale 1:73,700,000

2,500 MILES

PART I

The
Crisis of Containment:
1969–1972

CHAPTER

1

President Nixon and the Shift to Modified Containment, 1969–1970

The deterioration of the strategic, geopolitical, and economic positions brought about primarily by involvement in Vietnam combined to produce a crisis of strategy for the United States. The slippage of position with regard to ally and adversary alike raised the fundamental question of whether the global order which the United States had done so much to fashion after World War II and from which it had benefited so handsomely could be maintained and the American position of dominance within it restored. Or would the nation's strength be eclipsed from without by the growth in Soviet military power and eroded from within by the growth of allied economic power?

Of major importance was the relative shift in the strategic and conventional weapons balance in favor of the Soviet Union which, if not countered, would eventually put Moscow in position to dominate the entire Eurasian landmass. The sheer quantitative growth of Soviet military power was producing a qualitative change in political relations between Moscow and its neighbors. The United States could not hope to match the Soviet buildup with a commensurate one — even assuming that the U.S. Congress would commit sufficient resources to attempt it.

The growth in Soviet power and advantage meant that the United

States would be progressively less able to provide a credible deterrent and therefore less able to maintain the global position based on it. The Soviets could be expected to utilize their growing advantage by mounting pressure to edge the United States from its forward positions on the Eurasian landmass, country by country, region by region, as time, need, and opportunity allowed. It was this fundamental change of relationships that raised the issue of the continued viability of the containment strategy.

Richard Nixon had concluded that while containment could no longer be maintained in its pristine form, neither could it be abandoned altogether. His choice was to shift to a modified containment strategy, a choice implicit in his proclaimed objective of forging a "stable structure of peace."[1] The president's strategy would be to delay, offset, and if possible reverse the growth of Soviet power, while reordering the political relationships among the nations in the hemisphere so as to promote their continued reliance upon the United States and opposition to the Soviet Union.

During the first term Nixon's principal objective was to build on, to the extent possible, the adversary relationship which had developed quite independently of any American design between the Soviet Union and the People's Republic of China, while simultaneously constructing defensible positions of strength against Soviet expansion. The United States would attempt to facilitate a long-term Sino-Soviet confrontation by easing difficulties each faced in their respective rear areas.

In this conception, Europe was the rear area for the Soviet Union, and initial American policy was designed to foster the resolution of outstanding issues among the United States, Western Europe, and the Soviet Union. Negotiations on Berlin, the West German-Soviet friendship treaty, and a European security conference, for example, were all pointed toward the alleviation of pressure on the Soviet Union's western, or European, flank, permitting allocation of greater resources eastward toward China.

For the People's Republic of China the principal rear area was, of course, Southeast Asia. Here, Vietnamization and strong opposition to any suggestion of a Soviet nuclear strike against Beijing created the basis for rapprochement with China at an early date and normalization of relations at a later date. Initially, withdrawals of American forces from Vietnam permitted the reallocation of Chinese men and materiel northward to counter the large Soviet border buildup and encouraged Beijing's leadership to cooperate with the United States in the resolution of the conflict on mutually satisfactory terms.

Reducing pressures on the rear areas of both the Soviet Union and the People's Republic of China was also linked to the effort to build positions of strength around the Soviet periphery—modified containment—in Europe, the Middle East, Southwest and Southeast Asia, and the Far East. Fundamentally different conditions within each region, specifically the quality of United States relations with individual countries, the state of play as it were, would determine the application and timing of the president's strategy.

Assessment and Response: First Steps

At the strategic weapons level, President Nixon assumed office at an historic moment when the momentum of the Soviet Union's arms buildup would for the first time carry Moscow to the numerical lead in the deployment of land-based intercontinental ballistic missiles. Much would yet have to occur in the nature of qualitative improvements before the Soviet Union would be in a position to mount a credible first-strike threat against the United States. Nevertheless, the day when the Soviet Union would achieve this capability was more clearly visible than ever before, and delaying the emergence of this threat lay at the center of the president's strategic arms calculations.

The growing Soviet missile force did not yet present the United States with a direct homeland threat, but it would soon counterpose and to an increasing extent neutralize United States ability to project strategic power to areas of interest and concern, particularly on the Eurasian landmass, in support of friends and allies. Growing Soviet strategic power would soon enable Moscow to play a much more forceful role than hitherto in probing the containment structure. A fundamental assumption underlying and giving urgency to President Nixon's foreign policy formulation and execution therefore was the expectation that at some point Soviet leaders would attempt to translate strategic weapons power into geopolitical gain.

The basic dual thrust of President Nixon's policies was to shift the point of Soviet challenge as far forward in time as possible through qualitative improvements to American strategic systems, while simultaneously moving to consolidate United States global positions which could be expected to come under attack. The consolidation effort would involve extrication of the nation from the debilitating conflict in Vietnam in as honorable a manner as possible, reinforcement of positions of strength around the Soviet periphery, and the revitalization of the central American role within the Western alliance. Needless to say, these would be formidable tasks, and the United States would encounter tenacious resistance from every quarter.

Aside from the general question of how to handle Moscow's growing strategic weapons power, the foreign policy problems were legion. The conflict in Vietnam was the immediate difficulty on which action was necessary, yet it was also the most intractable. Over half a million American troops were engaged in a major war which had no clearly stated purpose or reasonable expectation of successful conclusion and which severely drained the resources of the nation. The president's minimum objective was to settle the conflict and extricate American forces. But, as luck would have it, the evolution of the Sino-Soviet conflict to the point of open hostilities in early 1969 offered the prospect of much more.

As war between Moscow and Beijing loomed from late 1968, Mao Zedong decided to signal Chinese willingness to improve relations with the United States in hopes of counterbalancing growing Soviet pressure. The Sino-Soviet conflict not only raised the possibility of improving relations with China, but of parlaying an improvement in relations with China into a settlement of the Vietnam war on mutually acceptable terms. The shift of China into the Western camp, in turn, would transform the structure of global politics. Thus, while the Vietnam War was the president's most pressing problem, it also offered his most promising opportunity—if properly managed.

Elsewhere, the prospects were grimmer and unrelieved by potential gains. In South Asia, the balance had already tipped irretrievably against Pakistan in favor of India, with little hope of restoring equilibrium. The administration's only hope here was to delay the inevitable for as long as possible and to minimize the damage when the crisis did come. But come it would as a result of the Soviet-Indian de facto alliance and the earlier withdrawal of the United States from the region. The stage was set for an Indian move to dismember Pakistan, once the opportunity arose.

The situation in the Middle East was not much better. If access to the region's petroleum resources was to be preserved, some form of collective security apparatus would have to be constructed—if only to replace the departing British—to withstand the Soviet-supported radical Arab efforts to destroy Israel. That would not be easy. The Johnson administration's shift to one-sided support of Israel had alienated the moderate Arab regimes and pushed them closer to the radicals while opening the door to Soviet manipulation of the geopolitical balance in this region as well. The Nixon administration's initial approach would be to attempt to develop a more balanced position—an "even-handed" position, it was termed—and to take steps which would lead to a negotiated settlement between Israel and Egypt, the core of any stable collective security arrangement.

Problems with the allies were of a different order. The growth of free world economic power combined with relative economic stagnation in the United States had literally transformed alliance economic relations. The growing strength of the West German deutschemark in the European Economic Community and the Japanese yen in the Pacific raised concern that the Bretton Woods monetary system forged at the end of World War II with the United States dollar as its centerpiece would be eclipsed by the emergence of separate currency blocs. Dissolution and transformation of the international monetary system would inevitably affect the political order that it underpinned, much to the disadvantage of the United States. Indeed, as one National Security Council report put it in 1970 forecasting long-term EEC economic prospects,

> In the long run we could be confronted by an "expanded Europe" comprising a Common Market of at least ten full members, associated memberships for the EFTA [European Free Trade Area] neutrals, and preferential trade arrangements with at least the Mediterranean and most of Africa. This bloc will account for about half of world trade, compared with our 15%; it will hold monetary reserves approaching twice our own; and it will even be able to outvote us constantly in the international economic organizations.[2]

Politically, former President Johnson's policy of encouraging East-West ties in Europe, the "building bridges" approach, had had mixed results. The Soviet crackdown in Czechoslovakia in 1968 not only reinforced the Soviet position in Eastern Europe but also accelerated trends already under way in Western Europe for accommodation with Moscow. European security, prosperity, and unity were old themes in continental intellectual circles dating back to the war, but the opportunity to pursue them had never before been realistic.

Now, as a result of the tremendous growth in European economic strength and the change in the United States-Soviet strategic balance, the idea of a unified Western Europe had taken on a new vitality. In some American circles European unity was viewed positively as a development which would strengthen the alliance. The evidence was not encouraging. Nixon administration officials were concerned that European unity would lead in the opposite direction, furthering the disintegration of the Atlantic alliance and the appearance of a Western Europe independent in world and economic affairs — a development that was decidedly not in American interests.

Relations with Japan presented a similar picture. Japanese economic strength had also increased dramatically in the previous decade. In terms of 1973 dollars, for example, Japan's gross national product in 1959 was 35.9 billion. By 1966 it had surpassed 100 billion. In 1968 it climbed to 143.1 billion and in 1970 reached 197.4 billion, and there was no sense that Japanese growth was reaching its natural limits.[3] By the same measure, United States gross national product grew from $486.5 billion in 1959 to $730.0 in 1966 and to $982.4 billion in 1970. The change in the *relative* size of the Japanese and American economies was staggering. Japan's GNP had increased by a factor greater than five over the decade, while the United States GNP had increased by a factor of less than two.

The growth in the West German GNP in comparison with the United States was equally impressive. In 1959 the West German GNP was 60.0 billion dollars; in 1966 it was 122.7 billion, in 1968 135.3 billion, and in 1970 it had grown to 188.0 billion. In less than

United States, West German, and Japanese trade surpluses (in billions of U.S. dollars)

Year	United States	West Germany	Japan	West Germany and Japan
1966	3.8	2.9	2.2	5.1
1967	3.8	5.2	1.1	6.3
1968	.63	5.6	2.5	8.1
1969	.60	5.1	3.6	8.7
1970	2.6	5.6	3.9	9.5

a dozen years, between 1959 and 1970, the West German GNP had more than tripled, and the Japanese GNP had expanded by a factor greater than six. Of particular concern was the shift in relative trade positions that was occurring between the United States and its two rapidly growing allies. Until 1966 West German trade surpluses were seldom more than one-third those of the United States; Japan was frequently in deficit until 1962 and actually did not begin to have consistent surpluses until 1964. But from 1966 onward, the combined trade surpluses of West Germany and Japan exceeded that of the United States, growing larger each year.

The United States had been urging West German and Japanese currency reevaluation as well as trade policy revisions to increase the cost of their exports relative to those of the United States and to assist in reaching an equitable trade and monetary equilibrium. Neither country was willing to reduce its advantage, although Bonn revalued its currency by 10 percent in 1969, an amount wholly inadequate to rectify the existing disparity. From the incoming Nixon administration's perspective and analyses, the foreseeable trends were for the continued growth of West German and Japanese economic power and the continued decline in the American share of the world product.

The problem for President Nixon, therefore, was how to forestall the disintegrating tendencies in the Western alliance represented by the rapid economic growth of the allies, especially West Germany and Japan, and to restore and preserve the dominant position of the United States. The initial approach was to enter into negotiations with West Germany, Japan, and the European Economic Community on political and economic matters in the hope of resolving diplomatically the difficulties confronting the administration. Politically, the Nixon administration hailed European efforts to promote greater unification, negotiated the four-power treaty regarding the status of Berlin, and concluded negotiations for the return of Okinawa to Japan, but parallel efforts to resolve outstanding trade and currency questions led nowhere.[4]

The Ideal and the Real

Proclaiming an "era of negotiation" upon entering office, President Nixon sought through diplomatic negotiation to curb the growth of

Soviet strategic power, settle the conflict in Vietnam, shore up the crumbling containment structure, and reestablish a healthy international economic and monetary environment. The much publicized five-part global order comprising the United States, the Soviet Union, Europe, China, and Japan reflected this approach.

It was obvious that the United States and the Soviet Union dwarfed the others in terms of pure military power, that China was neither a military nor an economic giant, that Europe was politically divided and Japan practically defenseless militarily though powerful economically. Nevertheless, there was purpose in establishing the concept of a five-part global order in which all five shared some presumed interest in a relatively stable equilibrium. It implied that the United States sought no special increase in advantage. Raising the Soviet Union to the level of superpower equal to the United States carried the same implication.

Such was the American public posture; reality was quite different. The shift in the strategic balance marked by the growth in Soviet military power at both the strategic and conventional levels inevitably foreshadowed a period of great instability as the Soviet Union sought to alter the geopolitical balance as far as its power would permit. It would have been politically irresponsible for the president to assume otherwise.

Furthermore, because of the anticipated Soviet challenge, the United States would have to become active to parry Moscow's thrusts. All this in an increasingly volatile world could easily lead to major confrontation — even war. The concept of the five-part global order therefore was designed primarily to facilitate change at the lowest possible level of conflict and thereby above all to avoid superpower confrontation, even while establishing a context for conflict management at lower levels.

The war in Vietnam was the president's most immediate problem, but shortly after the inauguration, it became his most challenging opportunity. The opportunity lay in the outbreak of open warfare between Soviet and Chinese forces along their common border and in this event's relationship to the conflict in Vietnam. Both Washington and Beijing faced the question of how to deal with growing Soviet power. For President Nixon the problem was how to counter Soviet strategic power and buttress the crumbling containment structure — both of which would take time.

Mao Zedong's needs, on the other hand, were more immediate. The

Soviet military buildup along the Chinese border had reached significant proportions by the spring of 1968 — between forty-five and fifty divisions depending upon how broadly one defined the term "border."[5] At that point, Mao had begun to terminate the Great Proletarian Cultural Revolution which had been wracking the country since 1965 and to reinforce China's northern defenses for what now appeared to be an impending showdown with the Soviet Union.

At the same time, on China's southern border in Indochina, the 1968 Tet offensive brought about a major increase in American troop strength in South Vietnam, to an authorized level of 549,500 men. In other words, Mao was faced with a major confrontation on the northern border with the Soviet Union and the possibility of the same on the southern border, if the United States were tempted to invade North Vietnam while Soviet and Chinese forces fought. In the event, caught in the tightening vise of a two-front conflict situation, Mao sought to extricate China from it by neutralizing the southern front.

From the beginning of its major troop deployment into South Vietnam, Washington conveyed assurances to the Chinese that American forces would not invade North Vietnam. The policy of graduated escalation was, in part, designed to reinforce this assurance. Still, Beijing was forced to construct its defenses on the basis of likely contingencies, not professions of good faith on the part of one of its major enemies. Accordingly, Beijing's major defensive deployments were along the northern border with the Soviet Union, the southern border with Vietnam, and China's east coast across from Taiwan.[6]

When the Tet offensive produced a public United States decision to negotiate rather than retaliate, fundamental signals were conveyed to both Beijing and Moscow that the United States would begin to move toward a settlement of the conflict one way or another. In November of 1968 — after the presidential election — Beijing indicated interest in exploring American attitudes further, requesting the resumption of the Warsaw talks which the Chinese had broken off six months earlier. Moscow, on the other hand, fully alert to the possibility of a Sino-American rapprochement, hastened preparations to deter it even if it required the use of force. In other words, by the time that Richard Nixon became president the basis for a coincidence of interest between China and the United States was already in embryonic existence. The question was, could the new president bring it to fruition?

The importance of China to the war in Vietnam was impossible to overestimate. Chinese territory constituted a secure and invulnerable logistical base in itself and, more importantly, a safe if not always secure railroad corridor for the transit of Soviet supplies to Hanoi. Including the Chinese corridor, there were but three logistical routes into North Vietnam by which to fuel Hanoi's war effort. The other two were by sea to Haiphong and Sihanoukville (Cambodia), both highly vulnerable to United States interdiction.

Between 1965 and 1968, despite the fact that Sino-Soviet relations worsened precipitiously and the Cultural Revolution periodically disrupted the flow of Soviet materiel across Chinese territory, the Chinese corridor was a critical supply route for the Vietnamese war effort. During this period Soviet and Chinese materiel shipments were roughly of equal quantity and significance as both communist powers sought to exert influence on Hanoi's conduct of the war. Moscow also sought to use support for Hanoi as a means of exerting leverage for reconciliation with Beijing.

The threat of armed conflict with the Soviet Union combined with the beginning of United States negotiations with Hanoi altered the equation for Mao Zedong. It now became manifestly in China's interest to improve relations with Washington—from the perspectives both of countering the Soviet threat and of resolving the Vietnam conflict on satisfactory terms. An improvement in relations would have both immediate and long-term benefits. Neutralizing the danger in the South, Beijing could redeploy its forces northward to meet the immediate Soviet threat.

In the longer term, relations with Washington would also serve Beijing's strategy in the whole of Indochina. Since 1954, when the Geneva conference restructured Indochina by dividing Vietnam in half and establishing neutral status for Laos and Cambodia, Beijing's strategy had displayed a remarkable consistency. Beijing sought to maintain the fragmented structure of Indochina to forestall the emergence of a major threat to its southern front. Even during the period of United States combat escalation, Beijing's policy was to support North Vietnam sufficiently to prevent defeat, but not enough to bring victory.

American strategy toward the region was similar. During the conflict Washington had done enough to prevent Saigon's defeat, but not enough to defeat Hanoi, which would have required an invasion of North Vietnam. The graduated United States war-fighting policy suggested that Washington too sought to maintain the fragmented structure of Geneva. Thus, from Beijing's point of view, American policy suggested that the basis for a coincidence of interest existed between itself and Washington.

The Soviet leadership was acutely conscious of the possibility that China and the United States would attempt to counter growing Soviet strength through a rapprochement. In the hope of forestalling that possibility, Soviet leaders moved early to employ carrot-and-stick methods toward each power. Moscow offered to cooperate with Washington on troublesome problems while generating renewed North Vietnamese military pressure against Saigon. Perhaps hoping to neutralize the Nixon leadership before the incoming administration got its bearings, on December 30, 1968, Moscow sent a formal note to the United States government suggesting cooperation on the Middle East and Vietnam. The president replied noncommittally on January 15, indicating that the new leadership would first need to conduct a full policy review.[7]

Then, on February 17, Soviet ambassador Anatoly Dobrynin, making his first formal call on President Nixon, delivered another note offering Soviet cooperation on a whole range of subjects, including Vietnam, the Middle East, Berlin, and strategic arms. The president again demurred, stressing "linkage," but agreed to establish a private communications channel between the Soviet ambassador and his national security adviser, Henry Kissinger.[8] A few days later, on the twenty-second, North Vietnam resumed military action in the South with a sharp, sustained offensive, the first since the abortive Tet offensive of the previous year. It was an abrasive answer to the discreet inquiries that the president had been making to Hanoi regarding a negotiated settlement of the conflict.

Moscow applied the same carrot-and-stick tactic to Beijing, but with heavier emphasis on the stick. While offering talks (a formal note was sent on March 29)[9], the Soviet Union generated intense military pressure along the Chinese border. Border tension had increased during the latter months of 1968 as reinforced Soviet military units conducted maneuvers, amid Chinese protests and counterpreparations.[10] On March 2 Chinese forces shelled a small Soviet unit on Damansky (Zhen Bao) Island in the Ussuri River on the Manchurian border,[11] marking the beginning of what would escalate into a protracted, six-month-long crisis between the two countries.

It seems clear that Chinese forces initiated this first clash, which was a small-scale spoiling action intended to disrupt the Soviet buildup on the island.[12] However, Moscow so enlarged the scope and scale of the action that it threatened to break out into full-scale war. Soviet forces initiated large-scale actions along the Manchurian border on March 14 and 15, May 12 through 15, 25, and 28, and in the west along the Sinkiang border on April 16 and 25, May 2 and 20, June 10, and August 13.[13] Moscow also augmented forces in Outer Mongolia. If the Soviet leadership hoped that these pressure tactics would intimidate or inhibit the Chinese from moving toward the United States, they would quickly be disappointed.

The North Vietnamese offensive against United States forces in South Vietnam and Soviet military pressure against the Chinese formed the crucible in which the first links were forged between Washington and Beijing. President Nixon's response to the Vietnamese attacks, which he interpreted as "a deliberate test, clearly designed to take the measure of me and my administration at the outset," was to authorize the bombing of Hanoi's border sanctuary areas in what was formally neutral Cambodia.[14] Acting with deliberation, the president himself ordered the first strike on March 16 after it had become plain that the Chinese were already delaying Soviet materiel shipments across their territory.[15]

In fact, Soviet military provocations gave Mao Zedong the excuse to do on a large scale what he had already begun to do on a small scale, which was to reduce the volume of Soviet supplies traversing the Chinese rail system to North Vietnam. After the March 2 clash the Chinese "halted all Soviet shipments to North Vietnam at the frontier."[16] On April 27, the Soviets charged that, where it had only taken ten to twenty minutes in the past for Soviet trains bound for North Vietnam to cross the border, Chinese officials were delaying trains for "weeks and sometimes months." One train, it was claimed, was kept three months and another was sent back in March. The Soviet report pinpointed the beginning of the slowdown to late January and made clear that it was deliberate policy by Beijing.[17]

Reduction of the Soviet supply effort and bombing of the Cambodian sanctuaries had an almost immediate impact on Hanoi's military operations. The level of fighting declined markedly over the next several weeks as did the rate of troop infiltration into South Vietnam. The Chinese decision to close off the invulnerable supply route into Vietnam was without exaggeration a crucial first step to what followed. It enabled the United States to conduct a successful withdrawal from South Vietnam and at the same time parlay a mutually acceptable Vietnam settlement into a long-term relationship with the People's Republic of China.

Since a satisfactory Vietnam settlement was the centerpiece of President Nixon's foreign policy, he would make no substantive movement in United States-Soviet relations until the key pieces were in place with respect to China and Vietnam. Even though he would enter into negotiations on two of the most important issues, the Middle East and strategic arms talks, there would be no progress in either area until the president was reasonably certain he would attain his objectives in Vietnam. To have agreed with Moscow, for example, to begin the strategic arms negotiations immediately upon taking office and before making the China connection would have signaled to Beijing that the United States and the Soviet Union were going to collude at China's expense. The same was true for the Middle East because of the logistical relationship to the Vietnam conflict. Thus, President Nixon's course was to put Moscow off pending completion of a full review of the issues.

United States Strategy in Practice, the China Connection

The exact date when President Nixon established a working understanding with Beijing is unclear, but the general time frame within which it occurred can be inferred. Although the president had made clear his intention of establishing contact with Beijing from the beginning, a working understanding was most probably reached with Beijing sometime after the president's May 14 peace proposal to Hanoi and before his message to Moscow of May 28 indicating that the United States was ready to begin discussion of Middle East matters.

The president's initial substantive signal to Beijing (aside from public remarks and comments made to foreign leaders, like French President Charles de Gaulle) came during a news conference on March 14, which was held against the backdrop of Moscow's heavy retaliation against Chinese forces in Manchuria for the March 2 incident. His signal was embedded in criteria established for determining the rate of American troop withdrawals from Vietnam. These criteria were the state of the Paris peace talks, the rate of Vietnamization, and the level of enemy combat activity. The Paris talks were stalemated, and it would be some time before the Vietnamization process would show results; but the remark about the level of enemy combat activity was directed to Mao and his indicated willingness to continue to slow down Soviet supplies to Vietnam.

Before any further signaling could occur, however, on April 14 a North Korean jet downed an unarmed navy EC-121 electronic reconnaissance plane. The American aircraft was conducting routine patrols well off the North Korean coast (some ninety miles) when it was attacked. All thirty-one crew members aboard were killed. Despite some intelligence suggesting that Pyongyang had made a mistake, the president believed that this time, too, "we were being tested," by what he termed "a calculated and cold-blooded challenge."[18]

Despite Kissinger's insistence that the United States conduct a bombing raid against North Korea and Nixon's initial inclination to meet force with force, the president's cooler instincts prevailed—particularly as Secretary of State William P. Rogers and Secretary of Defense Melvin Laird urged restraint.[19] The president decided not to risk action which could draw the United States into armed conflict against North Korea at a time when American forces were so heavily involved in Vietnam. United States military action in close proximity to China's northeastern and southeastern frontiers would clearly work against any possibility of rapprochement with Beijing.

President Nixon appears to have made four related decisions as part of his response to the EC-121 incident. First, he ordered the resumption of reconnaissance flights, but with armed escorts. Second, he made a show of force to Pyongyang by sending a large naval task force, Task Force 71, consisting of twenty-nine ships and four aircraft carriers, into the Sea of Japan. Task Force 71 would actually grow to forty ships before being withdrawn on April 26. Third, rather than retaliate with force against North Korea, he ordered a "second round" of bombing of North Vietnamese sanctuaries *in Cambodia!*[20]

Finally, the president publicly exonerated the Soviet Union from any direct responsibility. After all, there was little point in exacerbating relations with the Soviets over what was a relatively minor event. There were larger issues involved. At the same time, the president subtly indicated that he believed the Soviets were implicated in the incident. His "message" to Moscow came during his news conference on April 18 when he announced the decisions to resume patrols and send a naval task force. Demonstrating that the EC-121 had been in international airspace when attacked, the president said: "There was no uncertainty whatever as to where this plane was, because we know what their [North Korea's] radar showed. We incidentally know what the Russian radar showed. And all three radars [including the U.S.] showed exactly the same thing."[21]

The president certainly understood that by revealing American intelligence capability he would impair it, at least for a time.[22] Why had he done it? What Nixon had not said was important here. The president had not mentioned Chinese radar, which he knew also monitored the area. By omitting any mention of Chinese monitoring capability was the president attempting to send still another friendly signal to Beijing? At the very least, he chose to highlight American intelligence capability, superior to that of Moscow and not to embarrass the Chinese.

At any rate, President Nixon's second signal to Beijing, a discreet proposal backed by a subtle threat, came once again during heavy fighting on the Manchurian border in mid-May. Fighting had broken out on May 12 at Hu Ma on the Ussuri River and continued until the fifteenth. On May 14, in a television address, the president proposed an eight-point program to reestablish the status quo ante bellum according to the Geneva agreements of 1954.[23] Ruling out both the imposition of a "purely military solution," which implied an invasion of the North, and of a "disguised defeat" inherent in a unilateral withdrawal, the heart of President Nixon's proposal was the mutual withdrawal of all non-South Vietnamese forces from South Vietnam over a twelve-month period. Both the withdrawal and subsequent free elections would be supervised by an international supervisory body.

Even though mutual withdrawal was a change from former President Johnson's 1966 Manila formula of North Vietnamese withdrawal first, followed by United States withdrawal, the president expected little progress on the negotiating front. Nixon had already reconciled himself to the fact that Hanoi would not agree to any mutual withdrawal scheme. As Kissinger noted, the president "did not believe that negotiations would amount to anything until the military situation changed fundamentally. He thought Hanoi would accept a compromise only if it had no other choice. On the whole, he favored a policy of maximum pressure; he was not too eager for negotiations until some military progress had been made."[24] His offer, therefore, was directed to a different audience — in Beijing.

If spurned, the subtle threat was a unilateral settlement based on the Vietnamization program, which, the president asserted, had been "speeded up. . . . The time is approaching when South Vietnamese forces will be able to take over some of the fighting fronts now being manned by Americans."[25] In effect, the president was asking for Mao Zedong's concurrence to cooperate in the reestablishment of the 1954 political structure of Indochina, which after all was also the preferred solution from the Chinese leader's point of view. The failure to cooperate would mean loss of the opportunity to gain American support for China against the Soviet Union and any hope of ensuring that China's interests in Indochina would be served.

Following the May 14 speech, the president instructed Secretary of State Rogers to establish a secret channel of communication to Beijing through Pakistan.[26] Whether or not it was through this particular avenue or some other, sometime in late May 1969 the Chinese appear to have conveyed to President Nixon their willingness to cooperate on a resolution of the conflict in Vietnam. Establishment of the China connection would best explain the president's sudden readiness to move forward with regard to troop withdrawals from Vietnam and negotiations with Moscow, despite the continued adamant stand of Hanoi against any negotiated settlement.

First, Nixon sent a note to Moscow on May 26 communicating his readiness to begin discussions on the Middle East.[27] Second, after a hastily arranged meeting with South Vietnamese President Nguyen Van Thieu on June 8 at Midway Island, President Nixon announced the withdrawal of the first 25,000-man contingent of American combat troops from Vietnam.[28] The Paris peace talks were still stalemated and Vietnamization had only just gotten under way. The president's decision was obviously related to the reduction of enemy activity. Three days later, on June 11, Nixon informed the Kremlin that Washington was now also ready to commence strategic arms limitation talks.[29]

With the China connection presumably in place, Nixon now decided to "go for broke" in Vietnam. He would force the issue and "end the war one way or another — either by negotiated agreement or by an increased use of force."[30] In addition to dispatching a conciliatory letter to Ho Chi Minh offering to negotiate a settlement, on August 4 the president sent Kissinger to Paris for a meeting with North Vietnamese leader Xuan Thuy to deliver "what would in effect be an ultimatum" to Hanoi, demanding agreement to conclude the war by November 1.[31] Failure to agree would leave the United States no recourse but to "consider steps of grave consequence."[32] Hanoi would not be intimidated, waiting only a week to respond. On August 11, North Vietnamese forces resumed the offensive in South Vietnam, attacking over one hundred cities, towns, and bases, and ending the eight-week lull since June.

In the meantime, President Nixon embarked on his round-the-world trip, beginning with a stop at Guam to welcome the Apollo astronauts back from their successful flight to the moon. His trip included stops in the Philippines, Thailand, Indonesia, India, Pakistan, Romania, and also a brief unscheduled stop in South Vietnam. On Guam, July 25, he gave an informal briefing to newsmen. In the course of his remarks, in response to a question about Beijing's capability of inspiring wars of national liberation, Nixon replied, "Red China's capacity is much less than it was because of internal problems." A good indication of this, he said, was the "minimal role" that Beijing was then playing in Vietnam compared to the Soviet Union. "Three years ago, Red China was furnishing over 50 percent of the military equipment, the hardware, for the North Vietnamese. Now it is approximately 80–20 the other way around."[33]

The initial formulation of what would soon be termed the "Nixon Doctrine" overshadowed the president's revelation of his understanding of the role which the Chinese had begun to play in constricting Soviet supplies bound for North Vietnam. Discussing the future role of the United States in Asia, the president declared that the United States "will keep our treaty commitments . . . but . . . problems of internal security . . . except for the threat of a major power involving nuclear weapons . . . will be increasingly handled by . . . the Asian nations themselves."[34]

In the sensation generated by this announcement, initially dubbed the "Guam Doctrine," what was perhaps the most intriguing question was left unanswered. What had the president meant by the phrase "except for the threat of a major power involving nuclear weapons"? The only major power capable of making a credible nuclear threat against any Asian nation aside from the United States was, of course, the Soviet Union. Did the president mean to suggest, however obliquely, that the United States would extend its nuclear umbrella to cover China in case of a Soviet nuclear threat? At this stage of the evolving working understanding with Beijing the suggestion was left tantalizingly vague. Its clarification later in the year would confirm that Sino-American rapprochement was indeed under way.

From the outbreak of hostilities on the Ussuri the Soviets had raised the threat of nuclear retaliation against China as they strove to marshal the support of Communist party leaderships around the world.[35] In meetings of the Warsaw Pact countries and preparatory meetings for the coming World Congress of Communist Parties, the Soviets sought the endorsement of a tough stance against the Chinese, an effort in which they were largely successful, but the exceptions were notable. Nicolai Ceausescu of Romania and Josip Tito of Yugoslavia pointedly resisted Soviet demands for unity and condemned the Brezhnev Doctrine, because of its implications for themselves.

When the World Congress of Communist Parties did convene in June, speculation was rife that the outbreak of full-scale war between the Soviet Union and China was imminent. Reports were circulating in Moscow of a possible Soviet preventive strike against Chinese nuclear installations in Sinkiang.[36] Brezhnev's sharp denunciation of the Maoist regime at the congress, his proposal to create an Asian Collective Security System, and insistent demands for international solidarity fed those fears. After the congress, in July, Chinese officials uncharacteristically also spoke of war as "definitely imminent," possibly by October, and American officials noted intelligence reports that China had moved two armored and three anti-aircraft divisions to Lop Nor "to provide protection against a possible Soviet airborne attack."[37]

This, then, was the context within which President Nixon cautiously put forth his position on Guam. The president's oblique offer of support came just as the Sino-Soviet conflict was nearing its crisis point in mid-September. Undoubtedly, Romania's staunch objection to blanket condemnation of China at the Communist party congress was an important reason the president included Bucharest on his itinerary even though he protested that his visit should not be interpreted either "as an affront to the Soviet Union or as a move toward China."[38]

That Mao Zedong understood and responded to this latest signal also seems beyond doubt. As American combat forces were withdrawn from South Vietnam, Beijing began to shift Chinese forces stationed in southern China to the north, as well as to withdraw some 40,000 to 50,000 "service forces," mainly labor and engineer battalions, from North Vietnam. An early September report noted that the withdrawal of Chinese forces from North Vietnam had been completed "within the last two months or so."[39] It was accompanied by publicly expressed concerns that the Soviet Union was about to execute a nuclear strike against China and by increasingly visible war preparations on both sides of the border.[40]

In mid-September the Sino-Soviet crisis climbed toward its zenith as Moscow moved to the brink of a nuclear strike. Amid armed conflict and tension all along the frontier from Manchuria to Sinkiang, test firings of missiles, and lofting of reconnaissance satellites, Moscow issued what appeared to be an ultimatum, although its public aspect was of an indirect sort. On September 11, on his way back to Moscow after attending the funeral of Ho Chi Minh, Soviet Premier Alexei Kosygin held a brief meeting at Beijing airport with Chinese Premier Zhou Enlai. The topic of their "frank conversation" was not disclosed but was evidently related to the mounting crisis.

Then on September 16 there appeared an article in the *London Evening News* by one of Moscow's KGB "channels" to the west, Victor Louis. Entitled "Will Russian Rockets Czechmate China?" in allusion to the Soviet invasion of Czechoslovakia the previous year, the article moved the Sino-Soviet crisis to its highest point. Mr. Louis declared that the Soviet Union was prepared to go significantly further against China than it had gone against Czechoslovakia. There was no reason, he asserted, why the Brezhnev Doctrine should not be applied to China. Furthermore, Soviet rockets stood aimed and ready to destroy China's nuclear center at Lop Nor, Sinkiang. Finally, he said that there was evidence that anti-Maoist forces were emerging and "could produce a leader who would ask other socialist countries for fraternal help."

It appeared that as the Soviet Union increased pressure in the North, the United States relaxed pressure in the South. On the day the Victor Louis article appeared, President Nixon gave a speech in which he declared that "the time has come to end this war."[41] He announced a reduction in the authorized troop ceiling from 549,500 to 484,000 and withdrawal of an additional 35,000 troops to be accomplished by December 15. This would bring to 60,000 the number of troops withdrawn by the end of 1969.

Behind the scenes, Washington applied "diplomatic pressure" on Moscow throughout the next month.[42] Most importantly, "sometime in early October" the president with no public announcement placed Strategic Air Command on DefCon I, the highest level of nuclear alert.[43] Whatever the effect of United States actions on the Sino-Soviet crisis, the tension began to abate thereafter and in early

October both sides withdrew their armed forces out of direct contact. On the seventh, Beijing announced that it had agreed to enter into negotiations with the Soviets, but "should a handful of war maniacs dare to raid China's strategic sites . . . that will be war. . . ."[44]

Did the Soviet leadership conclude that the United States-China connection had already been made? Was the decision to terminate the crisis a reflection of that realization? Soviet policy behavior from this point suggests that Soviet leaders had indeed reached this conclusion. Having failed to prevent the beginning of a rapprochement between Washington and Beijing, Moscow now strove to avoid being odd man out. Improvement in Sino-American ties would be matched by improvement in Soviet-American relations—even while Moscow pursued the larger goal of moving toward overall supremacy.

The shift in Soviet policy came through clearly in an aide-mémoire delivered by Ambassador Dobrynin to President Nixon on October 20, the same day that Sino-Soviet border talks began. Only a fragment of the note has been published, but it is sufficient to indicate the Soviet interpretation of events. Peremptory in tone, the aide-mémoire stated:

> Moscow feels that the President should be frankly told that the method of solving the Vietnam question through the use of military force is not only without perspective, but also extremely dangerous. . . . If someone in the United States is tempted to make profit from Soviet-Chinese relations at the Soviet Union's expense, and there are some signs of that, then we would like to frankly warn in advance that such line of conduct, if pursued, can lead to a very grave miscalculation and is in no way consistent with the goal of better relations between the United States and the U.S.S.R.[45]

From the juxtaposition of the subject matter, it is evident that the Soviet leadership linked the Vietnam conflict, Sino-Soviet crisis, and Sino-American rapprochement. Despite the bluster about making "profit from Soviet-Chinese relations at the Soviet Union's expense," Dobrynin informed the president that Moscow was ready to begin strategic arms talks. (They would in fact begin on November 17.)

President Nixon responded to the Soviet diplomatic parry with the same connecting thrust, but he did so publicly. In a speech on November 3, while DefCon I alert was still in effect,[46] and following the expiration of the ultimatum to Hanoi, the president declared both his determination to see the Vietnam conflict through to a successful end and his intention to use America's nuclear power to "shield" the People's Republic from any Soviet nuclear threat.

President Nixon described the long road to American involvement in Vietnam from former President Eisenhower's initial commitment to the present. Pointedly noting that "the Soviet Union furnishes most of the military equipment for North Vietnam" he went on to explain how Moscow had declined to assist in bringing about a settlement of the war. Nor had there been any progress with Hanoi, which remained intransigent. Since neither Moscow nor Hanoi showed any inclination to work for a peaceful settlement, the president declared: "I, therefore, put into effect another plan to bring peace—a plan which will bring the war to an end regardless of what happens on the negotiating front."[47]

This plan was, of course, Vietnamization, which was public, and rapprochement with Beijing, which was not. Now, in line with what he termed "a major shift in U.S. foreign policy," President Nixon referred to his press conference on Guam. He then proceeded to develop the "two commitments" made on Guam into "three principles as guidelines for future American policy toward Asia." The first two principles were the same as those set forth on Guam, that the United States would keep all of its treaty commitments and furnish military and economic assistance to threatened nations, who would, in turn, provide the manpower for their own defense.

But it was in the third principle that the president, in effect, replied to Moscow's warning in the aide-mémoire. The United States, he said, *"shall provide a shield if a nuclear power threatens the freedom of a nation allied with us or of a nation whose survival we consider vital to our security."*[48] There was only the subtlest hint, recall, in his Guam remarks to match the specific declaration made now that the United States would extend its nuclear power as a shield to protect any Asian nation "whose survival we consider vital to our security." That nation, given the Sino-Soviet crisis and all that it implied for Vietnam in particular and for global stability in general, was, of course, China.

Three essential elements comprised Sino-American rapprochement as it evolved in 1969. First was agreement to seek a mutually satisfactory solution in Indochina. This meant a return to the status quo ante, the 1954 Geneva structure, a solution which would leave

Vietnam divided with a United States-supported South Vietnam within a region fragmented to satisfy Beijing's security concerns. Contrary to Beijing's propaganda statements, the least desirable outcome of the conflict would have been an outright conquest of the South by Hanoi. This would have resulted in the emergence of a "big Vietnam," which at the very least would have competed with China for influence in the region and at most would have cooperated with the Soviet Union against China.

Second, in return for Chinese cooperation, however obscured, in a mutually acceptable settlement in Southeast Asia, the United States would "provide a shield" against Moscow. Finally, the fruits of rapprochement could be anticipated in the extension of American assistance in China's development, facilitation of China's entry into the Western political and economic world, and ultimately establishment of full diplomatic relations. Most of this, naturally enough, was not visible in 1969, or even in 1970. It would not be until mid-1971 with Henry Kissinger's secret visit to China that the full dimensions of Sino-American rapprochement would begin to come to public light. But establishment of a working China connection in 1969 permitted the president to commence action on two related aspects of his strategy — the Middle East and strategic arms talks.

It is appropriate before proceeding to discuss the question of authorship of the strategy thus far outlined. Many accounts state or leave the impression that the originator of United States strategy, to the extent that the United States was perceived to have a strategy, was not the president but was his national security adviser, Henry A. Kissinger.[49] It is undeniably true that Kissinger would in time become the architect of American foreign policy, but this was not the case during the first two years of the Nixon administration. The originator of American strategy was the president, who very skillfully maneuvered the United States into a greatly improved position.[50] Not surprisingly, this view finds support from Henry Kissinger himself.

In his brilliant and disarmingly revealing book, *White House Years*, Kissinger's early policy recommendations show clearly that he neither comprehended nor was involved in the execution of the president's policy at this time. For example, his memorandum to the president of September 10, 1969, on "our present course in Vietnam," written just as the Sino-Soviet crisis was reaching its peak, betrayed no awareness of the emergence of the China connection described above,[51] nor of China's role in the Vietnam conflict. His textual analysis, on the other hand, written several years afterward, contrasts sharply with the memorandum.

Similarly, Kissinger perceived no relationship between the war in Vietnam and the situation in the Middle East. Even while acknowledging that he had no policy role in the Middle East until late 1971, he disparaged the president's "vague notion of a trade-off with the Soviet Union between the Middle East and Vietnam."[52] Assessing correctly that Nixon "let matters drift . . . [and] applied the brakes just often enough to prevent a coherent application of the State Department approach" to the region, Kissinger saw no connection between the two. It was, of course, as will be shown in the pages that follow, precisely President Nixon's policy, as Kissinger would later come to appreciate, to "let matters drift" in the Middle East *until* the principal pieces of the larger structure — China and Vietnam — were firmly in place.

Vietnam and the Middle East Connection

The immediate connection between the Middle East and Vietnam was the Suez Canal. Its closure during the 1967 war severely strained the Soviet Union's ability to ship war materiel to Hanoi. Using Suez, the route from Black Sea ports to Sihanoukville and the Haiphong port complex was some 7,000 miles. With Suez closed, the route more than doubled as Soviet ships were forced to steam around Africa to reach port. Furthermore, the Soviet shipping fleet was unable to increase sufficiently rapidly to compensate for the longer route. The outbreak of Sino-Soviet border hostilities put even greater pressure on the sea-borne shipment of Soviet supplies to Hanoi, as the rail route across China became virtually unusable. The consequences for Hanoi's war effort were obvious.

The Soviets needed and pressed for a settlement in the Middle East, promising far more than they could conceivably deliver, to bring about the reopening of Suez, which would in turn allow a quantum increase in shipment of military materiel to Vietnam. Reopening Suez was crucial to Soviet strategy, not only because of the relationship to the Vietnam conflict, but also in the way in which that conflict would affect Sino-Soviet relations. Even though Moscow's initial strategy of fueling conflict in Southeast Asia to induce a reconciliation with Beijing began to fail as a result of Sino-American rapprochement,[53] success in Vietnam remained a valuable objective in itself to create a containing position against China. Therefore, Moscow demanded early Israeli withdrawal from the canal zone as part of every proposal put forward for a Middle East settlement, and when all else failed, they shifted to achieve the objective by force.

The relationship of the Suez Canal to the Soviet supply effort to Vietnam determined the timing of United States Middle East policy, but not its content. Once the president was assured that he could close off all effective logistical access to Hanoi he would move forward substantively in the Middle East. Looking ahead somewhat, this meant that while the president would engage the Soviets in discussions on the Middle East, no concrete, feasible proposals would emerge until after the United States-South Vietnamese incursion into Cambodia in mid-1970, which secured the closure of the port of Sihanoukville. With Sihanoukville closed and Beijing sharply curtailing supplies into Vietnam as well, the president would then be in position to close off the remaining route of access, into Haiphong. From that position of leverage, then, in mid-1970, President Nixon would move ahead in the Middle East, knowing that Suez could not be reopened in time to thwart his objectives in Southeast Asia. Until then, he "let matters drift."

The content of the president's objectives in the Middle East was to a large degree a function of the changing United States-Soviet strategic weapons balance. Growth of Soviet strategic power would inevitably encourage Soviet leaders to play a more provocative role in attempting to improve their already formidable position in the region. Moscow was already supplying huge quantities of arms to Iraq, Syria, Egypt, Sudan, Algeria, and the Yemens. It would therefore be necessary to expand and consolidate the American position in order to withstand the expected pressures. A defensible collective security structure could, however, be achieved only by "broadening American relations with the Arab countries," an objective toward which the president "began taking steps" early in 1969.[54]

The president "was confident that a mutually acceptable compromise could be achieved [between Israel and Egypt] if the United States could establish a new relationship with Egypt and the Arab nations," but his longer-term goals involved broad structural change in the region.[55]

What I was trying to do . . . was to construct a completely new set of power relationships in the Middle East — not only between Israel and the Arabs, but also among the United States, Western Europe, and the Soviet Union.[56]

The principal target for both Washington and Moscow was Egypt, which for the former constituted the basis of any collective security arrangement with Israel and which for the latter was absolutely essential for maintaining the Arab pincer against Israel as well as for ensuring transit through Suez. Thus, on December 30, 1968, Moscow sent a formal note calling for full compliance by all parties with UN Resolution 242, a timetable for the withdrawal of Israeli forces to the pre-June 4, 1967, position and the return of the United Nations peacekeeping force to the Sinai.[57] Clearing of the canal would begin as soon as Israel had completed a partial withdrawal.

Washington replied to Moscow's note on January 15, 1969. Israel, the United States government believed, had accepted the United Nations resolution, but it was up to the concerned parties to agree on its interpretation. It was Washington's view that no solution could be imposed by outside parties; only the belligerents could resolve their differences. Finally, any Israeli withdrawal must be part of a comprehensive solution, and a solution must precede any withdrawal.[58] Moscow sought the obverse.

The exchange clearly indicated that Washington was in no hurry to settle anything, while the Soviets sought to reopen the canal. On the basis of the exchange the two powers began talks which were shortly expanded to include Great Britain and France. Considered useful, the talks went on inconclusively for several months. As a sign of good faith, President Nixon postponed delivery to Israel of a squadron of F-4 Phantom jets in early March. Further negotiations were placed in jeopardy when, on April 1, 1969, President Nasser announced the beginning of a new phase in the conflict, a "war of attrition" against Israel, as Egyptian artillery batteries began to shell Israeli positions in the heavily fortified Bar Lev Line along the canal.

To keep the discussions going, Washington transmitted a formal note to Moscow on May 26. This was, in fact, the first initiative to come from the new administration apart from responses to Soviet prodding. Recall, as noted above, Washington's intent was to keep Moscow engaged in the Middle East while the China connection was being forged. On June 11, Washington also signaled its readiness to begin strategic arms talks, but Moscow, wary of being boxed in, began to back off.

The Soviets responded on June 17, following the World Congress of Communist Parties, with a formal note that reverted to the earlier hard-line position on the Middle East.[59] The Soviets insisted once again on a timetable for Israeli withdrawal from all Arab territory and offered no proposals for direct Arab-Israeli talks. A formal peace would be declared only after a complete Israeli pullback; Sharm el Sheikh should revert to Egyptian sovereignty though placed under United Nations control. Moscow's note called for a demilitarized zone on both sides of the Egyptian-Israeli frontier and full restoration of Palestinian refugee rights.

The Soviet note was clearly designed to break off further talks. What had happened? One reason was that the "war of attrition" was going well for Nasser, making him less inclined to negotiate. Another, probably governing, factor was Moscow's growing realization that the United States-China connection was taking shape, and Moscow wanted to disengage temporarily from any Middle East entanglement to generate maximum pressure on Beijing in hopes of forestalling movement toward Washington. Soviet indifference to a political settlement in the Middle East became manifest during Assistant Secretary of State Joseph Sisco's trip to Moscow, July 9 through 17.

Three days later, however, on July 20, Israel initiated action which made Soviet disentanglement impossible. The Israeli Defense Force (IDF) commenced intensive and prolonged air strikes against Egypt, centering in the canal area and air defense sites covering the aerial approaches to the Nile valley. Whether or not comprehended by Israeli leaders, who were after all acting in their own self-interests, the air strikes served to create a de facto two-front conflict situation for Moscow between Egypt and China.

As Moscow mounted military pressure on Beijing during August and September, Israeli forces pounded Egyptian defenses. Indeed, by early September, just as the peak of the Sino-Soviet crisis was nearing, Egypt's ability to sustain continued air strikes came starkly into question, as the country lay prostrate in the face of IDF attacks. To compound Cairo's difficulties, the Israeli leadership announced in early September a "limited offensive" on the ground along the west bank of the canal.[60]

Then, during the height of the Soviet pressure on China, on September 19, Soviet Foreign Minister Andrei Gromyko caved in on the Middle East, offering in the United Nations what amounted to agreement to "work for peace" through negotiations. Gromyko's speech signaled the beginning of a major shift in Soviet policy which took place over the next month, culminating in the Soviet aide-mémoire to President Nixon on October 20. The speech reflected the Soviet leadership's realization that current trends were running against Moscow, which was overextended. In the Middle East, initial Egyptian success in the war of attrition had turned to ashes as Israeli retaliatory air strikes began to take a heavy toll on Cairo's defenses.

In the Far East, despite deployment of a huge ground force contingent along the Chinese border and generation of conventional military and nuclear pressure against Beijing, Sino-American rapprochement was rapidly taking shape. This would put Washington in position gradually to choke off Hanoi's war effort, with little that Moscow could do to prevent it. Finally, at the strategic weapons level, despite the imminence of Soviet ICBM launcher superiority, Washington's nuclear power was still decisive and promised to remain so with the decision to build an anti-ballistic missile defense system, authorized by Congress on August 6, and continuation of MIRV testing. These two decisions threatened to neutralize the Soviet effort to achieve superiority, or at the very least, to place the attainment of strategic weapons superiority much further into the future.

At this point, the Soviet leadership decided to refocus its efforts, concentrating on key areas in hopes of making a breakthrough which could be exploited. Thus, in regard to the Middle East, following Gromyko's United Nations speech, United States and Soviet negotiators hammered out the joint initiative which came to be referred to as the "28 October Rogers Plan," committing the United States to Israeli withdrawal from the West Bank and Gaza to lines "approximating" the pre-June 1967 borders.[61]

In the Far East, Moscow began the border talks with Beijing, dropping its belligerent stance of the previous six months. In Southeast Asia, Soviet leaders perceived that Sino-American cooperation threatened the Hanoi war effort and assumed that Washington would attempt to cut off the remaining two routes of access as soon as opportunities presented themselves. Therefore, following the visit of Pham Van Dong to Moscow in mid-October, the Soviet Union increased shipments of materiel, especially non-military supplies, to Hanoi.[62]

In Europe, October also saw Moscow step up efforts begun

following its invasion of Czechoslovakia to defuse tensions with Western Europe and particularly to improve relations with the Federal Republic of Germany under newly elected Chancellor Willy Brandt. During Warsaw Pact meetings in October and later in December the Soviet Union sponsored proposals for a European Security Conference to be held in the first half of 1970.[63] Finally, with regard to relations with the United States, Moscow agreed to begin strategic arms limitation talks on November 17. Soviet leaders had not yet formulated a full-blown counterstrategy to the one which they perceived the United States to be pursuing, but from late 1969, they adopted a damage-limiting approach to buy time while probing American positions further.[64]

Soviet leaders understood that a major shift was occurring at the strategic weapons level. Their objective therefore was to limit the amount of damage that could be done before the shift took place. Soviet policy in the period between late 1969 and late 1970 should be understood as a holding action combined with probes of United States positions. During this period Moscow would reach no meaningful agreements with Washington, even while engaging in negotiations. Thus, in strategic arms talks the Soviets would stall and in the Vietnam and Middle East negotiations backpedal — even on agreements they themselves helped formulate.

An exception was Europe, where the Soviets perceived an opportunity at small cost to recoup the damage done by the Czechoslovakian invasion and take a step toward the insertion of a wedge between West Germany and the United States by beginning negotiations for a mutual non-aggression pact with Bonn. Besides, a settlement on the European front would allow greater concentration of resources on problem areas in the Far East and the Middle East.

The Soviet decision to await further change in the strategic weapons balance coincided with the American decision to wait for the opportunity to take decisive action in Vietnam. Thus for several months through the winter of 1969–1970, both sides pursued parallel policies, doing only enough to prevent serious deterioration of existing positions. In one area, however, the Middle East-Horn of Africa, Moscow took action which ominously foretold of things to come.

In September, the United States had gained the compliance of the government of Somalia to prevent ships registered under its flag from shipping to Haiphong.[65] The governments of Singapore, Cyprus, and Malta were also approached. If implemented, the reduction of cargo carriers to Hanoi would have intensified the United States logistical squeeze on Moscow's effort to supply war materiel to North Vietnam. The military coup of Major General Muhammed Siad Barre on October 21 reversed the so-called "drift to the west" under the former Sharmarke government, returning it solidly to the Soviet camp, where it would remain until 1977.[66] Although Moscow was not directly involved in the coup, Soviet complicity was apparent.[67]

In the Middle East, publication of the 28 October Rogers Plan brought immediate Israeli condemnation. President Nixon's reaction was to say that he

> knew that the Rogers Plan could never be implemented, but . . . with the Rogers Plan on the record, I thought it would be easier for the Arab leaders to propose reopening relations with the United States, without coming under attack from the hawks and pro-Soviet elements in their own countries.[68]

All hope for a positive response from Arab leaders was dashed at the Rabat summit on December 20. Moscow, which had remained noncommittal until afterward, also rejected the Rogers Plan—this, despite the fact that it was a joint proposal incorporating more of the Soviet view than the American.

The Israeli leadership sought to forestall any further estrangement with Washington by escalating the level of conflict, which, it was hoped, would bring the United States around to full support of the Israeli position once again. In late January, declaring that "all of Egypt is the field of battle," the Israelis commenced long-range air strikes deep into the heart of Egypt.[69] Although the intensification of Israeli attacks produced a new crisis in Cairo that threatened to bring down Nasser, it failed to elicit the desired response from Washington. Instead, it was Moscow that responded, altering the nature of the problem entirely.

On January 31, 1970, Premier Kosygin sent his first personal note to President Nixon, in which he declared:

> We would like to tell you in all frankness that if Israel continues its adventurism, to bomb the territory of U.A.R. and of other Arab states, the Soviet Union will be forced to see to it that the Arab states have means at their disposal, with the help of which a due rebuff to the arrogant aggressor could be made.[70]

President Nixon's response was "carefully low-keyed," urging a more positive Soviet reaction to the Rogers Plan, offering to make a joint effort to limit arms supplies into the region, and deciding to "set aside" the latest Israeli request for twenty-four additional F-4 and eighty A-4 aircraft.[71]

In the meantime, Israeli attacks continued with devastating effect, rapidly destroying Egypt's entire air-defense capability and leaving the country progressively indefensible against air attack. By mid-March the Soviet decision on the defense of Egypt became apparent. Moscow had begun to supply Cairo with Soviet-manned SAM-2 and SAM-3 missiles and Soviet planes and pilots. In the face of Egyptian prostration the Soviet Union had decided to assume responsibility for much of Egypt's air defense, particularly the Suez Canal area and the Nile valley. For the first time, the Soviet Union had deployed its most advanced weaponry and military personnel to a non-communist client state in conflict with an American ally. Superpower crisis loomed in the Middle East.

The Soviet deployment to Egypt came at precisely the moment of the long-awaited opportunity to take decisive action in the Vietnam War. Kissinger's remarks at this juncture are most illuminating, though probably unintentionally so. For Kissinger "the proper response [to the Soviet move] would have been to increase military aid to Israel." We needed, he said, "to face down the Soviets and the Arab radicals. Otherwise, Israeli concessions would be perceived as resulting from the introduction of Soviet military personnel. Our position would deteriorate. . . ."[72]

President Nixon disdained his national security adviser's advice, doing precisely the opposite. Instead of increasing military aid to Israel, he decided "to postpone our delivery of Phantom jets to Israel."[73] Instead of facing down the Soviets, the president proposed a summit conference for later in the year. And instead of taking a tough line with the Arab radicals, following a fact-finding trip to the Middle East by Assistant Secretary Sisco in April, the United States now declared that it had a more "active interest" in the PLO, a shift from the long-standing American position of not dealing with that organization.[74]

As Kissinger noted uncomprehendingly, the president "spent much of his time on Cambodia."[75] Indeed, events were then occurring in Phnom Penh that would change the course of Soviet and

American strategy. This was the deposition of Prince Sihanouk and the assumption to power of Lon Nol on March 18, which opened up the possibility of closing off one of the two remaining logistics routes by which Moscow was continuing to supply Hanoi. Its closure, combined with the developing rapprochement with China, would place the United States in position to bring the conflict to a successful conclusion. In attempting to safeguard that opportunity, the president would try to engage, divert, and otherwise neutralize Moscow; thus the mild reaction in the Middle East and what many saw as aberrant behavior by the president.[76]

Cambodian Crisis — Turning Point in the Vietnam War

Prince Sihanouk's rule in Cambodia had been deteriorating for at least two years. By the time President Nixon assumed office three developments were coalescing to move Cambodia toward a crisis of the regime. These developments were: the increase in importance of Cambodia to the North Vietnamese war effort, which progressively alienated the urban elite; a growing domestic economic crisis, which disaffected the peasantry; and the beginning of armed resistance by the Cambodian Communist party, which affected both.

For Hanoi, Cambodia functioned primarily as a logistical supply line and sanctuary base area, functions which grew increasingly important as the war progressed. By early 1969, United States combat success on the battlefield had forced the removal of North Vietnamese bases out of South Vietnam proper for the most part, requiring increased use of Cambodian sanctuary bases. While it was American combat success which forced Hanoi's greater use of the sanctuaries, Cambodia's increased logistical role had its origin thousands of miles away, in Soviet policy toward China.

Moscow's buildup along the Chinese border involved a major redeployment of military power. As noted above, between forty-five and fifty divisions were moved across the limited capacity Trans-Siberian railway system to the Soviet Far East between 1966 and 1968. The Soviet border buildup took priority over Vietnam-end goods destined for transshipment across the Chinese railway system. The Cultural Revolution in China also made the China route unreliable. For these two reasons Soviet supplies to Vietnam were gradually rerouted by sea from Soviet and East European Black Sea ports to Haiphong and Sihanoukville.

One CIA field estimate claimed that up to 80 percent of Hanoi's war supplies were entering through Cambodia's main port of Sihanoukville by 1969.[77] While the percentage was probably exaggerated, the estimate of Sihanoukville's significance was not far off the mark. Military intelligence, for example, saw it as a "vital" supply line. General Westmoreland, field commander of American forces in South Vietnam, noted that between 1966 and 1969, 21,600 metric tons of military supplies and over 5,000 metric tons of nonmilitary supplies were transshipped from Sihanoukville across Cambodia to the North Vietnamese and Vietcong sanctuaries along the Cambodian-South Vietnamese border. "Using the figures for the year 1968 — the year of the enemy's highest expenditure of ordnance up to that time — the amount of arms and ammunition reaching the enemy through Cambodia was sufficient to meet the enemy's requirements at that level for at least eight years."[78]

The greater North Vietnamese troop presence in Cambodia — in the sanctuaries and along the supply line to the port — produced a seething discontent among Cambodia's political elite, particularly against Prince Sihanouk, who seemed powerless to preserve the nation's neutrality and who, indeed, appeared to be cooperating with the North Vietnamese. The political right, represented in particular by Sirik Matak, a long-time family rival of Sihanouk's, regarded the prince's efforts at dealing with the North Vietnamese as "totally inadequate to cope with the magnitude of the domestic security threat."[79]

Discontent was growing in the rural areas, as well. In the latter half of the sixties, partly as a result of the break with the United States in 1965 and partly because of market demand factors, Phnom Penh began to experience a serious revenue shortfall. Sihanouk's response was to reduce the price which the government paid for rice.[80] This policy exacerbated the problem as rural producers sold more rice on the black market, where the price was two-thirds higher than the government price. Indeed, in 1966 reportedly 40 percent of the rice crop was sold on the black market and smuggled to Vietnam.[81]

Sihanouk's solution for stopping black market rice sales was to step up government collection efforts. In January 1967, General Lon Nol set up "action committees" at the district, sub-district, and village levels, commencing a nationwide campaign to collect the rice crop.[82] Needless to say, such forced collections did not endear the regime to the peasantry. Rural discontent became fertile ground for opposition groups, especially the Cambodian Communist party (CPK), which began to show greater strength and cohesion by early 1967.

The "action committees" designed to ensure crop collection were also intended to establish Phnom Penh's presence in the countryside and displace the influence of the left in general and the communists in particular. Lon Nol utilized the opportunity of the crop collection campaign to strike preemptively at the growing Communist party, which, he had learned, was on the verge of shifting from a purely political program to armed struggle.[83] The harsh crackdown, however, simply provoked wider resistance and, in Battambang in the northwest, rebellion in the countryside.

Sihanouk's reaction was the traditional one of carrot and stick — on the one hand, bringing several leftist leaders into his cabinet and, on the other hand, ordering the arrest and execution of teachers and students suspected of being communists or supporting them. At the same time he banned associations of all types, including the Sino-Cambodian Friendship Association.[84] While the CPK was not a serious threat to Sihanouk's regime (the total number of men under arms was about 4,000 by 1969), growth of the party's ranks and increase of those who sympathized with it reflected the steady loss of allegiance to Phnom Penh.[85] Sihanouk himself, however, remained a popular figure with the peasantry.

Incoming President Nixon had few doubts about Cambodia's role in Hanoi's overall war scheme. In a January 8, 1969, memo to Kissinger, Nixon demanded a "precise report on what the enemy has in Cambodia" and called for a "definite change of policy toward Cambodia" as the "first order of business when we get in."[86] In retrospect, piecing together the strands of United States policy, it would appear that the president, perhaps comprehending the growing instability of Sihanouk's regime, made a basic decision early in 1969 to promote the conditions which would eventually lead to the closure of the Cambodian supply line.

Decisive action in Cambodia was contingent upon the establishment of the China connection, for to close Sihanoukville before reaching a working understanding with China would only increase pressure on Beijing to keep open its rail supply line across China. North Vietnamese operating needs were estimated at something like four to five tons per day; the Chinese rail system had the capacity to deliver over twenty tons per day. If need be, the Chinese could supply all of North Vietnam's military needs. Therefore, the opening to China was crucial, and President Nixon would take no action which would jeopardize it.

Once the president realized that Mao was closing off the Chinese supply line early in 1969, he decided to initiate pressure in Cambodia. First, as noted above, were the B-52 strikes against the North Vietnamese sanctuaries in Cambodia in March. Then, also in March, came increased American reconnaissance patrol activity into the sanctuaries from bases in South Vietnam.[87] The evidence also suggests that a gradual infiltration of Cambodia's armed forces by Cambodian units armed and trained by the CIA in South Vietnam began.[88] In any case, the president would authorize no decisive action in Cambodia until the China connection was secure.

It was the president's hope that Sihanouk, whose domestic position was growing weaker in any case, would perceive the change in United States policy and, rather than be caught in an impossible dilemma, act independently to limit Hanoi's presence in Cambodia. Clearly, Nixon understood the ramifications of overt American action against a formally neutral Cambodia. It would have been far better to achieve the objective of closing Sihanoukville without any direct role. Overt United States involvement would come only as a last resort, if all else failed.

United States bombing strikes thus constituted one horn of a growing dilemma for the Cambodian leadership. The other horn was Hanoi's growing reliance upon Sihanoukville as supplies coming across the China route dwindled. Sihanoukville, in particular, caused the North Vietnamese much worry because it was critical for support of Hanoi's war effort in the Mekong Delta and more vulnerable to interdiction than the Haiphong port complex.

As Hanoi's dependence upon the Sihanoukville port increased, the North Vietnamese deployed greater resources to protect it. In August 1969, newly appointed Prime Minister Lon Nol claimed there were between 35,000 and 40,000 North Vietnamese troops on Cambodian soil and the following February (1970) declared the number had jumped to 60,000.[89] Thus the dilemma: Growing North Vietnamese dependence upon Sihanoukville generated increased troop deployment on Cambodian territory. This, in turn, had precipitated intensive American bombing of the "sanctuaries," which compromised

Cambodia's fragile "neutrality" and made Sihanouk's political position increasingly tenuous.

Sihanouk did in fact attempt to extricate himself from this dilemma, which could no longer be ignored. In June 1969 he agreed to reestablish diplomatic relations with the United States, opening direct channels of communication with Washington. In May he began the "arbitrary seizure" of cargo coming through Sihanoukville.[90] When the People's Revolutionary Government (Vietcong) of South Vietnam was organized in June, Sihanouk promptly recognized it. He immediately commenced negotiations on use of the port, and the resulting agreement on "trade and payments" regularized port operations, providing greater information on the extent of Hanoi's supply effort.[91] At the same time, he made several direct appeals to Hanoi in the fall of 1969 to curtail use of Cambodian sanctuaries, but his pleas fell on deaf ears.[92]

At this point, in September 1969, whether authorized by Sihanouk or not, Prime Minister Lon Nol held secret talks with Son Ngoc Thanh, a Cambodian exile in South Vietnam long opposed to Sihanouk. Son was building an exile military force, the Khmer Serei, or "Free Khmer," under South Vietnamese and CIA auspices. Lon Nol wished to obtain Son's support for a more militant course against Hanoi, but Son was more interested in moving against Sihanouk himself. Lon Nol "remained uncertain as to the wisdom and possibility of either confronting Sihanouk or overthrowing him."[93] In these exploratory talks, it would be too much to say that Lon Nol "sought an alliance" with Son.[94]

Then, while in Paris for medical treatment in early 1970, Sihanouk and his prime minister Lon Nol evidently hit upon a risky scheme which it was hoped would enable them to extricate Cambodia from the deepening dilemma.[95] The scheme was for Sihanouk to travel to Moscow and Beijing to "implore the Soviet and Chinese leaders to exert pressure on their Vietnamese ally to withdraw from Cambodia."[96] Lon Nol, in the meantime, would return to Phnom Penh to stage anti-North Vietnamese demonstrations, with a threat to shift Cambodia into the American camp, to lend greater force to Sihanouk's requests. Implicit in this scheme, if indeed there was one, was the necessary deposition of Sihanouk should it fail.

Upon Lon Nol's return to Phnom Penh in mid-February, the prime minister took the first step by closing the port of Sihanoukville to communist use.[97] Then, in further talks with Son Ngoc Than, he took the next step. Lon Nol now gained Son's support for two contingencies in the event of a change of government: resistance either from army elements loyal to Sihanouk, or from "some form of intervention from the Vietnamese Communist forces in Cambodia."[98] After conferring and no doubt coordinating action with provincial governors in early March, on the eighth Lon Nol staged demonstrations in the border provinces against the North Vietnamese troop presence there.

Three days later in downtown Phnom Penh several thousand people, including fifty soldiers dressed in civilian clothes, students, Buddhist monks, and other civilians, marched on and ransacked the Vietcong embassy and North Vietnamese mission overturning cars, breaking windows, destroying furniture, and seizing documents. Few Western observers doubted that the attack had been authorized by the Sirik Matak–Lon Nol government.[99]

Immediately upon hearing of the attacks on the North Vietnamese and Vietcong embassies, Sihanouk gave an interview on French television to declare that "right-wingers in Phnom Penh had 'taken advantage of my long absence to try and change Cambodia's political orientation. They would like us to enter the American camp.'" He said that "there had been contacts between the rightists and the CIA and again warned of the danger of a coup."[100] Sihanouk's statement was consistent with the scheme to build the threat of a move into the American camp, as was his next act. Instead of returning immediately to Phnom Penh, which he should have done if he believed his position was in danger, Sihanouk remained in Paris for three more days and then proceeded to Moscow.

Meanwhile, on March 12, Sirik Matak, acting premier in Sihanouk's absence, cancelled the trade agreement which authorized North Vietnam's use of Sihanoukville, and Lon Nol issued an ultimatum demanding that Hanoi's troops leave the country within seventy-two hours.[101] (This was an extraordinary demand for a nation which was no military match for its occupier; Cambodia had a total of only thirty thousand poorly trained and armed men.) Up to this point, Lon Nol's actions remained consistent with the scheme to put pressure on Hanoi in Phnom Penh to support Sihanouk's talks with Soviet leaders in Moscow. But over the next few days a series of developments persuaded Lon Nol and Sirik Matak to turn the original scheme designed to support Sihanouk into a plan for his overthrow.

The first factor was evidently the information contained in the documents captured during the ransacking of the North Vietnamese and PRG (Vietcong) missions which revealed the extent of Hanoi's designs on Phnom Penh. Talks with North Vietnamese and Vietcong representatives on March 15 following the expiration of the ultimatum undoubtedly confirmed Lon Nol's worst fears of Hanoi's refusal to withdraw its troops from Cambodian territory.[102] The second was Sihanouk's violent reaction in Paris to the events of March 12. The prince's reported threats to imprison or execute his ministers suggested that Sihanouk was turning away from the scheme.[103]

Third, following Sihanouk's arrival in Moscow on the sixteenth, if there had been a scheme it fell apart as Soviet leaders flatly rejected the prince's arguments, terming him a "blundering fool" for believing that he could pressure Moscow with a threat to turn to the West.[104] Moscow's rejection would have left Lon Nol with no alternative but to take action. Finally, through clandestine contacts with United States representatives, Lon Nol may have been persuaded that the opportunity to turn away from Hanoi was ripe and that a coup was not only necessary in light of Moscow's refusal, but desirable in its own right as the only hope of containing the North Vietnamese.

It is highly unlikely that Lon Nol and Sirik Matak, both of whom had long-standing relations with the United States, would have carried out the coup against Sihanouk without receiving at least tacit assurances of American support. It follows then, despite professions of surprise and ignorance on the part of United States leaders, that Washington had advance warning of the coup. Given the importance of Cambodia in the broad-ranged effort to interdict supplies to North Vietnam, ignorance of events in Phnom Penh would have been nothing less than extraordinary.

The evidence of United States foreknowledge is persuasive. The Central Intelligence Agency had had extensive contacts for years with virtually every prominent personality in Cambodia, spanning the entire political spectrum and including all of the key players in the unfolding drama. These included Sihanouk himself, his deputy premier Sirik Matak, Prime Minister Lon Nol, and Son Ngoc Thanh, a prominent anti-Sihanouk exile in South Vietnam training Cambodian guerrilla forces under CIA auspices.[105]

In any case, on March 18, the Cambodian legislature voted unanimously (92–0) to withdraw confidence in Sihanouk as chief of state and transfer the reins of power to Lon Nol. Despite the Lon Nol government's declaration of its intention to continue Cambodia's long-standing policy of neutrality, the reality was that Phnom Penh was shifting toward the United States, a move which, if successful, would profoundly and decisively affect the future course of the war.

China's leaders, apparently taken by surprise, had quickly embraced Sihanouk, who arrived in Beijing the day after the coup. Beijing supported Sihanouk as insurance against the need to become more directly involved if it appeared that Hanoi would conquer all of Indochina. For the moment, however, that was a distant prospect, although the issue was far from settled. Consequently, even though the Chinese leadership had permitted Sihanouk to call for a general uprising against Lon Nol on March 23, Beijing's public reaction was delayed and the Chinese took no substantive action in support of Hanoi's effort to topple Lon Nol.

Sihanouk's broadcast brought forth large demonstrations in his support over the following few days, but produced only harsh reprisals by Lon Nol.[106] Hanoi responded quickly, within three days terming the coup a CIA plot, calling for support to overthrow Lon Nol the day after Sihanouk's broadcast, and breaking relations with Phnom Penh on March 27.[107] Beijing's reaction was much slower; they declared the coup a CIA plot only on March 26, called for support for an uprising only on April 5 when that prospect had already evaporated, and withdrew diplomatic personnel only on May 5, some seven weeks after the event.

If the deposition of Sihanouk did not take Hanoi and perhaps Moscow by surprise as well, it exposed a major miscalculation. The North Vietnamese in early 1970 were bent on a different objective — that of mounting a threat to the B-52 airbases near the Thai-Laotian border. In late January, Hanoi's forces launched a major offensive onto the Plain of Jars. The North Vietnamese thrust, if successful, would have placed great pressure on neutralist Premier Souvanna Phouma of Laos to withdraw permission for United States airstrikes against that portion of the Ho Chi Minh trail passing through Laotian territory.

If Laos capitulated and Hanoi's forces were able to exert pressure on Thailand, pressure would grow also on Bangkok to close down the United States air bases in Thailand.[108] Indeed, three major air bases were located close to the Thai-Laotian border and could conceivably have come under direct military pressure from Hanoi. It was to provide a protective shield for these crucial bases that the United States had for many years supported the neutralist regime in

Laos and supplied materiel for its army, especially the forces of Vang Pao and the Meo tribesmen that generally had controlled the plain.

When Laotian forces mounted a feeble counterattack on the Plain of Jars at the end of March, after the Cambodian coup, North Vietnamese forces promptly withdrew. The immediate danger lay in Phnom Penh. Upon assuming power, Lon Nol promptly reaffirmed the earlier closure order for Sihanoukville and renamed the port Kompong Som.[109] Permanent closure of the port, of course, would severely cripple Hanoi's operations, particularly in the Mekong Delta, and ease Saigon's pacification program there.

More importantly, in the overall logistical scheme, loss of the port would leave Moscow with only one route through which to supply Hanoi—the Haiphong port complex. Furthermore, unless Hanoi could regain access to Sihanoukville, the Haiphong port complex itself inevitably would become the next target, closing off all major external supply lines and placing a death-grip on North Vietnam's overall war-fighting capability. In short, the closure of Sihanoukville was of the utmost significance, affecting the immediate and long-term prosecution of the war on both sides.[110]

The Decision to Uphold Lon Nol

"From the first," following the coup, President Nixon wanted an "active policy" to support Lon Nol, but realized that any move the United States made would have to be carefully prepared in advance.[111] Therefore, his first step was to offer to "neutralize" Cambodia, a proposition which Henry Kissinger was instructed to put to Le Duc Tho during secret talks in Paris on April 4. The North Vietnamese negotiator flatly rejected the proposal outright on the grounds that the "conflicts in Indochina have now become one."[112]

In other words, Hanoi would not accept the closure of Sihanoukville without a struggle. Anticipating Hanoi's negative response, the next task was to pin North Vietnamese forces in the border sanctuaries and prevent a drive to topple the Phnom Penh regime and reopen the port. Toward this end, Washington quietly transferred three to four thousand Civilian Irregular Defense Group (CIDG) troops armed with captured AK-47 automatic rifles to Phnom Penh and authorized raids on the sanctuaries by Son Ngoc Thanh's Khmer Serei and South Vietnamese forces.[113]

For a brief moment, at this point, an opportunity arose to forestall further conflict when Moscow proposed on April 16 to reconvene the Geneva Conference on Indochina. Kissinger termed this a "sensational" proposal, which Washington would have been "most eager to explore," but Moscow withdrew it two days later.[114] Clearly, both Moscow and Hanoi had rejected neutralization of Cambodia in favor of a test on the battlefield. The decision to fight may have been made because North Vietnamese forces were successfully fighting their way southwestward along the Cambodian–South Vietnamese border in the direction of Phnom Penh.[115]

The inability of Lon Nol's weak forces to stop them, even with such South Vietnamese and American support as was rendered, forced the president to make a necessary but nonetheless momentous decision. The disposition of Sihanoukville was a strategic question commanding the highest stakes for all sides. For the United States, success in supporting the Lon Nol regime and keeping the crucial port closed would at a minimum enable the South Vietnamese to pacify the Delta and at a maximum put the United States in position to bring the conflict to a successful conclusion. For the Soviet Union, the failure of the North Vietnamese to regain control of the Sihanoukville supply corridor would make continued prosecution of the war very tenuous on other than a much reduced level.

The period between the coup and the United States–South Vietnamese "incursion" into Cambodia was a classic case of dissemblance and disinformation to confuse Soviet leaders regarding the main thrust of Washington's policy. First, regarding the events in Cambodia itself, the president, Kissinger, and Secretary of State Rogers each portrayed an administration that was confused and uncertain about the proper course to follow. For example, during a news conference on March 21, President Nixon stated:

> These developments . . . are quite difficult to appraise. . . . The Cambodian political situation . . . is quite unpredictable and quite fluid. . . . We have . . . estabished relations on a temporary basis with the government which has been selected by the Parliament and will continue to deal with that government. . . . I think any speculation with regard to which way this government is going to turn, what will happen to Prince Sihanouk when he returns, would both be premature and not helpful. . . . We respect Cambodia's neutrality. We would hope that North

Vietnam would take that same position. . . . And we hope that whatever government eventually prevails there, that it would recognize that the United States' interest is the protection of its neutrality.[116]

In mid-April, Kissinger, in private conversation with a Washington newsman, remarked that the United States "did not wish to have another client state in Southeast Asia . . . and . . . did not want to get deeply involved with Lon Nol in Cambodia." On the other hand, he said, it was a shame that the United States "could not provide help to a little country of seven million inhabitants begging for it."[117] Finally, on the day President Nixon made the final decision to go with the incursion into Cambodia, April 26, Secretary of State Rogers testified before the Senate Foreign Relations Committee on aid to Lon Nol. He blandly asserted what he knew to be untrue, that "North Vietnamese/ Vietcong operations in Cambodia had not changed much from what they were before Sihanouk's fall."[118]

Although many commentators interpreted these statements as representative of a leadership in disarray, they appear to have been part of a conscious effort to depict an administration uncertain of the course to pursue. These statements represented a consistent pattern that screened from public view the actual decision to take action in support of Lon Nol. The same pattern was evident in relations with Moscow.

From early April the president, seemingly eagerly, pressed for a summit meeting to be held in 1970, but Moscow declined to take the bait. After exploring the idea of a summit meeting in talks with Henry Kissinger on April 7 and 9, Soviet Ambassador Dobrynin went to Moscow for consultations. By the time he returned in early June the Cambodian incursion had already been under way for over a month, which prompted Moscow to interpret the president's summit proposal as a "maneuver." As Dobrynin noted to Kissinger: "The Kremlin's initial reaction had been favorable but then Cambodia had raised the thought that our proposal was a maneuver to obtain Soviet acquiescence in a tough Indochina policy."[119]

Yet another move in the general effort to divert Moscow on the eve of the Cambodian venture came during West German Chancellor Willy Brandt's visit to Washington in early April. Brandt had arrived greatly concerned about the American reaction to his policies of normalization and reconciliation with East Germany and the Soviet

Union. The president was indeed concerned about Bonn's eastward drift; but, for the moment at least, he took a different tack. When it mattered, the United States would insist that outstanding issues like Berlin, for example, be resolved in the four-power format and not by Bonn unilaterally. However, during Brandt's visit, the president surprised the German chancellor by giving his *Ostpolitik* policy a ringing public endorsement.[120]

As the time approached for action in Cambodia, the United States carried on policy as usual, convening the strategic arms talks as previously scheduled in mid-April. On the twentieth, the president also announced the withdrawal of an additional 150,000 troops from Vietnam to be carried out over the course of the next year. In other words, the administration's policy pattern manifested a persistent inclination to be conciliatory on areas of conflict with Moscow, while conveying indecision with regard to Cambodia. On April 26, after an excruciatingly detailed analysis of potential benefits and consequences, the president, believing that a "bold move" was necessary, made the final decision to "go for broke" in Cambodia.[121]

"Operation Rock Crusher" spanned approximately two months beginning April 28. It was far more than the advertised sweep into the "fishhook" and "parrot's beak" areas along the South Vietnamese-Cambodian border where Hanoi's sanctuaries lay. While twenty thousand American and South Vietnamese ground forces drove some twenty miles into Cambodian territory, ships and naval patrol craft blocked the port of Sihanoukville. Simultaneously, B-52s bombed supply depots and positions all along the Ho Chi Minh trail to North Vietnam.[122]

Although in his speech announcing the operation, the president declared that one of the main objectives was the capture of Hanoi's very elusive southern headquarters, or COSVN, this too was an attempt to disguise the actual objective. (COSVN was never found; it had been relocated some time before to Kratie.) A huge, three-kilometer-square underground facility was unearthed. Termed "the city," it contained medical, mess, storage, training, signal, and repair areas as well as enormous stocks of weapons, ammunition, equipment, vehicles, food, and documents.[123]

The objective of Operation Rock Crusher, however, was nothing less than the destruction of North Vietnam's formidable position in Cambodia and the elimination of any threat to Lon Nol's fledgling regime. Indeed, Hanoi would never be able to rebuild fully the positions which were destroyed. Because Sihanoukville remained effectively closed to Hanoi, the sanctuaries in the Delta became the end points of very long supply lines stretching up into North Vietnam instead of being the first stops afer unloading at Sihanoukville. Thus, for example, during the Easter invasion of 1972, Hanoi's attacks from the Cambodian sanctuaries were weakest and most easily contained.

The significance of the Cambodian incursion was strategic, notwithstanding the intense domestic opposition it provoked. Closure of two of the three logistics routes into North Vietnam meant that the president was now positioned to extricate the nation from its most disastrous war on satisfactory if not favorable terms. Reflecting this position of advantage, the president offered that fall to settle the conflict. In his speech on October 7, Nixon proposed a five-point plan to end the war.

First, he reiterated his call for an international conference. Second, a major inducement, he offered a "cease fire in place," which implied that Hanoi's negotiating position at a conference would not be insubstantial and that territorial adjustments were possible. Third, he declared the United States "ready now to negotiate an agreed timetable for complete withdrawals as part of an overall settlement." Fourth, he proposed the immediate and unconditional release of all prisoners of war held by both sides. And finally, the president called for a settlement based upon the "existing relationship of political forces in South Vietnam," which strongly implied Hanoi's continued influence in a coalition government through its PRG surrogate.[124]

By the fall of 1970 the United States had completed a major démarche regarding the Vietnam War and an opening to China. As the president undoubtedly expected, strategic action by the United States would produce strategic counteraction by the Soviet Union. The crucial questions were: How would Moscow react? The Soviets could hardly be expected to capitulate without a riposte. Could Washington sustain its advantage in the face of determined counteraction?

CHAPTER

2

Alliance Crisis and the Road to Detente, 1970–1971

The fall of 1970 was a time of decision for Washington encompassing a subtle but momentous shift of emphasis. By the fall, President Nixon had set in motion the essential policies of the first term toward China and with respect to the war in Vietnam. Much skill would be required to keep these policies on track, particularly during periods of disruption by the Soviets, such as in the Middle East and Caribbean in the summer and fall of 1970; but the strategic course had been set.

Increasingly from late in the year, the president turned his attention to problems of the Western alliance.[1] The trend toward European unity, the growth of West German and Japanese economic power, the continuing deterioration of the international monetary system — particularly the position of the dollar — and the burgeoning crisis in world oil were producing dangerous centrifugal forces that threatened to fragment the Western alliance. Indeed, one could speak of a structural crisis within the alliance by the end of 1970.

By the end of the year the magnitude of the Soviet strategic failure had become apparent. Washington's opening to Beijing was a serious blow to the Soviet global position and to further prosecution of the Vietnam conflict. Development of an effective coincidence of interest between Washington and Beijing promised not only to facilitate the extrication of the United States from its Vietnam quagmire, but also to alter the global political alignment to Moscow's disadvantage.

Furthermore, the failure to reverse the closure of Sihanoukville increased the likelihood that the conflict in Indochina would be resolved along lines favored by the United States and China.

From this position of advantage, President Nixon decided to offer detente to the Soviet Union. Detente with Moscow would not only ensure that rapprochement with Beijing and the denouement in Vietnam would occur peacefully, it would also provide the time necessary for Washington to concentrate on strengthening the Western alliance, and to initiate new policies in the Middle East and Southwest Asia. At the same time detente would offer the opportunity to shape if not arrest the further development of the Soviet Union's strategic weapons program and possibly Moscow's foreign policy objectives as well.

Following Moscow's unsuccessful riposte in the Middle East and Caribbean, Soviet-American relations moved to a very delicate point, prompting the Soviets to decide to accept Nixon's offer. Detente with Washington would give Moscow the time and opportunity to change failed policies in Asia and the Middle East while pressing forward with its strategic weapons buildup and attempting to restrain that of the United States. As it became clear that Washington's main concerns centered on its allies as opposed to its adversaries, Moscow mobilized resources for a drive to improve the Soviet Union's overall geopolitical position. For entirely different reasons, then, Washington and Moscow moved to embrace the strategy of detente in early 1971.

Soviet Riposte in the Middle East: May–September 1970

Within weeks of the Cambodian operation, the beginnings of a double-barreled Soviet counterthrust could be identified. Concentrated in the Middle East and the Caribbean, the Soviet move dashed hope for the time being of any early political settlement between Washington and Moscow as well as between Egypt and Israel, raising serious concern that the long-anticipated Soviet advance to the strategic offensive was commencing.

Moscow signaled in advance one focus of its activity on May 13, when the Soviet ambassador to the United Nations, Jacob Malik, delivered a vitriolic attack on United States Middle East policy, the most inflammatory statement since the height of the cold war. Then, in early June, events in Egypt and Jordan hinted at a coordinated pincer move in the region, which threatened to squeeze Israel and alter the Arab-Israeli balance. Since the commitment of Soviet forces to Egypt in early March, Moscow had restricted its role to SAM defense of the Nile valley and air combat patrols.

In early June, however, Soviet and Egyptian crews gradually but systematically began to move mobile SAM batteries toward the Suez Canal zone. The Israelis immediately reacted, Defense Minister Moshe Dayan declaring that Israel would oppose entry of Soviet-manned missiles beyond a line thirty kilometers west of the canal.[2] Several attempts by the Israeli Defense Force to destroy the missile bases were unsuccessful; and by the end of the month, six bases had been established, three just north of Cairo and three in Upper Egypt, operated by over 10,000 Soviet technicians.[3] The Soviet-Egyptian missile system had been moved toward a new line about thirty kilometers west of the canal, and a number of Egyptian-manned missile batteries had been stationed even closer to the canal (though no Soviet-manned batteries crossed that line).[4]

At the same time, on June 9 in Jordan, Palestinian guerrillas of the Popular Front for the Liberation of Palestine (PFLP) under the command of George Habash unsuccessfully attempted to assassinate King Hussein and also attacked American civilian and diplomatic personnel in Amman. The king was attempting to put a stop to the Palestinian terrorist and guerrilla raids on Israel from Jordan, which were bringing Israeli retaliation against Jordan itself. A complicating factor in the growing antagonism between Jordanian and Palestinian forces was Iraq, which promised to come to the defense of the Palestinians should King Hussein attempt to suppress them. Since the Six Day War Iraq had deployed some 17,000 troops in Jordan. The volatile situation prompted Washington to begin the evacuation of American citizens (approximately 536 in-country) from Jordan in mid-June.

The implications of these events were most ominous for the United States and its allies. If successful, the shift of SAMs up to and along the canal front would give Egypt control over the airspace on both sides of the canal and enable Egyptian forces to attempt a crossing to secure the east bank.[5] A successful crossing, in turn, would of course permit the reopening of the Suez Canal without need of a political settlement between Egypt and Israel, a development that would have obvious and profound consequences for Israeli security and American strategy in and beyond the region. In Jordan the prospects were equally bleak. The king's demise would alter the entire political equation. It could result in the removal of American influence and at worst the establishment of a Palestinian state on Israel's border.

Washington's reaction was to renew efforts, beginning June 12, to bring about a negotiated settlement between Cairo and Tel Aviv. An additional factor in favor of resuming the peace effort was the appearance of a potential rift between Nasser and the Soviets that was reflected in the Egyptian leader's May Day speech and the already noted May 13 Soviet attack on United States Middle East policy. In his speech, Nasser called upon President Nixon "as the central actor" to become more involved in establishing an arms balance — if not by ordering an Israeli withdrawal, then by refraining from furnishing additional weaponry to Israel.[6]

The United States reaction was the "second" Rogers Plan, which differed from the first in that it was wholly an American and not a joint United States-Soviet proposal. Broached on June 19, it called for a cease-fire of limited duration, the reactivation of the Jarring United Nations mission and acceptance of United Nations Resolution 242 as a point of departure for negotiations. Washington sought firm, written commitments from each of the belligerents — Israel, Egypt, and Jordan — to participate in talks along these lines, in return for which the United States would sponsor a limited ninety-day cease-fire.

The second Rogers Plan produced an immediate negative response from Egypt and an equally firm rejection from Israel, but after extended consultation with their respective allies, both sides moved toward acceptance.[7] President Nasser left for Moscow on June 29 for an unprecedented seventeen-day stay. In retrospect, it appears that it was during his stay in Moscow that Nasser and the Soviet leadership conceived of an extraordinary plan to gain control of the Suez Canal airspace by moving the SAM batteries up to the canal under cover of the cease-fire proposed by the United States.[8] That decision, of course, was unknown at the time to President Nixon, who attempted to sweeten the pot further for both the Soviets and the Egyptians.

While Nasser was still in Moscow, Washington sought to win over both sides to the peaceful approach by making a number of attractive proposals. The first was a substantial shift on Middle Eastern issues that exerted additional pressure on Israel and offered inducements to Egypt. On July 12, the State Department announced that it would henceforth replace only combat losses of Israeli aircraft, leaving the clear implication that further aircraft deliveries would be forthcoming only if the cease-fire and peace talks failed.[9]

On the same day, Undersecretary Joseph Sisco in an interview on "Meet the Press" revealed two additional shifts in the United States position. Asked about UN Resolution 242, Sisco declared that the resolution did not require Israeli withdrawal from *all* occupied territory, a definite change from earlier United States positions and an obvious inducement to gain Israeli agreement to enter the talks. During the same interview, however, Sisco declared that any just and durable peace must take into consideration the interests of the Palestinians (but not the PLO), with whom the United States was now prepared to communicate.[10]

On July 22, shortly after his return from Moscow, President Nasser communicated his acceptance of the American proposal, which was endorsed the next day by Moscow. Jordan accepted it on July 27, and on the thirty-first, Golda Meir, after repeated assurances from President Nixon himself that Israeli security would not be jeopardized, also agreed to the cease-fire and negotiations. For a brief moment, the Middle East crisis seemed to have been defused, and in that moment President Nixon sought to extend an additional concession to gain Moscow's agreement to continue with the peaceful approach. On August 4, Washington substantially shifted its position in the strategic arms control negotiations then under way in Vienna.

Washington's specific objective in entering the strategic arms talks was to reduce the ultimate maximum Soviet attack capability against Minuteman, the United States land-based intercontinental ballistic missile force, preserving its survivability. Since the opening of negotiations, however, Washington had made no serious effort to reach agreement. The two initial United States proposals — options C and D — offered earlier in the year were clearly designed as openers to probe Moscow's objectives and had no chance of being accepted.[11] Both were thinly disguised attempts to place strict limits on Moscow's heavy missile program.

Option C called for an aggregate limit of 1,710 on ICBM and SLBM launchers with a freeze on further silo construction and a sublimit of 250 for the SS-9, the heavy Soviet missile which alone possessed the potential to become a MIRVed weapon capable of threatening Minuteman, even though it carried only a single warhead at that time. This option also included a MIRV ban, which was to be verified by means of on-site inspection. Although this was a risky proposal for the United States to make, since it offered Moscow the chance to prevent the MIRVing of Minuteman then just commencing, given the historical Soviet aversion to on-site inspection proposals, there was little likelihood that Moscow would accept option C.

Option D would attempt to limit the SS-9 in a different way. Option D also stipulated an ICBM-SLBM aggregate launcher limit of 1,710, a freeze on further construction of silos, and a sublimit of 250 launchers for the SS-9 heavy missile. It differed from option C in that there was no MIRV ban, but the aggregate and sublimits were to be reduced over the course of a seven-year period by one hundred missile launchers per year. The first of the build-down proposals, option D provided that by the end of the seven-year period the aggregate total would be 1,000 launchers and the SS-9 sublimit total would be approximately 125.[12] Although more generous than option C, option D also sought to constrain the Soviet Union's growing capability to threaten Minuteman. Option C would allow 250 single-warhead SS-9 launchers, while option D — after seven years — would allow a MIRVed SS-9 force of 125 launchers, or a total of 1,250 warheads, assuming ten warheads per launcher.

Neither of the SS-9 missile force structures postulated in options C and D would present an overwhelming threat to Minuteman's 1,054 launchers. Standard targeting doctrine called for a capability to deliver two warheads on each missile launcher, while having one in reserve. By this calculation, to field a first-strike threat against Minuteman with its heavy missiles, Moscow would require 300 or so heavy missile launchers MIRVed with ten warheads each, for a total of 3,000 warheads. Option C offered a total of 250 warheads, while option D offered 1,250.

Now, on August 4, in an effort to induce Moscow to be cooperative, President Nixon offered a third option, option E, which went substantially beyond the parameters set forth in the first two proposals.[13] The United States now proposed an aggregate total of launchers, including long-range bombers, of 1,900, an ICBM-SLBM sublimit of 1,710, and a further sublimit for the heavy SS-9 of 250. Option E stipulated neither a MIRV ban nor a year-by-year force reduction. In effect, Washington had offered to accept the potential doubling of the Soviet Union's heavy missile force over the proposal in option D. Assuming ten warheads per launcher, 250 SS-9s (or follow-on generation of heavy missile) would be able to field up to 2,500 warheads, which could indeed present a significant threat to Minuteman once deployed and made sufficiently accurate.

Even though this would be the most generous offer the United States would ever make for the Soviet Union's heavy missile force, Moscow rejected it, stalling in the negotiations for the next several months. The American effort to promote a peaceful settlement failed. In the Middle East, even though both parties had agreed to a standstill cease-fire, which meant no movement of military equipment of any kind into the cease-fire zone thirty-two miles on either side of the canal, the Soviets, who were not formally bound in any case, and the Egyptians, who were, violated the terms of the agreement even before it went into effect on August 7 and repeatedly thereafter through August and early September. Washington was initially loath to acknowledge what was in effect a double-cross—a cynical abuse of an international agreement and an arrogant challenge to the United States—and professed to have no conclusive information on the continued movement of SAM launchers toward the canal, despite reliable Israeli and American intelligence detailing the violation from the outset.

In addition to U-2 and SR-71 high-altitude reconnaissance missions monitoring canal activity from August 9, in anticipation of the cease-fire the United States had launched a reconnaissance satellite on July 22, which enabled twice-daily photographic coverage of the canal zone throughout the period.[14] By the end of August, Moscow had succeeded in constructing at least 45 SAM-2 sites with 270 launchers within the canal zone, 30 during the cease-fire period. Israel claimed to have identified 90 sites, including several SAM-3s.[15] Whatever the exact figure, during August the Soviet Union had managed to erect a virtually impregnable wall of fire over both banks of the Suez Canal.

The United States had denied what was known to be a gross violation of the cease-fire agreement for two fundamental reasons. First, with the Sihanoukville closure accomplished, the president was now prepared to move forward on a settlement between Egypt and Israel, including the reopening of the canal. He was confident that the actual opening of the canal could be delayed beyond the point where it would have an adverse impact on United States objectives in Vietnam. Secondly, he persisted in the hope that the peace process itself could be superimposed upon any plans for further conquest. Simply put, the president believed that once negotiations began the United States could make the prospects for peace much more attractive than the prospects for war.

Deepening appreciation of the Soviet-Egyptian scheme, however, as well as a clearer outline of Moscow's move in the Caribbean, brought a shift in the United States position as Washington made another, albeit brief, attempt to include a role for Moscow in the negotiations. In a confidential press briefing on August 27, Henry Kissinger divulged that the United States was considering a plan for "joint great power peacekeeping operations under UN auspices."[16] (Earlier, on July 2, during a similar press backgrounder Kissinger had spoken of "expelling" the Soviet military presence from the Middle East.) Neither the "joint operations" trial balloon nor repeated protests against the cease-fire violations brought a response from either Moscow or Cairo, forcing Washington to conclude that the Soviets were intent upon pursuit of unilateral objectives. For the time being, therefore, the president set aside plans for a negotiated settlement and proceeded to reestablish the military balance, which had skewed unevenly toward Egypt.

The public signal marking a policy change came on September 1, when the Senate passed the Military Procurement Authorization Act, which contained a clause granting Israel the right to receive generous military aid on very favorable terms to counter "past, present, or future" Soviet arms deliveries to the Arabs.[17] Where Washington earlier had procrastinated, claiming that "we just don't possess equipment capable of destroying"[18] the SAM threat, the United States now rushed to equip Israeli forces with the necessary electronic countermeasure equipment and air-to-ground missiles, which were indeed capable of defeating the SAM threat along the canal. But before any action could be taken against the SAM sites, events in Jordan intervened to divert all attention away from the canal for the next several weeks.

On September 1 came a second attempted assassination of King Hussein, which led immediately to a tense situation in Amman as armed scuffling took place between the King's Legion and Palestinian guerrillas. Then, on September 6 and 7, the PFLP failed in an attempt to capture an El-Al jet but hijacked four Western airliners (Pan American, TWA, Swissair, and BOAC), flew them to an airfield in

Jordan twenty-five kilometers from Amman (except for the Pan Am airliner, which was flown to Cairo and blown up), and held the 475 passengers hostage. The hijackers demanded the release of all Palestinians then in prison in Europe and Israel (around 3,000), threatening to blow up the remaining three planes if their demands were not met within seventy-two hours.

One explanation of the PFLP's action was that it was "part of a broader plan devised by Palestinian organizations to prevent any settlement in the Middle East without their participation."[19] The trouble with this interpretation was that the hijackings occurred after any prospect for a settlement had passed. Furthermore, the action itself was immediately seen by Arab governments as damaging the Palestinian cause, not enhancing it, and without exception they denounced the PFLP.

On the other hand, there is little doubt that the PFLP had in recent months become increasingly responsive to Moscow's direction.[20] From Moscow's perspective the hijacking served the larger purpose of a diversion by shifting the focus to Jordan and preserving the Soviet position on the canal. It also broadened the threat to Israel's eastern as well as southern front. Indeed, the hijackings held only marginal relevance for the issue of Palestinian interests in a Middle East settlement, but were crucial for Soviet actions in the Middle East and, as we shall see below, for Cuba as well.

Washington's reaction to the hijackings was to lead a diplomatic effort to gain the release of the hostages and aircraft, while at the same time quietly shifting additional military power toward the region. This included a favorable decision on the long-deferred Israeli request for additional aircraft. On September 9, President Nixon informed Primer Minister Meir that the United States would ship Israel eighteen F-4 Phantom jet fighters. Washington also ordered deployment of a carrier task force off the Lebanese coast, shifted twenty-five United States F-4 Phantoms from bases in Western Europe to Incirlik, Turkey, and placed airborne units within the United States on alert. In the interval between the deployment decision and its execution Moscow moved SAM-3s for the first time on September 11 into the cease-fire zone and consolidated its defensive network along the canal.[21]

On September 12 the PFLP suddenly and inexplicably agreed to a settlement of the crisis substantially short of its original demands. In return for the release by Israel of 450 Palestinians who had been arrested *after* the hijackings occurred, the PFLP began to set free the hostages, holding 55 Israeli citizens among the passengers until the last. On the twelfth they also blew up the three airliners. While the exchange was under way but not yet completed, King Hussein moved to crack down on the increasingly uncontrollable Palestinian guerrilla groups in his country. Flagrant Palestinian disregard of Jordanian law, the emergence of what amounted to a state within a state, made a showdown inevitable sooner or later. On September 17, the king began a violent supression of thousands of Palestinians throughout the country, including those in population centers.

The king's choice of the precise moment to attack, however, came after consultation with Washington, which offered to neutralize any attempted intervention by outside forces, particularly Iraq or Syria. President Nixon would make this pledge publicly on the seventeenth in what was ostensibly an off-the-record discussion with editors of the *Chicago Sun-Times*, but which made the newspaper's early edition.[22] Washington wished the king to act while the hostage crisis was as yet unresolved, because it gave a rationale for the presence of American power in the region. In Kissinger's words:

> Whether because our readiness measures had given him a psychological lift or because he was reaching the point of desperation, the tough little King resolved on an all-out confrontation with the fedayeen.[23]

The buildup mentioned above was now nearing completion. Washington's "readiness measures" included the rapid deployment of three aircraft carriers into the eastern Mediterranean — two, the *Saratoga* and the *Independence*, from the Sixth Fleet, and a third, the *John F. Kennedy*, from its cruising area in the Caribbean. Dispatched to join them were an amphibious task force including 1,200 Marines just finishing maneuvers off Crete; the Sixth Fleet flagship, the cruiser *Springfield*; and the helicopter carrier *Guam*, sent from the United States.[24] Clearly, the United States was girding for confrontation in the Middle East.

Iraq had threatened to intervene if the king moved against the Fedayeen, but throughout the Jordanian crisis Iraqi forces kept a circumspect distance, declining involvement of any kind. It was Syria which actually intervened, sending several hundred tanks into northwest Jordan on the morning of September 19.[25] King Hussein immediately requested the promised American intervention, a request which presented Nixon with a dilemma.

Although the president had declared his intention to use American power to deter outside intervention, to do so raised the danger of Soviet involvement and the possibility of a major confrontation. On the other hand, if Nixon failed to act and Israel intervened, as there seemed a good possibility it would, the king would believe himself to have been betrayed, for he was adamantly against Israeli involvement on his behalf. And with good reason. Israeli intervention would seriously compromise the king politically in the Arab world—his position was already deteriorating as a result of his brutal suppression of the Palestinians—even if it succeeded in saving him militarily.

It was becoming increasingly apparent that Israel would act to secure its own interests. Tel Aviv could not tolerate the establishment of a hostile Palestinian state in Jordan and so would move to prevent the defeat of King Hussein, whether he liked it or not. Indeed, as soon as Syrian tanks appeared in Jordan, Israel began to mobilize its forces and by September 21 had concentrated two brigades on the Golan Heights with more on the way, threatening the Syrian flank.[26]

Meanwhile, in Washington, despite the president's publicly stated preference that the United States act, he quietly backed away from that commitment and instead attempted to prod Israel into action. On the evening of the twentieth, Kissinger called Ambassador Yitzhak Rabin, asking him to pass on a message to Prime Minister Meir, then in New York following her official visit to Washington. He said that "King Hussein has . . . asked us to transmit his request that your air force attack the Syrians in northern Jordan."[27] Suspicious, Rabin replied that he was "surprised to hear the United States passing on messages of this kind like some sort of mailman" and refused to accept the request until it was official.

After further discussion, which clarified that it was the United States, not Hussein, that wished Israel to take action, Rabin was instructed to say that Israel would intervene only if in a "written undertaking" Washington agreed to provide both additional weapons and an American umbrella "if the Soviet Union threatened Israel directly."[28] Contrary to Kissinger's assertion that United States forces "were best employed in holding the ring against Soviet interference with Israeli operations,"[29] he, in fact, declined to make any written commitment, agreeing orally only to provide additional arms.[30]

In the event, Washington was never required to make good on

either Hussein's or Rabin's demands. Whether the king from his more limited perspective felt that he had been misled or maneuvered by Washington into taking action, or whether he believed it necessary to preempt Israeli action, on September 22 he sent his air force against the advancing Syrian tank columns with great effect, forcing their withdrawal and bringing the crisis to rapid conclusion.[31] The presence of American and Israeli power not only encouraged and enabled Hussein to act, it evidently also deterred the use of Syria's air force, which, under the command of General Hafez Asad, never made an appearance.[32]

Moscow's behavior throughout the Middle East crisis centered on a single objective not immediately apparent — to keep Egypt isolated and dependent upon the Soviet Union. The Soviet leadership perceived that Egypt under Nasser was growing disenchanted with Moscow, and the Soviets sought to employ the continuing conflict between Egypt and Israel to drive a wedge between the United States and Egypt, preempting any rapprochement between them and strengthening the Soviet position in the process.

The point of decision for Moscow's Middle East missile scheme probably came hard on the United States incursion into Cambodia and Nasser's May Day speech, whose purpose Anwar Sadat later claimed was "to start a dialogue with the United States."[33] The subsequent plan to subvert the cease-fire, the triggering of the hostage crisis, and the Syrian intervention all bore marks of Moscow's hand in the course of events. The Soviet presence in manning the SAMs in Egypt and moving them in violation of the cease-fire requires no further elaboration; Moscow's influence in the PFLP was well known but difficult to document; and Syrian tank forces were accompanied by Soviet "advisers" literally up to the Jordanian border, at which point they departed.[34]

Soviet diplomatic interaction with the United States was an example of persistent duplicity throughout the crisis, but duplicity with a purpose. There was no intent to provoke a Soviet-American confrontation. For example, the Soviet Union never attempted to match the United States naval buildup in the eastern Mediterranean. What Moscow sought to do was prod the United States into openly siding with Israel and against Egypt.

Thus, Moscow initially adopted a "positive" attitude toward the cease-fire,[35] then proceeded to move SAMs directly into the prohibited cease-fire zone. When questioned, Moscow's answer was a semantic evasion: the Soviet Union could not violate an agreement to which it was not a party.[36] It goes without saying that Moscow did not join with the otherwise unanimous condemnation of the PFLP during the hostage crisis. Soviet diplomacy during the Syrian intervention was even more blatant. On September 18, Moscow sent a note to President Nixon saying that Syria was not moving its forces; the next day Syrian tanks moved into Jordan.[37] On the twenty-first, Moscow sent yet another note declaring that the Soviets were pressing Syria not to send additional tanks; the next day came more tanks.[38]

Soviet policy was designed to provoke the United States into siding openly with Israel, which would have bankrupted American credibility as an honest broker and forced Egypt back into dependence upon the Soviet Union. But the Soviet scheme failed. Washington refused to be drawn in—either out of design or by chance—and throughout maintained as balanced a position as possible even under the extreme provocation of the Syrian intervention.

In short, the failure of the Soviet ploy left open the door to improvement of Egyptian-American relations and kept alive the possibility of a political settlement between Egypt and Israel. On September 28, however, after having convened an Arab summit in Cairo to repair the damage done to the Arab cause by the recent crisis, President Nasser died. His death put an end, for the time being, to Soviet machinations in the Arab-Israeli problem. By then the American leadership had already turned to deal with the other barrel of Moscow's double-barreled initiative of the autumn of 1970—the construction of a submarine base in Cuba.

Diversion and Counterdiversion in Cuba

Although the story of Soviet base construction at Cienfuegos, Cuba, broke on September 25, United States intelligence and the top administration leadership had been closely monitoring Soviet activity in Cuba since at least mid-year. Moscow had undertaken a major global naval exercise—the first of its kind—in the spring of 1970, termed "OKEAN 70." As part of the exercise a Soviet naval task force had visited Cuba in April. By June subsequent Soviet activity in the area had fully sensitized United States naval intelligence to the potential dangers. In fact, the issue of a Soviet naval base in Cuba came up during closed-door hearings of the House Subcommittee on Inter-American Affairs held July 8 through August 3. Several speakers testified to the significance such a base would have for overall naval capabilities and for extended submarine operations off American shores.[39]

The United States government did not make an issue of the Soviet probe into the Caribbean at this time, first, because Soviet construction activity was in an embryonic stage. There was little to complain about, and Moscow's intent was as yet unclear. Secondly, the president saw no need to magnify an already complex situation then developing in the Middle East. It was only after the Middle East crisis had been surmounted that the administration turned to the issue of Soviet activity in Cuba, which only by then had become serious. As the Middle East crisis evolved, Moscow coordinated an acceleration of base construction on the small island of Cayo Alcatraz near the port of Cienfuegos with the rapid movement of SAMs up to the Suez Canal, the crucial phases of both operations coming during the period of the Middle East cease-fire and airline hijackings, from early August to mid-September.

There was nothing clandestine about Soviet construction activity near Cienfuegos. In fact, Moscow pointedly drew the administration's attention to Cuba just prior to the beginning of the Middle East cease-fire. This was probably as much an effort to divert the attention of American leaders away from the Middle East as it was to stress the administration's response and reaction capabilities to two crises occurring simultaneously. At any rate, on August 4, Soviet Chargé d'Affaires Yuli Vorontsov, acting for Ambassador Dobrynin, who was on leave in Moscow, conveyed the Soviet government's desire to "reaffirm" the 1962 Kennedy-Khrushchev understanding on Cuba.[40] Moreover, the Soviet government insisted that the United States "strictly adhere to the understanding," suggesting that Moscow had discovered a loophole which it obviously intended to exploit.

Nixon and Kissinger evidently concluded that the Soviets were attempting to whipsaw the United States in both the Middle East and Cuba, hoping to make a gain in one or both places. The United States response was to lead the Soviets into believing that they had indeed found a justification for doing what they wished to do, but, as soon as the Middle East crisis was resolved, the United States would close that loophole and remove any basis for Soviet activity in Cuba. When Kissinger responded to Vorontsov on August 7—the day the Middle East cease-fire formally went into effect—the Soviet Union had already begun rapidly moving SAMs into the canal zone. Kissinger's reply stated that the United States government considered the 1962 understanding in full force, defining it as prohibiting the emplacement of any offensive weapon of any kind or any offensive delivery system on Cuban territory.[41]

The national security adviser's carefully crafted reply said nothing about general Soviet activity in the Western Hemisphere, nor of the emplacement of any support facility for nuclear submarines. Restricting the reaffirmation to "Cuban territory" was a marked difference from the actual understanding reached by President Kennedy in 1962. Indeed, the operative statement made by Kennedy on November 20, 1962, was that there would be peace in the Caribbean

> if all offensive weapons are removed from Cuba and kept out of the Hemisphere in the future, under adequate verification and safeguards, and if Cuba is not used for the export of aggressive Communist purposes. . . .[42]

Comparing the two statements, as Soviet leaders most certainly would have done, clearly suggested that the United States no longer considered the Western Hemisphere an exclusive preserve.

Secondly, limiting the understanding to the emplacement of offensive weapons or delivery systems left open the most likely and in fact anticipated case—the construction of a support facility for a nuclear submarine. In Soviet eyes that which was not expressly prohibited was permissible. If Soviet leaders held any reservations that there was sufficient latitude in the 1962 understanding to permit construction of a nuclear submarine support facility—which probably generated the request for reaffirmation of the 1962 understanding and strict adherence to it in the first place—Kissinger's reply encouraged a positive interpretation. Yet, if Kissinger gave a green light to the Soviets in the Caribbean, from Washington's perspective his answer turned the Soviet diversion into an American counterdiversion, as Washington concentrated its attention on the crisis in the Middle East and officially disregarded Cuba for the time being.

Following Washington's "reaffirmation" of the 1962 understanding, the Soviet Union commenced construction of a nuclear submarine support facility on Cayo Alcatraz in earnest. The U-2 flight of August 11 showed nothing extraordinary, but the flight of August 26 indicated recent and ongoing construction activity.[43] The construction activity combined with additional intelligence of the movement of several Soviet ships en route to Cuba confirmed what up to this point had been only a tentative hypothesis.

Among the ships, particularly suggestive were a submarine tender and two eighty-foot barges. Upon inspection, the barges turned out to be storage bins for discharged radioactive waste from nuclear submarine reactors.[44] The function of the tender was self-evident. The ships reached Cienfuegos Bay on September 9. When Cuban MiGs scrambled after the next U-2 flight on September 14, forcing the aborting of its mission, and the next day intercepted a United States Navy antisubmarine aircraft out on patrol, the administration became fully alerted to the probability that construction was nearing completion.

A successful U-2 mission of September 16 confirmed the worst. That day in Chicago, Kissinger gave a background briefing dealing largely with the Middle East situation during which he conveyed a veiled warning to the Soviets to curtail their activity in Cuba. The president, during a meeting with the editors of the *Chicago Sun-Times* the next day, declared that the United States was prepared to intervene in the Jordanian crisis, which had just broken out. The "Cuban problem" then was set aside while the administration concentrated upon the crisis in the Middle East, which continued for the next week. It was not until September 24 that confirmation came of the withdrawal of Syria's tanks from Jordanian territory, and it was only then that the administration turned its full attention to Cuba.[45]

The following afternoon, the twenty-fifth, after the story of Soviet base construction had leaked to the press, Kissinger closed the loophole the Soviets thought they had discerned in the 1962 understanding. During an afternoon briefing, in response to a question on Cuba, Kissinger quoted in full President Kennedy's November 20, 1962, statement cited above, emphasizing the phrase "if all offensive weapons are removed from Cuba and kept out of the Hemisphere in the future." Then he said, "This, of course, remains the policy of this Government."[46] In a meeting with Ambassador Dobrynin later that day, Kissinger made plain the administration's position that "the base could not remain," dismissing Dobrynin's denial that the 1962 understanding had been violated as a "legalistic quibble." Tightening the loophole into a noose, he said: "Whatever the phraseology of the 1962 understanding, its intent could not have been to replace land-based with sea-based missiles."[47]

It would be almost two weeks before Dobrynin replied on October 6. The Soviet note denied that the Soviet government had done "anything . . . that would contradict" the 1962 understanding and reaffirmed that "the Soviet side strictly adheres to its part of the understanding."[48] The issue of what constituted a base, however, remained vague, and to establish a common definition, on October 9, Kissinger handed Dobrynin a "president's note" setting forth the United States conception.

> The US Government understands that the USSR will not establish, utilize, or permit the establishment of any facility in Cuba that can be employed to support or repair Soviet naval ships capable of carrying offensive weapons; i.e., submarines or surface ships armed with nuclear-capable, surface-to-surface missiles.[49]

On October 13, the Soviet news agency Tass published a communiqué in reply. The heart of it was that the Soviet Union "has not been and is not building its own military base" in Cuba. Although this did not directly address the presumed loophole of the 1962 understanding which did not specifically refer to naval support facilities, base construction was halted and no permanent shore facility was established in Cuba. Nevertheless, the end of the diplomatic contest did not mean an end to Soviet probing. For several months Moscow employed virtually every combination of port calls, submarine visits, and attempts to service Soviet missile submarines at sea from a sub tender based in Cuba to obtain United States tacit acceptance for the presence of Soviet missile submarines around Cuba. In every instance Washington objected, and each objection produced a new combination until early the following year when Moscow terminated its activity.

What is to be said of Soviet-American interaction in the autumn of 1970? From Moscow's point of view the moves in the Middle East and Cuba constituted spoiling-diversionary operations designed primarily to prevent the success of American efforts in the Middle East. If successful, they would have conferred more than the "petty advantage" Kissinger claims,[50] but nevertheless they amounted to less than a full response to what was a substantive American move to bring Egypt and Israel together as the future foundation of a collective defense structure for the region.

Soviet policy did, however, succeed in temporarily disrupting Washington's efforts, even though the crucial event—Nasser's death—was probably unanticipated and bought Moscow time to elaborate and initiate a more comprehensive response. Time was also important for Moscow's strategic weapons buildup, which was occurring at great speed, to reach politically useful proportions. Soviet policy in the autumn of 1970 may be viewed as strategic in the limited sense that in order for one's own strategy to succeed, he must first prevent the success of his adversary's strategy. The main thrust of Soviet policy, then, was to buy the time needed to build the strategic weapons which would neutralize the basis of American strategy.

Problems of Alliance and Collective Defense

The shift in the strategic weapons balance between the United States and the Soviet Union was only one of the significant structural shifts to occur during the previous decade. Equally if not more momentous was the shift of relative economic strength within the Western alliance—this also to the disadvantage of the United States. The combination of increased Soviet power and greater allied economic strength, particularly that of West Germany and Japan, was undermining the very foundations of the alliance structure.

Moreover, the adverse trend within the alliance was occurring as the American economic position was deteriorating badly as a result of the Vietnam War effort. Further compounding the United States difficulty was the failure to achieve the establishment of even an initial basis for constructing a strengthened collective defense in the Middle East. Finally, looming in the background but transcending the importance of any particular country or region were international monetary and energy problems which were rapidly approaching crisis proportions.

In Europe, dangerous conditions were evolving that could lead to greater West European integration and concomitant reduction of American influence. Indeed, by late 1970 there was substantial evidence of the trend toward unity and independence as well as a greatly enhanced German position in Eastern and Western Europe. Between the Hague summit in December 1969 and the Munich meeting of November 1970, the members of the European Economic Community (EEC) had taken several substantive steps toward the economic, monetary, and foreign policy integration of Western Europe. First, the community had decided at the Hague meeting to enlarge and strengthen its membership. The following March agreement came on a three-stage plan for full monetary and economic union by 1980. In July came the Davignon Report suggesting various ways to promote an integrated foreign policy, and in October the Werner Report outlined steps necessary to achieve full monetary integration. Then, in November 1970, the EEC members agreed to adopt a common voting procedure in the United Nations.

The general movement toward West European unity was complemented by West Germany's *Ostpolitik*, a policy of several years' standing, which had been given increased momentum under newly elected Chancellor Willy Brandt. Brandt's objective was the normalization of Bonn's relations with the countries of the East. By the end of 1970 he had already concluded the West German-Soviet treaty of peaceful cooperation (on August 12) and the treaty normalizing relations with Poland (on December 7). Similar negotiations were either scheduled or under way with Czechoslovakia, Bulgaria, and Hungary (and would be completed by 1973). Normalization negotiations between Bonn and the East German regime were also under way, as were four-power talks on the status of Berlin. Bonn's multiple initiatives were viewed by the Nixon leadership as containing the distinct prospect of "a more independent and a more national course by Germany."[51]

The West German-Soviet treaty codified the two parties' acceptance of the status quo in Europe and their common objection to the "threat or use of force . . . in any matters affecting security in Europe or international security, as well as in their mutual relations."[52] To the extent that the West German rapprochement with the Soviet Union reduced the need for a United States security guarantee, it opened the door for a gradual West German and, indeed, West European loosening of ties to the United States and perhaps ultimately disengagement. Moscow, of course, welcomed and encouraged Bonn's *Ostpolitik* as a means of defusing a potential two-front conflict situation then evolving from China's realignment with the United States.

Soviet interest in neutralizing any threat on its western or European front stemmed from two strategic considerations: first, the principle of avoiding entanglement in two-front conflict situations and, secondly, the opportunity of using the Soviet Union's growing strategic power to attempt to edge Western Europe into a more neutralist stance, driving a wedge between the United States and its NATO partners. The European anchor of containment was thus being weakened by the growth of West German economic power and the long-proclaimed but only recently feasible desires of the West European powers to develop a greater degree of unity among themselves. The logical consequence of both trends was the gradual de facto shift of Western Europe toward a central position within the larger structure of United States-Soviet relations.

While West Germany's leaders emphasized the strengthening of Bonn's political base, Japan's leaders were moving along another tack by attempting to develop an independent energy base. By the mid-sixties, Japan, like the European powers, had largely completed the transition from coal- to oil-based energy but had virtually no control over its energy supply. Over 80 percent of Japan's imported petroleum came from Kuwait, Iraq, Saudi Arabia, and Iran and depended upon the good will of the Arab countries and the disposition of the international, mostly American, oil companies. By 1970, Japan's consumption of energy had exceeded the annual equivalent of two hundred million tons of oil, placing Japan third behind the United States and the Soviet Union in total energy use. Conservative estimates projected that Japan's total energy demand would quadruple by 1985 and that the share of petroleum as a percentage of total energy use would increase from 60 to 75 percent.[53]

Anticipating this trend, in 1966 the Japanese government had embarked upon a major effort to secure greater control over its energy supply and by 1970 seemed to be on the verge of considerable success. During this period a consortium of Japanese companies had obtained through competitive bidding two major concessionary tracts in Abu Dhabi, which promised to make a significant contribution to alleviating Japan's anticipated petroleum needs by the mid-seventies. Greater use was also made of the Kafji field in the neutral quarter, originally developed by Japan in 1959, but only ineffectively exploited.

Negotiations were opened with the Soviet Union regarding the development of Siberian gas and oil. Such an arrangement, if completed, offered to provide Japan with approximately 15 percent of its imported petroleum. The government also purchased an interest in a Canadian company for joint exploration in Canada, including a tar sands project. The Japanese government formed an Alaskan Oil

Resources Development company and joined with Gulf Oil to explore prospects in Alaska. Japan also expanded its Indonesian Petroleum Development Company, financing the development of offshore discoveries in Northern Sumatra and Kalimantan.

Tokyo also purchased an interest in an Australian company for work in Australia and New Guinea and attempted to gain entry into the Latin American oil market as well. By 1970, Japan was involved in over fifty exploratory ventures, and the prospect was for as rapid a growth in Japanese-financed and -controlled oil production by the end of the seventies as the previous decade had been for Japanese oil consumption.[54] If successful, Japan's energy independence could pave the way for greater political independence at some point in the future.

Japan's search for energy independence was maturing at a time when the structure of world oil was undergoing rapid change. In September 1970 the decade of cheap petroleum had begun to close, with the first accession of the international oil companies to Libyan demands for price increases. The key event had occurred a year before in September 1969 when a young army captain, Moammar Gadhafi, engineered the overthrow of Libyan King Idris. Following the prompt and curiously uncontested ouster of American and British military bases from Libya in January 1970, the new revolutionary government initiated "negotiations" with the oil companies operating in the country for an increase in revenues. At this point, Libya was supplying a full quarter of Western Europe's petroleum imports and 41 percent of West Germany's import needs alone, placing Gadhafi in a very strong bargaining position.

When the oil companies resisted Gadhafi's demand for a forty-four cent-per-barrel price increase, he began to apply pressure. First, he reduced total oil production in Libya from the April 1970 high of 3.67 million barrels per day (b/d) to 2.9 million b/d in September. Then he forced the most vulnerable of the oil companies, Occidental Petroleum, an independent company controlled by Armand Hammer that had no foreign petroleum operation outside of Libya, to bear the brunt of the reductions imposed on the oil companies. Occidental's 800,000 b/d output was reduced to 680,000 b/d in May, 485,000 b/d in June, and 425,000 b/d in August.[55] Isolated and unable to obtain the support of the other oil companies, the pressure became irresistible for Hammer to capitulate to Gadhafi's demands.[56]

Other events also contributed to the growing pressure. In May the Trans-Arabia pipeline (TAPline) from Saudi Arabia to the Mediterranean was "accidentally" ruptured in Syria and purposely not repaired until January 1971, when Damascus obtained higher prices for transit rights. The closure quickly sent tanker freight rates up and tightened the oil supply situation. The market was further strained in July when Algeria, following lengthy and fruitless negotiations with France, unilaterally raised the price of oil to French companies from $2.08 to $2.85 per barrel.

At this point, in early September, fearing nationalization, Occidental's Hammer agreed to an immediate price increase of thirty cents a barrel (bringing the Libyan crude price to $2.53), a two-cents-a-year increase for the next five years, and an increase in the income tax rate from 50 to 58 percent. In return for this agreement, signed September 2, the Libyan government allowed Occidental to increase production to a rate of 700,000 b/d, still below its peak production rate.[57]

The Occidental capitulation was quickly emulated by the other producing companies in Libya, especially after Socal and Texaco, two important majors, agreed to settle in mid-October. Though small by current standards, at the time the Libyan settlement was impressive, creating a stir in high petroleum and government circles. For the first time, a producing government had prevailed in negotiations with the hitherto all-powerful international oil companies.

The Libyan settlement almost immediately had repercussions elsewhere. The first to react was the shah of Iran, who, shifting position, now also demanded a price increase.[58] The shah's long-held position, reaffirmed as recently as June 6, 1970, was:

> Our aim is not to get a higher price for Iranian oil; rather we are trying to increase our revenues through more production of crude oil.[59]

The shah's policy shift from demands for a production increase to demands for a price increase was quickly imitated by other Gulf producers. Dissatisfied with the oil companies' pronounced aversion to a price increase, leaders of the producing countries coordinated their strategy at the OPEC conference in Caracas, Venezuela, in December. At Caracas, the OPEC members agreed that those companies which had refused to meet minimum price demands would be denied access to oil supplies, and OPEC countries in that case would simply post their own prices.[60] The approach decided upon was to negotiate with the oil companies on a regional basis. Each of three groups of oil-producing countries (Persian Gulf, Mediterranean, and Venezuela-Indonesia) would negotiate their price objectives separately under the loose overall coordination of OPEC.

The emerging unity of the oil-producing countries under the OPEC umbrella paralleled a similar development on the part of the oil companies. By late 1970 the leaders of the international oil companies were themselves fully aroused and preparing to defend their interests. Whereas the oil producers sought split negotiations with the oil companies based on the regional approach, the oil companies had decided that their best approach lay in negotiating *en bloc* in order to obtain an overall agreement and avoid being trapped in an ever-escalating whipsaw sequence of price rises.[61] The stage was thus set for a major confrontation between the companies and the producing countries.

Changes in the world petroleum market were occurring against the backdrop of the disintegration of the international monetary system fashioned by the United States after World War II. When President Nixon assumed office in 1969 inflation was raging in the United States, and the dollar was seriously overvalued abroad. The stable international monetary regime which the Bretton Woods agreements were designed to promote had been thrown out of kilter during the sixties.

Under Bretton Woods, nations in balance of payments surplus and deficit were called upon to make adjustments to correct balance of payments disequilibrium. Nations in surplus were, in theory, to appreciate their currencies (value them upward), while nations in deficit were supposed to depreciate (value them downward). The inevitable bias in the system was, however, inflationary. Nations in deficit were more readily inclined to devalue to improve their competitive positions (except for the United States), while nations in surplus were persistently reluctant to appreciate their currencies and thus unilaterally deprive themselves of competitive advantages.

The American economy as the engine of the postwar international monetary system produced the necessary liquidity for the expansion of trade and economic growth largely by running persistent balance of payments deficits. The deficit position skyrocketed, as did world inflation, as a result of heavy Vietnam War costs. The obvious answer was for the United States to devalue the dollar in order to restore equilibrium to the system. In negotiations during 1969–1970, the

Nixon administration discovered that America's allies, especially the nations in surplus, were disinclined to permit the United States to devalue its currency and thus painlessly resolve its balance of payments problem. They "made it clear" that should the United States devalue unilaterally, they also "would devalue by an equal amount," thus nullifying the United States move.[62]

President Nixon's response, aside from calling for monetary reform, was to promote conditions which would make United States devaluation unavoidable and necessary, if not actually welcome. The essence of the policy, termed "benign neglect," was to do nothing to stem the growing outflow of dollars or to support the dollar in foreign exchange markets. Theoretically, as dollars accumulated abroad, dollar devaluation, or N-country currency appreciation, could become a simple function of an excess of supply over demand. To prevent appreciation of their currencies, which would reduce competitiveness by raising the price of exports, foreign central banks began to accumulate ever-greater amounts of dollars. But such a process could not continue indefinitely. At some point, dollar devaluation would become unavoidable.

The main, but not the only, accumulators of American dollars were West Germany and Japan, the two most important surplus nations. As United States credit conditions eased in the fourth quarter of 1969, lowering short-term interest rates, and as German credit conditions tightened and raised rates, there occurred an increase of short-term capital flow into Germany toward the higher interest rates. In 1970, the United States deficit reached a new high of nearly ten billion dollars and the nation moved into recession, while German dollar reserves increased to nearly six billion.[63] Japanese capital import controls mitigated the effects of the dollar flow somewhat, but Japan's central bank also accumulated dollars in unprecedented amounts. The scene was set for the final collapse of the fixed exchange rate system. By the end of 1970 the underlying structural trends in wealth, energy, and power were, from Washington's point of view, decidedly unattractive.

Detente, Dependence, and Defense

At the end of 1970 President Nixon adopted a complex policy mix in an effort to resolve these long-term problems. To correct the drift toward strategic weapons decline, the United States would offer detente to Moscow, which would include a strategic arms accord in the context of a general improvement in relations. Additionally, friendly engagement with Moscow would give Washington the opportunity to ease China into a new relationship with the United States without provocation to Moscow and reach a satisfactory settlement in Vietnam. Finally, a strong effort would be required to build a collective defense position in the Middle East–Southwest Asian region to compensate for the failure to promote an Egyptian-Israeli peace and in hopes of delaying if not preventing the anticipated collapse of Pakistan.

Most important, detente with Moscow would allow the United States to focus on its principal problem of rebuilding the Western alliance. That rebuilding process would essentially comprise several policies designed to promote the continued reliance if not dependence of the allies upon American strength and wealth. The principal drawback would be the continued growth of Moscow's military power and the leverage it gave future Soviet efforts to unhinge the Western alliance. Moreover, detente would encourage America's allies to emulate United States behavior and also seek improved relations with Moscow, thus accelerating the disintegrating tendencies already evident. But this was a course on which the allies were already embarked, so it was less risky than would otherwise have been the case.

The decision to offer detente to Moscow came at the moment when indications suggested strongly that the Soviet Union was poised for a major choice in its strategic weapons program. By late 1970, the Soviet strategic weapons program had produced 1,440 ICBM launchers (including early models), a figure which, incidentally, American intelligence had underestimated by nearly 150 launchers.[64] Soviet ballistic missile submarine construction continued apace with seventeen or eighteen Y-class boats operational and capable of firing between 272 and 288 missiles and another fifteen or sixteen boats under construction.

A crucial degree of uncertainty surrounded the SS-9, Moscow's heavy missile and the only one then able to provide the basis for a future counterforce capability against the United States. In the spring the Soviet Union had 282 SS-9s operational or under construction and in May had begun construction of 24 additional SS-9 silos. In October, however, just before the third SALT session commenced, the Soviets had begun to dismantle 18 of the most recent silo starts and to slow down construction work on some 30 more, limiting the number of operational SS-9s to around 250.[65]

Was the slowdown intended to signal acceptance of option E, which proposed a limit of 250 heavy missiles, as some in the SALT delegation thought? Or were the Soviets preparing to introduce a new generation of heavy missile?[66] The answer to these questions, of course, would indicate the fundamental direction of Soviet policy—whether to settle for equilibrium or strive for advantage—and have a decisive impact on United States policy calculations. As it turned out the questions were only partly answered when the SALT conferees assembled in early November for the third session (November 2 through December 18).

The immediate Soviet reply to option E was to stall, creating a deadlock in the negotiations. During the session Soviet negotiators insisted on an anti-ballistic missile (ABM) treaty only, their original position, declining to discuss any limitations on offensive systems, while insisting upon a redefinition of United States offensive systems to include forward bases.[67] (Although unappreciated at the time, the use of the "forward based systems" ploy would become one of Moscow's favored methods of stalling.) Thus, while it was clear at this point to the president, if not to members of the SALT delegation, that Moscow had not meant to signal agreement with option E by the October slowdown in silo construction, it was not yet clear precisely what the slowdown did mean.

But time was running out. If Moscow had decided to press for advantage, as expected, it was all the more necessary to be in a position to influence the buildup. SALT and detente would be the instruments of leverage, and the longer it took to reach agreements on strategic arms the more disadvantageous that agreement would ultimately be to the United States as the Soviet buildup proceeded. As we know in retrospect, Moscow's and Washington's policy calculations regarding the utility of improving relations were meshing, not diverging, though evolving from opposite strategic positions.

Moscow, too, had decided to adopt detente in an attempt to lock the United States into an inferior position while sharply increasing its strategic forces to desired levels. Thus, detente at its core, whatever else it might have been to others or whatever it evolved into once begun, was initially and essentially the agreement to freeze existing quantitative strategic weapons positions. Geopolitical rivalry continued under the rubric of detente, as Moscow sought to manipulate regional crises to advantage and Washington strove to negate Moscow's increasing foreign policy assertiveness short of the level of superpower confrontation.

When Henry Kissinger conveyed to Ambassador Dobrynin President Nixon's offer to build "a more constructive relationship" on December 22, 1970, he set out on the first concrete step toward detente.[68] Moscow returned an affirmative response on January 6, and it was agreed to establish a secret "back channel" through which the two countries could work out their differences at the highest and most confidential level. Three days later, on January 9, Kissinger proposed a solution to break the current deadlock in the strategic arms negotiations.

Washington had originally insisted upon a single treaty linking limits on offensive and defensive weapons. Moscow had just as doggedly pressed for an exclusive treaty banning missile defense. Only after conclusion of an ABM treaty would Moscow agree to begin discussion of offensive limitations. Now Kissinger offered a compromise. The United States, he said, would agree to conclude a separate treaty on defensive arms in conjunction with an accompanying five-year "interim agreement," or freeze, on deployment of offensive weapons. The linkage of offensive and defensive systems would be satisfied by virtue of the fact that the treaty and the interim agreement would be negotiated simultaneously.

Moscow replied on February 4, agreeing to the proposed compromise. Ironically, United States terms for the offensive freeze spurred an intensification of Soviet missile silo construction that same month. Since the "permitted levels would be the number of weapons operational or under construction on the date the freeze went into effect," Moscow immediately resumed silo construction while at the same time stringing out final agreement so as to ensure that the Soviet Union would possess a position of advantage when the agreement "went into effect."[69] Furthermore, since "modernization and replacement would be permitted . . . only by weapons of the same category," Moscow hastened to begin the deployment of two new generations of ICBM, the SS-18 which would eventually replace the SS-9 and the SS-19 which would replace the SS-11.[70] One cannot help but wonder why the freeze was not made retroactive to avoid the obvious and fully predictable moves by Moscow to obtain maximum advantage.

Moscow's negotiating approach was fully consistent with its policy objective. The Soviets needed time for silo construction to get under way and delayed reaching agreement. First, in early February, Dobrynin reverted to Moscow's original position that discussion of offensive systems could begin only after completion of the defensive treaty. Washington's objections only succeeded in further Soviet procrastination. Negotiations would resume following the Twenty-Fourth Party Congress (March 30–April 9). Following the congress, on April 23, Dobrynin did agree to discuss offensive limitations prior to completion of the defensive agreement, but then stalled once again.

Without warning, in early May, the Soviets shifted what up to this point had been private discussions between the White House and the Kremlin to the SALT delegations themselves. There, the chief of the Soviet delegation, Vladimir Semenov, restated the original proposal of defensive agreement first, then offensive, to Gerard Smith, chief of the American delegation, in effect starting over from square one. What had Moscow hoped to achieve by breaching the confidentiality of the secret back channel? Aside from angering and perhaps disillusioning the members of the delegation who believed they were the sole negotiators and thereby undermining morale, the main purpose of the Soviet maneuver seems to have been to buy additional time by generating domestic political pressure on the president. (The Soviet proposal was promptly leaked to the press, evidently from someone in the delegation.)

In any event, the Soviet ploy failed, and following strenuous objections from the White House, on May 12, both sides reached agreement on the so-called SALT "breakthrough," which was announced on May 20, 1971.[71] The announcement stated that the United States and the Soviet Union "have agreed to concentrate this year on working out an agreement" on anti-ballistic missile systems as well as "certain measures with respect to the limitation of offensive strategic weapons."[72] Yet, even then, after the announcement had been made, the Soviet leadership sought to obfuscate the terms of the agreement by wording the Russian language text to imply that offensive limitations would come only after conclusion of a defensive accord. The upshot of this final stall, when discovered, was that the agreed-upon official version of the May 20 announcement was retyped in the English language on Soviet embassy stationery!

Although Soviet diplomacy once again evidenced heavy-handedness and duplicity, the reason for the stall was obvious enough. Beginning in late January and continuing through October, the Soviet Union resumed construction at a rapid pace on ninety-one additional silos.

Twenty-five of these were clearly designed for the new generation SS-18, bringing the count for the SS-18/ SS-9 heavy missile up to the 308 figure,[73] while the remainder were for the SS-19/ SS-11 ICBM.[74] In other words, Moscow had commenced the construction of ICBM launchers in sufficient numbers to provide the basis for a Soviet missile threat to Minuteman, once the technical problems of multiple war-heads and pinpoint accuracy had been solved in the future. Kissinger, in commenting on the May 20 agreement, was less than candid in saying that the Soviet Union "had in effect accepted a freeze on new starts of strategic missiles."[75]

Countering Fractionation in the Alliance

From late in 1970, realigning the Western alliance and strengthening the United States' position within it became a high priority for the president. Policies were determined whose structural effects would not be felt immediately in all cases, for the consequences of earlier decisions made during the Johnson administration could not easily or quickly be undone. Indeed, some damage was irreparable. The long-term objective was to work toward a downward adjustment in the growth of allied economic power, particularly of West Germany and Japan.

The principal policy decision was to generate higher energy costs by promoting marginally higher petroleum prices, reversing a decade-long downward trend in oil prices. It was hoped that slower allied growth occurring within a restructured energy and monetary environment, which Washington was also attempting to bring about, would over time lead to a substantially strengthened American position in a more cohesive alliance system—one better able to withstand growing Soviet pressures. In mid-January 1971, the view of two economists on the NSC staff, C. Fred Bergsten and Harold Saunders, was that "the rise in the price of energy would affect primarily Europe and Japan and probably improve America's competitive position."[76]

Related to the intention to induce greater allied expenditures on energy was the effort to generate greater expenditures on defense. Both served the same general purpose of shifting resources from investment into capital goods to spending on what was in effect current consumption. The hoped-for combined effect would be to slow overall growth rates among the allies, harnessing them closer to the United States. Increased energy costs would work to the benefit of United States strategy in other ways as well.

Petroleum-producing countries such as Iran and Saudi Arabia would be able to devote increased resources to defense because of revenues that higher petroleum prices would bring. This would be true particularly for Iran, which the United States planned to strengthen as a bastion of defense for the larger Middle East–Southwest Asia region, an area of growing structural instability due to the disintegration of Pakistan (about which more below). In fact, the Western allies as the primary importers of Middle East petroleum would help underwrite the cost of strengthening the defenses of the region, even if they were reluctant to devote additional spending to their own defenses.

The petroleum price policy decision would also have a profound impact upon the world oil industry, whose structure had changed dramatically in the sixties. The position and profitability of the international (mostly American multinational) oil companies, the "majors," had deteriorated in the face of a growing oil glut. New discoveries of oil in the North Sea and Alaska promised to mitigate the problem of overdependence upon Middle East petroleum. It was estimated that the North Sea discoveries would make Great Britain and Norway self-sufficient for thirty years. (Gas had been discovered in 1965 and oil in 1969.) While Alaskan oil, discovered in 1968, would not place the United States in an analogous position, once developed it would provide an important offset to overdependence.

Libya and Nigeria were also bringing huge quantities of petroleum onto an already glutted market at prices below those set by the majors. Libya, in particular, had risen from virtually nowhere in 1960 to fourth place in overall production of crude oil by 1970. Leading independent oil companies, such as Occidental, Bunker-Hunt, Continental, Amerada-Hess, and Marathon were active in exploring and developing these new sources of petroleum. For instance, over half of Libya's crude output was under control of independent companies, not the majors.[77]

The appearance of new oil-producing countries and independent oil companies greatly eroded the controlling position over crude production that the majors once held. The abundance of oil had generated competition from independent companies and from producing countries. It was increasingly difficult for a handful of firms to control the world market from wellhead to consumer as once was the case. But it was not only the growing competition of foreign independents and the new interest of producing countries themselves in having a larger share in company profits that squeezed the majors.

Within the United States, the majors encountered burgeoning competition from private brand companies operating on narrower profit margins. The "private branders" were introducing new methods like self-service stations and opening new locations within an expanding superhighway and suburban road network. The net effect of entry into the market by the private branders and the independents at home and abroad was a progressive reduction in market share for the majors and, correspondingly, in their profits. By 1970, private branders had acquired 20 percent of the market in gasoline distribution within the United States.[78] From the point of view of the major oil companies the petroleum industry was entering a period if not of crisis, then at least of not fully desirable or controllable change.

The structural changes in the Western alliance and in the world petroleum industry were the determining factors accounting for the United States government's decision to seek higher oil prices, a decision that was carefully masked from the public. The conventional interpretation attributes a passive, reactive role to the United States government in response to an unsuccessful attempt by the majors to *hold back* a price increase that the producing countries were demanding.

According to this interpretation, the United States government, whose assistance the companies had sought, initially supported, then abruptly, inexplicably, undermined the negotiating position of the companies, which were left with no alternative except to acquiesce in a series of price increases, the Tehran and Tripoli agreements of February 14 and March 20, 1971, respectively.[79] This interpretation, while literally correct as far as it goes, is deceptive, misleading, and incomplete, and it fails to provide a satisfactory explanation of United States policy behavior.

Given the indisputable fact that higher prices meant greater company profits, the "resistance" of the major oil companies to higher prices, as John M. Blair notes, was "either an incomprehensible blunder or an elaborate charade, deliberately designed to divert attention away from policy decisions that had already been made at higher levels."[80] That the oil-producing countries demanded greater revenues was clear, whether derived from an increase in price, as in Libya's case, or from an increase in production, as in Iran's.

Furthermore, an oil price rise was in fact welcomed by most if not all of the consuming country governments, at least initially. The effect of very low-priced oil on other energy sources, such as coal and nuclear power, was to make their use progressively uneconomical and difficult to justify. Raising the oil price narrowed that differential. Thus, to some allies, such as Great Britain and West Germany, a rise in the price of oil improved the competitive position of the domestic coal industry, and to other allies, like Japan, a rise in oil prices allowed further development of the nuclear power industry. Even for the United States a price rise justified continued support for the relatively higher-cost domestic petroleum industry, not to mention coal and nuclear power as well. It was, as always, the individual consumer in all countries who would bear the burden of the added cost of petroleum.

While a rise in the price of oil made economic sense, there were also purely economic difficulties. The most important was the fact that the existing price of oil was already many times higher than cost. The estimated cost of lifting and producing a barrel of oil in the Middle East was then (and is today) approximately ten cents.[81] The higher the price of a barrel of oil, the greater became the differential between price and cost. The purely economic effect of a rise in price, therefore, was to generate greater competition among producers and drive prices down.[82] Furthermore, as long as prices remained far above cost, there was incentive for new companies to enter the market and to shave prices in order to gain and maintain market share.

A similar process operated among buyers. The many large and small oil companies that had gained entry into the petroleum industry survived by systematically undercutting the prices set by the majors. The purely economic effect of competition among buyers, too, was to bring prices down. This, in a nutshell, was the explanation of the sixties' price decline in the world oil market. It is this condition of the world oil market that substantially explains the role of the United States government in the negotiations between the oil companies and producing countries resulting in the rise of oil prices.

The difficulty was not in raising price, but in keeping it raised, which required restraining competitive behavior among and between buyers and sellers and narrowing the supply and demand ratio. United States policy from the fall of 1970 was, on the one hand, to promote the formation of an informal cartel among the major oil companies and independents and, on the other hand, to accept and support OPEC as a formal and legitimate cartel among the oil-producing countries.[83] Later, in 1974, it would be broadened to promote a formal cartel among the consuming nations.

While the concept was simple enough — promote concentration, restrain competition, and maintain high price levels — the execution of policy was extremely complicated. There was the matter of anti-trust regulations against cartels and collusion, to which government and companies alike were very sensitive. Therefore, the administration obtained specific written assurances (Business Review Letters) from the Justice Department to enable the companies to join together without fear of prosecution.[84] No overt collusion between the government and the companies occurred because it was unnecessary. The administration clearly signaled to all parties what was desirable and acceptable by what it did and did not do.

Raising the Price of Oil

The immediate thrust of Washington's policy — keeping the oil companies' production-distribution system in place — began to emerge in the fall of 1970 following the initial agreements between the oil companies and the Libyan government. In meetings with oil company executives convened by the State Department, the department's principal officer on oil matters, James Akins, stressed the importance of the companies' remaining in place in Libya and elsewhere — as controllers and distributors, even if not as price setters. The companies should maintain, Akins said, "a reasonable working relationship with the Libyans and with the other producers."[85] Of immediate concern was Libya, whose price demands Akins contended were "reasonable and the companies' position unwarranted."[86]

Akins strongly opposed the companies' inclination to resist Libyan demands and to attempt to block petroleum sales. He argued that if the oil companies resisted, Tripoli would nationalize the companies; and if they attempted to block sales of Libyan oil to Europe (which obtained a full 25 percent of its imported petroleum from Libya alone) through control of tanker operations or subsidiaries, then the European governments would nationalize the companies' operations in Europe as well.

Akins' explicit concern was that the European countries would skirt the oil majors' organization and establish direct access to Libyan oil, something to be avoided at all costs. In his view, confrontation with Libya would simply open the door to the Europeans, who "would have made their own deals with the Libyans," excluding the United States.[87] He believed that "the European countries under no circumstances would do without Libyan oil. . . . Europe, one way or another, is going to get Libyan oil."[88] The marked disinclination on the part of the State Department to back the companies in a confrontation against the Libyan government quickly led to settlements with Tripoli by the end of September 1970.

There would appear to have been nothing inevitable about this development. At the early stage in the crisis, concerted action by the United States and the oil companies could conceivably have produced a favorable outcome despite Gadhafi's boast that "people who lived without oil for 5,000 years can live without it again for a few years in order to attain their legitimate rights."[89] Washington could have brought the companies together to work out an insurance scheme to supply any company Gadhafi shut down. Had that been done, one or several companies might have been shut down, but the Libyan government would have been faced with substantial loss of revenue, as Gadhafi acknowledged.

The revenue lost to Libya would, of course, have been gained by other producers, who also would then realize the danger of attempting to pressure the consuming countries. Perhaps more important, as M. A. Adelman has noted:

> any Libyan commander of a division, brigade, or perhaps even a regiment could consider how he might gain a billion or several billions of dollars a year by issuing the right marching orders.[90]

While this was a feasible alternative course of action, it was not Washington's objective, even if it would have been successful in preventing a price rise. In any case, Libya's success was quickly emulated by other producing countries who demanded and received oil company offers for additional revenue. The cacophony of producer country demands now persuaded the oil companies, for the most part, to band together in an effort "to stem the avalanche."[91] In early January 1971, following renewed demands by the Libyan government for price increases over and above those just obtained the previous fall, chief executives of the oil companies, majors and independents, met with State and Justice Department officials to map out a joint approach.

The January 7 meeting produced a plan by which the companies would join together to engage OPEC in an "all-embracing negotiation," hoping thereby to preempt any tendency by the producers to "leapfrog" one price settlement with another. The oil chiefs also established a safety net agreement, an insurance scheme termed the Libyan Producers' Agreement, which would compensate any company shut down by Gadhafi with oil at or near cost. In preparation for the upcoming negotiations with OPEC the companies also set up policy groups in London and New York which incuded senior executives of all the participating companies to assist in developing a common negotiating position. Finally, the administration obtained provisional clearance (Business Review Letters) from the Justice Department for the companies to engage in what after all was collusive and oligopolistic behavior.[92]

Over the course of the next two weeks, by January 20, while leading the oil companies to believe that the United States government would support them against OPEC, Washington purposefully and deftly maneuvered the oil companies into new structural relationships with each other and with the oil-producing countries and a new regime of higher petroleum prices based upon assured supply. At the same time the Nixon administration would also obtain the acquiescence of the allied governments in the new pricing regime.

On January 15, the chief executives of the major and independent oil companies met again in the State Department, this time with Secretary of State Rogers, Undersecretary John Irwin, and Akins to discuss the forthcoming negotiations scheduled to begin in early February in accordance with the OPEC resolution taken at Caracas. The company executives urged the State Department "to enter into this thing and get the heads of the countries involved to moderate their demands, to persuade them at least to engage in fair bargaining practices. . . ."[93]

The State Department agreed to become involved, but not in the way that the company chiefs were led to expect. The administration decided to send Undersecretary Irwin to Iran, Saudi Arabia, and Kuwait; and, following a private meeting with President Nixon, Irwin departed for Tehran the next day, January 16.[94] That same day the companies sent a "message to OPEC," containing a proposal for an all-embracing negotiation with producers in both the Gulf and the

Mediterranean and a proposal to negotiate higher and escalating payments.[95] The stage was thus set for the decisive steps of the next few days.

If the companies thought that the purpose of Undersecretary Irwin's trip was to support the joint negotiations strategy and to ask the producers to "moderate their demands" on prices, they were completely mistaken. On the contrary, he went specifically "to seek assurances from the Gulf producers to continue to supply oil at reasonable prices to the free world."[96] His mission was to "prevent an imminent impasse in discussions between the oil-producing countries and oil companies from resulting in an interruption of oil supplies."

Thus, even though Irwin went to explain "why the U.S. government had taken steps to make it possible under American antitrust laws for the oil companies to negotiate jointly,"[97] that was not the position he supported. He went to gain security of supply from the Persian Gulf, not moderation of price. He would accept a price rise and separate negotiations in return for assurances that supplies would not be interrupted. Indeed, Irwin's actions after a discussion with the shah of Iran ensured that there would be both.

Arriving in Tehran on January 17, Irwin met with the shah and his finance minister, Dr. Jamshid Amuzegar. From what is known of their meeting, the shah argued strenuously against the companies' proposal for joint negotiation, which, he said, smacked of being a "dirty trick" against OPEC. If the companies persisted, he threatened, "the entire Gulf would be shut down and no oil would flow."[98] On the other hand, if the companies agreed to split negotiations between the Gulf and Mediterranean producers, the shah gave his assurance that any agreement reached between the oil companies and the Gulf producers would be upheld regardless of better terms gained by Libya in subsequent negotiations.

Following this single meeting, and without waiting to consult with the oil companies' negotiators, George Piercy of Exxon and Lord Strathalmond of British Petroleum, who were then en route to Tehran and scheduled to arrive on January 19, Undersecretary Irwin cabled the State Department to "encourage the companies to negotiate with the Gulf countries separately unless the companies had good reasons to the contrary."[99] Irwin then departed Tehran before Piercy and Strathalmond arrived, leaving them to face the shah alone.

Although the implication is that it was Undersecretary Irwin who, perhaps intimidated by the shah, made the decision on the spot to agree to split negotiations between the oil companies and the producing countries, it appears that such a momentous decision was not made unilaterally by a relatively middle-level official, who, moreover, was virtually unversed in petroleum matters. No, the decision was undoubtedly made in advance and, as John M. Blair suggests, "at higher levels."[100] But Irwin's trip served the important purpose of conveying to the producing countries that the United States government would *not* back the oil companies, which meant support for higher prices.

Indeed, as soon as Irwin's cable arrived, Secretary of State Rogers immediately "endorsed Irwin's recommendations," passing on the government's decision to the oil companies.[101] Washington had undercut their negotiating position even before negotiations had begun. When Piercy and Strathalmond objected to splitting the negotiations on the grounds that their respective governments would not agree, Dr. Amuzegar declared: "If you think you have a problem with your Governments, I am quite confident that they will agree to a regional or Gulf approach."[102] He then gave them a forty-eight-hour deadline to agree to "Gulf only" negotiations.[103]

While Undersecretary Irwin was conveying Washington's intentions for split negotiations — which everyone knew and understood would mean an upward racheting of prices — the Department of State was simultaneously active on another front. On January 20 the department convened a meeting in Paris of the members of the Organization of Economic Cooperation and Development (OECD) to gain their acquiescence if not their agreement to the anticipated changes. Although the discussion that took place was not made public, afterward an OECD spokesman declared that "contingency arrangements for coping with an oil shortage were *not* discussed."[104] In other words, the sequence of events in Tehran and Paris clearly conveyed to the oil-producing country leaders the idea that the United States and the industrialized countries were willing to accept a rise in price in exchange for continuity of supply.

The culmination of the negotiations, the Tehran and Tripoli agreements concluded February 14 and March 20, respectively, did indeed reflect higher oil prices and, on paper, also provided for security of supply. The Tehran agreement called for a graduated escalation of pricing arrangements over a five-year period. The immediate increase was thirty cents per barrel, rising to fifty cents by 1975. The total addition in revenue to the producing countries for the five-year period was estimated at $11.7 billion. The agreement included an anti-leapfrogging clause, stipulating that none of the Gulf producers would seek more advantageous terms should the companies subsequently agree to higher prices in negotiations with the Mediterranean producers.[105] This stipulation, like the five-year term, was violated within the year.

The Libyan settlement resulted in a substantially higher increase, raising Tripoli's "take" by 64 cents per barrel and the posting price to $3.45 per barrel. The result increased Libya's 1971 income from $700 million to $2.3 billion.[106] The much higher Libyan settlement prompted an immediate adverse reaction from the shah, who obtained an additional premium from the companies for "port costs," violating the clause assuring that Iran would not seek more advantageous terms in the event that Libya secured a better deal than the Gulf producers.[107] While small in light of the astronomical price increases which occurred after 1973 and 1979, the price increases of early 1971 were considered to be extremely high at the time — even if in reality not unwelcome. Indeed, one London financial analyst, Kenneth Hill, termed the Tehran and Tripoli agreements "truly an unexpected boon for the worldwide industry."[108]

Clearly, the United States government's role was decisive in bringing about a fundamental restructuring of world oil. Separate negotiations allowed the American-based international oil companies — the majors — to strengthen their positions within the Persian Gulf, especially in Iran and Saudi Arabia, while undercutting the position of the independents in the Mediterranean. Most of the change was accomplished over the next two and a half years prior to the October 1973 war.

The greatest changes involved the majors' success in regaining effective control of foreign and domestic competition while shifting the locus of industry profits from crude oil production to operations further downstream. From 1971 onward the majors' profits would come increasingly from distribution, refining, and related petrochemical operations and relatively less from extraction of crude oil in producing countries. Indeed, the very process that squeezed the majors at the producing end also acted with devastating effect to undercut many of the independent competitors, including crude-short national companies, as producing countries moved to increase their rate of participation, or more properly, their ownership share in foreign petroleum company holdings.

Washington (and the majors) had two objectives in the Mediterranean. First was to reduce the total output of Libyan oil, which would allow the Gulf producers to export more and gain proportionately larger returns with which to finance other, primarily defense, projects. Their second objective was, as Blair put it, to "eviscerate" the independents to prevent them from continuing to undercut prices.[109] The United States government kept pressure on the oil companies, both majors and independents, to maintain the joint approach among themselves, even though they were required to negotiate separately with the oil-producing countries. Of course, keeping the companies together prevented the independents from breaking away and making separate price-cutting deals.[110]

The weaker independents became prime takeover candidates for Gadhafi. Between early 1971 and late 1973 — *before* the October war and the very large price increases that accompanied it — not only had the independent oil companies been eviscerated, but total Libyan production had been reduced substantially. Oil companies holding over 80 percent of Libya's estimated reserves had either been nationalized or forced to relinquish 51 percent control of their companies. The Tripoli government nationalized British Petroleum, Bunker-Hunt, Amoseas, and Shell, while taking fifty-one percent control of Occidental, Oasis, Mobil-Gelsenberg, and Exxon.[111]

Even more significant from the perspective of larger American strategy, the Libyan government suffered a large cutback in production.

To the majors and the [U.S.] government alike, the reduction in Libyan output was the necessary prerequisite to the staggering price increases of late 1973 and early 1974. Had Libyan production by the independents and crude-long majors been running at the rate anticipated five years earlier by Exxon, the supply in 1973 would have been increased by some 1,500,000 b/d. Had it been necessary to find a market for such a quantity, the chances of making the 1973–1974 price increases stick would have been exceedingly remote. Whether anticipated or merely the product of fortuitous circumstances, the price increases of 1973–1974 had as their necessary prelude the unnoticed evisceration of a few independent oil companies operating in one of the world's most sparsely populated and little-known countries.[112]

While Libyan production was cut back, the Persian Gulf producers sharply stepped up their output, capturing market share and generating great revenues. The broadening of the revenue bases of Iran and Saudi Arabia, in turn, allowed a quantum leap in defense expenditures, which began in 1971 (U.S. fiscal 1972). For fiscal 1972, Iranian defense expenditures on purchases of United States equipment alone nearly doubled, to $524 million.[113] For fiscal 1973, prior to the jump in petroleum prices, procurement orders quadrupled to $2.1 billion. The order of magnitude nearly doubled again, to $3.9 billion for fiscal 1974, and only in fiscal 1975 leveled back to $2.6 billion.

Saudi Arabia, too, although on necessarily a much smaller scale due to the much smaller population base, nearly tripled its defense expenditures between 1971 and 1972, from $19 to $52 million. Overall United States arms sales also began to skyrocket. In fiscal 1974, total United States arms sales for the first time reached the $8.5 billion mark, of which nearly half went to Iran. It is in the context of increased oil prices, arms sales, and worsening balance of payments and trade positions that Washington acted to increase the liquidity in the already strained international monetary system.

Restructuring the International Monetary System

By the fall of 1970 the Bretton Woods monetary system, the financial underpinning of the American global position since its inception during World War II, was no longer tenable. The sharp deterioration that had occurred in the United States balance of payments and trade positions, war-induced inflation, intensive speculation in the dollar, and the anticipated effects of the petroleum price rise — all combined to convince the Nixon leadership that action had to be taken in defense of the United States international economic position. The first consequential steps toward establishment of the European economic and monetary union also undoubtedly affected the timing of the administration's actions. The Nixon administration's objective was to revitalize Bretton Woods and initiate the process of reforming the monetary system, reestablishing the dollar's preeminence, if possible, and accepting the larger role of the now much stronger German and Japanese currencies, if necessary.

In 1970 the United States economy had dipped into recession, in part the function of the cumulative inflationary effect of the earlier failure to finance Vietnam War expenditures through taxation. The balance of payments dipped as inflation rose, the deficit reaching almost $10 billion from a surplus of $2.7 billion the previous year, a twelve-billion-dollar swing. The trend continued into 1971, and by the second quarter the deficit was running at an annual and then unheard-of rate of $22.5 billion and careening downward. (The third quarter deficit rate would be $47.5 billion!)[114]

Over the same period the trade balance, too, became adverse for the first time since the end of World War II, moving from a $2.6 billion surplus in 1970 to a $2.3 billion deficit in 1971, almost a five-billion-dollar swing.[115] The foreign economic position of the United States was collapsing and rending to its foundations the international economic order which it had sustained for the previous quarter of a century.

During the same period the European Economic Community had also decided to move forward on the establishment of an economic and monetary union. Plans for the establishment of a European economic and monetary union had become far advanced by late 1970. The second Werner report in October had proposed among other things the reduction of existing parity margins among the EEC currencies, which subsequently became known as "the snake." The Werner report's recommendations had been accepted in principle by the EEC Council of Ministers in December and confirmed in a council resolution of March 22, 1971.[116] The "snake," whose central currency was, of course, the deutschemark, began to function in June 1971 and was the first small but necessary step toward European monetary union.

The just-concluded petroleum price rise agreements of February and March 1971 were yet another factor, auguring a major shift of monetary reserves into the hands of the oil-producing countries. It would be necessary to increase both the flexibility and liquidity of the system as a whole in order to cushion the effects of the movement of such enormous sums as they were recycled back into the industrial countries' banking systems. Inevitable speculation against the weakening dollar that would accompany this shift alone required compensatory action. Thus the administration moved to increase the exchange-rate flexibility of the dollar in order to minimize potential damage.

The two-tiered gold-price system established in 1968 still pegged the dollar to a fixed price of gold, even if the dollar was no longer freely convertible into it. Since the dollar was the numeraire under the Bretton Woods system, that is, the currency to which all other currencies were pegged, the United States could adjust its exchange rate only by changing the value of the dollar against gold, the other chief reserve asset.

But simply to revalue gold was not the answer. The gold drain of previous years had reduced United States holdings to around $10 billion, less than one-third of the dollar debt then outstanding. Raising the price of gold would mainly benefit those countries with large gold holdings, like France, Italy, South Africa, and the Soviet Union, and not solve the main problem of an inflexible and over-valued currency. United States policy therefore was not only to devalue the dollar in terms of gold, but to sever the connection to the precious metal entirely, a step which improved the dollar's position vis-à-vis other currencies and improved its flexibility as well.

In short, on August 15, 1971, President Nixon "temporarily" severed the connection between the dollar and gold, establishing what in effect was a pure dollar standard. It remained a fixed-rate system with all other currencies still pegged to the dollar, but the dollar was no longer tied to gold. At the same time, to encourage the allies to negotiate an equitable realignment of exchange rates, the president also levied a 10 percent surcharge on all imports, an act which immediately and as greatly improved the United States trading position as it angered the allies whose heavily subsidized export advantages were thus undercut. Finally, he imposed a ninety-day wage and price freeze in the hope of forestalling the rise in the domestic price level that invariably accompanies exchange rate devaluation. Thus fortified, the United States entered into protracted negotiations over the next several months with the members of OECD.

Following a crucial, decisive meeting between President Nixon and French President Georges Pompidou in the Azores, December 13–15, the final details were worked out in Washington three days later.[117] The Smithsonian Agreement of December 18, 1971, resulted in the removal of the 10 percent import surcharge in return for an across-the-board revaluation of exchange rates. The dollar was devalued in terms of gold by 8 percent, and OECD member currencies were appreciated vis-à-vis the dollar in varying amounts. The

Japanese, West German, Swiss, and Dutch currencies appreciated most—by 16.9, 13.6, 13.9, and 11.6 percent, respectively. The British, French, Italian, and Swedish currencies appreciated least—by 8.6, 8.6, 7.5, and 7.5 percent, respectively.

The monetary reorganization placed the United States in as strong a position as possible, under the circumstances, to meet the coming economic storms. Much of the overvaluation of the dollar had been wrung out, and no challenge could now come from the European gold bloc. President Nixon proclaimed the Smithsonian Agreement the "greatest monetary agreement in the history of the world" and may have believed that the United States could maintain the new fixed exchange rate and central role of the dollar. But he soon came to recognize that alliance economic relationships were not so easily adjusted.

Despite the agreement, OECD members intensified efforts to depress their currencies in terms of the dollar over the next year in a massive display of financial power. They succeeded in demolishing the exchange-rate relationships established at the Smithsonian. The result was a shift away from a fixed-rate system to a floating exchange-rate regime in February–March 1973 and the beginning of a new chapter of monetary and economic relationships with the allies.

But this gets us ahead of the story, for by the end of 1971 the Nixon administration had put the nation into a more competitive position vis-à-vis the Western allies with the monetary and oil agreements. The petroleum agreements, in particular, would build gradual upward pressure on energy costs for the Europeans and the Japanese, who were the principal importers of both Middle East and Mediterranean oil. It was hoped that increased costs of production would temper the rapid growth then being experienced by America's allies and allow for more orderly competition between them and the United States.

The rise in the price of oil would also facilitate the strengthening of Southwest Asia, an area of growing weakness and instability. The South Asian subcontinent was undergoing major change in the wake of Great Britain's withdrawal in 1967 and America's neglect since 1965. Indeed, Pakistan would be dismembered within the year (see below) as India with Soviet support would take the opportunity of internecine Pakistani civil strife to restructure the South Asian geopolitical balance to advantage. The new price regime would establish the revenue base for the buildup of Iran and Saudi Arabia as the "twin pillars" of United States policy in Southwest Asia to replace the collapsing India-Pakistan balance.

Finally, the nation was also well positioned to engage the Soviet Union in a greatly improved relationship as well. If there was to be a manifold increase in trade relations with Moscow as part of the detente process, some thought had to be given to increasing Soviet capacity to earn hard currency with which to pay for American goods. Since the Soviet Union traditionally earned between two-thirds and three-fourths of its hard currency through petroleum and gas exports, the rise in the price of petroleum would serve the purposes of detente as well. At this historical moment, however, by the spring of 1971, the stark outline of a well-conceived Soviet counterstrategy began to emerge, to which we now turn.

CHAPTER

3

The Soviet Counterstrategy, 1971–1972

T he winter of 1970–1971 was as much a time of reassessment for Moscow as it had been for Washington. From the Kremlin's viewpoint, the United States appeared to have had considerable success in blocking Soviet policy moves at several key points. In strategic weapons, even though the numerical growth of Soviet missile power promised eventually to eclipse that of the United States, Washington's decisions to MIRV the Minuteman and Poseidon missile systems and to protect its land-based missile system with an anti-ballistic missile system would significantly raise the cost of any attempt to achieve superiority—perhaps even make it unattainable as a realistic near-term objective.

In foreign policy, Moscow's effort to prevent Beijing from shifting toward the United States had failed. Moreover, de facto though not yet publicly acknowledged Sino-American cooperation was choking off North Vietnam's war effort, the continuation of which no longer served the original strategic purpose of driving China back into Moscow's embrace.[1] In the Middle East, the Soviet position hinged on the outcome of the leadership succession to Nasser. Any plans for reopening the Suez Canal would have to be placed in abeyance pending the resolution of the succession question. Finally, the attempt to establish a submarine base in Cuba had provoked a perhaps unexpectedly sharp rebuff from the United States.

The outlook was not entirely bleak, however. Moscow was in the process of successfully stabilizing the western flank, as relations with West Germany in particular improved and four-power negotiations over Berlin progressed. Nurturing Bonn's *Ostpolitik* offered an attractive means of gradually weakening the American position in Western Europe. This was a remarkable recovery from the apprehension generated in Western Europe by the Soviet invasion of Czechoslovakia just a brief two years before.

The rapidly evolving situation in South Asia also promised to make it an area of opportunity in the near future. The Soviet-Indian relationship had developed to the point where India now possessed an irreversible advantage over Pakistan, which, moreover, was moving into a period of internal crisis. The potential for a favorable shift in the South Asian geopolitical balance was extremely good. Lastly, it did not escape the Soviet leadership's notice that the energy and monetary relationships of the Western alliance were becoming increasingly crisis-ridden, offering additional opportunities to weaken the American global position.

Strategic Watershed — The Twenty-Fourth Party Congress

In retrospect, although formally inaugurating the policy of detente with the United States, the Twenty-Fourth Party Congress of the Communist Party of the Soviet Union, March 30 through April 9, 1971, represented the decision to initiate an aggressive counterstrategy in an attempt to defeat American strategy. The central purpose of detente from Moscow's perspective was as a political stratagem to halt further United States strategic weapons development, to weaken further the Western alliance infrastructure, and to strengthen the position of the Soviet Union. Indeed, Moscow did not conceal its intent to continue the political struggle with "imperialism" — a formulation which enabled the Soviet Union to pursue friendly relations with the United States while at the same time countering American policy wherever deemed desirable.

The decision to adopt an active counterstrategy was dependent upon a minimum condition — Soviet ability to neutralize American strategic weapons power, the foundation of the United States forward position around the Soviet periphery. An active course could only be pursued from a position of strategic weapons strength. Without such a minimum capability it would simply be infeasible and adventuristic to pursue policies that would inevitably produce confrontations with the United States in attempts to alter the correlation of forces to advantage, confrontations which the Soviet Union could not pursue to satisfactory conclusion.

The crucial question for Soviet leaders concerned Washington's strategic weapons position. The United States was several years ahead of the Soviet Union in ICBM technology, especially MIRV and guidance systems, and well over a decade ahead in ABM technology.[2] Even though many experts considered the level of American ABM technology to be unsatisfactory, to deploy a system that could be upgraded in the future would alter the nature of the subsequent Soviet offensive response.[3] The resources required to mount a credible threat against an undefended Minuteman were minuscule compared to those required to penetrate a steadily improving missile defense, even if such a defense did not match Soviet offensive deployments step by step. Not only would the cost of attacking a defended system rise significantly, but the uncertainty of the success of any attack would rise, perhaps exponentially.

From Moscow's viewpoint, therefore, the optimum outcome of the negotiations then under way to reduce arms levels was one in which the United States agreed to limit the number of offensive launchers it would deploy and also agreed not to defend them. For Moscow, any other outcome would most probably lead to the perpetuation of the American advantage and require deferral of a forceful counterstrategy. For this reason, since the start of the arms limitations talks in November 1969, Moscow's negotiators had stood rigidly upon the demand that both countries agree only to an ABM treaty prohibiting defense of their respective missiles and nothing more. Washington's position calling for limitations on both offensive and defensive weapons offered no inducement to Moscow for, if accepted, the proposal would only maintain the current situation of relative United States advantage.

Thus, when Henry Kissinger proposed in January 1971 to break the negotiating deadlock by offering an ABM treaty in return for a five-year interim offensive weapons freeze, Moscow readily accepted. The initial terms of the freeze—no new missile construction while negotiations were under way—provided a loophole for the Soviets to achieve all of their objectives. As recounted in the previous chapter, the Soviets agreed to Kissinger's proposal, then delayed the opening of negotiations, immediately commencing one of the largest silo construction efforts they had ever undertaken.[4] Ninety-one new silo starts would eventually be identified, giving Moscow the necessary heavy missile complement of 308 launchers with which to mount a serious threat to Minuteman in the future.[5] This missile force alone, mounted with ten warheads per launcher and made accurate, would be enough to target every United States missile launcher with nearly three warheads each (3,080 Soviet warheads versus 1,054 United States launchers), the optimum ratio considered necessary for success.

Whatever the American objectives were, Moscow had achieved its minimum condition. The existing number of United States launchers would remain fixed and essentially undefended,[6] while the Soviet Union would build launchers in sufficient number to provide the basis for a credible threat to Minuteman (not to mention the heavy investment in the research and development necessary to eliminate the American lead in ABM technology). What had occurred in May 1971, the so-called "breakthrough" agreement on SALT, was in fact the turning point in the United States-Soviet strategic weapons relationship.

Agreement on an ABM treaty gave Soviet leaders a strong incentive to strive toward the attainment of strategic weapons superiority. At the very minimum the growth of Soviet offensive missile power meant that in the near term Moscow could expect to deter the United States from employing its strategic power coercively in crisis situations. Beyond that, the Kremlin could hope to develop sufficient power to neutralize the United States strategic nuclear guarantee to its allies and potentially, in the yet more distant future, build the necessary missile force to employ strategic power in a coercive mode, too.

Once assured that Moscow would soon have the capability of deterring American strategic power, Kremlin leaders shifted from the essentially defensive strategy of the sixties to an offensive strategy. In retrospect, the strategy adopted around the time of the Twenty-Fourth Party Congress consisted of a complex set of policies designed to weaken American containment of the Soviet Union while strengthening Soviet containment of China. Specific policies included development of economic relations with Western Europe and Japan, revision of policy toward the war in Vietnam, utilization of the emerging opportunity in South Asia to shape the outcome to advantage, and consolidation of the shaky position in the Middle East.

Over the next several years, these policies would bring mixed results. Some would be more successful than others; some would fail.

Each policy would proceed on its own course and timetable according to the milieu in which it functioned. Therefore, the timing would be different for each. Detente with the United States, for example, would reach a high point in 1972 and vacillate thereafter, but Soviet relations with Western Europe and Japan would build upon the initial impetus. Detente, in significant ways, constituted an opening wedge by means of which Moscow gained access to American allies in hopes of undermining the alliance while simultaneously benefiting from improved relations.

In addition to political efforts to improve relations with United States allies, Moscow extended offers for improved economic relations. Energy, in particular, was an area in which the Soviets sought to alter the links between the United States and its partners. Partly in response to the higher prices already appearing in the world petroleum market, Moscow moved to increase petroleum and gas exports to both Western Europe and Japan.[7] Indeed, much of Soviet trade with Western Europe and Japan would center on the export of petroleum and gas in return for energy-related technology.

Apart from accumulating hard currency through petroleum and gas sales, Moscow sought to provide an alternative source of energy for America's allies, who would perceive detente increasingly to be in their own interests as a means of lessening dependence upon the United States and United States-controlled petroleum sources. This was, of course, not new. In the middle fifties, Moscow had attempted to wean Western Europe and Japan away from the United States with a vigorous petroleum export program and by the early sixties had brought its petroleum and gas pipeline system to the edge of Western Europe. Although the Soviets had some initial success in enticing energy cooperation, the drop in energy prices during the sixties demolished their energy strategy. The dramatic changes of the early seventies centering on detente, strategic weapons ascendancy, and rising petroleum prices made the fifties' approach seem viable once again.

Moscow's Decision Point in Vietnam

The decision to change strategy in Vietnam stemmed directly from the failure to break United States strategy, which was built upon Sino-American rapprochement and constriction of two of the three logistics routes connecting the Soviet Union to North Vietnam — the Chinese rail route and the port of Sihanoukville. The decisive point for Moscow was reached when it became clear that Hanoi could neither regain full Chinese support, reopen Sihanoukville, nor open an alternative logistics route through northern South Vietnam. But the critical moment was not immediately obvious because it occurred within the context of apparent defeat for American and South Vietnamese forces in the highly publicized Operation Lam Son 719, February 8 to April 8, 1971.

Operation Lam Son 719 had its genesis in Hanoi's reaction to the closure of Sihanoukville in the spring of 1970. Almost immediately afterward, North Vietnamese forces began to accelerate the movement of war materiel along the Ho Chi Minh trail in preparation for a counterattack. Their efforts intensified with the onset of the dry season in October, and by early December United States intelligence had identified major stockpiles in southern Laos around Tchepone, in base areas 604 and 611.[8] Military Assistance Command Vietnam (MACV) had concluded from the thrust of smaller-scale operations already under way that Hanoi would launch a major offensive as soon as its preparations were completed. Three military objectives were suggested by the logistical buildup: an invasion of military region one and an attempt to seize the key cities of Quang Tri and Hue; a drive against Phnom Penh in an effort to topple Lon Nol; and a continuing effort to fortify base areas along the Cambodian-South Vietnamese border.

The United States response was to mount a large-scale spoiling attack into southern Laos paralleled by a smaller drive into Cambodia in hopes of destroying Hanoi's military buildup and delaying an early offensive — at least through 1971. Seizure of territory was never contemplated. The United States-supported South Vietnamese incursion into Laos, Lam Son 719, largely achieved this objective,[9] but the manner of execution left doubts about the success of Vietnamization. The objective was to destroy Hanoi's supply base areas 604 and 611, located near the main communications junction at Tchepone, in southern Laos, some twenty-five miles west of Khe Sanh. The major difficulty was the political constraint enacted by the Cooper-Church amendment, passed on June 30, 1970, after the Cambodian incursion. It prohibited any direct United States ground involvement in either Cambodia or Laos.

Although United States air combat, artillery, and logistical support were permitted for this operation, American advisers normally present in South Vietnamese army units were not there to coordinate it. The Army of South Vietnam (ARVN) had never before attempted, nor even exercised, the kind of large-scale complex offensive they were asked to execute in Lam Son 719 and simply "did not yet possess" the necessary "adeptness and experience at fire coordination, resupply, and communications."[10] The consequence was that South Vietnamese forces undertook a major multi-unit operation, for which they had neither the experience nor preparation, into the heart of heavily fortified enemy territory.[11]

Washington wanted at all costs to avoid any threat to the evolving rapprochement with Beijing, a concern which, in retrospect, may have shaped the operational plan. The logical and obvious choice was for a multi-division-size thrust into southern Laos similar to that undertaken the year before in Cambodia. A mobile operation with no fixed positions, its size would have ensured safe resupply and evacuation from interior points. Moreover, it would have accentuated ARVN's chief advantage—superior firepower. Unfortunately, however, such a plan would have been difficult to distinguish from an outright invasion.

Lam Son 719 would not bear any resemblance to an invasion of Laos, which could rekindle thoughts in Beijing of an analogy with the Korean War. Therefore, instead of mounting a multi-division-size cross-border thrust toward Tchepone to destroy the supply buildup, Washington devised a plan which could not be mistaken for anything resembling an invasion, but which would also be riskier and result in higher casualties. The operational plan decided upon was to deploy some twenty-five mutually reinforcing firebases on either side of Route 9 between Khe Sanh and Tchepone, then send an armored force down Route 9 to Tchepone to destroy base area 604. Afterward, ideally toward the end of April when the dry season was ending, the firebases would be evacuated one by one as the armored force conducted a fighting withdrawal to the southeast, destroying base area 611 and reentering South Vietnam through the A Shau Valley.

The problem with this plan was that it depended heavily upon carefully timed coordination among firebases for mutual covering fire and between firebases and American rear units for air strikes, artillery support, helicopter reinforcement, resupply, and evacuation. Moreover, emplacement of over two dozen firebases in fixed positions played to the strength of Hanoi. As one military critique described it, "the firebases, dropped like islands in an enemy sea, did nothing but allow the NVA [North Vietnamese army] to encircle and attack at will, one at a time."[12] It was a plan which "invited disaster." Although what followed was not "disaster" in the literal sense, South Vietnamese and American forces took considerable losses, even while exacting a substantial toll of North Vietnamese men and equipment.

From the outset fierce resistance from NVA units, which outnumbered ARVN forces by two to one, and heavy rains hampering air cover and helicopter operations delayed the advance along Route 9.[13] After two weeks, when it looked like the drive would stall short of its objective, reinforcements were sent in, quadrupling the force from 5,000 to 21,000 and enabling the main force to reach Tchepone and base area 604 on March 6.[14] Although the American command urged South Vietnamese President Thieu to reinforce further to sustain operations in the Tchepone area until the monsoon season came in May, Thieu decided otherwise. Having determined from the outset to cut operations short after reaching 3,000 casualties, Thieu decided on March 9 to withdraw and conserve forces in anticipation of the eventual North Vietnamese invasion of the South.[15]

The withdrawal, back down Route 9 instead of to the southeast through base area 611 as originally planned, "became a nightmare by the time it ended."[16] North Vietnamese forces repeatedly ambushed the ARVN force as it attempted to return to Khe Sanh, and they sought to encircle and destroy each of the isolated firebases before they could be evacuated by helicopter. Although the withdrawal was conducted in tolerable fashion, some of Saigon's best units cracked under the pressure of NVA ambush and encirclement, raising questions about the success of Vietnamization.

President Nixon termed Lam Son 719 "a military success but a psychological defeat."[17] South Vietnamese losses were high, nearly 50 percent in some units. The ARVN suffered 1,529 killed, 5,483 wounded, and 625 missing.[18] North Vietnamese losses were, however, staggeringly high. There were an estimated 19,360 killed and 57 captured. According to official figures, approximately half of the North Vietnamese troops committed to the operation were killed. United States losses were eventually disclosed as 219 killed, 1,149 wounded, and 38 missing. American forces lost 107 helicopters, while 618 more were damaged, many beyond repair.[19]

At high cost in men and materiel on both sides, Operation Lam Son 719 removed any possibility for a North Vietnamese offensive in 1971, but it was Beijing's response which removed any doubt that

Moscow's Vietnam strategy had failed. As soon as the incursion began, the Soviets welcomed Hanoi Politburo member Le Thanh Nghi to Moscow to sign an agreement for the Soviets to provide further "technical assistance."[20] Moscow press and radio immediately portrayed Lam Son 719 as an invasion of Laos and the "Koreanization of Indochina."[21] Moscow saw this as a threat to Chinese security and urged a return to "united action."[22] Privately, the Soviets offered to reconcile differences with Beijing.[23]

At first it appeared that Beijing might alter its policy, but by the end of February that prospect had evaporated. Le Than Nghi returned to Hanoi via Beijing, where on February 15 he accepted a "supplemental economic and military aid agreement."[24] Meanwhile, China's official news agency, Hsinhua, reacted strongly to the ARVN drive into Laos, terming it "a grave menace to China. The Chinese people absolutely will not remain indifferent to it!" Reaffirming support for the Laotian people, the statement declared that "China's territory is their reliable rear area."[25] A *People's Daily* editorial of the fourteenth rejected the Nixon administration's view that the operations were limited and did not "pose a threat" to China by asserting that China and Laos "are as close to one another as lips and teeth."[26]

Even though the Chinese media rejected President Nixon's press conference statement of the seventeenth reiterating that the operations in Laos "present no threat" to China, which, he therefore believed, had no "reason . . . to react," it may have had a reassuring effect.[27] Beijing briefly picked up the Korean analogy on February 20 and declared that Nixon was taking the path trod by President Truman,[28] but this was the high point of Beijing's hostile public reaction, which subsided thereafter.

Zhou Enlai made an unannounced trip to Hanoi in early March (5–8) to reiterate Chinese support for North Vietnam, where he publicly repeated the characterization used earlier for Laos, referring to China as a "reliable rear area" and positing the "lips and teeth" relationship. But in the joint communiqué issued at the end of his visit Zhou carefully indicated that China would do nothing unless the United States widened the war further.[29]

> Should U.S. imperialism go down the road of expanding its war of aggression in Indochina, the Chinese people are determined to take all necessary measures, not flinching even from the greatest national sacrifices, to give all-out support and assistance

to the Vietnamese and other Indochinese peoples for the thorough defeat of the U.S. aggressors.[30]

Even reports from Hong Kong that China was bolstering anti-aircraft defenses in South China, deploying additional aircraft to Hainan Island, and calling up reserves in Kwangtung, Kwangsi, and Yunnan provinces emphasized the defensive nature of the preparations.[31]

Beijing's position quickly became clear after Zhou's trip to Hanoi. The Chinese leadership rejected Moscow's offer to reconcile, and Beijing's media quickly resumed their acid criticism of Soviet policy. Chinese strategy continued on the course of preserving the fragmentation of the region, which required not only that North Vietnam not be defeated (hence necessitating military aid to Hanoi), but that South Vietnam not be defeated either (hence prohibiting direct intervention).

In any case, for Moscow, Lam Son 719 was the last straw. From the Soviet perspective of early 1971, the war could not be won given existing conditions. Soviet leaders had to assume that any near-term attempt to increase the level of supplies through the remaining port of Haiphong in support of a major increase in the level of conflict would inevitably precipitate a United States closure of the remaining route of access. This would leave Hanoi no recourse but reversion to low-level guerrilla warfare, which would serve no larger strategic purpose. Remaining American forces would in any case bear the brunt of any attack in the near term, leaving South Vietnam's military position essentially unaffected and perhaps improved.

On the other hand, from a longer perspective, once the United States had completed its withdrawal another offensive could be mounted. Even if that were to fail, Hanoi would have dealt a weakening blow to the forces of South Vietnam and at a minimum be in a better negotiating position to bring the current phase of the conflict to conclusion. At that point it would be possible to determine the feasibility of resuming the effort to topple the South. Finally, demonstration of some degree of restraint at the outset of detente could be interpreted as a gesture of goodwill and the intention to work toward improved relations with the United States.

Thus, Soviet policy toward North Vietnam was to cut military supplies through the summer of 1971. It would not be until August that large-scale shipments of military goods would be resumed in preparation for the 1972 spring offensive. This decision was taken despite the vigorous protests of Le Duan and Pham Van Dong, who traveled to Moscow immediately after Hanoi's forces had foiled Saigon's thrust into southern Laos. Le Duan would remain in the Soviet capital for forty-three days, from March 27 until May 9, pleading the case for continuation of the counteroffensive; but his arguments fell on deaf ears. Moscow's immediate course was set. Indeed, there were other, more serious problems and more attractive opportunities which then preoccupied the Soviet leadership.

Structural Crisis in the Middle East

By the turn of the year the foundations of the Soviet position in the Middle East had become extremely shaky. The region, politically unstable since the departure of the British in 1967, offered a myriad of opportunities which, however, Moscow seemed on the verge of botching due to its usual heavy-handed tactics. In the eastern Mediterranean the outcome of the Egyptian leadership struggle would have a significant impact upon the emerging structure of the entire region. In the Red Sea-Persian Gulf area, Soviet support for the new state in Aden and involvement on the republican side in the Yemen civil war had spurred cooperation between Saudi Arabia and Iran. In Somalia, on the Horn of Africa, Soviet support for the regime of Said Barre (who had come to power in October 1969) offered the possibility of establishing a formidable Soviet position astride the southern end of the Suez-Red Sea waterway.

Soviet objectives from early 1971 onward were to consolidate positions and prevent the politically amorphous situation from slipping out of control. The general approach was publicly to support Arab unity and independence but privately to spur pro-Soviet and communist elements into action to press for policies compatible with Moscow's objectives. The supply of arms, of course, continued to be essential for support of those leaders who leaned toward Moscow, and the extension of "friendship" treaties was a useful device by which to strengthen relationships, or at least to prevent their further deterioration.

The attempt to influence the succession struggle in Egypt was central to Moscow's effort. The Soviet approach was to maintain formally correct relations with Cairo but behind the scenes to encourage the pro-Soviet group in Egypt led by Vice-president Ali Sabri to unseat Anwar Sadat. Between Nasser's death and the end of the year, even though Sadat had been elected president in mid-October, Sabri's position was powerful enough to prevent any fundamental change in Egypt's policies. Thus, for example, in an interview with the *New York Times* published December 23, the new president took a hard line on the Israeli issue. Vice-president Sabri, then visiting Moscow, released a communiqué three days later echoing the same stance.[32]

By early February, 1971, however, Sadat's position had strengthened, and the president seized the opportunity to propose a new course for Egypt. Weaving together the objectives of both the United States and the Soviet Union, on February 4 Sadat proclaimed a thirty-day extension of the cease-fire and offered to reopen the Suez Canal in return for a partial Israeli withdrawal. Eleven days later, on the fifteenth, he went further, stunning the international community by declaring Egypt's willingness to accept a peace settlement with Israel.[33]

Taken by surprise, the Israeli leadership stalled. In the meantime, both Moscow and Washington—for different reasons—extended support to Sadat's plans. In March, following an unannounced trip by Sadat to Moscow,[34] the Soviets began delivery of an extensive shipment of largely defensive weaponry, pointedly declining to provide any offensive weapons.[35] At the end of March, Washington, also following Sadat's lead, proffered another "plan" to reopen the Suez Canal. Washington's plan centered on a two-stage withdrawal by Israel.[36] After a cease-fire and an initial Israeli pullback, dredging would begin on the canal. In the second stage, Israel would withdraw twenty-five miles and the canal would then be opened for the use of all countries. Again, the Israeli leadership balked, but Sadat, undeterred, pressed forward with his proposal for a partial settlement.

Having set in motion his plans for a settlement with Israel and improved relations with the United States, President Sadat began to chart a new role for Egypt in the Middle East. His principal initiative was for a federation of Egypt, Syria, Libya, and the Sudan based upon joint coordination of foreign policy. Second, Sadat sought to enhance Egyptian regional security by pressing forward with rapprochement with both Turkey and Iran, a process begun earlier. Third, he sought and obtained West European financial support for the construction of a Suez-Middle East (Su-Med) pipeline, a project which would enable Egypt to compete with Israel in the shipment of oil to the eastern Mediterranean without reference to the eventual fate of the Suez Canal and at the same time significantly increase the total volume of petroleum flowing to Western Europe. These steps, with their decidedly Western orientation, crystallized opposition to President Sadat both inside Egypt and in the Soviet Union.

Following extensive negotiations, the leaders of Egypt, Libya, and Syria signed the federation agreement on April 17, 1971, in Bengazi, Libya. President Jafar Muhammad Numayri of the Sudan declined to join in the federation at this time because of the precariousness of his own domestic position (see below), but he would join later in the summer. In signing the agreement Sadat had been forced to override the objections of Vice-president Sabri and his supporters, who strenuously opposed Egypt's participation in the federation.

Upon his return to Cairo, Sabri demanded that the issue of the federation be put to a vote of the eight-man Politburo of the Arab Socialist Union (ASU), Egypt's ruling body, where he controlled a voting majority. Sabri marshaled a five-to-three majority to defeat Sadat's federation plan, but the president immediately demanded, in turn, that the issue be taken up in the ASU Central Committee. In the larger body, where Sadat held a huge majority, the federation proposal was "ratified unanimously," easily overturning the Politburo rejection.[37]

The vote on the federation starkly drew the lines of battle as both sides now prepared for a showdown. Before Sabri, whom Sadat termed "the chief Soviet agent in Egypt," could act, on May 2 the president dismissed him from his position as vice-president and placed him under house arrest.[38] At the same time he informed the Soviet ambassador of his action in an effort to forestall an unfavorable reaction from Moscow. Sadat's arrest of Sabri had come less than forty-eight hours prior to the arrival in Cairo of Secretary of State Rogers, whose visit was the first by a high-ranking American leader since Secretary of State John Foster Dulles' visit in 1953. The Rogers-Sadat talks were described as "productive," but produced no immediate, tangible result. Through early May the tension mounted as Sadat foiled at least one planned assassination attempt. Then, on May 13, he arrested Sabri's supporters and carried out an extensive government reshuffle.[39]

Following Sadat's wholesale purge of the pro-Soviet group in Egypt, at the end of May Moscow responded to this adverse turn of events. Moscow's response was twofold: On the one hand it involved an effort to stabilize relations with Cairo to the extent that it was still possible. On the other hand, the Soviet Union began to shift its position to improve relations with other Arab states. The first step was toward Cairo. Giving Sadat only forty-eight hours' advance notice, President Nikolai Podgorny flew to Cairo on May 25 and demanded that Sadat agree to conclude a Soviet-Egyptian treaty of friendship—a demand to which Sadat acceded two days later.

The treaty, designed to forestall the complete rupture of Soviet-Egyptian relations, described Egypt as a "socialist country" but abjured the usual references to the advance toward revolutionary democracy that were commonly included in treaties between the Soviet Union and its client states. The Soviet position was circumscribed to the provision of military-economic aid and training. In short, although not immediately apparent, the Soviet-Egyptian treaty formalized and greatly constricted Moscow's involvement and role in Egypt, in return for Egypt's agreement not to join in any alliance hostile to the Soviet Union.[40]

Moscow's second step was to strengthen its position with the other Arab states, especially Syria, Iraq, Sudan, Somalia, and North and South Yemen. Here results were mixed. While the Soviets managed to improve relations with Syria, Iraq, and Somalia, mainly through increased arms deliveries, relations with the two Yemens were complicated by Soviet efforts to retain influence in regimes which were becoming increasingly antagonistic to each other. But it was the Soviet relationship with the Sudan which fell apart completely in the summer of 1971, precipitated by the issue of Sadat's federation plan.

When the Numayri regime emerged victorious from the coup of May 31, 1969, the junta had offered a role in the new government to the Sudanese Communist party. Despite Moscow's insistence that the party cooperate with the junta, it split. The majority faction, led by the party chairman, Abdul Khaliq Mahgoub, refused to cooperate on the grounds that the junta was a transitional body that would soon be replaced by a genuine revolutionary regime. The minority chose to obey Moscow's directive, cooperated with the junta, and attempted to gain power from within it. Thus, there existed an uneasy truce between the junta and the Sudanese Communist party from the beginning.[41]

When Numayri traveled to Moscow in November 1969, Soviet leaders were extremely conciliatory, agreeing to provide a major military and economic aid program to the regime which had the largest and best-organized Communist party in the region. By the following spring the Soviet Union had substantially equipped most of the Sudanese army, including the insertion of Soviet advisory personnel down to the brigade level. Even so, the military leadership supported Numayri's plans to join the federation. Numayri withdrew because of violent Communist party objections and out of concern that Moscow's opposition to the federation would result in a crisis between the regime and the Communist party which would shake his own position.

Numayri's trip to Moscow in late April and Sadat's showdown with the pro-Soviet group in Egypt in early May persuaded him that the danger of continued cooperation with the communists was too great and so resolved to crush them just as Sadat had. Following delivery of a major policy statement on May 25, in which he castigated the Sudanese Communist party, Numayri began to arrest leading communists in the party, trade unions, and other state organizations. Ordering the expulsion of Soviet advisers, Numayri set about remodeling the Sudanese political structure along the lines of Sadat's Arab Socialist Union.

By July, those remaining communists who had not been arrested had joined together with pro-communist elements in the army to stage a coup d'etat. Anticipating their move, Numayri executed a preemptive counter coup which he then expanded into a large-scale purge of the non-communist left as well. By July 20, the Soviet press began to express dismay over what was viewed as an "hysterical bloodbath and anti-communist campaign" in the Sudan, but Moscow was helpless to prevent the destruction of the Communist party apparatus that it had labored so hard to build. Throughout the crisis, Sadat openly supported Numayri, who had all along favored joining the federation. When the purge was completed in late July, he promptly aligned the Sudan in the federation with Egypt.[42]

Moscow's position in the Middle East, and certainly the reliability of its centerpiece—Egypt—had crumbled, requiring a significant realignment. Despite the friendship treaty, Soviet leaders clearly perceived that Sadat was in the process of forging an independent position for Cairo which involved a distancing from the Soviet Union and movement toward the United States. Whatever other plans the Kremlin may have contemplated for the region that included Egypt's active collaboration would now have to be postponed indefinitely—hence, Moscow's intense activity to secure its position in Syria, Iraq, Somalia, and the Yemens. For the moment, the summer of 1971 was an inauspicious beginning for the new Soviet strategy.

The Soviet Union had not only suffered a setback in the Middle East. In a bolt out of the blue, on July 15, the United States and the People's Republic of China made public what Kremlin leaders had known privately to have been building for many months: a rapprochement was under way between the two powers. The significance of the announcement that Henry Kissinger had visited China and that President Nixon would do the same sometime in early 1972 was not that Moscow was taken by surprise at the relationship, but the damage that would occur to Soviet strategies by virtue of the fact that everyone else now knew about it, too. Now all other concerned leaders would begin to calculate the consequences for their own policies of Sino-American cooperation — in Vietnam and elsewhere. Not all of the consequences were bound to be negative. Indeed, in one case at least the results were most positive for Moscow — the case of Soviet relations with India.

Opportunity to Restructure the South Asian Balance

For some time, since putting forth the proposal for an Asian Collective Security System in early 1969, Moscow had been pressing Indira Gandhi to enter into a treaty relationship, but without success.[43] Indian adherence to Moscow's "system" would strengthen containment of China as well as the Soviet position in South Asia. By the spring of 1971 a constellation of factors had converged to produce an unprecedented opportunity for the two powers in concert to restructure the subcontinental political balance to mutual advantage.

Foremost among these was the Soviet decision to adopt a more aggressive foreign policy based upon the strategic weapons shift Soviet leaders perceived to be under way at that time. A second factor was a growing disposition on the part of India's leadership to utilize its growing military predominance over Pakistan, particularly in light of that country's deepening internal crisis, which severely weakened Islamabad's capacity for defense. Finally, the factor that was decisive in swinging Indian calculations around to acceptance of a treaty relationship with the Soviet Union was Sino-American rapprochement, which became public knowledge in mid-1971.

In retrospect, it is clear that the power balance between Pakistan and India had begun to tip heavily in India's favor following their 1965 conflicts over Kashmir and the Hindu Kush, when India established a firm arms relationship with Moscow.[44] Between 1965 and 1970, India, under Indira Gandhi's leadership, had devoted an increasingly larger share of national resources to a military buildup, roughly four times that of Pakistan (57 million rupees to 13.8 million). Moreover, during the same period, while publicly proclaiming pursuit of an evenhanded policy, the Soviet Union delivered $730 million worth of arms and equipment to India *and* only $8 million to Pakistan.

China, on the other hand, was able to supply Pakistan with only $133 million worth of materiel, while the United States, continuing an arms embargo placed on both South Asian countries in September 1965, made no significant military contribution to Pakistan's defense. American supplies to India *and* Pakistan during these years totaled only $70 milllion in nonlethal goods and spare parts for previously supplied equipment. Even more significant was Indian qualitative superiority.[45]

By the spring of 1971 Indian military superiority over its rival was accentuated by Pakistan's divisive internal condition. Elections held in December 1970 with the hope of strengthening Pakistani unity had had the opposite result. Sheikh Mujibur Rahman's Awami League based in East Pakistan obtained a majority of the seats in the National Assembly (169 of 313), while Zulfikar Ali Bhutto's People's Party held sway in West Pakistan. Although President Yahya Khan had announced the convocation of the National Assembly in March, Mujib refused to attend. Mujib and the Awami League began to govern East Pakistan as a de facto independent state "in the name of the people of Bangla Desh."

After unsuccessful attempts to reestablish unity, on March 25 Yahya banned the Awami League, arrested Mujib for treason, and ordered the Pakistani army to restore the authority of the national government in East Pakistan. The next day, the insurgents proclaimed the independence of East Pakistan, and civil war began. Throughout the spring and summer violent clashes between insurgents and the army took place on a large scale. By autumn it was estimated that over three million people had been killed, twenty-five million rendered homeless, and another seven million made refugees, who sought safe haven in India. By fall, however, the Pakistani army was well on the way toward regaining control.

From Delhi's perspective, successful suppression of the rebellion would mean loss of the opportunity to become the hegemonic power in South Asia, by weakening Pakistan. It was thus in Delhi's interest to prolong the crisis until conditions were judged to have evolved to the point where action could be taken to restructure the balance of power in South Asia to advantage. Initially, Indira Gandhi sought to achieve her objectives in East Pakistan independently and at the least cost in terms of expended resources and related political commitments.

At this stage of Delhi's calculations the principal threat to Indian objectives was China. From early spring onward, as India moved five divisions to the East Pakistani border and began a "crash program" of defense preparations,[46] Chinese leaders publicly pledged support to Pakistan, leaving the clear impression that Beijing would intervene on behalf of Pakistan should India attack.[47] Indian plans were to wait until late in the year to take action, when the monsoon had ended and snow began to fall in the Himalayas, hindering Chinese troop movements.

In the meantime, Gandhi's policy was to stoke higher the flames of resistance in East Pakistan, even while piously preaching a peaceful solution. Thus, in mid-April Gandhi permitted the establishment in Calcutta of a Bangladesh government-in-exile and throughout surreptitiously supported extensive guerrilla operations of the so-called "Mukhti-Bahini," Indian-trained and armed Bengali refugees who were then returned to East Pakistan.[48]

Up to midyear, even though Moscow publicly supported India's actions and privately promised to deter Beijing in case the Chinese intervened,[49] Gandhi nevertheless declined to enter into the formal treaty relationship for which Moscow was pressing. From Delhi's point of view this was simply good politics as well as good strategy. A formal link with the Soviet Union would undoubtedly provoke a corresponding linkage on the Pakistani side. It therefore made sense to attempt to keep the potential coaliton of forces that India would have to face as small as possible. The July 15 announcement of Sino-American rapprochement forced a change in Indian calculations.

Taken by surprise, the Indian leadership was now required to consider the possibility of American as well as Chinese intervention. Sino-American rapprochement might also include some form of cooperation over Pakistan with which both powers had a security relationship (even though the United States had been decidedly ungenerous with military supplies for the past several years). In an effort to counterbalance if not neutralize a potential Sino-American joint effort to preserve Pakistan's rapidly disintegrating territorial integrity and thus frustrate Indian ambitions, Indira Gandhi agreed with the Soviets to conclude the treaty which had been under discussion since 1969.

The twenty-year treaty of "peace, friendship and cooperation," signed with the Soviet Union on August 9, 1971, now made it possible for Indira Gandhi to proceed with her plans to divide Pakistan, on the assumption that Moscow would deter both Beijing and Washington. Exhibiting the usual hypocrisy of Soviet peace treaties, Article 4 declared Soviet respect for India's policy of "nonalignment," despite the obvious fact that the document itself demonstrated the very opposite, and India's respect for the "peace-loving" policy of the Soviet Union, despite the obvious fact that the treaty was designed to free India to make war. Article 9 stipulated that an attack on either party would be met by mutual consultation with a view toward eliminating the threat and also that each party agreed not to assist any nation at war with the other.[50]

Whether the Nixon leadership understood the relationship between the United States-China announcement of July 15 and the Soviet-Indian treaty of August 9 is unclear. The fact is, however, that the treaty put Washington into the position of providing full support to Pakistan, or acquiescing in that country's dismemberment. Washington's response was to intensify efforts to bring about the peaceful, political partition of Pakistan, which in any case had been long-term United States policy.[51]

In other words, Washington accepted the reality of East Pakistani autonomy. What American leaders sought to avoid was the impression that the Soviet Union was now strong enough to use force with impunity to achieve geopolitical ends at the expense of the United States. Therefore, Washington's principal objective was to forestall a military conflict whose consequences might very well include the collapse of West as well as East Pakistan and which would most certainly demonstrate Moscow's ability in conjunction with its allies to manipulate the geopolitical balance to the detriment of the United States and its allies.

It is the last resort of the power playing the weaker hand in a crisis to offer to act jointly with the power in the stronger position. The objective is to dissuade the stronger power from playing its hand out to the full. This tactic invariably fails and actually confirms weakness, removing any doubt that the stronger power can proceed with its plans. On October 9, Kissinger made such an offer to the Soviet Union. In a conversation with Ambassador Dobrynin, he said of the United States that "we were prepared to consider acting jointly with the USSR to defuse the crisis" and lamented the fact that "the offer was never taken up."[52] Indeed, once Kissinger admitted, in effect, United States inability to control events, there was no need for Moscow to take up the offer.

Indo-Pakistani War and United States-Soviet Relations

Despite the fact that Yahya, now fully aware of the danger, agreed on October 11 to convene a new National Assembly before the end of the year, submit a constitution to it, and turn over power to a civilian government, it was too late. Soviet and Indian preparations were in final stages of readiness. At the end of October the Soviet Union commenced a large military airlift to India which was accompanied by daily consultations between Soviet and Indian officials. Materiel deliveries ceased just prior to the Indian attack, but resumed once hostilities began. Indira Gandhi in the meantime had embarked upon a world tour that included Moscow, Washington, and several European capitals.[53] Upon her return to Delhi she declared, on November 13, that the world now held a fuller appreciation of the seriousness of the crisis on the subcontinent and the course of action India would take to resolve it.

On November 21, 1971, India attacked East Pakistan.[54] Indira Gandhi, incredibly declaring that Pakistan was preparing to attack India, sent Indian forces into East Pakistan "in self defense" against "approaching" Pakistani tank forces. The 70,000-man force that Yahya had deployed to East Pakistan to regain control of the rebellion was in no position to contemplate an invasion of India from any quarter, let alone from East Pakistan and against the 200,000-strong armed force Delhi had deployed on the border. Moreover, the dozen combat jet aircraft based in East Pakistan were no match for the some two hundred fighters Delhi had mobilized for the conflict.

In any event, Indian forces struck at five key areas in East Pakistan—Jessore in the west, Hili in the northwest, Rangpur in the north, the Sylhet area in the northeast, and the Chittagong port area in the southeast.[55] Within ten days, by December 1, Indian troops had gained command of the fighting on the ground in East Pakistan, having surrounded or otherwise isolated Pakistani units, and had eliminated the Pakistani air force there as an effective force.[56]

Once it became clear that Indian forces would be victorious in East Pakistan, the question was whether India would attempt to defeat West Pakistan as well. On December 2, Indian troop redeployments westward alarmed Yahya sufficiently for him to invoke Article I of the 1959 bilateral agreement between Pakistan and the United States, which stated:

> In case of aggression against Pakistan, the Government of the United States of America, in accordance with the constitution of the United States of America, will take such appropriate action, including the use of armed forces, as may be mutually agreed upon and as is envisaged in the Joint Resolution to Promote Peace and Stability in the Middle East, in order to assist the Government of Pakistan at its request.[57]

The 1959 agreement was the baseline agreement between the two countries that had been reaffirmed publicly and privately on several occasions afterward by Presidents Kennedy and Johnson. But that agreement involved a security guarantee against attack by "communist" forces, not India, as Yahya well knew. Yahya was clearly signalling his need for assistance, hoping to obtain American support on the basis of the 1959 agreement without having to reveal that the United States had also made a secret commitment in 1962 to come to Pakistan's aid against *Indian* aggression.[58] Unfortunately not privy to this commitment, the Department of State responded by vacillating while correctly suggesting that the 1959 commitment was not "binding."[59]

Washington equivocated, and perhaps because it did so the war spread to West Pakistan. On December 3, Yahya sent the bulk of his remaining, serviceable combat aircraft on a "totally ineffective attempt at a pre-emptive strike" against airfields in the Indian portion of Kashmir and Punjab.[60] The air strike was not accompanied by a major ground assault. Yahya's action had minimal effect on India's westward redeployment and only allowed Gandhi to justify her planned attack on West Pakistan as coming in response to an actual attack from Islamabad.

More ominous, the spread of the war to West Pakistan, which stood little chance of holding its own against India's vastly superior forces, raised the question of third-power entanglement, which was probably the purpose of Yahya's spoiling attack. Yahya may well have gambled, given the hopelessness of his position, that increasing the Indian threat to West Pakistan would precipitate American and Chinese involvement on his behalf.

Meanwhile, the Soviet role in the events on the subcontinent closely resembled United States behavior of an earlier day, when Washington had acted from a position of strategic weapons strength. The super-power role was to deter all other powers from intervening to defeat the objectives of its client in a crisis. It was this role that Moscow sought to assume, even though the Soviet Union did not yet possess strategic weapons superiority over the United States and at best enjoyed only sufficient power to neutralize part of the American nuclear shield over some of its clients. Yet the direction of change in the strategic weapons balance was unmistakable, and the Indo-Pakistani crisis would con-stitute a barometer of sorts, registering just how far the balance had shifted, or was perceived to have shifted.

In other words, the emerging crisis on the subcontinent forced the Nixon administration to reveal its priorities. The question was, were the stakes sufficiently high in South Asia to risk nuclear confrontation with Moscow? While there were clearly defined areas where the United States had declared its intention to "extend its nuclear shield," such as over Western Europe, Japan, and lately China, Soviet leaders calculated that South Asia was no longer in the same category, given the evolving nuclear balance.

From Moscow's point of view, of course, a political resolution was readily available, but this would not demonstrate the change in the Soviet-American strategic relationship that the crisis was in part designed to reveal. Certainly, the extent to which the U.S. Depart-ment of State attempted publicly to extricate itself from treaty com-mitments to Pakistan could only strengthen Soviet calculations and firm Moscow's resolve to play out the deterrent role.[61]

Moscow's deterrence package contained a range of components from soft to harsh. On the soft side, Moscow clearly must have hoped that announcement of the Soviet-American summit on October 12 would be an inhibiting factor for the United States. Throughout the crisis, moreover, Moscow's diplomats in Washington were soothing and conciliatory, replete with denials that India had any intention of dismembering West Pakistan by seizing Azad Kashmir, an area in dispute since 1947 and fought over in 1965.[62]

At the diplomatic level, in the United Nations, the Soviet Union used its veto in the Security Council to prevent passage of any resolution that might hinder India's action. Thus, when the United States sought to gain UN Security Council approval for a cease-fire on December 4, after fighting had spread to West Pakistan, Moscow vetoed the United States resolution. Moscow also vetoed a second United States resolution put forward the next day, which labeled India the aggressor in the conflict.

It was only by shifting the question from the Security Council to the General Assembly that the United States was able to obtain passage of a cease-fire resolution under the Uniting for Peace clause of the UN Charter. The assembly voted overwhelmingly, by a 104-to-11 margin, for an immediate cease-fire and withdrawal of all forces to their own territories. The vote had no effect beyond emphasizing India's political isolation. India disregarded, indeed denounced, the resolution. It was not until December 21, five days *after* fighting had ceased, that Moscow permitted passage of a Security Council resolution demanding withdrawal of forces, but not before India had succeeded in establishing the independence of East Pakistan as Bangladesh.

Toward India, Moscow displayed firm public support while at the same time attempting to manipulate the Indian leadership into decisions that would achieve the maximum gain short of provoking American and/ or Chinese intervention. Chinese intervention was unlikely, given the turmoil which continued in military ranks after the Lin Biao crisis of mid-September, in which the minister of defense and China's second in command was ousted and killed in a confrontation with Mao.[63] Nevertheless, intelligence regarding Chinese troop movements could not be discounted.

On the harsh side, on December 4, a Tass bulletin denounced Pakistan and declared that "in the event" of interference by outside forces the Soviet Union would not "remain indifferent to the developments taking place in direct proximity of the borders of the U.S.S.R. involving her security interests."[64] Soviet Ambassador to India Nikolai Pegov then assured Indira Gandhi that the Soviet Union would deter both the United States and China. He declared that the Soviet fleet, "now in the Indian Ocean . . . will not allow the Seventh Fleet to intervene" and promised that "in case of Chinese attack across the Himalayas," then "Moscow would open a diversionary action in Sinkiang."[65] Gandhi's reaction was to invoke Article 9 of the Soviet-Indian treaty, which required joint assessment of the threat to India's security and the measures necessary to remove it.

At this point, in Washington, intelligence received from a source "in Gandhi's cabinet"[66] that India had decided to liberate West Pakistani-controlled Kashmir, persuaded the president "that the best hope to keep India from smashing West Pakistan was to increase the risk for Moscow that events on the subcontinent might jeopardize its summit plans with the United States."[67] A message from Nixon to Soviet leader Leonid Brezhnev was sent to this effect, but the Soviet reaction was to stall, which the White House interpreted as an intent to see the war continue. When Brezhnev did reply formally on December 9, his proposals for a cease-fire and negotiations amounted to an attempt to buy more time for India to finish off its conquest.

Moscow had a nominal contingent of four ships on station in the Indian Ocean when India attacked Pakistan on November 21, 1971. These were a destroyer, a minesweeper, a tank-landing ship, and a diesel-powered attack submarine. On December 5, a SAM-equipped destroyer and a second minesweeper entered the Bay of Bengal. Whether intended as relief for the ships already on station or not, "routine rotation became a timely reinforcement."[68] A few days later, on December 9, two more ships — a Kynda-class, cruise-missile-carrying cruiser and a similarly fitted submarine — were sighted passing through the Tsushima Strait between Japan and South Korea on their way to the scene. (They would reach the Bay of Bengal on December 18.)

Even if only as a prudent measure to counter possible United States deployments, Moscow was gradually augmenting its naval force in the bay. The Soviets would ultimately have over thirty naval craft in the Indian Ocean, but only a third of them would be combatants. At this point, with no American ships in the vicinity, Washington was left with two alternatives: either accept the defeat of West Pakistan as a fait accompli, which the loss of Azad Kashmir would accomplish, or meet the challenge Moscow was so subtly orchestrating.

On December 10, President Nixon decided to meet the challenge, in part because Yahya now invoked the 1962 commitment. Calling in Dobrynin's deputy Vorontsov, Kissinger revealed to him the secret aide-mémoire to Pakistan of November 5, 1962, in which the United States promised to assist Pakistan in case of Indian aggression. "We would honor this pledge," he warned.[69] Revelation of the secret

United States commitment to aid Pakistan produced an immediate reaction in both Delhi and Moscow as each dispatched delegations to the other's capital for consultations.[70]

To reinforce his warning, the president now ordered a previously alerted aircraft carrier group of ten ships to move to a position off Singapore, at the eastern entrance of the Malacca Strait. Designated Task Force 74, the naval group consisted of the nuclear attack carrier *Enterprise*, the helicopter carrier *Tripoli*, three guided-missile escorts, four destroyers, and a nuclear attack submarine.[71] The deployments were made "ostensibly for the evacuation of Americans but in reality to give emphasis to our warnings against an attack on West Pakistan."[72] Moving Task Force 74 was designed not only to deter an Indian attack westward, but also "to have forces in place in case the Soviet Union pressured China."

The Soviet response was to move additional units of its Pacific fleet toward the combat zone.[73] At the same time, continuing to stall, Moscow pulled out all of the propaganda stops, condemning the "gunboat diplomacy" of President Nixon and denying that the Indian Ocean was "an American lake."[74] Meanwhile, toward Beijing, the Soviets issued thinly veiled threats of a nuclear strike should China intervene. In a Chinese-language broadcast, a Soviet commentator declared: "Everyone knows that the expansion of a regional war into a large-scale nuclear war would annihilate the peoples of all countries, including the Chinese people."[75]

Time was rapidly running out. Indian forces would be in position to commence an attack on West Pakistan by December 15 or 16.[76] Therefore, in a last attempt to deter an Indian attack, on December 12 the president decided to intensify the pressure on both Moscow and Delhi. In an Oval Office meeting on the morning of the twelfth attended only by the president, Kissinger, and Alexander Haig, "the first decision to risk war in the triangular Soviet-Chinese-American relationship was taken."[77] In a Hot Line message to Moscow, the president declared that he had "set in train certain moves" that could not be reversed, although he was "still prepared" to accept a standstill cease-fire on the battlefield and the beginning of immediate negotiations.

Pakistani sources claimed that the president also sent a letter to Indira Gandhi on the twelfth issuing a "categorical warning" regarding the possibility of direct American military intervention in the conflict.[78] Although in their memoirs neither Nixon[79] nor Kissinger mentions a message to Gandhi, it would of course have been both logical and consistent, if not mandatory, to have sent one, given the imminent entry of the United States naval task force into Indian waters. Kissinger does note that Ambassador to the United Nations George Bush was instructed to demand a public statement from India that it harbored no territorial ambitions in West Pakistan *and Azad Kashmir.*[80]

At any rate, the Indian response came in a letter from Indira Gandhi to President Nixon on December 15. In it, Gandhi denied having any territorial ambitions but continued to evade the central question of whether India would attack Kashmir. Gandhi declared:

> We do not want any territory of what was East Pakistan and now constitutes Bangladesh. We do not want territory of West Pakistan. . . . But will Pakistan give up its ceaseless and yet pointless agitation of the past 24 years over Kashmir?[81]

Still on the twelfth, to strengthen and elaborate on the Hot Line message, the president instructed Ambassador Jacob Beam to inform the Soviet leadership personally that the "president's trip to Moscow might be jeopardized by India's 'dismemberment' of West Pakistan."[82] Finally, the president ordered Task Force 74 into the Bay of Bengal from its holding position off Singapore.

Ambassador Beam's personal reinforcement of the Hot Line message and intelligence regarding the movement of Task Force 74 reached the Soviet leadership the next day, December 13, along with news that Beijing had begun large-scale troop movements at points adjacent to the Indian protectorates of Sikkim and Bhutan, where the passes were still open.[83] Although it would not become clear until afterward, the combination of the president's threat to scuttle the summit, movement of the carrier force into the combat zone, and the parallel development of Chinese troop movements persuaded the Soviet leadership that it was time to settle.

On the thirteenth, Moscow communicated its views to the Indian leadership through its emissary Vasily Kuznetsov, who had just arrived, and Ambassador Pegov. Pegov, while reassuring the Indian leadership that the Soviet Union "would not allow the Seventh Fleet" to "bully India, to discourage it from striking against West Pakistan," urged that India quickly conclude its operations.[84] He said:

> India should try to occupy Bangladesh in the quickest possible time and that it should then accept a ceasefire. . . . India has

achieved a marvelous military victory, Pakistan is no longer a military force, and it is therefore unnecessary for India to launch an offensive into West Pakistan to crush a military machine that no longer exists.[85]

Kuznetsov, on the other hand, said that the Kremlin was "impatient with the Indian armed forces for their inability to liberate Bangladesh within the ten day time frame mentioned before the outbreak of hostilities." While affirming that Moscow would "continue to use its veto to stall any efforts to bring about a ceasefire for the present, he stressed the importance of quick and decisive Indian action."[86]

On that same day, December 13, the Soviet Union vetoed for a third time an American proposal in the UN Security Council for an immediate ceasefire.[87] At the same time, Moscow replied to the president's Hot Line message, a reply which was received in Washington at 3:00 a.m., December 14. The Soviet leadership now professed to see a "considerable rapprochement of . . . positions." Moreover, the message continued, there were now "firm assurances by the Indian leadership that India has no plans of seizing West Pakistani territory."[88]

Concerned that Moscow was continuing to stall and therefore that an Indian attack on West Pakistan was imminent, Kissinger made public the president's private threat to cancel the Moscow summit and also threatened a reevaluation of the entire Soviet-American relationship. In a backgrounder given later, on December 14 aboard Air Force One, while the president and he were en route home from their meeting with French President Georges Pompidou in the Azores, Kissinger declared that Soviet conduct during the affair was "not compatible with the mutual restraint required by genuine coexistence. If it continued, we would have to reevaluate our entire relationship, including the summit."[89]

Although Kissinger implies that it was his threat of December 14 to cancel the summit that was decisive in Moscow's calculations, in retrospect it is clear that the decisive events occurred earlier. It was the series of decisions taken on December 12 by President Nixon, which included his own privately communicated threat regarding the summit and the orders to send in Task Force 74 that, combined with the additional factor of possible Chinese intervention, persuaded the Soviet Union to urge restraint upon the Indian leadership. Kissinger's public threat was a hasty and unnecessary overreaction.[90]

The fall of Dacca, capital of what was East Pakistan, on the sixteenth was immediately accompanied by an Indian declaration of a cease-fire. The Indian leadership repeatedly and vehemently denied that Moscow had brought any pressure to bear on its decision not to attack in the west. It also rejected any notion that either the presence of United States naval power or the threat of Chinese intervention was a factor. All such talk, of course, falls into the category of after-the-fact rationalization.

The president's own evaluation of the crisis on the subcontinent was that "the Soviets . . . tested us to see if they could control events. . . . Part of the reason for conducting our Vietnam withdrawal so slowly is to give some message that we are not prepared to pay *any* price for ending a war."[91] He believed that the war "involved stakes much higher than the future of Pakistan — and that was high enough. It involved the principle of whether big nations supported by the Soviet Union would be permitted to dismember their smaller neighbors. Once that principle was allowed, the world would have become more unstable and unsafe."[92]

While the United States ultimately had proved willing to defend West Pakistani teritorial integrity and thus had met the Soviet "test," it was not able to maintain the structural integrity of the subcontinent, which was now altered irrevocably in India's favor. The chief beneficiaries of the Indo-Pakistani war were clearly the Soviet Union and India. India emerged from the conflict the dominant power on the Asian subcontinent, surrounded by weak states. Victory laid open the possibility for further Indian gains against smaller neighboring states. (In fact, India would annex the small mountain kingdom of Sikkim in 1974 and make threatening troop movements toward Pakistan the same year.)

For the Soviet Union the restructuring of the South Asian political balance held broader significance beyond the region. In terms of Sino-Soviet relations, the partition of Pakistan removed a pro-Chinese buffer state between China and India and replaced it with a pro-Indian one. In this sense, the Soviet Union strengthened its "containment" of the People's Republic. Regarding the Soviet-American balance, the Soviet Union struck a sharp blow at the overall American geopolitical position. Apart from the defeat of an American ally, the dismemberment of Pakistan destroyed the one key state in the linkage between the NATO and SEATO treaty structures around the Soviet Union. While West Pakistan remained allied to Turkey and Iran, the removal of East Pakistan from the Pakistan state structure made SEATO membership irrelevant for West Pakistan, which withdrew in November 1972.

Finally, for the first time since the late fifties, the Soviet Union, for the most part successfully even though engaging in a high degree of bluff, carried off the role of a superpower in a geopolitical conflict involving its client against an American one. Soviet behavior would be markedly different in Vietnam over the course of the following year, not because strategic conditions had changed, but because Soviet policy was designed to achieve different ends.

Moscow Shifts Course in Vietnam

From the Soviet perspective of the spring of 1971, the probable outcome of the Vietnam conflict was a gradual return to the status quo ante bellum. Hanoi would become progressively incapable of waging large-scale warfare and Saigon increasingly able to defend its territory. Objectively, Moscow's leaders could afford to reach no other conclusion. Barring an unforeseen turn of events, the United States would have extricated its forces successfully from the region while maintaining a position there through its client in Saigon.

The threat to China's southern flank would be eliminated. North Vietnam would remain a small state like North Korea, hedged in on the north by Beijing and on the south by a United States ally. Moreover, Sino-Soviet hostility would be perpetuated as Beijing was drawn into the Western political-economic network. In short, Soviet strategy had failed to keep the United States pinned down in a draining conflict, to bring about an improvement in relations with China, or to unify Vietnam under Hanoi—and that strategy had to be changed.

Moscow's new approach was to continue to seek the unification of Vietnam under Hanoi, but now as an end in itself in order to establish a strong client state in a containing position on China's southern flank. Initially, Soviet strategy had sought to embroil the United States in a debilitating conflict, which, it was hoped, would generate sufficient danger to China's security to bring about an improvement in Sino-Soviet relations to meet the threat. The new turn in Soviet policy was to facilitate what the United States was successfuly accomplishing in any case—the withdrawal of its forces. At the same time, Moscow sought to put Hanoi in a position from which it could carry on the struggle for unification after American withdrawal was completed. Only after the withdrawal of American forces would resumption of the offensive become feasible.

There was, of course, no guarantee of success. Nevertheless, the present course would produce only negative returns and had to be altered. The Hanoi leadership was understandably opposed to Moscow's new course. It was not at all clear to the North Vietnamese leadership that delay was in its interests. If Vietnamization succeeded and Sino-American interests remained coincident, resumption of the offensive after American withdrawal offered only the slimmest of prospects and then only if Moscow *re*-engaged and Washington did not.

Indeed, the fear that the Soviet Union was preparing to cut its losses in Vietnam, much as it had in Geneva seventeen years earlier, led to an effort to improve relations with Beijing in the fall. In the meantime, Hanoi's leaders insistently pressed Moscow to provide sufficient material support to complete the conquest of the South while Saigon was at its weakest — in the immediate wake of the United States withdrawal but before Vietnamization had become fully effective. In practical political terms, the question at issue was the timing of the spring offensive.

Except for Hanoi, there evolved an independent and implicit convergence of interests among Washington, Beijing, and Moscow on the timing of the 1972 offensive. For different reasons, each of the major participants sought to delay the start of the offensive until after President Nixon's trip to Beijing in late February. The seasonal monsoon pattern was a primary consideration in their separate calculations. The dry season, during which major military operations were most feasible, encompassed the period from October to June, give or take a week or two at either end. When the spring rains or, more accurately, deluge came, military operations dependent upon tracked or wheeled transport became virtually impossible. In short, the earlier in the dry season an offensive began, the better were its chances of success. And vice versa.

Washington's interests were most straightforward. American leaders sought to delay the offensive to reduce its chance for success. (It was also true that the monsoon brought heavy cloud cover, making air operations in the South extremely difficult.) Delay was also sought to avoid placing the Chinese leadership in a compromising position. For this reason Beijing, too, sought to delay the offensive until after the president had departed. Despite some propaganda commentary to the contrary, China sought to perpetuate a divided Vietnam to preserve its security in Indochina and maintain some degree of hegemony there. An offensive begun in February while the president was in the Chinese capital would, aside from having a better chance of success, place the Chinese leadership in a delicate and contradictory position. Beijing would be required to proclaim support for Hanoi against the United States, even while negotiating a relationship with Washington that undoubtedly diverged from Hanoi's interests.

Moscow's position was least clear. On the surface it might appear that the Soviet Union would have preferred an offensive to coincide with the president's trip to Beijing in order to exert maximum pressure on both. Though both Washington and Beijing feared this would happen, such was not Moscow's objective. An offensive begun while Nixon was in Beijing would be seen as an obvious attempt by the Soviet Union to embarrass them and to signal hostility to both, which was manifestly no longer Moscow's intent. This, in turn, could lead to cancellation of the Moscow summit, from which the Soviet Union expected to derive the major benefit of the ABM treaty.

The strategic shift embodied in the ABM treaty combined with a significant improvement in overall relations would have the utmost importance for Moscow's global position for the foreseeable future. An early offensive would also make doubly difficult either the improvement of relations with, or exertion of pressure on, Beijing. Finally, an offensive begun in February, early in the dry season, would stand a good chance of success and thus hinder if not forestall United States withdrawal. (It could not be assumed that Washington would stand aside and allow Saigon to fall.) Since the Soviet objective was to facilitate American withdrawal, not prevent it, Moscow too sought to delay the offensive.

The basis of Moscow's policy shift was partly in reaction to the evolution of the administration's peace terms toward Vietnam, particularly the offer of a cease-fire in place, first put forward on October 7, 1970, and developed further in the secret seven-point peace proposal of May 31, 1971.[93] The latter proposal, in particular, formulated solely by Kissinger and his staff, offered "to set a terminal date" for *unilateral* withdrawal of American forces and proposed a "ceasefire in place throughout Indochina," in return for "immediate release of all prisoners of war and innocent civilians."

It would be left to "the Vietnamese and the other peoples of

Indochina . . . [to] discuss among themselves the manner in which all other outside forces would withdraw from the countries of Indochina." Once the cease-fire went into effect "there should be no further infiltration of outside forces into the countries of Indochina." Finally, the cease-fire would come under "international supervision," both sides agreeing "to respect the 1954 and 1962 Geneva Accords," which "could be formalized at an international conference." As Kissinger later described it, the May 31 proposal was "a turning point in our diplomacy in Vietnam . . . [which] in its essence . . . was accepted sixteen months later by Hanoi."[94]

From Washington's perspective the plan offered the prospect of a return to the status quo ante bellum, or, in other words, a successful outcome to the conflict. Unilateral withdrawal was American policy in any case. The cease-fire in place was not expected to leave Hanoi in a strong position in the South for three reasons. First, there were few North Vietnamese main force units in the South at this point, virtually all having withdrawn because of the success of United States combat operations and the increasing difficulty of supporting a large force.[95] Second, the ban on infiltration contained in the administration's proposal meant that those forces that did remain in the South could neither be reinforced nor supplemented and in time would atrophy and wither. Third, Saigon's forces, strengthened by the Vietnamization program, could be expected to deal successfully with the less well-equipped Vietcong and People's Liberation Armed Forces (PLAF) in the South.

The very strength of the United States proposal also contained its principal weakness. Given the weak position of Hanoi's forces in the South, it was obviously necessary at some point prior to a negotiated settlement to mount an invasion. This had to be attempted not with any expectations that Hanoi could defeat Saigon — American power would deny victory — but primarily to place forces into positions of strength in the South on the basis of which Hanoi could negotiate an end to the current stage of the conflict.[96]

The weakness in the proposal was not in offering the cease-fire in place, but in setting a time for it to take effect, which was "at the time . . . US withdrawals began based on a final agreed timetable."[97] This formulation meant that although Saigon might have the advantage for the moment, the United States would be committed to a cease-fire in place even after a Northern offensive would inject substantial main force and other smaller units into the South, significantly changing the balance of forces. (It should not escape the reader's notice that Kissinger's May 31 formula was precisely the same in its political effect as the one he had offered earlier in the year to Moscow on strategic arms. In both cases—an offensive weapons freeze and a cease-fire in place—an initial advantage was turned into a serious disadvantage between the time the proposal was accepted and the time it went into effect.)

Thus, the Soviet policy shift in Vietnam would involve three steps. First, it was necessary for North Vietnam to mount a major offensive in order to inject forces into South Vietnam. Second, once in position, Hanoi would negotiate a settlement that would permit American withdrawal to be completed in a formal sense and make it virtually impossible for Washington to "jump back in." Finally, once withdrawal was complete, Moscow would support the resumption of Hanoi's assault on Saigon at some propitious later time. Soviet policy was thus highly compatible with United States policy as it had evolved through early 1971, except presumably for the last step—the final defeat of South Vietnam.

In preparation for Hanoi's offensive, the Soviet Union began sending large quantities of heavy military equipment—T54 tanks, 130mm artillery, and SA-7 hand-held anti-aircraft missile launchers—to North Vietnam by seaborne transport from August of 1971 at about the same time that it commenced training Vietnamese tank crews at the Odessa armor school.[98] By that time the Chinese too had become active in an effort to affect the timing of the invasion. In late September, Chinese Vice-premier and Politburo member Li Xiennien went to Hanoi to negotiate the annual aid agreement. Li's reception in the North Vietnamese capital was cool and correct. Even though he subsequently agreed to double China's military aid commitment to Hanoi for the coming year, a chill remained evident in Sino-Vietnamese relations.[99] Chinese aid deliveries would be correlated to, and a function of, the timing of Hanoi's invasion.

Joint high-level Soviet-North Vietnamese planning for the offensive reached the substantive stage a few months later with Soviet President Nikolai Podgorny's trip to Hanoi, October 3–8, 1971. Podgorny may well have taken the North Vietnamese leadership aback by also arguing for a delay of the offensive until after Nixon's return from China. But the reasoning was straightforward. Once the offensive began, the United States would be expected to mine the harbors and cut off further delivery of Soviet seaborne aid.

Beijing would then hold the key to the ultimate development of the offensive. Unless Sino-Vietnamese relations were repaired beforehand, there was little chance that Hanoi could expect any assistance from Beijing, which would spell certain defeat. This would be true particularly if North Vietnam chose to start the offensive while President Nixon was in Beijing in contravention of the Chinese leadership's wishes. If begun later, then the pressure would be on Beijing to contribute assistance from the only supply route not under American control.

The Soviet preference for delaying the launch of the offensive also clearly involved the larger consideration of relations with the United States. An offensive begun while President Nixon was in Beijing would place great pressure on the American president to cancel the scheduled Moscow summit meeting — and with it perhaps even the strategic arms agreements. This was clearly too much to risk, given Soviet dependence upon the SALT and ABM agreements for all their other plans. If, on the other hand, the offensive were delayed, the question of whether or not to go through with the summit would shift to Moscow, thus removing any danger of cancellation.

Thus, while Podgorny was still in Hanoi, the North Vietnamese leadership's attitude toward Beijing underwent a substantial transformation. Hanoi's leaders began publicly to refer to assistance from China and aid from the Soviet Union in their speeches, a new development. By the end of November, a rapprochement of sorts seemed to have been accomplished. Pham Van Dong went to Beijing for a week, November 20–27, where he was feted regally and in turn placed heavy emphasis on the importance of Chinese aid, which he said was always given "in the spirit of proletarian internationalism."[100]

By the end of the year a high level of interaction was apparent between Hanoi and each of the two communist powers (although obviously not between Moscow and Beijing) as both pumped large quantities of military and other supplies into North Vietnam for the coming offensive. Hanoi, too, was actively preparing its cadre for the offensive. A series of articles in North Vietnam's military press late in the year set out to explain the need for a basic shift from guerrilla to large-unit combat, and COSVN directive 42 issued in December 1971 established Hanoi's basic objectives for the coming campaign.[101]

There can be little question of deep Soviet involvement in — indeed, it would not be too strong to say dominance over — Hanoi's policies, just as there can be little doubt of the North Vietnamese leadership's resentment that its interests were being subordinated to and integrated into the Soviet Union's larger strategy. This is not to say that Moscow dominated every issue and made every decision; it is to say, however, that Moscow ultimately determined the general course of Hanoi's policies. Nor is there any question that the North Vietnamese strenuously attempted to bend Soviet policy to their own policy preferences. The record of their interaction is voluminous.[102]

Moscow dominated Hanoi's policy-making process in the period from late 1971 onward because Hanoi simply and literally had nowhere else to go. Hanoi's and Beijing's interests were clearly divergent. Even when Beijing provided aid, both knew that the Chinese would not assist Hanoi in defeating Saigon as long as there was some hope that Beijing's objective of a fragmented region was still within reach. Sino-American rapprochement left Hanoi no alternative to Moscow, and it is in this sense that Moscow dominated Hanoi's policy-making process.

The Podgorny mission marked the beginning of a virtually continuous high-level Soviet interaction with the Hanoi leadership. Podgorny's delegation, for example, included Politburo member Kiril Mazurov, Secretariat member Konstantin Katushev (who managed the "Hanoi account"), General Sergei Sokolovsky of the Defense Ministry, Deputy Premier V. Novokov, Nikolai Firyubin of the Foreign Ministry, and I. Grishin of the Foreign Trade Ministry.[103] The Soviet press described Podgorny's relations with the North Vietnamese in terms of "fraternal friendship, solidarity, and complete mutual understanding." The considerably more restrained accounts in the North Vietnamese press omitted any reference to "complete mutual understanding."[104]

Although Podgorny and Katushev returned to Moscow on October 8, the others remained in Hanoi for almost six months, departing in late March of 1972 on the eve of the offensive.[105] They were replaced at the end of the month by another delegation, headed by Air Marshal P. Batitsky, whose task was to establish an anti-aircraft defense system over the Haiphong-Hanoi area.[106] A similar pattern was evident in Moscow.

Indeed, there was probably no period of greater Soviet interaction with North Vietnam's representatives than during the month of February 1972. Politburo members Alexei Kosygin and Andrei Kirilenko met with the North Vietnamese ambassador no fewer than five times, and Konstantin Katushev met with other North Vietnamese officials in Moscow on two other occasions.[107] This was partly, to be sure, to formulate the kind of response Hanoi should make to Washington's revelations in late January of the secret negotiations with Hanoi, which exposed North Vietnam's intransigence, but mainly to ensure that the offensive would occur as planned.[108]

The Easter Invasion and the Prelude to Negotiations

American intelligence had noted and followed the North Vietnamese buildup from early fall both in the area north of the demilitarized zone and in the sanctuaries. An invasion was believed to be "imminent" from early January, and in hopes of delaying it for as long as possible, air strikes were conducted against the border sanctuaries (but not in North Vietnam proper) from the last week in December. When the expected offensive failed to materialize, American leaders explained Hanoi's inaction in terms of the preemptive air attacks.[109]

At the same time the administration muted domestic criticism of its disruption tactics. On January 13, the president announced that 70,000 more troops would be withdrawn by the first of May, leaving a total of 69,000 in country, only 6,000 of which were combat troops. On January 25, he disclosed that the United States government had been holding secret talks with Hanoi's representatives for the past two years. The president also revealed on this date that the latest United States peace offer of October 11, 1971, to which Hanoi had never responded, proposed the date of July 1, 1972, for the final withdrawal of all American troops.

In the event, the president's trip to Beijing went off without hindrance. The United States and the People's Republic of China established the basis for normalizing relations while making public their common opposition to Soviet hegemony. In the Shanghai Communiqué, expressing the new relationship, the Chinese generalized their support for Hanoi to the "peoples of Vietnam, Laos and Cambodia in their efforts for the attainment of their goal [sic]," without, however, specifying the goal. And in the communiqué's review of the "long-standing serious disputes between China and the United States," no mention was made of Vietnam at all.[110] Zhou Enlai's hurried, secret visit to Hanoi immediately after President Nixon's departure could not offset Hanoi's growing sense of isolation.

North Vietnamese forces commenced an all-out assault on South Vietnam in the early hours of March 30, 1972, a month after the president's return from China. The strategic plan, as William S. Turley correctly notes, was "to attack on widely separated fronts, draw the ARVN away from populated areas, break up Saigon's outer-most ring of defense, and help local lowland forces carry the attack into the enemy's 'secure rear areas.'"[111] Ultimately, fourteen divisions and twenty-six independent regiments would take part in the invasion.[112] Every regular division except for one in Laos would be committed, leaving no regular ground forces in North Vietnam.[113] The offensive was completely unlike anything Hanoi had ever attempted previously; it was not a guerrilla-style attack like Tet of 1968, but a conventional invasion employing several hundred tanks accompanied by massive artillery barrages.

Overall, Hanoi opened four fighting fronts. Initially, North Vietnamese forces mounted two armored, regiment-size thrusts—one directly across the demilitarized zone toward Quang Tri City, which was taken on May 2, and a similar drive farther south from bases in eastern Cambodia at An Loc, a town sixty-two miles due north of Saigon.[114] While these two attacks were under way, the North Vietnamese assembled three divisions spearheaded by yet another armored regiment for a drive on Kontum in the central highlands; it began later, on April 23. The attack in the central highlands threatened to divide South Vietnam in half and was probably the principal military objective. Hanoi also marshaled four regiments from the Cambodian sanctuaries for attacks on lightly defended outposts in the Mekong Delta thirty-five miles from Saigon.

Once the offensive began, Soviet policy entered its most delicate phase, for it was crucial that Hanoi's action not provoke Washington into cancellation of the coming summit. It was Soviet Ambassador Dobrynin's task to be in close and frequent contact with the White House to keep summit preparations on track and to minimize the implications of the Vietnamese offensive for overall United States-Soviet relations. Thus, for example, from the beginning of the offensive on March 30 until Kissinger's unannounced, secret trip to Moscow on April 20, a period of three weeks, Dobrynin met with Kissinger personally on at least eight different occasions and was in almost daily telephone contact.[115]

Throughout, the Soviet ambassador insisted that Moscow had played no role in Hanoi's decisions—something that both men knew to be a fiction but which, to some extent at least, allowed the Soviets to separate the issue of Soviet-American relations from the war. With the single exception of Brezhnev's letter to President Nixon on May 6, which Kissinger dismissed as "distinguished by its near irrelevance to the real situation," the Soviets would maintain this clearly specious position in the face of mounting administration public accusations of Soviet responsibility for Hanoi's offensive and even direct American air strikes on Soviet ships in Haiphong harbor.[116]

In a meeting with Kissinger on April 12 "to review summit preparations," Dobrynin reassured the national security adviser that Moscow was "not interested in a showdown" over Vietnam. Indeed, he declared that Kissinger's long-contemplated visit to Moscow "was now urgent." The Soviet ambassador said that "the agenda could be Vietnam, as well as accelerated preparations for the summit."[117] Agreeing to April 20, Kissinger viewed the trip as "the vehicle by which to separate Moscow's interests from Hanoi's."[118] To test Soviet forbearance and "to make sure that both Hanoi and Moscow understood our determination," Kissinger said, "I had recommended, and Nixon had approved, a dramatic two-day B-52 attack on fuel storage depots in the Hanoi-Haiphong area together with a shore bombardment by naval gunfire."[119]

Whether it was intended as a test of Soviet forbearance, as an expression of Washington's "determination," or was completely accidental, the April 15–16 B-52 attacks produced a very serious provocation to Moscow, for American planes struck and damaged four Soviet merchant ships in Haiphong harbor, and the attack resulted in significant loss of life to Soviet seamen. Nevertheless, when Dobrynin met with Kissinger at his home that same evening he said nothing about the incident, which had already hit the headlines. Indeed, he was "extremely friendly," saying pointedly that "great powers must be able to put local differences aside to settle fundamental issues."[120] Only the next day, April 16, did Moscow lodge a formal diplomatic protest declaring that the attack "seriously complicates the situation," a protest that Kissinger described as "restraint of a high order."

As a continued expression of Soviet "restraint" Dobrynin accompanied Kissinger aboard the presidential aircraft on the trip to Moscow, an unprecedented gesture. Upon their arrival on the evening of the twentieth, they were joined in Kissinger's lodgings by Foreign Minister Gromyko, who struck the theme which Soviet leaders would play throughout the four-day visit. Gromyko affirmed Brezhnev's readiness to discuss the war in detail, but "spent most of his time stressing the importance that the Soviet leaderhip attached to the summit."[121] In their meetings Brezhnev was most conciliatory—on Vietnam, on SALT, and on everything else, leading Kissinger to conclude that *he* was successfuly manipulating the Soviet leader, little realizing that Brezhnev was engaging in a considerable degree of manipulation himself.

During their first meeting on April 21, the Soviet leader "effusively expressed his commitment to the success of the forthcoming summit."[122] Referring obliquely to the ongoing Vietnamese offensive and United States air strikes as having "dampened the atmosphere somewhat," Brezhnev hastened to add that "I am not saying this will reduce the prospects for our meeting." On the contrary, he insisted that they must "reach results." Kissinger, on behalf of the president, expressed his commitment to a successful summit but stated bluntly that Hanoi's offensive presented a serious threat to it. If it continued unchecked, he said,

> either we will take actions which will threaten the summit or, if the summit should take place, we will lose the freedom of action to achieve the objective. . . .[123]

Brezhnev's response to this thinly veiled threat to take strong retaliatory action against Hanoi was "mild in the extreme." The Soviet leader stated lamely that "only the Chinese . . . opposed the summit," only they stood to benefit from its cancellation.

Kissinger correctly concluded that Brezhnev would not allow a strong American reaction in Vietnam to jeopardize the coming summit. Aside from "wondering" whether the United States would accept a cease-fire in place, expressing his conviction that the North Vietnamese leaders were ready for serious talks, and sending Katushev to Hanoi to prod them, Brezhnev raised no other issues regarding Vietnam. His interest was in the coming summit and the SALT negotiations.

Here the Soviet leader was willing to make concessions. He now agreed to accept as part of the ABM treaty terms the formula allowing each side to protect its capital, plus one other site; a five-year offensive freeze instead of three years, and also the inclusion of SLBMs in the offensive freeze, with a ceiling of 950 missile launchers. Other subjects that Brezhnev and Gromyko probed included the Middle East, Western Europe, improved economic relations, and an "understanding" regarding the mutual non-use of nuclear weapons—all of which Kissinger diverted into innocuous channels.[124]

Kissinger's secret April trip to Moscow held as much if not more significance in the realm of American domestic politics—that is, regarding the growing differences between the president and his national security adviser—as in American-Soviet relations, although the two were connected. More will be said on this subject as it related to Vietnam and, indeed, to United States global strategy in the next chapter. For the moment, the April trip served the purposes of both countries. Moscow gave the necessary assurances that the Soviet leadership would go through with the summit even under extreme provocation, while Washington made it clear that it would soon take strong measures to defeat the Vietnamese offensive, enabling the president to proceed with the summit.

Following the April meeting the way was now clear for the United States to take the steps that both sides long anticipated would be the countermove to an offensive by Hanoi: the mining of the Haiphong port complex. On May 8, President Nixon announced that

> to keep the weapons of war out of the hands of the international outlaws of North Vietnam. . . . I have ordered . . . [that] all entrances to North Vietnamese ports will be mined to prevent access. . . . United States forces have been directed . . . to interdict the delivery of any supplies. Rail and all other communications will be cut off to the maximum extent possible. Air and naval strikes against military targets in North Vietnam will continue.[125]

The president coupled his announcement with a new peace proposal which called for "an internationally supervised cease-fire throughout Indochina," the return of all American prisoners of war, followed by "complete withdrawal of all American forces from Vietnam within four months."[126]

Mining North Vietnam's harbors had an electrifying effect on the main axes of the offensive. The move affected primarily Soviet and East European ships sending supplies to Hanoi, decisively undercutting North Vietnam's ability to sustain the multipronged offensive. The power and thrust of the invasion, designed as it was around tanks and artillery heavily dependent upon seaborne logistical support, was also its main weakness. Closing off access to the ports meant that as Hanoi's limited inventories of petroleum, ammunition, and spare parts were exhausted, the offensive would eventually and inevitably grind slowly to a halt.

At this juncture, Mao Zedong held the key to Hanoi's successful continuation of the invasion. If Beijing reopened rail lines greatly constricted since 1969 and allowed Soviet use of southern China ports, there was a good chance sufficient supplies could be funneled to Hanoi's forces to permit continuation of the offensive. (Of course, such a decision would carry larger political implications for Beijing's relations with Moscow and Washington.) Despite considerable Soviet propaganda commentary to the contrary, however, Beijing *did not initially* resume support to Hanoi, nor did it allow Moscow to use either the Chinese rail system or any ports in southern China.

The inevitable battlefield result was that during the course of the next month South Vietnamese forces were able to cap the four main salients of the invasion. The An Loc front stabilized by mid-May, Kontum in the Central Highlands by the end of May, and early in June Saigon's forces secured a defensive perimeter at the My Chanh River just north of Hue.[127] Hanoi's weak attempt to open a fourth front in the Mekong Delta some thirty-five miles from Saigon never amounted to anything, giving ringing testimony to the impact of the closure of Sihanoukville.

Once it was clear in late May that the offensive would not succeed in defeating South Vietnam, Beijing began in June to permit limited Soviet supplies to transit Chinese territory and also to provide some petroleum and other supplies from its own stocks.[128] It was not sufficient, nor was it designed, to enable Hanoi to continue the invasion, but only to strengthen the defense of North Vietnam against the increasingly devastating bombing strikes of the United States.[129] At any rate, it was in late May (22–29), under conditions indicating that South Vietnamese forces had recovered from the initial shock of the invasion, that the Moscow summit took place.

The Moscow Summit and Vietnam

The Moscow summit was a dramatic event in Soviet-American relations. It visibly and formally established Soviet "equality" with the United States enshrined in the concept of "detente." For Moscow, the arms control agreements constituted the formal centerpiece codifying the change in the correlation of forces that was under way. The ABM treaty and the five-year offensive freeze fixed the United States strategic weapons posture and opened the way for a move to a position of advantage from which the Soviet Union could begin to put to greater political use the enormous investment in strategic arms made over the previous decade.

The ABM treaty precluded any meaningful American effort to protect its Minuteman III missile complexes, which in 1972 were the principal threat to the Soviet Union. The offensive freeze limited the number of missile launchers each side could deploy and thus on paper placed a general limit on the number of warheads each side could deliver against the other. The upper limit was not expressly defined because the freeze included only launchers and not warheads. SALT I thus placed no limit on the number of warheads each side could deploy except that inherent in the capacity of the missiles themselves and the scientific ingenuity of each side.

The aggregate ICBM and SLBM totals for deployed missile launchers permitted during the freeze period were 1,710 and 2,350 for the United States and the Soviet Union, respectively. The Soviet edge in launchers was offset by the larger number of deliverable warheads of the United States. At the time the agreement went into effect the United States had deployed approximately 3,500 warheads to the Soviet Union's 2,050.[130] This was explained by the fact that the United States had already begun to MIRV its land- and sea-based systems, while the Soviet Union had not yet done so. Moreover, the United States held a very large advantage in long-range strategic bombers, some 450 (B-52s) to approximately 150 (Bison and Bear) for the Soviet Union, an advantage greater than the numbers indicated because of the low quality of the Soviet bomber force.

In a very real sense, the SALT I agreements at the Moscow summit represented a snapshot of two ballistic missile programs on divergent courses at the moment of near intersection. The United States advantage in deliverable warheads and long-range bombers at the time of the agreement was real enough, but the momentum of the Soviet program would soon carry it ahead of the American one in the crucial category of time-urgent, counterforce weapons. Of course, this would not happen immediately. The Soviet Union would begin to MIRV its heavy missile force in 1975, and within five years would have fielded over 750 counterforce missiles armed with over 5,400 highy accurate warheads (150 SS-17s with four warheads per launcher, 308 SS-18s with eight to ten warheads, and 300 SS-19s with six warheads). This formidable force would constitute only slightly more than one-half of the land-based force of 1,400 launchers.

The United States force was limited to 1,054, and only a portion of it would ever be MIRVed.[131] At the time the agreement went into effect the United States had MIRVed 210 Minuteman III missiles with a total of 630 warheads. The Minuteman III program would be completed in 1975 with 550 missiles carrying 1,650 highly accurate warheads. The remaining 450 Minuteman IIs and 54 Titan missiles were not MIRVed. The SLBM MIRV program was actually further along in 1972 than was Minuteman. There were already 12 submarines equipped with 192 Poseidon C-3 launch tubes with 10 to 14 warheads per missile, for a total of 1,728 warheads.

Even though the American SLBM program proceeded steadily, quadrupling the number of warheads at sea by the end of the decade, the sea-based missiles on both sides were insufficiently accurate to function in a counterforce role and would remain so until the end of the eighties. In other words, for the next decade and a half, the Soviet counterforce threat to Minuteman would only increase over time, raising the possibility of a Soviet first-strike capability, while the reverse would not be true for the United States against Soviet land-based launchers. Only in 1989 with the deployment of Trident II, a counterforce SLBM, would that equation begin to change.

For the moment, however, in 1972 an uneasy balance of mutual vulnerability obtained. As long as Soviet weapons were not MIRVed and not accurate, sheer numbers of launchers alone did not constitute a threat to the United States. Nevertheless, Moscow had completed the first stage of its three-stage program (launcher stage, MIRV stage, refined guidance stage) to build a counterforce threat, and the United States would have to take measures to keep ahead. Since the offensive freeze prohibited the deployment of new weapons and since it would take from five to ten years to go from drawing board to deployment for any new system, there appeared to be ample time for both sides to prepare for the next advance. In short, the "freeze" did not constrain the programs of either side and implicitly raised the question of its relevancy for arms control.

In historical perspective, the significance of the strategic arms control talks lay (and still lies) far more in the negotiating process itself than in the actual agreements. Negotiations allowed both leaderships to engage in a broad-based strategic dialogue which involved virtually continuous mutual assessment of the rapidly evolving correlation of forces. Ongoing talks also reduced to a minimum the possibility of miscalculation during a period when each side's vital interests were being dramatically affected.

This was doubly important because the two sides were playing different games, as it were. The United States was engaged in a multilevel (and, in truth, multilayered) process of restructuring the global order—an order in which the Soviet Union was playing an increasingly important, even if mostly destabilizing, role. Moscow, on the other hand, was busily engaged in building the necessary power and geopolitical positions to enable the shaping of the global order in its own design at some future time.

At the end of the summit, having achieved the principal objective of the ABM treaty, the Soviet leadership turned once again to the task of bringing the current stage of the Vietnam conflict to an end. During the last private conversation between Nixon and Brezhnev, the Soviet leader proposed sending Podgorny to Hanoi in order to "restrain" the North Vietnamese leaders, "if" the United States "would consider it helpful."[132] It was obvious to both the president and Kissinger that the Russians wished to send a senior leader to Hanoi for their own purposes regardless of what the Americans thought, but they agreed to explore the matter.

The Soviet leader expressed the hope that the United States would cease the bombing raids in the North while Podgorny was in Hanoi and then asked, in reference to Nixon's January 25 peace proposal, whether South Vietnamese President Thieu would be willing to resign two months (instead of one month) before the elections that would follow a settlement. President Nixon readily agreed to two months instead of one, as long as all other terms of his proposal were accepted, and he also agreed to exempt both Hanoi and Haiphong from bombing raids while Podgorny was in North Vietnam—as long as he did not stay too long.[133]

Although Kissinger believed that the Soviets wished to send Podgorny to Hanoi in order to "placate" the North Vietnamese, it is far more likely that the senior Soviet leader went to communicate a policy change. At any rate, a change of policy is what followed Podgorny's trip on June 15. Almost immediately, Hanoi began to change its battlefield tactics, communicating to its troops in the field that the initial phase of the invasion was over, and began to prepare the groundwork for a settlement.[134] By this time, too, the mining of the harbors and intensive bombing strikes had begun to take their toll on the extensive logistical systems that supported the offensive. But while Saigon had succeeded in blunting the main thrusts of Hanoi's forces, tying up most of their reserves in the process, vast areas of the countryside now opened up to low-level guerrilla action and political infiltration.

From mid-June, Hanoi's main effort shifted from attacking Saigon's armies to regaining a political base in the countryside. Both the American and South Vietnamese sides perceived the shift of tactics but either discounted or misunderstood it. Kissinger, discounting the possibility, asserted that he "did not agree with those of my staff who thought Hanoi would choose protracted warfare after the offensive." It would be "technically difficult," after having "committed its regular forces," and psychologically difficult as well. On the other hand, he acknowledged that "Hanoi might adopt such a strategy if everything else failed; it would not choose it if other options were available."[135] President Thieu also noted Hanoi's "dispersal" of forces, but believed it to have been a major error by Hanoi which enabled Saigon's forces to beat back the invasion.[136]

Sir Robert Thompson, head of the British military advisory mission to Vietnam, reached much the same conclusion as President Thieu. General Giap, he believed, had

> made the fundamental strategic error of dispersing his forces in order to attack on three main fronts instead of . . . concentrating his main forces to achieve a penetrating thrust at one point and to maintain momentum.[137]

Thompson attributed this otherwise elementary military blunder to Giap's "arrogance." Nevertheless, he perceived that the "effect of the dispersed attacks was to allow the South Vietnamese to commit more of their forces to the battle." That, of course, was precisely the objective. Hanoi's strategy was to tie down the major portion of Saigon's forces on multiple fronts while resuming the struggle for control of the countryside. Above all, Hanoi had to recapture a political base—a base which had been systematically denied them in the previous three years of pacification and Vietnamization. Without it there was little chance that Hanoi could compete successfully for political control after a settlement.

Before the invasion Saigon had controlled the vast majority of the countryside, conceding only *seven* hamlets to the so-called Provisional Revolutionary Government (PRG). By the fall, however, the government in Saigon officially acknowledged that some 1,400 hamlets were under PRG control and a large but undetermined number of others was being contested.[138] The contest for the countryside clearly indicated the previous degree of success that Saigon had achieved in the pacification program and also the main point of Hanoi's June tactical shift. It was under conditions of intensifying political struggle for the countryside that Hanoi agreed to resume negotiations with the United States.

Le Duc Tho had begun to meet with Kissinger in Paris at roughly two-week intervals from mid-July onward. During these meetings, Hanoi's negotiating position softened bit by bit until at the September 15 meeting, Le Duc Tho proposed that the two sides agree "in principle" to "a certain timetable."[139] They decided on a target date of October 15. Hanoi now moved with all deliberate speed toward a settlement which it hoped to conclude before the November election.

The shift was based on the assumption—sound from Hanoi's perspective—that more favorable terms would be available before the election than afterward because it was now obvious that President Nixon would win the election and be in a position to drive a hard bargain afterward.[140] By this time, too, Hanoi's position in the South Vietnamese countryside had improved to the point where the North Vietnamese cadre would be able to mount a formidable challenge for political control.

Thus, in early October, at a meeting between Le Duc Tho and Kissinger on the eighth, the North Vietnamese negotiator offered a complete draft agreement which essentially incorporated Washington's peace proposals of May 31, 1971, and May 8, 1972. As eventually worked out, Hanoi's offer called for a cease-fire in place, no infiltration after the cease-fire had gone into effect, the withdrawal of all United States forces within two months, and the simultaneous release of all prisoners of war. The proposal dropped all demands for President Thieu's prior removal and the establishment of a coalition government.

Instead, there would be a vaguely defined National Council of Reconciliation and Concord which would administer national elections in the South at some future, unspecified date. In the meantime, both the Saigon government and the communist PRG would continue to coexist. Beyond this, all other political questions would be settled by the two South Vietnamese parties. Extremely conciliatory, Hanoi also agreed that the United States could continue to provide military aid to Saigon under the concept of replacement of armament on a one-for-one basis. Finally, Hanoi agreed to a cease-fire in Laos as well, and to withdraw all forces from both Laos and Cambodia.[141]

These terms, of course, were too good to be credible. If actually carried out, they would have amounted to a "total surrender" by Hanoi — as some of Nixon's senior advisers noted.[142] This, of course, was unlikely in the extreme. The North Vietnamese were not likely to engineer their own defeat. Hanoi's proposal was designed to achieve one objective — to generate irresistible pressure on the United States government to agree to a final settlement *before* the election.

A pre-election settlement would also restrict to a minimum the amount of time that the United States would have to send reinforcements to Saigon's forces, which had been severely weakened by the impact of the invasion. Hanoi was undoubtedly aware that Washington in mid-October was well along in a massive resupply effort for ARVN. Appropriately termed "enhance plus," it amounted to one-third of the 1973 military aid allocation and was intended to provide South Vietnam with as strong a position as possible to enable its forces to sustain themselves without the direct support of American ground forces. It would also establish a high base upon which to calculate compliance with the proposed one-for-one replacement rule.

The negotiations stalled in late October because of President Nixon's second thoughts as well as violent objections by President Thieu. When the United States failed to be stampeded into a pre-election settlement, Hanoi reverted to its former hard-line position, retracting concessions made earlier and revealing its October peace proposal for the gambit it was. One chief reason the North Vietnamese were unwilling to reach the same agreement immediately after the election that they were willing to enter into before it, was the disastrous consequence of a miscalculation made in late October.

Assuming that the United States was committed to a pre-election settlement, an assumption Kissinger encouraged, Hanoi had surfaced its cadre in the South for a last-minute land-grab.[143] Unfortunately for Hanoi, the United States declined to settle before the election. Moreover, Saigon's leadership anticipated Hanoi's maneuver, and its forces decisively beat back the land-grab attempt.[144] Ambassador Ellsworth Bunker's report from Saigon concluded that "there was a large gap . . . between the enemy's capabilities and his intentions." The result was, he said, that the land-grab had been "a complete failure."[145]

The decimation of its political cadre in South Vietnam, and the edge Saigon's forces would gain by virtue of the United States resupply program were the principal reasons for Hanoi's stall. The North now needed time to regain the advantage by rebuilding its cadre infrastructure and accumulating military stocks before entering into a settlement. After all, from Hanoi's point of view, the settlement would only be the prelude to the final struggle for control of South Vietnam. The result was that when negotiations resumed in late November after the election, Hanoi gradually backed away from its earlier proposal.[146]

Saigon's demands for numerous changes in the draft agreement provided a convenient pretext for Hanoi's shift but were hardly the cause of it. Kissinger belatedly recognized what had happened. As he reported to the president on December 7:

> What they have done is . . . to modify their strategy by moving from conventional and main force warfare to a political and insurgency strategy within the framework of the draft agreement.[147]

This, of course, was exactly what Kissinger had predicted Hanoi would *not* do.

After another week of negotiating impasse, the United States acted to force Hanoi back to the bargaining table by a massive show of American power—the so-called Christmas bombing of December 18–29. Contrary to the many hysterical media predictions that the bombing would destroy all prospects for a negotiated settlement, the reverse happened. On December 26, Hanoi agreed to resume talks to "settle the remaining questions with the U.S. side."[148]

Meanwhile, Moscow had reentered the picture in full support of North Vietnam's position. When the Christmas bombing commenced, Moscow sought to exert pressure on the United States to stop it. Employing the much-ballyhooed Nixon concept of "linkage" themselves, the Soviet Union threatened, in a Tass statement of December 21, that the future of Soviet-American relations depended upon bringing the conflict to a prompt conclusion. At the same time, Moscow used the negotiating impasse to advantage by mounting a resupply effort to North Vietnam — mostly by air — that helped to replenish some of Hanoi's losses.[149]

The final negotiations took place January 8–13, and the "Paris Peace Accords" were signed formally two weeks later, on January 27, 1973. While the Christmas bombing had brought Hanoi back to the bargaining table, it did not soften its position. Despite the fact that North Vietnam now lay prostrate, it was the United States that capitulated in the January negotiations. The final agreement contained only a few minor changes from the original draft as it had stood before the bombing had begun, and these were clearly incommensurate to the resources expended to gain them.[150] Aside from allowing virtually unrestricted aid to Saigon, which the United States could in any case do within the terms of the one-for-one replacement rule, the remaining changes were semantic and not all in Washington's favor.

Amending the agreement's reference to the "three nations of Indochina" to the "states of Indochina" was an improvement, for the former implied that North and South Vietnam were one state instead of two. The term "administrative structure" was dropped from the National Council of Reconciliaton and Concord because its rendering in Vietnamese also meant government, thus clarifying the intent that the council would have no governmental functions. But denying the council any role in preserving the cease-fire and peace was essentially meaningless because it had no power in any case.

Reaffirming the DMZ, as Kissinger put it, "in the precise terms of the provisions that established it in the Geneva Accords" of 1954 was no advance at all. Indeed, it was a major concession. The 1954 accords specifically established the DMZ as a temporary armistice measure; in no way was it to be a permanent political or territorial boundary.[151] Reaffirming the DMZ in these "precise terms" in fact further undermined the legitimacy of South Vietnam. Finally, extracting Hanoi's promise not to use Laos and Cambodia as staging areas was as enforceable as the International Control Teams were useful — both required voluntary compliance by the communists to act against their real interests.

What accounts for this last-minute capitulation by the United States? Was it Congress that would not permit the president to "press his advantage"?[152] Were the North Vietnamese simply tougher bargainers?[153] Was Washington satisfied that South

Vietnam was sufficiently strengthened to hold its own, or simply eager to have done with it? Were there larger reasons encompassing the Vietnam settlement that required action in early 1973? Whatever the reasons, which will be explored in the next chapter, the administration delivered an ultimatum to its ally of almost two decades that failure to sign the "Peace Accords" would leave the United States no choice but unilateral action,[154] marking a shabby conclusion of America's longest war.

For the Soviet Union and its ally North Vietnam, the signing of the Peace Accords was a major victory. The day after the accords were signed, Moscow sent a congratulatory telegram to Hanoi, warmly celebrating the "glorious exploit" of their "joint victory."[155] Soviet policy had negotiated a complicated course in Southeast Asia that saw the withdrawal of the United States from the region and the isolation of South Vietnam. A major step had thus been taken toward the larger geopolitical objective of containing Beijing by establishing a strong client state on China's southern border.

In the larger context of overall Soviet strategy, the two years since embarking upon its new policy course marked significant gains. There were setbacks, to be sure, such as the failure in the Middle East, which will be discussed in chapter six from the perspective of United States policy. But the major gains were clearly the shift in the correlation of strategic weapons, the arms control agreements which strengthened it, Moscow's first successful endeavor in superpower diplomacy in South Asia, and the denouement in Vietnam.

CHAPTER

4

The Domestic Determinants of American Foreign Policy

Throughout most of the first term of the Nixon presidency, the main policy thrust had been to attempt to maintain, though in modified form, the containment structure that had evolved since World War II. However, while some notable steps had been taken during the first term, Washington's efforts to rectify underlying adverse trends in both the American-Soviet strategic weapons balance and in the United States economic relationship with the European allies had met with but minimal success. The failure to check these negative trends precipitated a prolonged, intense, and well-guarded debate that rent the American leadership establishment and displayed all of the characteristics of a classic power struggle encompassing issues of strategy, policy, and personality.

On one side was the president, who argued for continuation of the modified containment approach, and on the other side was his national security adviser, Henry Kissinger, who pressed for the adoption of a new, bolder, and more complex strategy. The strategic debate, particularly its central question of what the American position in Asia should be after Vietnam, would be resolved against the president, ironically just after he had been reelected for a second term. Thereafter, the United States would embark upon a new strategy espoused if not conceived by Henry Kissinger, who would inaugurate and execute its several policy parts.

Persistence of Adverse Strategic Trends
and the Crisis in United States Strategy

Two negative trends were the mainsprings driving the policy debate within the administration. The first was the evolution of the strategic weapons balance as Soviet missile power increased. The ABM treaty and SALT I agreements, even though presented to the public as a panacea, had not provided and in truth had not been expected to provide a definitive solution to the problem of containing the momentum of Moscow's buildup, which continued. At best, SALT established a common basis for evaluating the complex power shift then under way. While the United States would retain the advantage in deliverable warheads due to its lead in MIRV technology for several years (Moscow would not begin to deploy MIRVed weapons until 1975), the Soviet missile buildup was gradually eroding Washington's capacity to maintain the credible security guarantee that was the backbone of the Western alliance.

It was not that the American homeland was coming under direct threat; that would not happen until Soviet missile accuracy improved to the point where Minuteman silos could be attacked successfully—a development thought to be many years off—and then only if the United States took no countermeasures. The point was that the shift in the strategic weapons balance was making it progressively difficult and risky to maintain and sustain a forward position in the Eastern Hemisphere. The absolute growth in Soviet power was gradually weakening the nuclear adhesive that bound and protected the Western alliance. As Henry Kissinger put it:

> It was not necessary to postulate a Soviet advantage in strategic weapons to be concerned about the altered military balance. Even U.S.-Soviet equality in strategic weapons implied a revolutionary change in the assumptions on which the West's security had been based in the entire postwar period.[1]

Second was the qualitative change in the Western alliance as European (especially West German) and Japanese economic power grew. It had become painfully apparent well before the end of 1972 that American efforts to negotiate a readjustment of economic relations among the allies had reached a dead end. The West German and Japanese leaders, in particular, had built positions of substantial economic strength for their respective countries and declined to relinquish them. Generally speaking, a reversal of economic positions had occurred between the United States and its principal allies since World War II.

To place the shift in perspective, recall that during the Bretton Woods negotiations in 1944, the European allies had feared that the United States would emerge from the war in a structurally hegemonic position requiring that balance of payments adjustments, for example, would fall primarily and perpetually on the countries of Europe.[2] Their fear was that the United States would become a permanent creditor and they permanent debtors. Thus, one of the principal points in John Maynard Keynes' proposal for a new postwar monetary system was the establishment of an adjustment mechanism that would work more or less automatically and facilitate the economic restoration of the European powers. American leaders rejected Keynes' proposal.

Ironically, the reversal of positions that had occurred over the subsequent quarter of a century now led American negotiators to propose a plan remarkably close to the one Keynes had put forth at Bretton Woods. Of course, the parallel was not exact. The United States was a formidable economic power in 1972 compared to the extremely weak position of the European powers at the end of the war. Nevertheless, it was now the European powers' turn to reject the American proposal, in hopes of keeping the United States in a relatively inferior position. The Europeans sought, as one economist described it, "an American balance of payments that was strong enough to prevent international monetary turmoil but not so strong as to reestablish American dominance."[3]

A few key indicators will illustrate the shift that was under way. The 1971 devaluation and demonetization had failed in its fundamental purpose. The United States trade balance, for example, went from a deficit of $2.2 billion in 1971 to a deficit of $6.4 billion in 1972. In the same two years the West German trade balance increased from a surplus of $6.3 billion in 1971 to $8.3 billion in 1972, while the Japanese trade balance went from a surplus of $7.7 billion in 1971 to $8.9 billion in 1972. The United States was, in other words, gradually losing its leading position and was experiencing a declining share of world economic product.

The economic power shift was further illustrated by the change in reserve positions among the three powers. In 1964, the reserve holdings of foreign exchange and gold by the United States, West Germany, and Japan were roughly 17, 6, and 3 billion dollars, respectively. By the end of 1972, the figures were $11 billion for the United States, $22 billion for West Germany, and $17 billion for Japan. To put this even more graphically, where in 1964 the United States held almost twice as much in reserves as West Germany and Japan together, by 1972 the West German and Japanese combined total was more than triple the holdings of the United States.[4] The situation for the United States had reached a critical point. Some attempt would have to be made to halt the slide, if not to reestablish a preeminent position, before it was too late. Clearly, the American leadership would not simply acquiesce in the nation's continued slippage vis-à-vis its principal allies.

In the world of oil a similar negative trend was in full swing, threatening American command of the Western alliance's energy supplies. Intensifying oil-producer demands for a larger share of the petroleum business were rapidly fracturing the structure of the global petroleum industry as it had evolved since World War II. Following the August 1971 decoupling of gold from the dollar, OPEC producers strove to minimize the effects of further inflation expected to flow from that decision.

In further negotiations with the oil companies, OPEC sought agreement to index the price of oil to the inflation rate of the dollar and also to increase producing country "participation" (that is, ownership) in oil company operations.[5] By the fall of 1972 the petroleum-producing countries had succeeded on both counts. Not only was the price of oil indexed, OPEC and the oil companies entered into a general agreement which called for a gradually increasing rate of participation from 20 percent to 51 percent over the next decade. Specific implementation of the general agreement was left to individual country-company negotiations.[6]

The shah of Iran had held separate and parallel negotiations with the oil companies' consortium during 1972 that produced an even more remarkable agreement. In late February 1973, in St. Moritz, Switzerland, the parties concluded a twenty-year agreement replacing the 1954 consortium agreement (which was not due to expire until 1979).[7] Ratified by the Iranian Majlis in July, the agreement transferred ownership of all in-country consortium operations to Iran in return for guaranteed, long-term, and exclusive supply. The oil companies, in short, were relinquishing ownership of their facilities in return for assured access, a process that was quite far advanced by 1972.

The very fact of increasing "participation" was having a perhaps not unexpected or unintended effect. Once the oil-producing countries gained a stake in the companies' operations they also acquired a common interest in raising price and therefore profits. This changed the former attitude toward low-price, high-volume sales, in which revenue was largely based on taxation of output. The shift to increased participation gave the oil-producing countries a greater interest in price over volume as taxation of company output became increasingly secondary. And once price became the decisive factor, the way was cleared for consideration of restricting supply to maintain or increase price. In sum, participation established, in the words of a leading petroleum expert, a "bilateral symbiotic oligopoly" between the oil-producing countries and the oil companies.[8]

By the end of 1972, the very sinews of economic and military power which formed the infrastructure of America's global position were undergoing deep and systemic change. The threat to American preeminence contained in these rather fundamental changes formed the backdrop to and provided the explanation for the debate within the American leadership. The country was at a strategic crossroads. In the largest sense the United States leadership faced the question: What is to be done? The resulting debate sundered the leadership, producing the most far-reaching domestic political crisis since World War II, if not in the entire history of the republic.

As the strategic debate took shape in Washington during 1971 and 1972, irreconcilable differences led to factional conflict, even though only a handful of those who were involved fully comprehended the significance of what was taking place. As in all such cases where alternatives are diametrically opposed and compromise is thus impossible, policy issues would be settled by the political defeat of one of the protagonists. In this context, the Watergate affair stands in sharp relief as the phenomenon which not only brought about the political defeat of the president but also determined the outcome of the strategic debate. The result was the adoption of a new American strategy in early 1973, a strategy which has governed American foreign policy ever since, surviving persistent attempts to reverse it.

President Nixon's policies clearly prevailed through the first two years of his presidency, as the analysis in this volume attests. But, as the failure to check the adverse trends with regard to the Soviet Union and the Western alliance became apparent, in what was perceived to be a time of growing crisis, Henry Kissinger's views and prescriptions for remedying the difficulties facing the nation increasingly diverged from those of his chief. The strategic debate that followed thus set the president against his national security adviser, who presented markedly different views.[9]

President Nixon's position in the debate was based on the assumption that the United States could maintain a position of strength in the Eastern Hemisphere. This had been the essence of his policy approach since he took office, and he hewed to it. He proposed to continue a modified containment strategy, strengthening the bipolar geopolitical stucture against the Soviet Union. In Asia, he sought to accomplish this objective through the inclusion of China in the Western camp and the restoration of South Vietnam as a viable client state in a fragmented Indochina reconstructed along the lines of the 1954 Geneva settlement. In other words, the United States would continue to maintain its presence on the mainland rim of Asia, but now buttressed by the addition of China in the American camp.

In Southwest Asia, Nixon planned to press the further buildup of Iran and to a lesser extent Saudi Arabia to compensate for the deterioration of South Asia as a result of Pakistan's dismemberment. In the Middle East, he sought to broaden the American position through the promotion by diplomatic means of an Israeli-Egyptian settlement. Regarding the United States relationship to its European allies and Japan, President Nixon hoped to negotiate further adjustment of the modified economic and monetary regime adopted in August of 1971 while retaining the dollar as the central reserve currency in a fixed-rate system. In sum, the central thrust of the president's thinking was continuity of strategy even while conceding the necessity for modification of policy to sustain the commitment to a strong American position on the Eurasian landmass at key points around the Soviet periphery.

Kissinger's position was based on his pessimistic assumption that the United States could neither indefinitely maintain the bipolar structure nor keep a forward position in the Eastern Hemisphere. In his view, Soviet power had simply grown to the point where the costs to the United States of maintaining its formerly hegemonic position were too high. America's allies should be required to assume a greater share of the security burden based upon their growing economic strength. In brief, Kissinger proposed to reshape American strategy based on the gradual withdrawal of the United States from vulnerable positions on the mainland of Eurasia and the substitution of viable, collective security structures for direct American presence.

Initially, the United States would hold its position in Western Europe and, with modification, in the Middle East, but would pull back to the offshore island chain in the Pacific. Eventually, as time and circumstance allowed, the United States would withdraw its direct military presence from the Eurasian landmass entirely, retaining only an island presence in the Eastern Hemisphere. This new position would enable the United States in the future to deal with both its allies and adversaries with greater flexibility and less vulnerability than was currently possible. Using the policy concepts of "trilateralism" and "tripolarism," Kissinger proposed through the former to strengthen the United States position vis-à-vis Europe and Japan and through the latter to play China off against the Soviet Union.

Kissinger's differences with the president were strategic — that is, structural and fundamental. Where President Nixon sought to preserve the bipolar order through modification of containment, Kissinger proposed to dispense with it and move gradually to a multipolar order repositioning American power from its forward position around the Soviet periphery. Through a broad-based accommodation with the Soviet Union, involving dramatically improved political, economic, and cultural relations, it was hoped that the United States would obtain sufficient time to make the desired structural changes in the proposed new order.

Indeed, detente with the Soviet Union was indispensable for Kissinger's proposed strategy to succeed, for the structural shift could not be undertaken in the context of cold-war confrontation with Moscow. It was assumed, however, that the United States would gain leverage on Soviet policy as the fruits of cooperation became evident to the Soviet leadership. In Kissinger's view, the Soviets would forgo, or, at least temper, their desire to adopt more aggressive policies commensurate with the growth of their strategic and conventional weapons power as economic relations with the West in general and the United States in particular improved.

In the Pacific, the main objective of Kissinger's "tripolar" policy was to build on the adversary relationship between Beijing and Moscow while shifting the United States to an offshore position. This required the reversal of long-standing policy toward South Vietnam and, eventually, toward South Korea as well. Presumably, Moscow would seek to fill the vacuum in the Pacific and leave Beijing no feasible alternative but to rely on the United States for support against the Soviet Union. The geopolitical shift, which was designed to perpetuate conflicts of interest between the two communist powers and was combined with improved economic relations with Beijing, would theoretically put the United States in position to manipulate one communist power off against the other. It would also lead to enhanced ties to Tokyo, the anchor of the American Pacific position, whose leaders would perceive the need to improve Japan's security through closer cooperation with Washington.

Kissinger's policy proposals for strengthening the United States position within the Western alliance, the "trilateral" concept, were enmeshed with policy toward the Middle East. At this point, in these two areas, the differences between the national security adviser and the president appeared to be principally of degree rather than of kind, unlike their clearly divergent strategic precepts for the Pacific. It had been the president, recall, who had initiated the policy of gradually increasing oil prices as a means of diverting allied resources from investment in capital construction to consumption in order to slow down their rates of growth and who had promoted the "benign neglect" monetary policy to adjust exchange rates. But Kissinger sought to intensify both of these processes, connecting the increase of oil prices to a quite different approach to the Arab-Israeli problem, as will be discussed in detail in chapter six.

Watergate as Intra-party Conflict

As several of the president's policies began to fall successfully into place in the course of 1971 — the strategic weapons agreements with Moscow, rapprochement with Beijing, the extrication of American troops from Vietnam, the economic revaluation agreements with the allies — his political standing strengthened immeasurably. His bold foreign policy moves overshadowed the underlying structural problems, which in any case were lost upon the electorate, making his reelection a virtual certainty.

The political implications of the president's reelection, coming at a time when fundamental strategic choices would have to be made, were ominous for those who opposed the president's prescriptions. Once reelected, the president would be free to make policy unbeholden to former political constituencies. In short, fundamental strategic choices would be made when the president's political strength was at its zenith and those who opposed his strategic views were at their nadir.

Under these circumstances, with arguably the most important strategic choices, both foreign and domestic, in the history of the republic weighing in the balance, and with so little prospect of prevailing, the president's opponents, essentially the Eastern wing of the party political establishment, resorted to what was a desperate gamble to regain political leverage on policy. This was the genesis of what came to be known as "Watergate," which in retrospect appears not as a matter of Republicans versus Democrats but as the opposition of one wing of the Republican party against the other, with the Democrats as foil.[10]

The initial objective was not in any way novel to the American or, for that matter, any other political system; it was a pure-and-simple attempt at political blackmail to gain policy leverage. The concept was straightforward enough: implicate the White House in illegal activity during the election campaign; elicit a cover-up to avoid a pre-election scandal; then, afterward, threaten to expose the president's criminal involvement in an obstruction of justice.[11] In this way, presumably, the Eastern group could obtain the necessary leverage over the decision-making process that it could not otherwise hope to possess after the president's reelection. The scheme succeeded beyond its perpetrators' wildest imagination as the president himself provided the opportunity for his opponents not simply to gain leverage over, but to capture control of, the office of the presidency.[12]

It was inconceivable to the president's adversaries that so skilled a politician as Richard M. Nixon would so ineptly respond to what was actually a rather crude, muddled, and transparent entrapment scheme, opening the way to his political downfall. Within weeks following his landslide reelection, Richard Nixon acceded to the strategic arguments of the Eastern group, which, through Henry Kissinger, proceeded to inaugurate a new American strategy. His refusal to capitulate precipitated the Watergate scandal which eventually brought about his political demise.

It is beyond the scope of this or any other volume, and perhaps beyond the capacity of any historian, to weave together the entire extraordinarily complex fabric of Watergate. With considerable hindsight, however, it is possible to discern the main pattern of intra-party factionalism, out of which the scandal grew.[13]

Factional skirmishing began soon after the administration took office. The wiretapping of high-level aides during the first two years was evidently the means by which the president attempted to obtain information on the source of press leaks of highly sensitive foreign policy moves early in the administration. Who was the president's target? Although never publicly disclosed, the individuals tapped bore mute testimony to the president's objective.

Seventeen persons were tapped: seven on the National Security Council staff, three White House staff members, four prominent reporters, two officers at the Department of State and one at the Pentagon.[14] It would seem obvious that Nixon believed the source of leaks was the National Security Council and particularly its chief, Henry Kissinger. The taps never yielded compromising material, and the president terminated the program on February 10, 1971, because, in his words, it produced nothing more than "gossip and bullshitting."[15]

It is difficult to assess whether the decision to stop the wiretaps was made on its apparent lack of merit or was a function of more important developments occurring at that time. As detailed in previous chapters, the winter of 1970–1971 was an extremely crucial period, in which the issues of future relations with Moscow, Beijing, and the Western allies were beginning to be addressed. To maintain a confidential record of the internal debate, ostensibly for historical purposes, President Nixon installed a voice-activated tape-recording system in the Oval Office, cabinet room, Lincoln Sitting Room, Executive Office Building hideaway, and in the Aspen Lodge at Camp David.[16]

The president ordered the Secret Service to install the system in February 1971, just as the wiretap program was being discontinued, allowing only the few people who managed and serviced it to know of its existence. Even the Army Signal Corps, normally responsible for White House communications and which had installed President Johnson's taping system, was kept ignorant of it. Significantly, among those who did not know of the existence of the taping system was Henry Kissinger. Indeed, it would appear that one, if not the principal, function of the tapes was to establish a record of the policy debate between the president and his national security adviser.

The matter of a record became particularly important as Kissinger was entrusted with greater responsibility for the actual management of foreign policy from 1971 onward. From the president's point of view it was imperative that he have some means to check Kissinger's growing policy assertiveness and independence—that is, his divergence from the president's policy positions. H. R. Haldeman delicately put it this way:

> One of the prime focal points of Nixon's concern was the unpredictable Henry Kissinger. Nixon realized rather early in their relationship that he badly needed a complete account of all that they discussed in their many long and wide-ranging sessions. He knew that Henry was keeping a log of these talks, a luxury in which the President didn't have time to indulge. And he knew that Henry's view on a particular subject was sometimes subject to change without notice. He was frequently given to second thoughts on vital matters that the President assumed had been settled.[17]

Meanwhile, having discontinued the wiretaps, Nixon felt the increasing need to obtain more information on his NSC chief to supplement the taped policy discussions. Enter "the Plumbers" in mid-1971. The specific origin of the Plumbers, formally a White House investigation unit personally authorized by the president, grew out of the publication of the Pentagon Papers by the *New York Times*, June 13, 1971. A secret Defense Department study of the Vietnam War through 1968, commissioned by former Secretary of Defense Robert McNamara, the papers had been leaked to the *Times* by Daniel Ellsberg. Ellsberg, a former Rand employee, Defense Department official, and student of Henry Kissinger's, had participated in the formulation of foreign policy options early in the Nixon administration.

The president was far less upset by the publication of the papers than was Kissinger, who, besides being concerned that his relationship with Ellsberg might compromise him, also fumed that the papers might undermine his credibility in Beijing, for which he was scheduled to depart on a secret mission in early July. Kissinger's concern was genuine on both counts. He had been an early pessimist on the possibility of victory in Vietnam, an opinion which he shared with Ellsberg in 1965 and 1966.[18] Fear of being compromised by Ellsberg led Kissinger into a violent denunciation of his former student.

More important was the credibility consideration. The Pentagon Papers themselves, especially volume one, which contained substantial amounts of hitherto classified material regarding Washington's behind-the-scenes role during the 1954 Geneva conference, established beyond doubt that the United States had shaped the 1954 settlement and implied that it was a long-term American strategy which the current administration wished to reestablish.[19] Thus Kissinger's concern. The Pentagon Papers suggested a strategy different from his own, which may also explain why the president showed no particular alarm over their disclosure, since they reflected his own strategy preference.

While the president voiced little concern over the release of the papers,[20] he employed the incident to justify a renewed effort to "plug leaks" in the government, especially in the NSC. Nixon's remarks to his top aides in early July when the Plumbers were organized testifies that his main concern was Kissinger. For example, on July 2, he assigned John Ehrlichman responsibility for the Ellsberg case and ordered him to put a staff man on it full time. Four days later, Nixon noted to Ehrlichman that we "can't assume NSC staff not participants"; and on July 9, while Kissinger was away in Beijing, Nixon declared to both Ehrlichman and Haldeman that the NSC "staff must be cleaned out."[21]

Upon his return from Beijing, Kissinger quickly became suspicious that he was the target of the Plumbers' efforts, the reason being that David Young, one of Kissinger's own aides with whom he had had a falling out, had been assigned to the unit.[22] Young had met Kissinger when both worked on Nelson Rockefeller's presidential campaign in 1968. After Nixon's election, Kissinger brought him onto the NSC staff to assist him in handling his personal matters. Young therefore knew enough about his chief's affairs to probe sensitive areas.

It is evident that Nixon recruited Young precisely because he hoped the disaffected aide would help keep tabs on his former boss. Under the direction of Egil Krogh, the president's trusted aide and chief of the Plumbers unit, Young was given the task of investigating Kissinger's role in NSC staff leaks, although his job was innocuously described publicly as handling "declassification matters for the president."[23] Kissinger was furious, for Young "knew far too much," but he reluctantly accepted Nixon's decision.

A cardinal rule of political factionalism is to infiltrate any organization that potentially could cause harm to your side and attempt to turn it to your own purposes. The Plumbers were a case in point. As the unit was being formed, more professional staffing beyond Egil Krogh and David Young was deemed necessary. Thus, in July, two additional operatives were added, G. Gordon Liddy and E. Howard Hunt. These two men, along with James W. McCord, would in different ways play critical roles in the entrapment of the president in the Watergate affair.

G. Gordon Liddy was a former FBI agent turned politician who had been placed at Treasury by influential political friends following his electoral defeat in Dutchess County, New York, by incumbent Congressman Hamilton Fish, Jr.[24] Liddy was an extraordinary person of high principle, but reckless in word and deed and childlike in his fascination with adventure, guns, cars, and women. He moved over to the Plumbers from Treasury where he had come to be viewed as a political embarrassment after publicly lobbying vigorously against government-sponsored gun-control legislation. Liddy would eventually become the "fall guy" of Watergate.[25]

The second addition to the Plumbers was E. Howard Hunt.[26] Hunt was a career CIA agent, a veteran political operative who had been involved in agency clandestine affairs since virtually the beginning of the agency. Among his many "credits" had been a role in planning the overthrow of Guatemalan President Guzman Arbenz in 1954, the training of the Cuban emigre force prior to the Bay of Pigs invasion, and serving as chief of the agency's domestic operations division during the sixties.

Hunt had "retired" on May 1, 1970, and the following day had gone to work for the Robert R. Mullen Company, a CIA "asset," or front organization, in downtown Washington, D.C. Hunt's retirement was in reality a move under cover in order to resurface at a later time for work which could not be done as an agency employee. The agency's decision to maintain his covert security clearance confirms this interpretation.[27] At Mullen, Hunt performed what amounted to odd jobs in the public relations field until July of 1971, when he prevailed upon Charles Colson to bring him into the White House.

Hunt had met Colson at a Brown University Club of Washington function in the late sixties. They subsequently became close friends and were active in the alumni club; Hunt became vice-president and Colson president. After Hunt retired from the CIA, Colson, now President Nixon's special counsel with the task of keeping track of and confounding White House opposition (the enemies' list was Colson's project), sought to place him in the White House.

First, Colson attempted to set him up as director of a Republican "think tank" that the White House was contemplating establishing to counter the influence of the Democratic party's counterpart, the Brookings Institution. So Colson sent Hunt to see Jeb Magruder, who was in charge of the project. Initially impressed, Magruder eventually decided that Hunt was not the right man for the job. It seems that Hunt, in sending Magruder a memorandum developing his thoughts on his potential role as director, had outlined how such a think tank could become a base for covert political activity, which was not what the White House had in mind.[28]

When Colson heard that the White House was setting up an internal investigation unit, he sounded out Hunt's attitude. Hunt expressed intense interest. Colson quickly arranged for him to meet with Ehrlichman about a job possibility in early July, but Colson was unable to convince the president's counsel to hire Hunt on with the Plumbers. Ehrlichman did agree, however, to allow Colson himself to engage Hunt as a White House consultant, which was done on the spot.[29] Hunt was given a small office in the Executive Office Building and worked under Colson's direction for the next year. But Hunt's relevance to this history has less to do with his work for Colson than it has with his work for Egil Krogh, for within two weeks of his joining the White House staff, Hunt had managed to catch on with the Plumbers.[30]

Hunt immediately began to cultivate Gordon Liddy, titillating him with tales of agency derring-do; and before long they had developed what Liddy thought was a close personal relationship. They planned several adventuresome escapades that were not carried out, such as an attempt to break into and pilfer the files of the Brookings Institution, where the Pentagon Papers were supposed to be hidden.[31] However, they did carry out the break-in of Ellsberg's psychiatrist's office in Los Angeles on Labor Day weekend, 1971.

The break-in of Dr. Lewis Fielding's office established the team and set the operational mode for the later break-in at the Watergate. Liddy was nominally in charge, but Hunt supplied the men and made the local contacts. Hunt employed the assistance of "friends" in the Los Angeles area during the Fielding job and enlisted several of his former CIA charges, Cubans from the Bay of Pigs force living in Miami. In fact, Hunt had contacted them in April 1971, even before he had been hired at the White House.[32] At least one of these, Eugenio Martinez, was still on the agency's payroll, reporting to his case officer on a monthly basis.[33]

The Plumbers were disbanded in the fall of 1971, and jobs were sought for the men elsewhere in the administration. Hunt for the time being was shifted back to Colson. Liddy, on the other hand, was hired on at the Committee to Reelect the President (CRP) as general counsel and head of a newly formed intelligence-gathering organization for the coming campaign. There can be little question that the president himself insisted on the establishment of such a campaign organization, but he failed utterly to anticipate the use to which CRP's intelligence-gathering group would be put. It would, of course, be through the CRP intelligence-gathering unit that the scheme to entrap the president would be carried out.

Entrapment of President Richard M. Nixon: Step One, the Break-in

Evidence strongly suggests that the entrapment scheme was directed at the top from origin to denouement by the president's close colleague and friend, John Mitchell, whose higher allegiance to the Eastern wing of the Republican party led him into a Judas-like turn against the president.[34] Mitchell appears in the historical record as the key player at every crucial decision point. As attorney general, Mitchell placed personnel in appropriate positions, established the campaign intelligence-gathering system and determined its principal mission. Then, as chairman of the Committee to Reelect the President, he authorized the funds for the operation, decided on the Democratic National Committee as a target, and sent Gordon Liddy and his men back for a second, fateful entry. When they were arrested, Mitchell, from the position of a private but still extremely influential adviser, inspired the cover-up which implicated the president in the obstruction of justice by eliciting White House "hush money" payments for the Watergate defendants.

While so much seems cut and dried in retrospect, the temptation to view the fall of Richard Nixon as inevitable must be resisted. The fact is that the scheme very nearly did not succeed, and indeed would not have succeeded, had Bob Haldeman not made the mistake of allowing the White House to become directly involved in blackmail payoffs to the Watergate defendants. Yet even this almost did not happen, for throughout the campaign the president and his chief aides successfully avoided direct entanglement. It was only after the election that Haldeman committed the blunder of directly involving the White House and entrapping the president in the criminal obstruction of justice which would eventually bring him down.

By all accounts it was the president himself who determined the need for political intelligence in the coming electoral campaign. Several ideas were considered, and the issue boiled down to where an intelligence organ should be located. Initially, some thought was given to employing a private investigating firm to create an independent intelligence-gathering organization, a "Republican intertel," which would moreover possess a "black bag" capability.[35] Unfortunately, as it turned out, that idea was discarded in favor of lodging the unit within the campaign headquarters of the president.

In the fall of 1971, then, within the context of obtaining election campaign intelligence, Attorney General John Mitchell authorized the estabishment of an intelligence-gathering unit in the Committee to Reelect the President. Mitchell specifically sought someone with both a legal and an investigative background to direct the unit and found him in G. Gordon Liddy. After one brief interview, on November 24, Mitchell hired Liddy to be legal counsel and intelligence chief for the Committee to Reelect.[36] Liddy began work December 13, 1971.

It would appear that the Eastern wing had discovered in Gordon Liddy exactly the sort of individual who could be played as the fall guy in their scheme to entrap the president. He was not a conscious part of the scheme and, naturally if ironically, throughout believed himself to be acting on behalf of the president. The decision to set Liddy up was probably made sometime in the fall of 1971, once his propensities for the daring and adventurous had become clear in his Plumbers exploits. Liddy, in short, would be the unwitting dupe whose connection to the White House would ultimately ensnare the president. It was not an extraordinary quirk of fate but careful forethought that placed him in position to start Richard Nixon on his road to ruin.

By the time Mitchell had hired Liddy, he had already brought onto the committee the man who would ultimately spring the entrapment, James W. McCord. McCord was yet another "former" CIA agent, who had "retired" August 31, 1970, after a lengthy and highly distinguished career.[37] (Former CIA Director Allen W. Dulles had once described McCord as "my top man" in the agency, the highest accolade.)[38] Upon retirement McCord taught a course in industrial and retail security for Montgomery Junior College in the Washington suburbs as a part-time instructor and also became active in community affairs. He had been hired as part-time "security coordinator" for the Committee to Reelect on October 1, 1971, and became full-time chief of security as of January 1, 1972. His firm, McCord Associates, Inc., was given a contract to provide "security services" for both the Committee to Reelect and the Republican National Committee. The firm had no other clients.

As soon as Liddy went to work for the committee, McCord began to cultivate him just as Hunt had done earlier in the Plumbers. McCord had been an FBI agent prior to moving over to the CIA, and the two men thus had a bit of common background. Before long they developed a personal and professional relationship as Liddy frequently consulted McCord on "technical matters."[39] In early February, too, again at Colson's urging, Hunt was transferred over to CRP, and by the spring of 1972 the three men had become something of a team.[40]

Curiously, when Hunt moved over to CRP he feigned any previous acquaintance with McCord, yet the two men had known and worked with each other for most of their professional lives in the CIA, dating back at least to 1963, if not to 1954 when they both were posted to Taiwan.[41] So effective was their mutual dissemblage that Liddy believed that he knew McCord better than Hunt did though he had met him only a few months before.[42] But this gets slightly ahead of the story. The decision to set the campaign intelligence program in motion against the Democrats, the vehicle for the entrapment scheme, was made slightly earlier.

Upon hiring Liddy, Mitchell had instructed him to prepare an intelligence-gathering plan for the coming campaign, promising a budget of a million dollars.[43] Liddy thereupon set to work, collaborating closely with Hunt and to a lesser extent with McCord.[44] On

January 27, 1972, Liddy presented his plan to Attorney General John Mitchell at a meeting in Mitchell's Justice Department office, a meeting attended only by Mitchell's protege John Dean and Nixon's man Jeb Magruder. Liddy's plan, each facet of which was given the name of a different gem, was code-named "Gemstone" (at the suggestion of Howard Hunt). It was a wild, mind-boggling scheme including the use of thugs to rough up hostile demonstrators, prostitutes to compromise rival candidates, and specially trained teams to conduct electronic eavesdropping, bugging, and burglary.[45]

Much to Liddy's disappointment, Mitchell considered the plan "beyond the pale," though he did not reject it outright. Instead, he instructed Liddy to "tone it down a little, then we'll talk about it again."[46] Though crushed by the rejection, Liddy agreed to revise his plan, at half the original cost, eliminating the mug squads and, reluctantly, the call girls, concentrating as instructed on wiretapping. He regained his enthusiasm a few days later when in a conversation with Dean he was told that the prospects for approval of a revised plan were good, but that "some means would have to be found for deniability for Mr. Mitchell" and "a method of funding . . . arranged so that the funds would not come through the regular committee."[47]

Liddy presented his revised plan to the attorney general in his office on February 4. Once again, Dean and Magruder were the only others present. Dean wrote that he arrived late to the meeting and heard only that ". . . there was talk of 'targets' and 'surveillance.'"[48] Magruder says simply that "once again Dean joined us,"[49] while Liddy says that Dean, while arriving late, was in plenty of time to participate in the main part of the discussion.[50] In any case, at the meeting Liddy's revised plan was further refined to establish a priority list of targets, with the focus on electronic eavesdropping. Objectives in rank order were to be the Watergate office of the chairman of the Democratic National Committee, Larry O'Brien; O'Brien's hotel suite in Miami during the convention; and finally the campaign headquarters of whoever became the Democratic nominee.[51]

Mitchell also expressed an interest in burglarizing the office of Hank Greenspun, publisher of the *Las Vegas Sun*, partly because of Greenspun's claims to have damaging evidence against potential Nixon rival Ed Muskie, but also because of what he might possess regarding Nixon's relationship to Howard Hughes.[52] O'Brien had at one time represented Hughes as his Washington consultant, and there was some concern that Greenspun, who had also had an alliance of sorts with Hughes before subsequently falling out with him, might have passed on to O'Brien information damaging to Nixon.

In the course of their discussion, Dean recalls, he "was surprised, and it came to me that Mitchell was perfectly capable of approving a scaled-down version of the Liddy plan."[53] It was evidently this realization that prompted him to say, "I don't think this kind of conversation should go on in the attorney general's office," although his remark was understood differently by all of the others. Liddy recalls that what Dean actually said was, "Sir, I don't think a decision . . . should come from the attorney general's office. I think he [Liddy] should get it from . . . completely unofficial channels."[54] Magruder's version tends to support Liddy. According to Magruder, Dean said, "I think it is inappropriate for this to be discussed with the attorney general. I think in the future Gordon should discuss his plans with Jeb, then Jeb can pass them on to the attorney general."[55]

Dean claims that after their meeting, while outside in the hallway, he realized that Liddy had misinterpreted his remarks, thinking that he had said he should communicate through Magruder to Mitchell in order to protect the attorney general. But what Dean insists he meant to convey was that there should be no decision at all.[56] Both Liddy's and Magruder's accounts concur that Dean's remark was designed precisely to protect, that is, to give deniability to, the attorney general. Furthermore, Mitchell's reaction supports the understanding of Liddy and Magruder. The attorney general, agreeing with Dean's suggestion that no decision be made in the attorney general's office, declared that he would "think about it" and let Liddy know later.[57]

Thus, while John Mitchell was still attorney general, no decision was made on Liddy's watered-down Gemstone plan at the February 4 meeting—although target priorities and procedure had been established. The decision to proceed came only after Mitchell had resigned as attorney general to become head of the Committee to Reelect the following month. Mitchell resigned as attorney general on March 1, moving immediately to assume the chairmanship of CRP and from that position made the decision to go forward with a still more narrowly focused penetration scheme.

The decision to proceed was made on March 30, in Key Biscayne, Florida, during a meeting attended only by Mitchell, Magruder, and Mitchell's confidant, Fred LaRue. According to Magruder,

Mitchell . . . scribbled on the paper Liddy had prepared, which listed the amount of money he wanted, and the number of men and types of equipment he'd need. Finally, Mitchell told me that he approved the plan, but that Liddy should receive only $250,000. We discussed the targets of the wiretapping program, and it was agreed that Liddy should go ahead with the wiretapping of Larry O'Brien's office at the Watergate, then we'd see about the other possible targets.[58]

Mitchell denied having approved this or any other plan, but even his confidant LaRue says otherwise.[59] It was, of course, highly unlikely that money could have been disbursed without Mitchell's authorization. On April 7, when Liddy requested an initial payment of $83,000 from Campaign Treasurer Hugh Sloan, Sloan checked with Maurice Stans, Finance Committee chairman. Stans, in turn, called Mitchell, who confirmed the legitimacy of Liddy's request, and the funds were then duly handed over to Liddy.[60]

Shortly after Mitchell had moved over to CRP in early April he engaged James McCord to provide protection for his wife and young daughter. The FBI team that had provided protection while Mitchell was attorney general had been withdrawn upon his resignation. Whatever McCord's relationship to Mitchell had been prior to this point, and that is unclear, from this point onward McCord became quite involved with Mitchell's personal and family affairs. For several weeks he personally drove Mitchell's daughter to and from school.

In mid-April, upon becoming an integral part of Liddy's "team,"[61] McCord hired a former FBI agent who had fallen on hard times, one Alfred Baldwin, to take over the job of providing security for the Mitchell family.[62] Baldwin remained in that job only a few days before being found unsatisfactory by Martha Mitchell. Nevertheless, McCord kept Baldwin on, assigning him various surveillance duties, one of which was in connection with the plan to eavesdrop on the Democratic National Committee.[63]

At the end of April, Magruder had relayed instructions from Mitchell that Liddy's "team" was to break into the Democratic National Committee offices to implant room and telephone bugs, as well as to photograph what looked promising.[64] Within a few weeks they were ready, and on the weekend of May 26–28 the team (comprised of Liddy; McCord and his man Al Baldwin; Hunt and his men, the Cubans, Bernard Barker, Eugenio Martinez, Virgilio Gonzales and Frank Sturgis) set out on its mission.

The effort was under the formal leadership of Gordon Liddy but under the operational control of James McCord, who was the only one of the three CRP men actually to go in with the Cubans. (Liddy and Hunt stayed in their room at the Watergate Hotel, and Baldwin stayed in his room across the street at the Howard Johnson Motel as lookout.) The group made four attempts to gain entry into the committee's offices — on Friday, Saturday, and Sunday evenings — before finally succeeding.[65]

Once inside the Committee's offices McCord pretended to install two bugs, one in O'Brien's telephone and one in the telephone of another DNC official, O'Brien's aide, Spencer Oliver. (In fact, McCord installed no bugs at all according to FBI and Chesapeake and Potomac Telephone Company technicians who examined the DNC premises immediately following the June 17 break-in.[66] As bizarre as it seems, McCord was enagaged in a completely different clandestine operation, for which his CRP job was cover.[67])

The Cubans, meantime, took photographs of some documents, but much to their consternation McCord cut short the mission as soon as he had finished his "installation."[68] The initial euphoria over a successful penetration dissipated within a few days. The "take" from the bugs was meager; moreover, McCord declared that he was unable to pick up the tap on O'Brien's phone, saying that it was either defective or that the signal was being blocked by shielding of some sort within the building structure.[69]

It was not until June 8, eleven days following the break-in, that Liddy was able to accumulate a packet of materials taken from the DNC office. He gave it to Magruder to transmit to Mitchell, according to the procedure agreed upon at the February 4 meeting. The next day, Magruder met with Liddy and said that the material was "hardly worth the effort, risk and expense."[70] When told of the defective bug, Magruder asked whether it could be made to function. Liddy then informed Magruder that he planned to "hit" McGovern's headquarters on the weekend of June 17 and would be bringing the Cubans up from Miami for the job. He could do both jobs over the weekend, he offered, "if it were just a quick in and out" with a key man, guard, and wire man.[71]

It was at this point, between June 10 and 12, when the photographs taken during the break-in had been developed and shown to be of little use, that the decision was made to go back in a second time.[72] The decision itself, however, was not simply for a "quick in and out" to replace the defective bug, but for a major penetration to photograph as much of O'Brien's correspondence in the DNC files as possible. On June 12, Magruder called Liddy into his office to convey the new instruction, telling him to "go in there with all the film, men and cameras necessary to photograph everything in his [O'Brien's] desk and in his files."[73] To Liddy, this now meant that McCord's role would be to go along "merely as an unpaid electronic hitchhiker, free to leave when he was through," while the Cubans remained for as long as was necessary to photograph O'Brien's files.

The decision to enlarge the reentry from a "quick in and out" to a major penetration suggests two inputs. The decision to go back in was Mitchell's; Magruder could convey but had no authority to make such a decision. Magruder, however, was Haldeman's man at CRP and undoubtedly made the earlier "take" available to him. Upon learning that a second attempt would be made, Haldeman ordered the expanded mission. In this, Haldeman may well have been responding to what he perceived to be Nixon's interest in O'Brien and seized the opportunity presented by the decision to reenter the DNC. Whatever the reason, the decision to expand the mission also facilitated the entrapment scheme, which would have occurred anyway.

The tragic irony was that the files were worthless as campaign intelligence. O'Brien had already departed for the convention in Miami, taking his most important files with him—a fact which everyone involved knew and from which some, like Liddy and Hunt, drew the obvious conclusions. There was no point in risking a second, let alone prolonged, entry. Yet the order was firm: go back in.[74] However valuable it might have been to install a working tap on O'Brien's phone for whatever reason, there was no justification for having a team of men spend *several hours* in the committee's offices to photograph worthless files. It was a major blunder, perhaps born of curiosity, to assume that O'Brien's files might contain something damaging about the president. Yet the main purpose for returning was to obtain O'Brien's files; the defective bug simply offered the inducement.

Here was the set-up: McCord and the Cubans would break into the DNC a second time. McCord would stay a few minutes and depart, but the Cubans would spend several hours there and be caught photographing the committee's files. The evidence strongly suggests that McCord's role was to lead the others into a trap without being caught himself. When the Cubans were arrested, the trail would inevitably lead to Hunt and Liddy through CRP to the White House. There was nothing to connect McCord to the Cubans. The trap sprung, McCord would return to the operation he was really conducting, for which surveillance of the DNC had been the initial justification.[75]

Of course, McCord was caught within minutes of entry into the DNC offices. His apprehension along with that of the others came because of an unanticipated delay. Gonzales, who was the "key man" responsible for picking the lock, was unable to open the door and they all, including McCord, had to pull off the entire door by removing its hinges, a process that consumed over half an hour. In other words, what should have taken a few minutes took over half an hour, throwing off the timing of the entrapment and making it impossible for McCord to get away before the police arrived.

This explains how McCord was caught but does not explain why he participated in the scheme to entrap the president. The motive for McCord's double-agent role emerges clearly from some of his comments made while he was awaiting sentencing for the break-in. As he wrote in December,

> Never in our nation's history has the integrity of the national intelligence system and especially of the FBI been in such jeopardy. . . . When the hundreds of dedicated fine men and women of CIA can no longer write intelligence summaries and reports with integrity without fear of political recrimination — when their fine director is being summarily discharged in order to make way for a politician [James Schlesinger] who will write or rewrite intelligence reports the way the politicians want them written, instead of the way truth and best judgment dictates, our nation is in the deepest of trouble and freedom itself was never so imperiled. Nazi Germany rose and fell under exactly the same philosophy of governmental operation.[76]

McCord evidently saw Nixon as inimical to everything he believed in, and this view is what allowed him to become involved in the scheme. This, by the way, tends to place the role of the CIA in somewhat better perspective. CIA men, "retired" or not, are found strewn all over the schematic landscape.[77] Was the agency acting under Director Richard Helms' instructions to subvert the presidency? I think not, but agency involvement is undeniable. It is this author's view that Helms was prevailed upon by the powers that be in the Eastern wing of the Republican party to contribute human and material agency resources to the scheme, resources which were also employed in a dual capacity in the case of McCord. The CIA was not directly engaged in an independent institutional conflict with the president of the United States, but it clearly served as a resource of expertise for the Eastern wing. At least that is a view consistent with what is currently known.

Agency involvement prompted the president to attempt to employ the "CIA defense" as a means of avoiding entanglement himself. Nixon insisted that they "take care of their own"—that is, provide the necessary funds for the Watergate defendants, an undertaking which would not only implicate but also silence the CIA. Helms refused to go along, and after the November election Nixon would fire him. In a November 20 meeting attended only by the president, Helms, and Haldeman, none of whom has divulged the contents of what transpired, it might be surmised that Nixon accused Helms of complicity in Watergate and dismissed him for that reason, even though he was "promoted" to the ambassadorship of Iran.[78] But let us return to the story.

Entrapment, Step Two: Cover-up

Once the break-in occurred, the next step was to draw the White House into a criminally culpable role. John Mitchell, who resigned on July 1 as chairman of the Committee to Reelect the President, now attempted to prod the White House into making hush-money payments to provide for the Watergate defendants' legal expenses, salaries, and family support. He was, however, initially unsuccessful. In the ensuing struggle, which was essentially Mitchell versus Ehrlichman and Haldeman, each side attempted to maneuver the other into arranging for provision of financial support for the defendants.[79]

Although there was never any question that support would be forthcoming from some source or other, Ehrlichman and Haldeman stood firmly against any direct White House involvement in money payments. To break the impasse, Mitchell suggested that Nixon's personal lawyer, Herbert Kalmbach, be asked to raise the money secretly, which would mean no direct involvement by the White House. Kalmbach agreed to take on the job, which was a minor victory for Mitchell, who knew that Nixon's personal attorney would not have agreed to do the job without the president's approval. At any rate, between late June and mid-September, Kalmbach raised $220,000, most of which he passed clandestinely to Howard Hunt's wife, Dorothy, for distribution to the Watergate defendants.[80]

By mid-September, Nixon believed that he had won the battle to contain the Watergate problem and prevent it from spilling over and damaging his reelection bid. The grand jury indictments handed down on September 15 named only those directly involved in the break-in (Liddy, Hunt, McCord, and the four Cubans, Barker, Martinez, Gonzales, and Sturgis). The Justice Department announced that there was "no evidence to indicate that any others should be charged." The trial date for the "Watergate Seven" was set for November 15, a week after the election.

In a meeting with Haldeman and Dean on the day of the announcement of the grand jury indictments, the president was understandably exultant, knowing with reasonable certainty that he would win the election after months of gnawing doubt that Watergate would somehow erupt into a major scandal and defeat him. His euphoria included an edge of rage against ". . . all those who tried to do us in." The president remarked that while he had not "used the power" of the presidency the first four years, "things were going to change." Threatening his unnamed opponents, he said: "They didn't have to do it. . . . But now they are doing this quite deliberately. And they are asking for it, and they are going to get it!"[81]

By mid-September, then, the White House had successfully avoided all but the most marginal of entanglements in the cover-up — that of Kalmbach's fund raising and distribution — and now moved to cut that off, too. A few days after the grand jury indictments, Kalmbach turned over the role of paymaster to Mitchell. In a meeting of Kalmbach, Dean, Mitchell, and LaRue, it was decided after lengthy discussion that Mitchell's man, Fred LaRue, would take over Kalmbach's role.[82] Foisting the money payment role onto Mitchell suggests a bit of "turnabout is fair play" by the president. But Nixon's eagerness to get even affected his better judgment.

While it was undoubtedly true that neither side wished to be tied to hush money, assigning the task to Nixon's private lawyer,

Kalmbach, was in retrospect the best solution, for it enabled the president to retain control of the problem within the letter of the law without becoming directly involved. Nixon could always ensure that the defendants' needs were taken care of and their silence maintained. When the job of raising money was shifted back to Mitchell through LaRue, it undoubtedly gave the president's men a sense of satisfaction with having foiled an attempt to put the president in a potentially very difficult situation, but it also put Mitchell into a position to sabotage the containment effort. And this is precisely what occurred.

When LaRue took over the role of paymaster, he simply declined to make any payments to the Watergate defendants, except for a single payment sent to Hunt's lawyer, William O. Bittman, on October 20.[83] And this, according to Hunt, who happened to be in Bittman's office when the money package arrived, "was far less than what was owed my attorney. And of course there was nothing in the package for family support for myself or for Liddy, McCord or the Miami men."[84] Cutting off the money payments placed great pressure on the White House to become involved, for it led the defendants to conclude that they had been abandoned and increased pressure upon them to talk. Despite the growing pressure, for the moment the containment held. Watergate had no discernible effect upon the election of 1972, which Richard M. Nixon won by a landslide.

After the election the money question immediately came to the fore once again. One week later, on November 14, Howard Hunt telephoned Charles Colson demanding support money for himself and the others by November 25. The clear purpose of Hunt's call, which was followed by a memo to Colson a few days later detailing the financial "requirements" of each of the defendants, was understood to be blackmail. According to Dean, Hunt's memorandum spelled out "the money demands of each of the seven Watergate defendants. . . . Salary, family upkeep, incidentals and lawyers' fees. Month by month. Due dates for cash deliveries stretching to the early months of 1973 [sic]. The total was staggering."[85] The pressure was on.

The Hunt memorandum, with its implicit threat that he would talk and expose White House involvement in Watergate in return for immunity from prosecution, precipitated another round of contention between the White House and John Mitchell. Ehrlichman, communicating through John Dean, urged Mitchell to "take care of

Mr. Hunt's problem," meaning that he should raise the money to meet Hunt's demands.[86] But, once again, Mitchell refused. Nor would LaRue help, lamenting in a subsequent meeting with Dean, "I can't raise this kind of money."[87]

Though the pressure to respond grew, the White House still refused to be drawn into the money trap. Mitchell now raised the possibility of using the White House "slush fund" to pay off Hunt. On Thanksgiving weekend, Mitchell telephoned John Dean, who had gone with his wife to his parents' home in Greenville, Pennsylvania, for the holiday. He wanted to know whether "anything had been done." When Dean replied in the negative, the following exchange took place:

> Mitchell: Well, I think Ehrlichman and Haldeman are finally coming down from Camp David tomorrow. So I understand. Don't you think maybe you ought to get back there and see that something's done about this? I don't think we can let it slide.
>
> Dean: I know we can't, but I'm not sure my talking to them will do any good.
>
> Mitchell: Well, you just think about it. . . .
>
> Dean: I'll see what I can do. Maybe I can handle it on the telephone. What do you think I ought to tell Bob and John?
>
> Mitchell: I think they've got a few reserves sitting around down there that they could help us out with. They've got to pull an oar in this thing. . . .
>
> Dean: I think it would be pretty dangerous to use any of that money, John. There's already been a lot of heat about it.
>
> Mitchell: Well, we may not have much choice. Think about it.[88]

Still Haldeman and Ehrlichman refused to budge. Dean returned to Washington the following day to meet with the two White House chiefs, who disdainfully brushed off his representations with the comment that Hunt was "Mitchell's problem." Dean relates of this meeting: "Each of them offered a few words of encouragement for me to pass on to LaRue but refused to discuss the matter further."[89] Mitchell persisted, giving what turned out to be the final turn of the screw a few days later, in early December. Still communicating through Dean and having failed to budge Ehrlichman, Mitchell told the White House counsel to "ask Haldeman for a 'loan' from the $350,000 slush fund." Haldeman, in a fateful decision made on the spot without consultation with either Ehrlichman or the president, said,

> Well, if Mitchell says there's no choice and you don't have any better ideas, then go ahead and do it. Just make goddam sure you get that money back, and fast. Make it clear it's a loan.[90]

An initial loan was quickly extended and immediately repaid by LaRue, as Haldeman demanded. But in a few days the pressure for more became so intense that Haldeman agreed in exasperation to transfer all of the funds remaining in the slush fund to LaRue.[91] Although Haldeman specified that his aide Gordon Strahan, who delivered the money, obtain a receipt, when he handed it over LaRue flatly refused to give him one. Donning a pair of rubber gloves to handle the cash, LaRue replied, "You'll have to talk to John Dean about that. . . . I never saw you."[92]

With the payment of White House funds directly to Hunt, presumbly for distribution to the Watergate defendants, the noose was slipped firmly around the president's political neck. Whatever else would occur, the president's opponents now had evidence of his direct complicity in a criminal obstruction of justice. It would be impossible to argue at this point that the president was not fully involved in the cover-up, even though as Haldeman claims, he may in fact have not known "of any of these fund-raising, payment, or money-transfer activities at the time."[93]

In a meeting with Haldeman, on December 5, Dean summarized the dilemma that now faced the president. The president had sought to persuade Dean to write a report in which he would declare that he had as the president's counsel investigated the Watergate affair and concluded that the White House was not involved in the matter.[94] But Dean resisted on the grounds that any such report would reopen the grand jury and lead to indictments not only of CRP officials Mitchell and Magruder, but also of the president's top aides. To Haldeman's "startled" response, "What do you mean?" Dean replied,

> Well, Bob, Mitchell and Magruder know about all these money payments. So do all the defendants and a lot of other people.

Everybody's going to have to trust everybody else to commit perjury. If even one person cracks and starts looking for a deal, we're in an obstruction-of-justice situation.[95]

Over the next several days, no later than the second week in December, the president capitulated to his opponents, relinquishing his decisive voice on foreign policy to Henry Kissinger. It would seem that the president did not intend to accept permanent surrender at this stage. He was, after all, still president and in the process of completing plans for the reorganization of the executive branch, which would involve a wholesale personnel shakeup and purge. With these changes the president would be prepared to retrieve what he had just relinquished.

But this, of course, was not to be. As the Watergate noose began to tighten early in 1973 with Senate hearings, the testimony of John Dean, James McCord's accusations of cover-up, and the revealing news stories tracing the scandal, the president was forced into greater and greater concentration on the matter of self-preservation; and the issue of control over American foreign policy slid permanently out of his hands.

CHAPTER

5

Watergate and Vietnam

We are now in position to explore in greater detail the relationship of the Watergate drama to the sea change that took place in American foreign policy in late 1972, centering on Vietnam. When the Vietnam negotiations are placed side by side with the unfolding Watergate events it becomes evident that the successful entrapment of the president in an obstruction of justice led directly to his capitulation to the Eastern wing of the Republican party on the final terms of a Vietnam settlement. President Nixon's capitulation, in turn, opened the door to Kissinger's de facto assumption of control over American foreign policy. It cannot be overemphasized that the choice of final terms for Vietnam was not made by cool, rational deliberation, but was the result of bitter, heated argument between the president and Kissinger, an argument that was not finally decided until the president's defeat on the domestic political front.

The principal policy question at issue was the nature of the Vietnam settlement. It would determine whether the United States would maintain the containment structure in the Pacific, as Nixon preferred, or move toward Kissinger's proposed tripolar order. Thus, Nixon's settlement terms would produce a restoration of the status quo ante bellum, while Kissinger's would lead directly to a new structure — complete withdrawal from mainland Southeast Asia. This outcome would leave China pinned between the Soviet Union in the north and a unified Vietnam in the south, theoretically perpetuating an extensive conflict of interests between the two communist giants and positioning the United States to manipulate one against the other. The differences between the president and his national security adviser, of course, were not merely the egoistic squabbles of two individuals, but the focal point of a leadership-elite conflict, which was rending the very fabric of American life.

The Nixon-Kissinger Cleavage

The first clash over the nature of the Vietnam settlement occurred in 1972 during Kissinger's April 20–24 trip to Moscow. His trip came during Hanoi's Easter offensive, which had commenced in late March. The offensive, recall, had been anticipated for several months as Hanoi's final attempt to establish a strong bargaining position for the negotiations that would follow its inevitable collapse. When the attack began, therefore, the American leadership understood that the nation was entering the final phase of its longest and most divisive war.

The cognoscente also clearly understood from all that had gone before that the president would insist on overruling his national security adviser and executing his preferred policy choice. Thus, in late March the Eastern group gave the go-ahead to John Mitchell to commence the entrapment of the president, hoping that when the moment of decision arrived they would have accomplished their scheme to blackmail him into compliance on Vietnam. This, by the way, may also explain Kissinger's extraordinary behavioral turnabout in Moscow, a turnabout which can only be described as the usurpation of presidential authority. Indeed, Kissinger's authority derived as much from his position in the Eastern political elite as from his actual position as national security adviser.

Prior to Kissinger's departure for Moscow, the president instructed him to engage in discussions of a "Vietnam settlement as a prerequisite for discussions on any other subject." If Soviet leaders "proved recalcitrant on this point, he [Kissinger] should just pack up and come home."[1] For Nixon, then, the failure to obtain Soviet agreement on satisfactory settlement terms over Vietnam would trigger cancellation of the upcoming Moscow summit and implicitly threaten the collapse of the ABM treaty which the Soviets so eagerly sought.[2]

The president was playing for high stakes. As he described it in his memoirs, "If he [Kissinger] had followed my instructions and insisted on a Vietnam settlement as the first order of business, perhaps Brezhnev would have dug in, called his bluff, and told him to go home—and that might have meant the end of the summit, with everything that it could accomplish, while still producing no progress on Vietnam. *That was a risk I had thought worth taking.*[3]

But Kissinger did not follow the president's instructions because, as he candidly explained in his memoirs, they had produced "a difference that was fundamental."[4] Kissinger had his own scheme, which was "to shift the risks and the onus for cancellation to the Soviets and to use Moscow's eagerness for the summit as a device for separating Moscow from Hanoi."[5] Thus, rather than press the Soviets on Vietnam as a prerequisite to any discussion of summit matters as the president had instructed him to do, Kissinger did the opposite.

Opening his meeting with Brezhnev, he expressed "on behalf of the President our *commitment* to a successful summit."[6] For Kissinger to express commitment to a successful summit in advance was hardly the way to separate Moscow from Hanoi. Indeed, it simply removed any leverage the United States might have had in parlaying Moscow's desires for a successful summit into cooperation on a Vietnam settlement.

Kissinger persisted on his own initiative in defiance of the president's explicit instructions. During the second meeting, on April 22, he subtly offered a fateful compromise on Vietnam whch would affect all subsequent negotiations. He had put forward according to instructions the president's proposal for "withdrawal of those North Vietnamese units that had entered South Vietnam since March 29, respect for the DMZ, immediate exchange of prisoners who had been held for more than four years, and a serious effort to negotiate a settlement within an agreed time period."[7] Brezhnev's response to this proposal was extremely cautious. As Kissinger described it, the Soviet leader's "extraordinarily conciliatory" reply was to "wonder" if "perhaps," without raising any "conditions," the United States would be willing to accept "a cease-fire along existing lines with all units staying in place?"[8]

Kissinger's counterproposal was indeed the "veritable diplomatic bomb" it was described as being at the time, even though the reporter who made the charge misunderstood what was in fact occurring and despite Kissinger's subsequent denial.[9] Kissinger declared to Brezhnev that "it is imperative, if we are to stop the bombing, that they withdraw the divisions that crossed the DMZ, and that henceforth the DMZ be respected." In other words, Kissinger had retreated completely from the president's instuctions, which called for "withdrawal of those North Vietnamese units that had entered South Vietnam since March 29," by saying that *only* those "divisions that crossed the DMZ" need be withdrawn.[10]

In reality, this was a difference of more than ten divisions. Hanoi's assault force which had crossed the DMZ amounted to between three and four divisions; but ten other divisions had entered South Vietnam through the Central Highlands and at An Loc, not to mention the twenty-six independent regiments that were also part of the invasion. Far from requiring Hanoi to withdraw its forces from South Vietnam, Kissinger was offering to allow virtually its entire force to remain, as Brezhnev had proposed!

It was no wonder that at this reply Brezhnev became suddenly "eager to get on to other business," while sending an emissary immediately to Hanoi to convey the new United States offer. Nor was it any wonder that the president warned his national security adviser against making a "deal" on Vietnam.[11] Indeed, the president was so concerned about this possibility (perhaps infuriated is a better description of his reaction) that he ordered Kissinger "to cut short the talks and return home."[12]

What was most extraordinary was Kissinger's reaction, for he flatly refused to obey the president's orders. In his words, "I judged this to be dangerous and unwise and I therefore went to the limits of my discretionary authority and proceeded to the rest of the agenda."[13] Faced with what amounted to a fait accompli, the president in a face-saving gesture *after the fact* authorized his national security adviser to stay on in Moscow "provided it was warranted by 'progress on the Vietnam question.'"[14]

Vietnam was central to the president's concerns and he acted on the assumption that Moscow held the ultimate controls on Hanoi's policy behavior. Not so Kissinger, who was operating on a quite different premise, which he revealed in a subsequent cable: "I cannot share the theory on which Washington operates. I do not believe that Moscow is in direct collusion with Hanoi."[15] The president's post-trip assessment laid starkly bare the obvious fundamental cleavage between the two men. Referring implicitly to his initial instructions, the president said that "it seems to me that their primary purpose of getting you to Moscow to discuss the summit has now been served while our purpose of getting some progress on Vietnam has not been served. . . . " Despite some ambiguous progress on strategic arms, he concluded, "the main issue was Vietnam and there we had failed."[16]

Vietnam Endgame and Nixon's Entrapment

As the Vietnam negotiations moved toward denouement from October through the following January, the differences between the president and Kissinger sharpened, particularly over the timing of the settlement. The final negotiations passed through four distinct stages: October 8 to November 7, November 20 to November 25, December 5 to December 14, and January 8 to January 13. Throughout the negotiations Kissinger's objective was to bring about as rapid a settlement as possible, preferably before the November election. When the president refused to be rushed into a pre-election settlement, Kissinger shifted tactics, offering tougher, post-election terms to provoke Hanoi's objection and to justify the application of massive American power to reach the same end, a quick settlement. President Nixon continued to reject Kissinger's initiatives for a quick settlement, including his proposals to resort to massive bombing of North Vietnam, until he was compromised domestically in Watergate, from which point, December 11, 1972, he acquiesced to Kissinger's view.

Why a quick settlement? To reiterate, Vietnam was the key to the first stage of Kissinger's preferred strategy. The sooner the conflict was brought to an end and American withdrawal completed, the sooner would South Vietnam fall prey to the North. The unification of Vietnam in turn would produce an Asian power balance that would have China locked between the Soviet Union in the north and a pro-Soviet Vietnam in the south, with the United States in an offshore position, now unencumbered and theoretically able to manipulate one communist power against the other.

On the other hand, the danger for Kissinger in protracted negotiations was that even congressional determination to conclude American involvement in the conflict would not be sufficient to overrule a president pledged to secure South Vietnam's survival against a North Vietnamese regime openly bent on conquest. White House polls taken in 1972 confirmed that the vast majority of the American people fully supported the president's quest for "peace with honor."[17] Thus, Kissinger strove to avoid protracted negotiations, which would inevitably be portrayed as evidence of Hanoi's determination to take over the South and would work in favor of Nixon's strategic objective of maintaining support for South Vietnam over the long term as part of an overall containment structure.

Determination to achieve a quick settlement led Kissinger after the election to espouse the massive bombing of Hanoi. Massive bombing would force a settlement but at the same time make one impossible to maintain. The more massive the bombing to bring about a settlement, the more difficult it would be to resume bombing later to enforce one. It would achieve other objectives as well. Not only would bombing coerce Hanoi, it would also remove any ground for Saigon's refusal to come to terms and silence critics on the American domestic right who were saying that Washington was not being tough enough. Thus, Kissinger's recommendation for massive bombing after the election had the objective of producing a quick settlement and speeding up disengagement from Southeast Asia.

In the first stage of the negotiations, between Hanoi's peace offer of October 8 and the November 7 election, Kissinger attempted to stampede the president into acceptance of a pre-election settlement. Curiously, as the negotiations progressed Kissinger's position paralleled Moscow's and Hanoi's in pressing for a quick settlement, while Nixon's reflected Beijing's and Saigon's interests in seeking a return to the status quo ante bellum. Kissinger's strategy, particularly its tripolar stage, fit nicely in structural terms with Moscow's version of the "containment" of China. Both called for the establishment of a unified Vietnam. Nixon, on the other hand, sought to strengthen United States containment of the Soviet Union by incorporating China into what Beijing also viewed as an anti-Soviet "united front."

As the October 8 meeting neared, President Nixon adopted a go-slow approach, fully realizing that this would be the last negotiating opportunity for Hanoi to bid for a pre-election settlement. In the president's view "it seemed unlikely that, even if the North Vietnamese wanted to, we would be able to negotiate an acceptable agreement in just five weeks."[18] As Nixon saw it there was only an "outside possibility" for a pre-election settlement at this point, and that would require Hanoi's acceptance of Washington's terms, which would amount to its own defeat.

Nevertheless, if Hanoi did make a reasonable offer, the United States, he felt, would be bound to act upon it. Under such circumstances, if President Thieu then rejected it, *he* and not the leaders in Hanoi would appear to be the main obstacle to peace. In early October, therefore, the president sent Alexander Haig to Saigon to reassure Thieu that the United States "would not rush headlong into an agreement," but also to caution him about the political implications in a last-minute peace offer and, no doubt, to urge him not to complicate matters by an outright rejection.[19]

In the event, Hanoi did what Nixon feared and offered settlement terms which, if actually implemented, meant "complete capitulation."[20] Although Le Duc Tho had made his proposal on October 8, Kissinger had revealed none of its terms, not even the fact that there had been an offer, to the president (beyond cabling cryptic hints about "progress") until his return to Washington and his personal meeting with Nixon on the evening of the 12th.[21] It was at this meeting, over a dinner of steak and wine the president had ordered to "toast Kissinger's success," that the national security adviser sprang the surprise which made Nixon's worst fear a reality.[22] He informed the president that the negotiating schedule would lead to a completed and signed agreement within three weeks!

Kissinger and Le Duc Tho had agreed upon a schedule — without consulting the president even though Kissinger knew that Nixon preferred to wait until after the election to settle — that would produce a settlement one week before the election.[23] Kissinger claims that although he had agreed to the schedule, he had had no hand in devising it. The schedule "was one that Hanoi was pressing upon us. At no point did I seek to speed up the process."[24] But of course! It could hardly have gone any faster, or more to Kissinger's liking. The schedule called for Kissinger to return to Paris for a brief, final negotiating session on October 17 to iron out the two remaining issues, Vietcong prisoner release and weapons replacement. On the eighteenth, he was to fly to Saigon for several days of sessions with President Thieu. Assuming Thieu's concurrence, no easy assumption, Kissinger would then fly to Hanoi on the twenty-fourth to initial the final agreement and return to Washington. On the twenty-sixth, President Nixon would announce the final agreement, which would be signed on October 31.

In truth, Kissinger had maneuvered the president into a tight corner. Nixon did not want a quick settlement, but at the same time did not want to be seen as rejecting a reasonable offer. If he rejected Hanoi's offer, moreover, there was little doubt that Kissinger himself would leak word to the press (as he had been doing all along) and that would indeed have a negative effect on the electorate, as well as on the powerful figures in the establishment upon whose support the president also depended.[25]

Therefore, the president acceded to Kissinger's preemptive schedule, but with little intent to adhere to it. His only recourse now was to delay and string out the negotiations until after the elections and for as long as was necessary thereafter to fortify the Saigon government for the struggle which would inevitably resume once the United States had withdrawn. There were no illusions about Hanoi's ultimate intentions. All understood perfectly that although what was being negotiated was the face-saving withdrawal of the United States, the issue being decided was the future of South Vietnam's government.

Kissinger flew to Paris on October 17 for what he anticipated would be a final wrap-up session with Xuan Thuy, Le Duc Tho's deputy; but their meeting dragged on inconclusively, consuming most of the afternoon and evening. Realizing that further delay would jeopardize a pre-election settlement, Kissinger became highly agitated, "almost hysterical" according to one source; and finally, an hour before his scheduled departure for Saigon, he told Xuan Thuy that he had to leave if he were to maintain the schedule.[26] As Kissinger prepared to depart, Xuan Thuy declared that "if you go to Saigon, we'll never settle it," to which Kissinger responded, "We'll solve it by cable."[27] Kissinger's reaction suggested that he was more eager for a pre-election settlement than the North Vietnamese were, and his subsequent behavior left little doubt about it.

From the plane en route to Saigon, Kissinger cabled Hanoi that his trip to the North Vietnamese capital could take place only if there were a firm agreement. He sent along proposed texts on the two remaining disputed points regarding resupply provisions and the timing of the release of Vietcong prisoners held by Saigon. Then he sent another message, this time in the president's name, reiterating that a visit to Hanoi would be impossible as long as any main issues were still "outstanding."[28] That was where matters stood when Kissinger and his entourage arrived in Saigon October 19 to hold the first of several difficult meetings with South Vietnamese President Nguyen Van Thieu.

Meanwhile, the leadership in Hanoi, as anxious to lock Kissinger into a quick settlement as he was to be locked into one, acted to preempt anticipated resistance to their offer in Saigon. Late on the

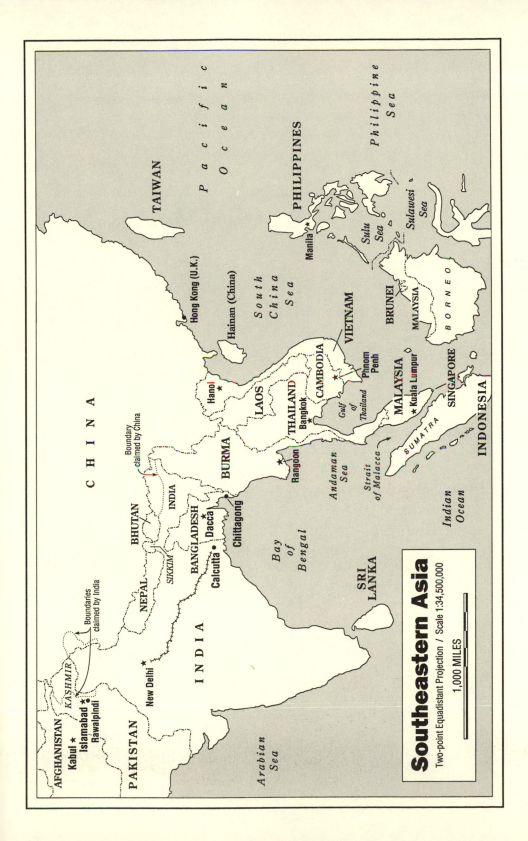

Southeastern Asia

Two-point Equadistant Projection / Scale 1:34,500,000

1,000 MILES

AFGHANISTAN

Kabul ★
Islamabad ★
Rawalpindi ●

KASHMIR

Boundaries
claimed by India

PAKISTAN

New Delhi ★

I N D I A

NEPAL

BHUTAN

SIKKIM

Boundary
claimed by China

C H I N A

BANGLADESH
Dacca ●
Calcutta ●
Chittagong ●

BURMA

Rangoon ★

LAOS

Hanoi ★

THAILAND
Bangkok ★

CAMBODIA

VIETNAM

Phnom
Penh ★

TAIWAN

Hong Kong (U.K.) ●

Hainan (China)

South
China
Sea

Pacific
Ocean

PHILIPPINES

Manila ★

Philippine
Sea

Sulu
Sea

Sulawesi
Sea

BRUNEI

MALAYSIA

B O R N E O

MALAYSIA
Kuala Lumpur ★

SINGAPORE

SUMATRA

INDONESIA

Gulf
of
Thailand

Andaman
Sea

Strait
of Malacca

Indian
Ocean

Bay
of
Bengal

SRI
LANKA

Arabian
Sea

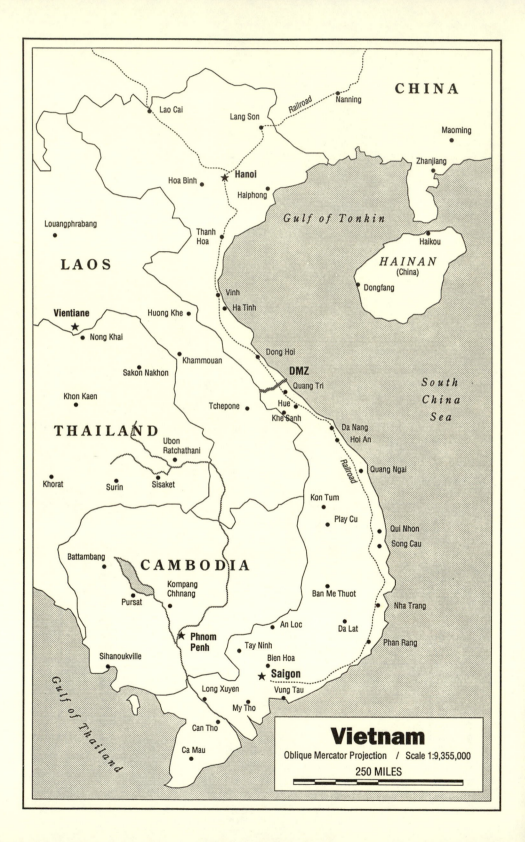

CHINA

Lao Cai

Lang Son

Railroad   Nanning

Maoming

Zhanjiang

Hoa Binh

Hanoi

Haiphong

Gulf of Tonkin

Haikou

Louangphrabang

Thanh
Hoa

LAOS

HAINAN
(China)

Dongfang

Vientiane

Huong Khe

Vinh

Ha Tinh

Nong Khai

Khammouan

Dong Hoi

Sakon Nakhon

DMZ

*South
China
Sea*

Khon Kaen

Tchepone

Quang Tri

Hue

THAILAND

Khe Sanh

Da Nang

Hoi An

Ubon
Ratchathani

Railroad

Quang Ngai

Khorat

Surin

Sisaket

Kon Tum

Play Cu

Qui Nhon

Song Cau

Battambang

CAMBODIA

Kompang
Chhnang

Ban Me Thuot

Nha Trang

Pursat

An Loc

Da Lat

Phan Rang

Sihanoukville

**Phnom
Penh**

Tay Ninh

Bien Hoa

Saigon

Gulf of Thailand

Long Xuyen

Vung Tau

My Tho

Can Tho

Ca Mau

Vietnam

Oblique Mercator Projection / Scale 1:9,355,000

250 MILES

evening of October 19, Hanoi cabled its acceptance of the United States position on the remaining two outstanding points of disagreement, including the text Kissinger had proposed. This meant that Hanoi now agreed to Washington's position regarding the replacement of military materiel on a one-for-one basis as well as agreeing to omit from the final settlement any provision requiring the simultaneous release of Vietcong prisoners held by the Saigon government and American prisoners of war held by Hanoi. Indeed, Hanoi appeared with its cable to have removed all grounds for refusal by either Washington or Saigon to sign the peace agreement forthwith.

As soon as he received Hanoi's cable, Kissinger attempted to preempt Nixon and Thieu. Without consulting Thieu or contacting the president, later that same evening he sent a return cable to Hanoi in the president's name, declaring that, except for unilateral understandings relating to Laos and Cambodia, "the text of the agreement is considered complete."[29] Hanoi immediately cabled back its confirmation, and by October 20, the next day, the deal was sealed. Or was it? Had Kissinger gone too far? Did the president in fact agree with or even know of Kissinger's action? The evidence strongly suggests that the president had no idea that such a message had been sent, despite Kissinger's later claim that Nixon had been given a copy of every message sent in his name and could "countermand any message . . . [but] never did so."[30]

On October 20, the day Kissinger sent the acceptance message to Hanoi in the president's name, a story appeared in the *Los Angeles Times* by Robert Toth based on high White House sources conveying the message that no breakthrough was expected before the election.[31] That day, too, Nixon met with soon-to-retire Army Chief of Staff General William Westmoreland, to whom he emphatically declared that he would not "be pressured by the forthcoming election into premature signing of the agreement."[32] After the president's conversation with Westmoreland, he sent Kissinger a cable, the fifth in four days, according to Kissinger, all stressing disregard of the approaching election as a factor in the negotiations and emphasizing the necessity of supporting Thieu. Thieu's acceptance, the cable read, "must be wholehearted. . . . We must have Thieu as a willing partner in making any agreement. It cannot be a shotgun marriage."[33]

The newspaper article expressing Nixon's view, the personal reassurances to Westmoreland, and the cable to Kissinger clearly mark the president's position. What is most important, particularly about the president's message to Kissinger of October 20, is what he did not say. There is no inkling, no hint that the president knew of Kissinger's confirmation message sent to Hanoi in his name. The president's October 20 message to Kissinger was drafted hours after Kissinger's cable to Hanoi had presumably passed through the White House communications center. Kissinger's confirmation cable was supremely important — critical — and it is inconceivable that Nixon would have ignored it had he in fact seen it. Kissinger had moved sharply and openly into opposition to the president.

If Kissinger believed that he could talk Thieu into agreement, he misjudged the South Vietnamese leader badly. His "stampede" scheme fell completely apart in Saigon. In four days of meetings, October 19–23, the South Vietnamese president and his advisers remained unmoved by Kissinger's arguments, refusing to countenance any "peace" plan that left over 300,000 enemy troops on their soil, established what they believed was the nucleus of a coalition government, and left vulnerable the demilitarized zone to North Vietnamese transgression.

Tactfully at first and then with increasing emotion, Thieu and his advisers let Kissinger know unequivocally that the agreement was unacceptable. This, however, did not deter Kissinger from sending periodic cables to the president claiming that he was making progress and that a breakthrough with Thieu was near. Without exception, Nixon's messages to Kissinger while he was in Saigon express the position he had taken from the start, namely, that Thieu must willingly accept the agreement and that a post-election settlement was preferable to a hasty agreement beforehand.[34]

After Kissinger's climactic meeting with Thieu on Sunday, October 22, he cabled the president the news of Thieu's final rejection and offered two options. In the first he requested that he be permitted to go on to Hanoi according to the schedule and shuttle between Hanoi and Saigon until an agreement was reached. He also recommended that the United States discontinue all air support for Saigon's forces until Thieu acccepted the agreement, a part of the option that Kissinger mentions only in a separate context and not in conjunction with the trip.[35]

His second option was that he return to Washington forthwith and attempt to obtain Soviet assistance to restrain Hanoi from drawing away from the negotiations altogether. (Kissinger claims that he had already rejected the first option of going on to Hanoi before the president sent his reply, but his explanation is unconvincing.[36]) While awaiting the president's return cable, on October 22, Kissinger sent yet another message to Hanoi in the president's name, reaffirming American commitment to the draft agreement but explaining that Kissinger was being recalled to Washington because of "difficulties in Saigon."[37]

Whatever the truth regarding Kissinger's proposal to go on to Hanoi (the record is ambiguous)[38] and his recommendation to pressure Saigon by a bombing halt in the North, Nixon seized the opportunity to establish in no uncertain terms his opposition to a pre-election settlement. In his reply cable the president "vehemently rejected the option of going to Hanoi," called his adviser back to Washington, and let it be known within the NSC that "this time Henry's gone too far. He's through as a negotiator."[39] Before departing for Washington, however, on October 23, Kissinger sent one last message to Hanoi—again in Nixon's name—apologizing for the failure to gain Thieu's acquiescence and precluding his trip to Hanoi. He proposed that he and Le Duc Tho meet in Paris to reconcile remaining issues. "The President reiterates his firm belief that an agreement is obtainable in the very near future."[40]

Kissinger had not given up. He "knew that there would be strong temptations in Washington to jettison the draft peace treaty [sic] and to go for broke after the election. I was determined to preserve the draft against all the passions that would soon descend. . . ."[41] In his view, "the time for a settlement had arrived." The concern in Washington was that Hanoi might make the negotiating record public and place the administration in the embarrassing position of failing to sign an agreement whose terms were better than those ever publicly demanded of Hanoi. Thus, Nixon instructed Kissinger to hold his first-ever press conference in an attempt to preempt Hanoi.[42] But it was too late. On October 26 Hanoi revealed the essential elements of the negotiations since October 8, including Kissinger's "presidential" cables confirming the agreement.

There was now all the more reason for Kissinger to give his press conference, not only to reassure Hanoi of American readiness to conclude the agreement but also to reassure Saigon, whose leaders were severely compromised by the revelations. Most important, however, it was Kissinger's last chance to prod Nixon into accepting a quick settlement. Thus his famous phrase, "peace is at hand," which sparked renewed domestic debate over the negotiations at a time when the president's most fervent wish was to make the issue of Vietnam disappear for the few remaining days until the election.[43]

Nixon, understandably, was furious. Once again, Kissinger had boxed him into a corner.[44] He had given Hanoi the impression that the United States had no choice but to have peace, on conditions which it was bound to accept after just one more negotiating session. The president moved immediately to undercut the groundswell of public sentiment which the statement was calculated to produce, even as Kissinger argued strenuously that the president must not "back off from what he [Kissinger] had said."[45] That very evening on the campaign trail in Ashland, Kentucky, Nixon acknowledged the reports of progress, but reaffirmed that peace was not yet at hand. "The day has not yet come. There are still some differences that must be resolved." Furthermore, he said, he would not agree to any settlement unless it would "discourage aggression in the future rather than encourage it."[46]

Then, a few days later, on November 2 in a televised address to the entire nation, the president, determined not to "allow the impression to remain that a settlement would be the guaranteed outcome of the next Paris meeting," declared that he would not

> allow an election deadline or any other kind of deadline to force us into an agreement which would be only a temporary truce and not a lasting peace. We are going to sign the agreement when the agreement is right, not one day before. And when the agreement is right, we are going to sign, without one day's delay.[47]

As one account described it, "the president was virtually in open warfare with Kissinger."[48] Indeed, he was; and at this point he had already won if not the war then a very important battle with his national security adviser. There would be no headlong rush to settlement before the election. Moreover, Nixon now spoke openly to aides that Kissinger must go as soon as the peace talks were concluded.

November Round: Kissinger Changes Tactics

Having failed to stampede the president into a pre-election settlement during the October round, Kissinger now changed tactics. He still sought a quick settlement, but realized that the changed military situation on the ground in South Vietnam now made an early settlement less, not more, likely. What had happened was this: Hanoi had assumed that a settlement would occur according to the agreed schedule by October 31 and had already surfaced its cadre in the South for extensive land-grabbing operations. A settlement with its accompanying cease-fire would have frozen South Vietnam's countermove and left Hanoi's minions in a strong position. When it failed to materialize, their cadre were exposed to the well-prepared counterattacks of South Vietnamese forces and decimated.[49] It was therefore obvious that Hanoi would attempt to stall and string out the negotiations to play for time to rebuild their positions.

How long Hanoi would stall could not be estimated. Of course, if negotiations dragged out long enough Congress might very well move to legislate an end to it all; but if that occurred it would take time, and Kissinger was in a hurry. Whatever his reasons, and undoubtedly anticipating Hanoi's shift, Kissinger, too, changed tactics. Instead of pressing for a settlement as he had in October, he now provoked Hanoi into doing what it had decided to do anyway by altering the terms of the settlement.

Now all sides, Hanoi, Kissinger, and the president, had decided to change tactics, but with different ends in view. Hanoi wanted to stall for time, but Kissinger wanted to provoke North Vietnamese intransigence in order to justify the application of massive American power to compel an early settlement. On the other hand, the changed situation on the ground now led the president to conclude that the terms of the agreement were acceptable, and he sought to direct Kissinger toward a settlement.

Hanoi had initially agreed to resume talks on November 14 but put them off until the twentieth.[50] When they recommenced, Le Duc Tho immediately led off with a prepared denunciation of the United States and the insistence that Washington sign the October draft as it stood. Kissinger, in his turn, undoubtedly took the North Vietnamese leader aback by putting forward sixty-nine changes which Washington and Saigon wished to make in the draft agreement. Among the changes demanded, seven were major issues which, if accepted, would alter the terms of the settlement substantially in Saigon's favor.

Kissinger sought to strengthen the DMZ as a demarcation line between north and south and to limit and gain greater control over Hanoi's transit into the South. He attempted to obtain the withdrawal of substantial numbers of North Vietnamese troops from the South and to remove any possibility that the National Council of National Reconciliation and Concord could function as a supranational government, superseding the government in Saigon. Kissinger also insisted that the coming elections be for the office of president, rather than for a new Constituent Assembly, and he sought to link the cease-fire in Laos and Cambodia to the one in South Vietnam. Finally, he demanded that all references to the Provisional Revolutionary Government (PRG), Hanoi's political organ in the South, be deleted from the text.[51]

Kissinger had made no distinction between the changes that Saigon had insisted upon and those which Washington desired. He claimed in his memoirs that "all the sixty-nine changes [were] requested by Saigon,"[52] but Nixon notes that "there were changes and clarifications we wanted."[53] Indeed, Kissinger gave the impression that he put forward the "preposterous" list of changes "to avoid the charge that we were less than meticulous in guarding Saigon's concerns," but this could hardly have been the case, since that had given him no qualms whatsoever in October when Saigon's interests were ignored completely.

Although Kissinger regarded this as "a major tactical mistake" from the point of view of provoking the North Vietnamese, it was strategically correct, for, as he observed, it simply "strengthened Hanoi's already strong temptation to dig in its heels."[54] Le Duc Tho's reaction "was predictable." He threatened that "if these changes were presented as an ultimatum the war would go on another four years."[55] Kissinger's reply was classic: "I would put it this way. It is our final proposal, but it is not an ultimatum."[56] At this, Le Duc Tho asked for an overnight recess, and the first meeting ended.

When they met again the next afternoon, November 21, Le Duc Tho opened the meeting by declaring that the changes Kissinger "was demanding were not just 'technical' but substantive, not few but many."[57] And he rejected all but a handful of minor ones. For example, he agreed to insert a clause requiring that both parties respect the DMZ and the territory under the control of each party, so long as the DMZ was clearly identified as "provisional and military" in character and not in any way a political boundary.[58] He also agreed to drop the six-month deadline for elections and accepted Kissinger's proposals to add references to the "sovereignty of South Vietnam" in several places in the text.

But he reopened several issues of his own, seeking once again to obtain the release of Vietcong prisoners held by Saigon at the same time that Hanoi released American prisoners of war. He also demanded that all American civilian technicians withdraw along with the military forces. Nevertheless, at this early stage of the negotiations, Kissinger viewed all this as simply "old-fashioned hard bargaining. . . . At a minimum Le Duc Tho kept his options open. He could settle quickly, but he could also hang us up indefinitely."[59]

At the third session, on November 22, Kissinger dropped the vast majority of Saigon's "less important nitpicks" and "returned to essentials." He demanded reductions in North Vietnamese troop strength in the South, controls on movement across the DMZ which would obstruct Hanoi's access, and the establishment of sizable international control machinery to monitor troop movements. He wanted to loosen restrictions on provisions for weapons replacement for forces in the South, redefine the National Council into a powerless, paper organization, and tie the cease-fire in Laos (withdrawing the Cambodian cease-fire demand) to the one in South Vietnam.[60]

The overall effect of these provisions, if accepted, would have been to make Hanoi's position in the South untenable for any length of time and to ensure the viability of the government of South Vietnam. Kissinger's "essentials" were, of course, unacceptable to Hanoi — as he knew they would be. Le Duc Tho agreed to a looser interpretation of weapons replacement but would not budge on anything else.

Afterward, Kissinger sent a message to the president saying that the session "had been another tense and totally unproductive meeting." In reply, on November 22, "in an effort to get the negotiations moving," the president sent Kissinger a message "in the form of a directive,"[61] which he could show to Le Duc Tho *if* he thought it would make the North Vietnamese leader more cooperative. It read:

> The President is very disappointed at the tone as well as the substance of the last meeting with Le Duc Tho. Under the circumstances, unless the other side shows the same willingness to be reasonable that we are showing, I am directing you to discontinue the talks and we shall then have to resume military activity until the other side is ready to negotiate. They must be disabused of the idea they seem to have that we have no other choice but to settle on their terms. You should inform them directly without equivocation that we do have another choice and if they were surprised that the President would take the

strong action he did prior to the Moscow summit and prior to the election, they will find now, with the election behind us, he will take whatever action he considers necessary to protect the United States' interest.[62]

Kissinger's treatment of this message in his memoirs is strange, giving the impression that it was an unsolicited intrusion into the negotiations. He suggested that the message was the product of their deteriorating relationship, that the president was somehow goaded into sending it on the incompetent advice of "public relations experts" surrounding him at Camp David where he was "ensconced." Lastly, he insinuated that the president was not following and did not actually understand the negotiations and that he actually wanted to break off the talks after only forty-eight hours.

None of this was true. Nixon's message was a reply to Kissinger's own and was designed to give him additional negotiating leverage by offering, "if and when he saw fit—or not at all," the old tough guy-nice guy routine.[63] The threatening message would enable Kissinger to present himself as the "nice guy" whom the North Vietnamese could help in fending off the "tough guy" Nixon—if only they would make a few concessions. This, of course, was an old negotiating tactic and, in truth, simply a variation of the "madman concept" the president and Kissinger had employed on several occasions previously.[64] After the fact, Kissinger was attempting to turn Nixon's message against him, suggesting that the president was in favor of breaking off the talks and resuming the bombing, which was clearly not the case, as the subsequent record amply attests. The opposite was true.

The next day's meeting, on November 23, produced six more hours of give and take. According to Kissinger, Le Duc Tho offered "a semi-concession on the DMZ in return for altering other parts of the agreement" (although Kissinger doesn't say what the semi-concession was)[65] and proposed a de facto withdrawal of an unspecified number of North Vietnamese forces from the South, but would put nothing on paper. Kissinger believed Le Duc Tho's response to be "a significant degradation of the October document." After the morning session, he cabled Nixon to say that "while we had achieved some marginal improvements, the North Vietnamese had pulled back somewhat, leaving the overall agreement slightly *worse* than the one negotiated in October." It is the phrase "slightly worse" here that jars. For Kissinger's recommendation, coming after only one more negotiating session — when there was still some, even though slow, progress — was to "break off the talks and resume bombing north of the twentieth parallel," that is, to bomb Hanoi.[66]

Kissinger set his recommendation in terms of two options: either "settle for the improvements in the draft agreement already achieved" or "break off the talks and resume bombing." Nixon states in his memoirs that the bombing option "was the option Kissinger favored," but Kissinger says lamely that he "hinted at" a preference for settling.[67] Fully understanding the difficulties that settling would produce with Thieu, Nixon nevertheless "strongly opposed breaking off the talks and resuming the bombing unless it was absolutely necessary to compel the enemy to negotiate."[68] In his return cable to Kissinger, Nixon declared that the bombing option was no longer open. "We must recognize the fundamental reality that we have no choice but to reach agreement along the lines of the October 8 principles."[69]

"Almost immediately," however, the president had second thoughts. Concerned that he had undercut Kissinger's bargaining leverage vis-à-vis the North Vietnamese, Nixon sent another cable the next morning, November 24, saying that "*if* the Communists remained intransigent, he [Kissinger] could suspend the talks for a week so that both sides could consult with their principals. I said that I would be prepared to authorize a massive bombing strike on North Vietnam in that interval." His message continued:

> I recognize that this is a high-risk option, but it is one I am prepared to take *if* the only alternative is an agreement which is worse than that of . . . October 8. . . .[70]

Kissinger's treatment of Nixon's November 24 message is a major distortion, having the same objective as his treatment of the November 22 message — to give the impression that the president favored massive bombing of North Vietnam. Kissinger says that Nixon "sent another cable suggesting that I interrupt the talks after all, on the pretext of giving the negotiators an opportunity to consult their principals. In that case he would authorize a massive air strike against North Vietnam during the recess. This was not my preference. I favored resumption of bombing north of the twentieth parallel only if the talks broke down altogether, and we had not yet reached that point."[71]

When the two accounts are compared, the distortion is obvious. What Kissinger had done was to assume the very position Nixon had taken in the November 24 message, while attributing to the president his own preference to break off the talks and resume heavy bombing. Kissinger does not include in his memoir that part of Nixon's message in which the president gave his opinion, but the president does. Kissinger says that Nixon was "suggesting that I interrupt the talks," but what Nixon actually said was "*if* the Communists remained intransigent, he *could* suspend the talks." Even the president's authorization for "a massive bombing strike" was conditional: "*If* the only alternative is an agreement which is worse than that of . . . October 8. . . ." In other words, Nixon's instructions were to keep the talks going; a suspension would be considered *only if* the talks broke down completely.

At this point, Kissinger took the unauthorized and most unusual step of suggesting that he and Le Duc Tho meet alone "each accompanied by just one adviser."[72] (As might be expected, the record here becomes quite murky and contradictory, for no note-takers would be present.) About the only thing the Nixon and Kissinger accounts agree on regarding the November 24 meeting is that it occurred. According to Nixon, when Kissinger informed Le Duc Tho that the president was prepared to take strong measures "the North Vietnamese immediately became more conciliatory," confirming his suspicions that Hanoi's "intransigence was in fact a negotiating tactic. They did not want the talks to end any more than we did and were therefore prepared once again to engage in serious negotiations."[73]

Kissinger's account of the November 24 meeting is completely different. He said that after reading "to my interlocutors the starchier of Nixon's telegrams, especially those emphasizing his willingness to run military risks . . . Le Duc Tho maintained his position."[74] In other words, where the president believed that there was now every possibility of making progress, Kissinger concluded that the talks had reached a dead end! After the meeting, Kissinger cabled Nixon seeking permission to postpone the talks. Nixon's reply was an emphatic no.

It was important to keep the negotiating channels open and working. I considered Thieu's position to be ill-advised, and I felt more strongly than ever that if we could get a good agreement, we should do so and let Thieu make his choice accordingly. I immediately replied to Kissinger that I thought it preferable for him to stay in Paris and continue talking as long as there was even a remote chance of reaching an agreement. I said that I would even "take risks in that direction."[75]

Again, Kissinger's account is at odds with the president's. He claims that Nixon's message ordering him to stay on in Paris came "after the recess had already been agreed," then acknowledges that the president's message arrived late on November 24 while the meeting with Le Duc Tho at which he requested the recess occurred the next morning.[76] In other words, Kissinger brought the November round of talks to a close against Nixon's instructions. When he returned to Washington he went immediately into a meeting with the president. There, Nixon expressed in person the opinion he had been pressing on Kissinger in his cables.

I had to back him off the position that we really had a viable option to break off the talks with the North and resume the bombing for a period of time. It simply isn't going to work. While we must play the card out with the North Vietnamese *as if it would work that way*, we must have no illusions that we now have no option except to settle.[77]

In evaluating the negotiations up to this point, despite Kissinger's blatant deviation from the president's instructions, Nixon still appeared to be in overall policy control.

December Round and the Watergate "Coup"

At the outset of the December round it appeared as if President Nixon would succeed in negotiating a settlement which reestablished the status quo ante bellum, despite Henry Kissinger's machinations. Although on October 20 the president had ordered the massive resupply of South Vietnam's forces, the Enhance Plus program,[78] Kissinger had almost immediately sabotaged it: "I had slowed down these shipments to Saigon after Thieu rejected the agreement."[79] But when Nixon discovered what Kissinger had done he reissued the orders to get the supply effort going again, and by the end of November it was nearly completed.

With the failure of Hanoi's earlier land-grabbing venture, Saigon's forces were now in rough balance with those of North Vietnam. Additionally, the president was making arrangements to employ American air power as an indefinite guarantee of the settlement; and he moved during this round to communicate his intentions secretly to Thieu, hoping to gain the support of the South Vietnamese leader. In short, conditions had evolved to the point where the president believed a settlement could be sustained. Therefore he was now determined to reach a settlement, regardless of Thieu's attitude and virtually on whatever terms Hanoi demanded.

Prior to the beginning of the December round, on November 30, the president convened a meeting of the Joint Chiefs of Staff, Secretary of Defense Melvin Laird, and Kissinger. Assuming an active, dominant role in the proceedings, President Nixon raised two issues. First, what should be done in the event of a breakdown in the coming negotiations? Second, what steps should be taken in the event a settlement was reached, and subsequently breached by Hanoi? In the first case, the president wanted contingency plans prepared for three- and six-day bombing strikes against North Vietnam.[80] In the second case, Nixon

> was adamant that our response be swift and strong. "If Hanoi violates an agreement, our response must be all out," [he] said. *"We must maintain enough force in the area* to do the job, and it can't be a weak response. Above all, B-52s are to be targeted on Hanoi. We must have our own unilateral capability to prevent violations."[81]

Admiral Elmo R. Zumwalt, chief of naval operations, whose notes on the meeting described the president's dominant participation, makes it clear that Nixon was preparing to deploy American power to secure the continued viability of South Vietnam over the long term.[82] In any event, it is evident that the president was now prepared to reach a settlement of the Vietnam conflict during the coming December round. Not so his national security adviser, who intensified his pursuit of a negotiating breakdown to justify a bombing-induced settlement, just as he had attempted to do during the November round.

At the first session on December 4, which Kissinger had arranged as another closed session attended only by himself, Haig, Le Duc

Tho, and Xuan Thuy, he presented a "stripped-down version of the minimum changes for which we would settle."[83] Le Duc Tho responded by requesting changes of his own on what had already been agreed. After some mutual haranguing the session ended with each side's having laid out its positions, undoubtedly in the expectation that there would be further compromise as negotiations proceeded.

Kissinger's report to Nixon that evening, however, was remarkably alarmist considering that only a single day had passed. "Hanoi," he said, "has apparently decided to mount a frontal challenge to us such as we faced last May."[84] Le Duc Tho would not have taken such a strong position, he declared, unless he was "willing to risk a break-off." The "only hope of averting a collapse," he shrilled, was to prod Moscow into exerting pressure on Hanoi. Toward this end, therefore, Kissinger had sent a thinly veiled message to Dobrynin stating that the negotiations were "approaching a situation comparable to last May, requiring the same kind of reaction."[85] That comparable situation and reaction, of course, was the United States decision to bomb and mine the North.

To give Moscow time to make its influence felt, Kissinger requested a twenty-four-hour recess, the two sides to reconvene December 6. During the brief recess, a flurry of cables went back and forth between Kissinger and the president in which the national security adviser now strove to gain Nixon's acceptance of his recommendations. Curiously, Kissinger's recommendation to *avoid* a collapse of the talks was "to pursue a course that involved a high risk of a break-off."[86]

Nixon's account, quoting Kissinger's recommendation directly from the cables he sent on December 5, is much more explicit. Kissinger declared: "I believe we must be prepared to break off the negotiations. The question is how we do it."[87] In other words, after a single day's negotiations, and in flagrant opposition to the president's desire to settle, Kissinger was pressing the same recommendation in the December round that he had argued for unsuccessfully during the November round: break off the negotiations and bomb.

The question was, Kissinger proposed, How do we do it? His recommendations *for breaking off the talks* were: either offer to sign the agreement reached in the November round as it stood, or provoke Hanoi more directly by seeking additional changes sought by Thieu.[88] Since Hanoi was highly unlikely to accept either proposal outright, this would precipitate a breakdown in the talks, which would enable the United States to resume bombing. Kissinger's expectation was that the bombing would have to be maintained *for six to eight months* before Hanoi would agree to Washington's terms. Therefore, to "rally" the American people on what would be a resumption of the war "with no end in sight," he proposed that the president announce the bombing plan in a televised address to the nation.[89]

Nixon, of course, refused Kissinger's recommendation to precipitate a break-off of the talks and resume the bombing accompanied by a presidential speech explaining the failure of the negotiations. He declared himself "unconvinced of the wisdom and the feasibility of this course of action. It was my firm conviction that we must not be responsible — or be portrayed as being responsible — for the breakdown of the talks." As the president put it, "There was clearly a difference of opinion between Kissinger and me regarding the best *strategy* to pursue."[90] Referring to the November negotiating round, he said:

> *Once again* he [Kissinger] felt that we had reached a point where the only thing we could do was break off the talks and step up the bombing to make the North Vietnamese agree to a settlement. And *once again* I believed it was important to keep the talks going for as long as there was even a remote chance that they might yield a settlement.[91]

Kissinger was not at all pleased with the president's response, declaring in his return cable that "we had better face the facts of life." If there was no agreement in the next forty-eight hours, he said, a stalemate would be evident, in which case

> we have only two choices: to yield or to rally American support for one more effort which I do not believe the North Vietnamese can withstand.[92]

Moscow, in the meantime, replied to Kissinger's message, counseling patience and assuring him that, just as Le Duc Tho had said on December 4, Hanoi was "still ready to sign an agreement within the October framework."[93]

The two sides reconvened December 6, but after a six-hour session positions remained essentially unchanged, and it was agreed to make a final effort the next day. Both Kissinger and Nixon agree in their accounts on the outcome of the December 6 meeting but differ markedly on what happened immediately afterward, specifically regarding Kissinger's reporting cable to the president. According to Kissinger, he "warned" the president that the negotiations were "almost bound to fail," and that "even if there was a last-minute breakthrough" the settlement would quickly disintegrate because of "the total hatred and pathological distrust between the Vietnamese parties, and knowing as well that Hanoi has no intention of giving up its strategic objectives."[94]

Kissinger then characterized the president's reply cable as being in agreement with his own view and containing instructions "to try to pin Hanoi to a series of intransigent positions to strengthen the record in case the talks should recess or break up. "[95] Kissinger declined to include *any* of the president's cable text, choosing instead to describe its contents, for a very good reason. Nixon's account of what transpired after the December 6 meeting is entirely different!

According to the president, who quoted extensively from both his and Kissinger's cables, Kissinger once again put forth "two options" for consideration. Option one involved making one last attempt to reach a settlement, which, in the unlikely event it was accepted by Hanoi, would precipitate a crisis with Saigon. Thus, Kissinger recommended against his "option one." As he put it: "Unless you are prepared to undertake such a confrontation you should *not* instruct me to follow this course."[96] Option two, like his cable of December 4, reiterated preference for provoking a break-off of the talks by making some unacceptable demand and resuming massive bombing, which Kissinger wanted to continue for six months. In other words, Kissinger was now openly rejecting the president's instructions for a negotiated settlement and demanding the authority to provoke a break-off of the talks!

Recognizing that he and his national security adviser were at an impasse and realizing that Kissinger could destroy any possibility of a settlement if he chose, Nixon sought the advice of his closest advisers. He had already canvassed the views of John Connolly, Chuck Colson, and Ron Ziegler. Now on December 6, he called on John Ehrlichman, whose advice had never before been requested on a foreign policy matter. Ehrlichman's views were sought because of Kissinger's insistence that Nixon deliver a major televised address to "rally" the people.

In order to give Ehrlichman the full background of the problem, Haldeman showed him the cable traffic of the Paris talks, remarking,

> I don't know if you realize it, but Henry was very "down" when he left for Paris. . . . *He's been under care.* And he's been doing some strange things. When he was in Saigon [in October], twice he cabled the North Vietnamese in the President's name to accept their October proposal. Henry did that over Al Haig's strong objection and beyond any Presidential authority.[97]

Ehrlichman's advice was the same as that of the others. "The president should explain successes. The staff explains failures," he said. Therefore no speech. But the key question was how to get Kissinger home before he wrecked any possibility of a settlement. After thinking the matter over, the president decided upon a set of "step-by-step instructions" which would bring Kissinger home without arousing his suspicions.

In his reply cable, the president stated that "before a decision of this importance [the bombing option] is made, it is imperative that I talk with you personally."[98] Therefore, at the next meeting, he instructed: "Go down a list of specific questions on all of the proposals that are contained in your minimum position. . . . I then want you to ask them what is their final offer. You will then tell them that you will report . . . to the President directly. . . ."[99] Hoping to persuade Kissinger to accept his line of reasoning, Nixon promised that if the next meeting did not end in a settlement, even though "there is a very remote possibility that you will make a breakthrough on the settlement side, we will embark on a very heavy bombing in the North."

Kissinger explained the "stiff tone" of his return cable as reflecting "a certain lack of spontaneous warmth in the relationship between President and adviser," but the fact was that he was not fooled by this disguised order to return home. In his memoir, of course, Kissinger attempted to leave the impression that the president had agreed with him on everything but "sequence."

> Thank you for your message of December 6. Your instructions are understood and will be followed. However, I believe the tactical sequence in carrying them out should be different. At this afternoon's session I will first push for Hanoi's acceptance of our minimum position which you approved (Option I). If Le

Duc Tho rejects this position I will ask the series of questions you have listed. . . . I will then ask for a recess to enable me to return to Washington and consult with you. . . .[100]

Interestingly, Kissinger's reply also suggested that the president still retained ultimate control over the negotiations and that his objective remained a negotiated settlement.

At the December 7 meeting, Le Duc Tho, sensing that a critical juncture had been reached and perhaps hoping to forestall a recess, became more conciliatory. "He started giving some ground." Speaking of Le Duc Tho's "concessions," Kissinger noted that "on the first day he had reneged on nine of the twelve changes he had agreed to in November; he now gave back six." He also dropped an earlier demand that Saigon release Vietcong prisoners when Hanoi released American POWs. Yet, inexplicably, Kissinger concluded from all this that the December 7 meeting "marked the beginning of the real deadlock."[101]

In his memoirs, Nixon also declared that "very little was accomplished" at the December 7 meeting.[102] Yet, something must have come out of it or a recess would have been called, according to the president's instructions of the day before. Instead, the meetings continued.

Kissinger's meetings of December 8 and 9 now brought results, and the president, buoyed by the prospects, indicated in his cables "that he would prefer almost any agreement to a recess."[103] By the 9th, all differences had been resolved save one defining the DMZ in a way which kept open the legal justification for Hanoi's troop presence in the South. The next meeting was scheduled for Monday, December 11, and the president now allowed himself "to begin feeling optimistic about the possibility of having an agreement before Christmas."[104] As he put it:

For better or for worse, we are on a course now where we have no choice but to make the very best settlement that we can and then to do the best that we can to see that it is enforced.[105]

The president sought to obtain Soviet leverage on Hanoi and toward this end called Ambassador Dobrynin to request his government's assistance in persuading Hanoi to accept the November formulation on the DMZ. In order to give Moscow time to put pressure on Hanoi, the president sent a cable to Kissinger on December 10 instructing him to shift that day's meeting time from morning to late afternoon. At the Monday afternoon meeting, Kissinger was instructed to "hold tough on the DMZ issue. . . . If Moscow's assistance is evident, we may then find Hanoi caving."[106]

> If not . . . we must not break off the talks on Monday. In that event you should return for a new session hopefully as early as possible on Tuesday morning. . . . On Tuesday you should again enter the talks in a tough posture by which time Moscow's ultimate leverage should be evident if, in fact, they exercise it at all. If Le Duc Tho is still intransigent, you should then try our compromise as the final US concession. If even this fails, *the President . . . would even be willing to cave completely* with the hopes that we can still bring Thieu around.[107]

To summarize, the president's instructions to Kissinger were to hang tough on Monday. If no settlement was reached they were to meet again on Tuesday and, if necessary, cave in completely to Hanoi's demands, but *reach a settlement*. When Kissinger and Le Duc Tho met on Monday, the North Vietnamese leader toughened his position, making it clear that "he wanted no agreement, at least on this round." Nevertheless, as Kissinger reported to Washington, "It is not impossible that we could conclude the agreement tomorrow, but nothing in their behavior suggests any urgency and much in their manner suggests cock-sure insolence. . . ."[108] The president's reply of December 11 was an order to Kissinger "*to stay as long as there was any hope of a settlement*; to return for consultations if I judged the deadlock to be unbreakable; to recess but not to adjourn the talks; and to brief the press if he [Nixon] decided to resume bombing."[109]

President Nixon's position could hardly have been more consistent throughout the negotiations. Time and again he insisted that Kissinger negotiate a settlement, rejecting the bombing option that his national security adviser repeatedly urged upon him. The evidence for this view is overwhelming and conclusive through the November and December negotiating rounds—up to December 12. At this point the president did an abrupt one-hundred-and-eighty-degree turnabout. His cable to Kissinger for the meeting of December 12 "contradicted his instruction of the previous day to cave in as a last resort . . ."[110] He now instructed Kissinger:

Tell Le Duc Tho that in no circumstances would we make the wrong kind of settlement and that until there was an end to North Vietnamese intransigence there would be no further American concessions.[111]

What had happened? Nixon's turnaround occurred *before* the meeting of December 12, at which Le Duc Tho informed Kissinger that he would return to Hanoi two days hence. Thus, the reason for Nixon's reversal cannot lie in the negotiations themselves, but outside them. It was here, it seems, that the Watergate crisis intersected with Vietnam.

At the point when a settlement appeared to be within reach and for little evident reason discernible in the course of the negotiations themselves, the president suddenly reversed his position. Between December 10 and 11 he turned abruptly away from an insistence upon a settlement and acquiesced in Kissinger's demands that the United States break off the talks and commence a major bombing campaign against North Vietnam. Nixon's reversal cannot be explained in terms of a negotiating impasse, for Hanoi's stall, the reason given for the Christmas bombing, did not become plain until *after* the president's turnaround.

The author's conjecture is that at some point after the December 10 cable and prior to the president's cable to Kissinger for the December 12 meeting, Nixon was confronted (perhaps by the senior figures in the political establishment) with the evidence of his entrapment in a criminal obstruction of justice, and he was required to relinquish his authority over the Vietnam negotiations in particular and over further direction of foreign policy in general.[112] Whatever the explanation for Nixon's reversal, which can only be conjecture, there can be no doubt that it occurred at this point.

Indeed, what is also beyond doubt is Richard Nixon's withdrawal from any further authoritative participation in the foreign policy process once the decision to embark upon the Christmas bombing was made. This is true not only regarding Vietnam, but also in foreign policy in general. In what can fairly be described as a bloodless coup, Henry Kissinger assumed command of American foreign policy in late 1972 and immediately set a new strategic course for the United States.

Nixon makes no mention of the turnaround cable in his memoirs, which from this point onward contain little information regarding his conduct of United States foreign policy — itself remarkable, mute testimony to his removal from the decison-making process. Once the decision to embark upon the Christmas bombing was made, on December 14 in a meeting attended only by the president, Kissinger, and Haig and at which no records were kept,[113] Nixon abjured further involvement in the final scene of the Vietnam drama.

According to Seymour Hersh, the president "did not deal at all with the substantive issues of the peace agreement, nor did he discuss the negotiated compromises and the secret commitments at the end. He accepted Kissinger's account. . . ."[114] It is Hersh's view that Nixon's fall occurred in early 1973, although he is not specific. "Sometime in these first few months of 1973 . . . Nixon's active collaboration with Henry Kissinger came to an end."[115] It is doubtful that there ever was the "active collaboration" that Hersh suggests, but it is clear from the foregoing that Nixon's "substantive" role was finished by mid-December 1972.

The historian is struck by this extraordinary episode in American political history, in which the unelected, hired subordinate of the president of the United States successfully refused to execute policy instructions — not just on a single occasion, but over a period of months. It confounds all notions of the democratic process but confirms the hypothesis offered here of a fundamental division within the American leadership over national strategy, a cleavage which resulted in the defeat of a president and the assumption to power in a de facto sense of Henry Kissinger, who would become what can perhaps best be described as the first American shogun.

PART II

Detente and Transition: The Kissinger Shogunate, 1973–1976

It is characteristic of periods of upheaval that to those who live through them they appear as a series of haphazard events. Symptoms obscure basic issues and historical trends. The urgent tends to dominate the important. Too often goals are presented as abstract utopias, safe-havens from pressing events.

— Henry Kissinger, "Pacem in Terris," October 8, 1973

The world is extraordinarily different and more complex than the world we knew in 1950, and so are the problems confronting it. However, one striking parallel remains: Once again, as after World War II, we are at a watershed in history. We are living in a period which, in retrospect, is going to be seen either as a period of extraordinary creativity or a period when the international order began to come apart—politically, economically, morally. We are at one of those rare moments when, through a combination of circumstances and design, man is in a position to shape his future. Thus the central challenge before American foreign policy is to take advantage of this open moment in history.

— *United States Foreign Policy, An Overview*
Department of State, May 1975

If you act creatively you should be able to use crises to move the world towards the structural solutions that are necessary.

—Henry Kissinger, interview with Murray Marder
Washington Post, November 1, 1976

CHAPTER

6

War and Realignment, the Middle East, 1973

In early 1973, the United States began to unveil a bold and complex strategy designed to reshape the global order in a manner designed to arrest the adverse trends under way since the mid-sixties and preserve the preeminent position of the nation. The new course provided a definitive answer to the strategic question posed at the outset of the first Nixon administration—whether it would be possible to maintain the containment structure. The new strategy acknowledged that the old global order was beyond recapture and indicated that the United States was determined to take action before the continuing shifts in major power relationships proceeded too far to be remedied.

Under Henry Kissinger's direction, Washington adopted a new strategy comprised of two broad policy sets. One was the "tripolar" set, whose objective was to establish a new equilibrium with the two communist giants, the Soviet Union and the People's Republic of China. The other was the "trilateral" set which sought to reinforce the partnership with the allies in Western Europe and Japan.

Henry Kissinger in fact described the new strategy and United States objectives in a speech delivered late in 1973. Billed as a "year-end review," the speech was a remarkably candid admission that the United States was deeply involved in a broadly based effort to construct a new international order according to a clearly conceived and carefully developed design.

> By the time the second term of the President started, we faced an international situation in which the basic assumptions of the immediate post-war period had been substantially altered. The rigid hostility between the communist world and the non-communist world had been altered first by the divisions within the communist world itself and by the amelioration of relations between the Soviet Union and the United States, as well as the People's Republic of China and the United States.

> Europe and Japan had gained strength and political self-confidence. The economic system that had been created in the immediate post-war period had become fluid and was in need of redesigning. So the great task before this administration . . . has been to construct an international system based on a sense of justice so that its participants would have a stake in maintaining it; with a sufficient balance of power so that no nation or group of nations would be dependent entirely on the good will of its neighbors, and based on a sense of participation so that all nations could share in the positive aspirations.[1]

This was, Kissinger observed, "the basic architectural design," which involved several broad policy choices. These policy choices were: "detente" with Moscow and Beijing; continued "Atlantic" cooperation with an "emerging unified Europe"; development of a "new and mature partnership" with Japan, which "should be an integral part of the relationship we are also attempting to develop with Europe"; and a new approach to the Middle East, which posed "a number of profound issues" for the United States, transcending the region itself. Lastly, there was the international economic system, which "was in need of redesigning," a self-evident mandate in late 1973 as the world entered the early stages of the energy and monetary crises following the Yom Kippur War.

In retrospect, the means chosen to bring about the new international order Kissinger described were daring, devious, and strategically preemptive, but only partially successful. The central approach was to hedge Soviet power by engaging Moscow in a friendly and rewarding relationship while reshaping the geopolitical order in

Western Europe, the Middle East, and Asia. The main function of detente would be to buy the time necessary to effect the structural disengagement of American power from its forward position around the immediate Soviet periphery. Friendly relations with Moscow, it was hoped, would dissuade the Soviets from attempting to employ their growing military power to upset Washington's plans.

It was vitally important to convince Soviet leaders that they could not utilize strategic weapons in the same coercive manner that the United States had done in the fifties and sixties when Washington had held a decisive strategic weapons advantage. Presumably, the SALT process, even though it had not placed any limits on Moscow's strategic weapons buildup, had gone a considerable distance in achieving this objective by positing the notion that any use of nuclear weapons would be mutually destructive.

In any case, Kissinger sought to reinforce this idea in his year-end review. We do not accept, he said, that "detente can be used for military expansion or for threatening weaker countries, or for undermining our traditional friendships." Disavowing completely the concept of nuclear coercion, Kissinger declared that "no responsible statesman can base his policy on the constant threat of . . . [nuclear] holocaust."[2]

Furthermore, he went on, because what had occurred in the past twenty years was "a fundamental change in the international environment compared to any other previous period," there was, he said, quoting former President Eisenhower, "no longer any alternative to peace." Toward this end, we have made "a conscious effort to set up rules of conduct and to establish a certain interconnection of interests, and above all to establish communications between the top leaders . . . that makes it possible in times of crisis to reduce the danger of accident or miscalculation."

The "certain interconnection of interests" to which Kissinger alluded was, of course, a vastly enlarged and rewarding economic relationship between East and West. Indeed, East-West trade would skyrocket beginning in 1973, particularly Soviet and Eastern-bloc imports of grain, high technology, and credit. Even though the percentage of Western trade with the Soviet bloc would never exceed five percent of any Western nation's bilateral total trade volume and never more than three percent of United States total trade volume during this period, the dollar value of trade was, relatively speaking, extremely valuable to Moscow.

Kissinger's objective was to enmesh the Soviet Union and its allies in a web of beneficial relationships which, ideally, would incline them to forgo the struggle for power and geopolitical advantage and develop a commitment to maintaining the stability of the newly emerging order. At a minimum it was hoped that detente would buy sufficient time for the United States to adjust its own global position[3] and at a maximum evolve into a new noncontentious relationship with the Soviet Union which would be the fulcrum of stability on the Eurasian continent.

Washington attempted to reshape its position around the Soviet periphery in several ways, but two deliberate acts of omission stand out as decisive, one in Southeast Asia and the other in the Middle East. In Asia, refusal to uphold the provisions of the just-signed Paris Peace Agreements would lead to the defeat of South Vietnam and the emergence of a unified Vietnam under Hanoi. This change would transform the shape of mainland Asia, locking China firmly between the Soviet Union in the north and a powerful Soviet client state in the south.

In theory, this would leave Beijing with no alternative to close cooperation with if not reliance upon, the United States and would enable Washington from an offshore position to play off Beijing against Moscow and maintain a tripolar equilibrium. The advantage of the leverage gained from withdrawal was judged to outweigh the negative impact on national will and morale that would inevitably flow from the decision to accept defeat in Vietnam. (See chapter 9 for discussion of the tripolar set.)

In the Middle East a similar act of omission would set Egypt on course for war against Israel — a conflict whose outcome would transform the shape of the Middle East fully as much as American withdrawal from Vietnam would restructure Asia. The war, so long as the outcome was not an outright defeat for Egypt, would establish the basis for negotiation between the two nations and lead to Cairo's shift into the Western camp. This shift would transform the region by securing Israel's southern flank and strengthening its overall position. Thenceforth, Israel would no longer be faced with a two-front conflict situation, but could orient its defenses northward. Splitting of the Arab coalition, in turn, would undercut Soviet ability to increase pressure against the allies of the United States. Moscow would find itself shunted to the periphery as Washington became the chief power broker in the region.

The Middle East conflict would have consequences beyond the immediate region, affecting the Western alliance. The war would trigger a sharp rise in the price of petroleum *above that already scheduled by OPEC* for the fall of 1973. Theoretically, the resultant energy crisis would exert a braking effect upon the rapidly growing economies of the Western allies heavily dependent upon low-cost Middle East petroleum, but not on the economy of the United States, which was much less dependent upon Mideast imports. Because oil was priced in dollars the rise in energy costs would also strengthen the dollar's role in the international monetary system, undercutting the drift toward separate monetary blocs. The overall hoped-for effect was to strengthen the position of the United States within the Western alliance in terms of energy, finance, and trade and, ultimately, to bring the alliance itself into stable equilibrium. (See chapter 8 for discussion of the trilateral set.)

Ideally, if all went well, the new international order would see Western Europe and Japan strengthened militarily, even if accumulating economic wealth at a slower rate, but firmly linked in a "trilateral" relationship under the leadership of the United States. The trend toward alliance disintegration (as evinced by growing European unity and Japanese economic strength) would be moderated if not halted.

The new structure would also see the emergence of a "tripolar" order consisting of the United States, the Soviet Union, and the People's Republic of China, with the United States having friendly relations with both but in position to benefit from the adversary relationship that had characterized Sino-Soviet relations since the late fifties and which showed little sign of abating. Finally, the new international monetary system would include a heretofore unattainable automatic balance-of-payments adjustment mechanism which would in effect maintain equilibrium within the Western alliance and close off the neomercantilist accumulation strategy of the allies.

Like all things temporal, however, the new American strategy was beset with difficulties almost from the moment it was put into effect. Unexpected reactions by allies and adversaries forced early and continuous corrective action. Indeed, it would be fair to observe that serious miscalculations lay at the heart of each of the policy initiatives of which the new strategy was composed. Although part of the structural outcome sought by the United States was achieved, it occurred in an unexpected way and at very high cost.

The result was that, far from reestablishing American preeminence in a restructured global order, the years of the Kissinger Shogunate marked the low point in America's post–World War II stature. As will be analyzed below in some detail, Henry Kissinger, and the American leadership that supported him, miscalculated the impact of the Yom Kippur War on Israeli politics, the allies' reactions both to the war and to the energy crisis it exacerbated, the Chinese reaction to American withdrawal from Vietnam, and the Soviet reaction to the temptations offered by detente.

Impasse and Opportunity in the Middle East

The expulsion of Soviet advisers from Egypt in July of 1972 was the first step in Anwar Sadat's plan to put Cairo into a position from which — one way or another — he would be able to settle the conflict with Israel and get on with Egypt's modernization. Central to his calculations was the conclusion that continued dependence upon the Soviet Union for support would mean perpetuation of the "no war, no peace" condition that had obtained since 1967. As Sadat came to realize, the Soviet Union could not deliver the political solution he wished. Only the United States possessed sufficient leverage with Israel to offer even the prospect of a settlement.

Thus, Sadat's policy was to shift Egypt away from Moscow and toward the United States. The February 1971 offer to Israel of an interim settlement based upon a partial Israeli withdrawal from the Suez Canal, the agreement to seek a final settlement and willingness to sign a peace treaty, signaled the beginning of this shift. Although it was necessary to deny publicly Egypt's willingness to reach a separate peace with Israel, this was in fact what was being proposed, as all of the principals to the dispute understood. Sadat's reassurance to fellow Arabs was to establish an Arab federation consisting of Egypt, Syria, Libya, and the Sudan; but the shift of Egypt out of the Soviet orbit was apparent despite this, as Sadat also improved relations with Turkey, Iran, and several European and African states.

Moscow responded to Sadat's policy shift in two different ways. On the one hand, the Soviet Union sought to halt Egypt's drift, or at least to limit it, by insisting that Cairo enter into the friendship treaty of May 1971. The treaty marked out a reduced Soviet role in Egypt in return for a promise that Cairo would not join an anti-Soviet alliance. Sadat accepted the treaty, as he put it, "to allay the fears of Soviet leaders" and "to prove our good intentions."[4] On the other hand, Moscow moved to shore up its overall position in the region, particularly in Syria and Iraq, for implicit in Egypt's shift was the evolution of a de facto one-front conflict situation for Israel against Syria and Iraq, which would place those regimes increasingly at a disadvantage.

Thus, in early 1972 Moscow entered into an agreement with Syria to strengthen that country's defenses and into a friendship treaty with Iraq. The improvement of Moscow's position in these two countries did not imply improved cooperation between them. Long-standing antipathies kept Syrian-Iraqi relations cool, at best. Moscow also attempted to strengthen its position through increased arms deliveries, with some success in Somalia and the two Yemens. However, the Soviets suffered a severe setback in the Sudan, which, expelling Soviet advisers in the summer of 1971, promptly aligned itself in federation with Egypt.

Washington attempted to match Sadat's initiatives with a partial settlement proposal, yet another Rogers Plan, the third. The two-staged plan of July 1971 involved continuation of the cease-fire and an initial Israeli troop pullback from the canal in a two-year-long first stage. Israel was to withdraw twenty-five to forty miles from the canal, which would be dredged and then opened for the use of all nations. A token Egyptian military force of 750 men would be stationed on the east bank of the canal with a United Nations buffer force deployed between the two forces in the Sinai. Ultimately, after the October war, the initial stage of the Egyptian-Israeli settlement would look remarkably like this plan. At this point, however, the Israeli leadership balked, refusing to commit itself to a timetable (while privately demanding a ten-to-fifteen-*year* first stage) and flatly rejecting any Egyptian presence on the east bank.

Israeli intransigence blunted the American initiative. What had appeared to be a promising opening led instead to a refreezing of positions. Israel was unwilling to make the kind of strategic shift the United States urged. Paradoxical as it may seem, the optimum Israeli position was the *status quo*, in which a threat to its security guaranteed United States support and also restricted Washington's influence in the region. From the perspective of the Israeli leadership no other condition offered the same advantages. As Prime Minister Golda Meir put it in March of 1973, "We never had it so good."[5]

The United States, too, had been satisfied with this condition until four developments produced a new outlook. First was the failure to check Moscow's strategic weapons buildup, which led to the decision to change strategy. The shift away from containment required the restructuring of regional balances around the entire periphery of Soviet power to withstand anticipated Soviet pressure on weak points. Second was the emergence of Anwar Sadat himself, who pressed for resolution of the conflict with Israel even at the cost of a separate peace and potential Egyptian isolation in the Arab world. Third was the resolution of the Vietnam conflict, which no longer required blockage of the Suez Canal. Fourth were the growing fissures within the Western alliance as West Germany and Japan sought to parlay increased wealth into greater political influence at Washington's expense, including independent access to Middle East oil.

For the United States, therefore, Sadat's emergence and determined movement out of Moscow's orbit offered the opportunity of building a collective security structure on the basis of an Egyptian-Israeli rapprochement—if the Israeli leadership could be persuaded that such a shift was in its interests. The problem was that throughout Nixon's first term the United States would gain preliminary acquiescence only to have Israel retreat into intransigence, essentially on the grounds that the current situation was better than any alternative that implied trusting the Arabs.

Furthermore, an Egyptian-Israeli rapprochement would increase Washington's leverage within the region and on Israel as well, raising the possibility that at some future date Washington would find it beneficial to shift further toward the Arabs rather than to retain Israel as its primary influence vehicle in the Middle East. No number of reassurances or promises of support could alter this impression, which was, moreover, carried forcefully to the American leadership as treasonous by the American Jewish intellectual community. As Premier Meir herself put it in a speech to the Knesset on October 26, 1971, "Israel is not prepared to agree to political conditions that harm our security, even in return for promises of vital military equipment."[6]

As Israel's position hardened and relations with Washington became embittered, a similar development was occurring between Egypt and the Soviet Union. The central and continuing issue was Sadat's insistence that Moscow supply "decisive" weapons to Egypt for the battle with Israel. By "decisive" was meant such weapons as the MiG-23 tactical fighter, the SCUD surface-to-surface tactical missile, and the SAM air-defense system. By late 1971 it had become apparent, particularly after the Indo-Pakistani conflict, that Moscow would not provide decisive weapons to Egypt in time for action in 1971.[7] In early 1972, after his visit to Moscow, Sadat began to shift ground in an attempt to resolve the Israeli "problem" by either diplomacy or war. In either case, his objective was not to drive Israel into the sea (as was Asad's of Syria), but to recover the territories Egypt had lost in 1967.

Stressing the need for Arab self-sufficiency, Sadat made opening overtures to Saudi Arabia, the country with which it would be essential to have close relations if there were to be any hope for independent action.[8] The main sticking point in an improvement in relations with Saudi Arabia was Egypt's relationship with the Soviet Union. Thus, a readjustment of the Egyptian-Soviet relationship would serve multiple purposes. Not only would it remove any constraints that the Soviets could place on Sadat's war plans and simultaneously open the way to an improvement of relations with the United States, it would also open the treasury of King Faisal for the purchase of the arms necessary to carry forward plans for limited conflict. Even though the arms would ultimately come from the Soviets, censuring Moscow reassured Faisal that Sadat was in command of his own house and not in any way subservient to the Russians.

Sadat's establishment of "back channel" contacts with Washington in the spring of 1972 just prior to his expulsion of Soviet advisers ensured that Washington would be fully apprised of Egyptian expectations for an improvement in relations with the United States.[9] Following the ouster, Sadat sought to arrange a meeting between his own national security adviser, Hafez Ismail, and Henry Kissinger; but the United States side deferred any substantive contact until the presidential elections were over and the complex and time-consuming Vietnam negotiations had been completed. Thus, it was not until late in February 1973 that a meeting was held.

Sadat had charted his course carefully, but in a way which necessarily left his ultimate choices in the hands of others. In preparing for a move toward the United States he had demonstrated his independence of the Soviets without, however, burning his bridges to them. He had, for example, renewed Moscow's access to port facilities at Alexandria in December 1972.[10] Thus, if the shift to the United States failed to produce a negotiated solution, Sadat was prepared to force negotiations by military means. Nevertheless, Sadat's course would depend heavily upon the United States, whose response would be decisive.

By the time that the meeting between Sadat's national security adviser and Henry Kissinger took place in late February 1973, the issue of overall United States strategy had been resolved. Kissinger's views would prevail for the Middle East just as they had for Vietnam. President Nixon's preference for an early opening to Egypt, after which the United States would exert diplomatic pressure on Israel to accept an "interim settlement,"[11] would be shelved in favor of Kissinger's alternative. Kissinger rejected any approach requiring Israel voluntarily to relinquish territory won in battle. As he perceived it, "a strategic shift was in train" in the Middle East by the end of 1972 which opened up an opportunity for the United States to bring about "a reversal of alliances in the Arab world."[12]

Kissinger saw Sadat in a dilemma. An all-out attack on Israel would not succeed because the United States would not permit it, and the "mere disengagement of forces along the Suez Canal" was domestically unsupportable within Egypt. For Kissinger, it followed that "nothing could happen without our cooperation."[13] Indeed, he believed that Egypt "had no choice but to await the American diplomatic initiative."[14] That initiative, when it came in the February meetings between Kissinger and Ismail, was not the Nixon preference for opening diplomatic relations with Egypt followed by the exertion of political pressure on Israel for a settlement, but Kissinger's decidedly *un*diplomatic alternative.

The new American strategy pursued by Kissinger from early 1973 was to set Egypt on a course which Anwar Sadat was in any case prepared to undertake — limited war with Israel. The war would act as a catalyst for resolution of both the Middle East and Western alliance problems bedeviling the United States. The rejection of Nixon's "gradualist approach" to the reintegration of the Western alliance made a new approach necessary there, too. It had been the president's decision some two years earlier to attempt a gradual diversion of alliance resources from capital construction to current consumption. The gradual rise of petroleum prices, monetary devaluation, and demonetization, plus political pressure for greater allied defense spending, had had little perceptible effect on the neomercantilist accumulation strategies being pursued in Western Europe, particularly West Germany, and Japan. Now the Middle East-Western alliance connection would be tightened another notch.

As envisaged, the conflict in the Middle East would enable the United States to commence the restructuring of the regional balance based upon a separate peace between Egypt and Israel. Egypt would complete its shift into the Western camp with all of the benefits that shift would confer, and the process would transform Israel's strategic position from a two-front to a one-front conflict situation, breaking the Arab encirclement. The war would also precipitate a sharp rise in the price of petroleum, which, it was hoped, would at last bring about the desired slowdown in allied wealth accumulation as well as reinforce the political-economic role of the United States in both regions.

It was risky, of course. There was no guarantee that a limited war in the Middle East could be controlled and not explode into a superpower confrontation. There was no guarantee that if the conflict remained limited as planned the result would lead to a mutually satisfactory settlement between Egypt and Israel. There was no guarantee that a sharp rise in the price of oil would in fact achieve the desired results. Nor was there any guarantee that the United States could be insulated against the inflationary effects of an oil price explosion, or that the net result would be to improve the American position within the Western alliance.

On the other hand, the trends both in the Middle East and within the Western alliance, not to mention in the United States-Soviet strategic equation, had passed the point where the continuation of existing policy could hope to produce the desired results. Israeli intransigence, the changing power relationships within the world of oil, and allied strength were not only the obstacles to the achievement of American goals, but also the underlying reasons for action. The new approach, even though risky, had to be taken.

Washington Prepares for Structural Change

From late February 1973 onward, Kissinger and the American leadership initiated several steps, which together set the stage for the structural changes they hoped to effect in the Middle East and in the Western alliance. Washington would set Egypt irrevocably on course for war, prepare the nation to absorb the economic shocks of the conflict, offer an improved relationship to its Atlantic partners, attempt to shape Moscow's attitude, and deter any preemptive action on the part of Israel.

In several ways the new American strategy bore a vague, nearly inverse relationship to that pursued in the mid-fifties which led to the Suez crisis. The outcome then had been the restructuring of the regional balance under the Eisenhower Doctrine. The subsequent imposition of the petroleum import quota redirecting Mideast petroleum flows to Europe and Japan had undercut the Soviet petroleum offensive of that time, which had threatened to weaken the preeminent United States energy position in the Western alliance. The proximate cause then, as in the current instance, was the perceived shift in the strategic weapons balance in the Soviet Union's favor. Of course, in the former case the shift had failed to materialize, while in the current instance the shift was all too real.

The major differences between the conditions in the fifties and the current situation were that in the earlier period the principal threat to United States interests in both the Middle East and the alliance came from without—from the Soviet Union. Thus, in the fifties Washington's approach had been to split Egypt and Saudi Arabia, securing control over petroleum supplies and subsequently integrating the Western alliance based upon inexpensive energy.

In the current instance, the problem was more complicated, in that the threat to American interests came both from without and from within due to the growing independence of the allies. Thus, in 1973 the approach was to reintegrate Egypt into the Western camp in order to strengthen the region against Soviet pressures and to raise the cost of energy to the allies whose economic strength was producing fissures in the alliance.

The first step, as in 1956, was to nudge Egypt toward war. The opportunity came during the visit of Hafez Ismail, Sadat's national security adviser, to Washington in late February. Ismail had been invited for an official visit on February 23 after months of procrastination by the American side. He was received by the president and met with top State Department officials, but he did not meet with Kissinger or any of his staff during the official visit,[15] which was a cover for a more serious meeting.

The real purpose of Ismail's visit, to which the State Department was not made privy, was to meet secretly with Kissinger and a few of his trusted aides at a private home in the New York City suburbs, for a "full, private review of Egyptian-American relations."[16] It was an extraordinary procedure for a "review," to say the least. Moreover, it was a review which removed any hopes Sadat may have had that

Washington would attempt a diplomatic settlement, and it persuaded the Egyptian leader that war was the only course available to break the negotiating logjam with Israel.

Earlier in February, Sadat had reopened negotiations with the Soviets, sending the same Hafez Ismail and Egypt's war minister, Marshal Ali Ismail (no relation), on separate trips to Moscow, where they conveyed the nature of the predicament Sadat was preparing to pose for the Soviet Union. Sadat's envoys informed the Soviets of his intention to initiate another war against Israel barring a positive response from the United States, and of his expectation of Soviet support. Sadat undoubtedly made clear that failure to support Egypt would threaten the destruction of what influence the Soviet Union had left in the Middle East.

Moreover, Sadat's threat was credible. He possessed sufficient weaponry to begin a war whether Moscow agreed to supply additional arms or not.[17] Of course, as he understood, Egypt could not win such a war. But Moscow would be the bigger loser, for Syria would undoubtedly also be defeated under those circumstances; and the result would be the eradication of the Soviet position there and particularly of any hope of reopening the Suez Canal.[18]

Thus, if Moscow declined to help and the Arabs lost, the entire Soviet position in the region would be dealt an irreparable blow. On the other hand, if the Soviets did assist them and the Arabs still lost, at least the magnitude of defeat could be minimized and the Soviet overall position could be preserved, if not enhanced. In short, Moscow had no satisfactory option other than to support Sadat, and it would do so. However, the Soviets strove to manipulate both their support and Sadat's perception of the achievable before, during, and after the war in the hope of not only retaining the strong Soviet position in Syria, but also of maneuvering Egypt back into a position of dependence.

The fact was that the Soviet Union was not at all averse to a limited conflict that served larger purposes. The Brezhnev leadership would support a limited war whose minimum outcome would be to reopen the Suez Canal, an assiduously sought-after objective since its closure during the Six Day War. Beyond the however-small Arab victory such an outcome would represent, and beyond reinforcing Moscow's position in the region, reopening the canal would shorten and strengthen the Soviet supply line to Hanoi when that conflict resumed — as it surely would once the euphoria of the Paris agreements had dissipated and the United States had fully withdrawn its forces.

This, after all, had been the deeper purpose underlying the missile crisis along the canal in 1970—a purpose which had been frustrated by Nasser's death. In fact, it would be precisely the presence of Moscow's SAM air-defense system that would be the crucial arms element enabling Egyptian forces to cross the canal in the 1973 war by neutralizing Israel's air superiority.

Following Ismail's visit to Moscow, Brezhnev sent a message to Washington on February 18, setting out the substance of the talks with the Egyptian envoy and the Soviet position. In essence, Moscow would not countenance a separate peace between Egypt and Israel disguised as an interim settlement. An Egyptian-Israeli settlement was acceptable, Brezhnev said disingenuously, as the first phase of a comprehensive settlement "within a framework of a single plan" agreed upon in advance by all concerned parties.[19]

As Brezhnev knew very well, and as past experience had shown clearly, requiring a comprehensive agreement as a condition of a partial settlement in effect ruled out any diplomatic settlement at all, for it was extremely unlikely that the concerned parties would agree to "a single plan." The Soviet leader then concluded his message with the thinly veiled warning that there soon would be war in the Middle East:

> We have got an impression from our talks with Mr. Ismail that, if . . . no progress is reached toward [a] political solution . . . the Arabs can turn to the use of other possible means. . . .[20]

Thus, when Ismail arrived for his secret "review" with Kissinger, the United States national security adviser had a clear understanding of Moscow's and Sadat's positions and the possibilities contained in them. He knew, in other words, that Washington held the key to Sadat's decision for war or peace. If the United States decisively opposed a conflict, promising to undertake a strong diplomatic initiative, then Sadat would make no military move. He had no interest in a military conflict for its own sake, nor would he recklessly confront the United States.[21]

Contrary to what Sadat hoped for, a solution in fact that the president preferred, Kissinger declined to proffer an American diplomatic initiative. His tactic was later revealed by the Israeli side following Kissinger's visit to Tel Aviv after the war. During a conversation with Meir, Kissinger reportedly said:

> Do you remember . . . when I reported to you on my meeting with Hafez Ismail in Washington? What did I do in those conversations? I talked with him about the weather and every subject in the world just so we wouldn't get to the subject the minister thought most important. I played with him. I toyed with him. My aim was to gain time and postpone the serious stage for another month, another year. . . . Ismail told me several times that the present situation could not continue. He asked me whether the United States did not understand that if there weren't some [negotiated] agreement then there would be war.[22]

Sadat put Kissinger's rebuff much more diplomatically. He described the outcome of the Kissinger-Ismail meeting to be that "the United States regrettably could do nothing to help so long as we were the defeated party and Israel maintained her strategic superiority."[23] Nor can there be any doubt that Kissinger understood that Sadat would draw the appropriate conclusion from the refusal to undertake a diplomatic move. The fourth Arab-Israeli war became inevitable as a result of the meeting between Kissinger and Ismail in late February 1973.

In the course of his discussions, Kissinger had perceived the common ground in the positions of the interested parties. While all of the participants gave lip service to the ultimate objective of a comprehensive settlement, each recognized that the likely outcome would fall short of this. Indeed, all — including the Israelis[24] — had come to the position that an interim agreement which included disengagement along the Suez Canal as a first step toward a comprehensive settlement was a viable short-term solution to the existing impasse.

But it would take a war to clear away the debris of the past and establish the basis for negotiating the common position. By declining to undertake a diplomatic initiative, therefore, Kissinger had purposefully set Egypt on a course whose logical culmination would be war. Having set the wheels in motion toward conflict, American leaders now moved to put the nation into a position from which to exploit the coming crisis to advantage.

Economic Contention in the Alliance

Paralleling Kissinger's efforts on the Middle East, the administration under George Shultz as secretary of the treasury put an institutional mechanism in place which, it was hoped, would enable Washington to become competitive with the allies in international trade over the long term. Throughout the first term, administration officials had striven to persuade the alliance partners of the need to reform the monetary system which was miring the United States in an increasingly unsustainable and ever-enlarging deficit position.

The United States was simply losing its share of the world product at a rapid pace, while West Germany and Japan were surging forward, building positions of wealth through the accumulation of vast reserves. It was further evident that these two nations sought to translate growing wealth into greater political power and influence and were seemingly oblivious to the impact such a redistribution of power would have upon the structure of the alliance. EEC members were in the process of establishing an economic and monetary union which would form the financial infrastructure for future political union, while Japan continued its efforts to establish an independent energy base for itself through extensive bilateral agreements with oil-producing countries.

American efforts to slow down this process, President Nixon's "gradualist approach," had been judged a failure. The gradual increase in petroleum prices, efforts to induce increased defense spending, the revaluation of the dollar, and attempts to reform the monetary system had all failed to brake the allies' neomercantilist drive for wealth and power. Now the administration tried again. The previous year, in the fall of 1972, the United States had unexpectedly put forward a series of proposals for "orderly" reform of the international monetary regime, which would restore equilibrium and also eliminate what were considered to be unfair trade and investment arrangements.

Initially devised by Treasury Undersecretary Paul Volcker, the United States proposal was set forth by Secretary Shultz in a speech at the annual meeting of the International Monetary Fund on September 25, 1972. Shultz proposed the creation of an exchange-rate adjustment mechanism which would automatically keep the system in equilibrium and prevent any nation or group of nations from accumulating exorbitant surpluses or deficits.[25] The secretary singled out in particular the function of capital controls which, he said, should not be used to maintain an undervalued currency. Hinting at what was to come, Shultz noted that although most countries wished to maintain a fixed-rate system, some provision "needs to be made for countries which decide to float their currencies."

While public reaction to the American proposals was favorable, the immediate effect was to galvanize the Europeans into accelerating efforts toward union. When the enlarged EEC met in Paris a month later, on October 19–20, the delegates affirmed their determination "to strengthen the Community by establishing an economic and monetary union."[26] Although the target date for full union was set for the end of 1980, several steps were to be taken immediately. Viewing a fixed exchange-rate system as the "necessary basis for achieving monetary union," the European leaders agreed to set up a European monetary cooperation fund prior to April 1, 1973, in order to support stable parities among member currencies.[27]

Moreover, to enhance effective economic coordination among the member states, it was agreed to establish a European Development Fund by the end of 1973. A few weeks later, in November, when the newly formed Committee of Twenty charged to explore reform measures met at the International Monetary Fund, their determination to resist any substantive change in the international monetary system along the lines proposed by Secretary Shultz was apparent.

In sum, the United States had prodded the European leaders into taking what was perhaps a premature step toward union, thereby forfeiting any role they might have played in changing the monetary system by negotiation and opening the way for the United States to take the initiative. That intiative came during a major foreign exchange crisis in the second half of January 1973. It would afford the United States an opportunity to make fundamental changes: in the international monetary order, in the United States trade position, and in policy governing the importation of petroleum from the Middle East—all of which would have a profound impact on the structure of alliance relations thereafter, even up to the present time. In the short run, however, most of the changes would work to the *dis*advantage of the United States.

Pressure began to build on the lira in mid-January, prompting the Italian government to announce on January 20 the establishment of a two-tier foreign exchange market intended to discourage the outflow of capital.[28] The measure had the opposite effect. As funds immediately surged into Switzerland, Swiss authorities "panicked," allowing the franc to float three days later. Market jitters spread, and by early February it was evident that a major foreign exchange crisis was under way, now sharply focused upon West Germany and Japan.

During the first nine days of February the Bank of Japan purchased $1.1 billion to keep the yen from appreciating, then closed its foreign exchange market. During the same period, the Bundesbank purchased $5.9 billion and imposed additional exchange controls on capital inflow to prevent the mark from rising.[29] Rumor had it that the German authorities were about to float the mark. In an atmosphere of crisis, the European exchange markets closed on February 12.

The markets had been closed in an attempt to neutralize the impact of an imminent announcement from Washington, the result of a week-long series of secret negotiations between the United States and the allies. On February 6, in response to the initial outbreak of the crisis, Undersecretary Volcker had been sent first to Tokyo, then to Bonn, London, Rome, and Paris for an intense round of consultations, returning on February 12, the day the European markets closed.[30] That same evening, Secretary Shultz announced that since progress by the Committee of Twenty on monetary reform had been "too slow" the United States had decided to give it "renewed impetus." Accordingly, after consultations with allies, the United States was devaluing the dollar by 10 percent.

Furthermore, he stated that the president would shortly be sending to Congress a comprehensive set of proposals on trade legislation designed to improve the nation's trading position and declared that by the end of the following year, 1974, the United States would have phased out all capital controls. Finally, he announced that Japan had decided to let the yen float, which meant that the yen, the Swiss franc, the lira, and the Canadian dollar were then floating in relation to the American dollar.

Washington had sought to obtain agreement for a general float, but the Europeans led by Bonn demurred, preferring that the United States devalue unilaterally.[31] When the European exchange markets reopened on February 14, however, they were immediately deluged by large speculative capital flows which became so intense over the following two weeks that the markets were forced to close again on March 1. The West German authorities, perceiving an opportunity to bring about the early monetary unification of Western Europe under Bonn's aegis, proposed a joint float of all European currencies against the dollar, but neither Great Britain nor Italy consented.

The markets would remain closed until March 19 while renewed negotiations with the United States took place. On March 9, at a meeting in Paris of the United States, Japan, Canada, Sweden, Switzerland, and the nine EEC members, EEC finance ministers put several proposals to Secretary Shultz designed to test Washington's willingness to maintain the current monetary structure. They demanded that the United States intervene in the market to maintain the dollar, issue long-term Treasury bills, absorb Eurodollars, retain capital controls, and raise interest rates.

Although offering to be "cooperative," Secretary Shultz "politely rejected" each demand.[32] With the ball now squarely in the European court, it was announced two days later, on March 11, that six of the nine—West Germany, France, Belgium, Luxembourg, the Netherlands, and Denmark—would allow their currencies to float jointly against the dollar. Norway and Sweden shortly joined them. On the surface, it appeared that the way had been cleared for a major step toward the establishment of West European monetary union; but these prospects were fleeting and would be dashed with the onset of the oil crisis in October. Nevertheless, by the middle of March 1973 an historic development had occurred. Japan, Canada, the United States, and most of Europe were in a floating regime. Declared to be temporary until monetary reform could be worked out, floating would in fact become the norm, but not in the manner expected.

Step two occurred on April 10, when the president submitted to Congress sweeping trade legislation which would give him the power to conclude trade agreements, eliminate tariffs, remove non-tariff barriers, grant export preferences to underdeveloped countries, and grant most-favored-nation status. It also authorized him to retaliate against unfair trade practices and levy trade restrictions, including import surcharges, if deemed desirable.

The new trade bill signaled the clear intention of the United States to compete seriously with the Europeans and the Japanese in the world market, a significant shift from the basic inward orientation of past American economic activity. American trade negotiators were enjoined "to obtain full reciprocity and equal competitive opportunities for U.S. commerce." The House Finance Committee declared in reporting the bill that

the United States can no longer afford to stand by and expose its markets, while other nations shelter their economies—often in violation of international agreements — with . . . a host of other practices which effectively discriminate against U.S. trade and production.[33]

Passage of the trade act was delayed by almost two years, however, as the bill stalled in Congress over the issue of granting most-favored-nation status to the Soviet Union, which would have opened the way for extension of sizable credits to Moscow. Passage was delayed by the introduction of an amendment by Senator Henry Jackson barring United States trade concessions and most-favored-nation status to the Soviet Union until it permitted free emigration of its Jewish citizens.[34] A compromise was eventually reached in October 1974 whereby the president was empowered to issue an eighteen-month waiver of restriction after he had received assurances from Moscow that it would move "substantially to free emigration."[35] The bill passed on December 20, 1974, and was signed into law on January 3, 1975.

The third policy change, regarding the importation of Mideast petroleum, came in mid-April. It provided for the complete removal of quotas, which had been placed on the importation of foreign oil into the United States in 1959. There had been some relaxation of the terms of the quotas beginning in 1970 in conjunction with Nixon's gradualist efforts to increase pressure on the allies. Now, on April 18, they were removed entirely.

In world oil, as discussed in the previous chapter, by the end of 1972 not only was the nature of the relationship between the oil companies and the producing countries undergoing fundamental change, the market itself had begun to tighten markedly in the course of the year as a function of changing supply and demand factors. In the course of 1972 world economic growth and energy demand were greater than they had been forecast to be. At the same time energy production in both petroleum and non-petroleum fuels (such as coal and nuclear energy) was much less than projected.

Libya, Kuwait, and Venezuela had cut back petroleum production.[36] Oil from Alaska, scheduled to come onstream in 1972 or 1973, was blocked by environmental opposition (until 1974); and crude oil production in the United States itself had peaked in 1970 and begun to fall. In 1970, the United States had produced 9.6 million barrels per day. By 1973, production had dipped to 9.2 million barrels per day, which, although a small decrease in itself, was almost a million barrels per day below the 1970 projections for 1973.[37] These supply and demand factors produced a growing crunch on petroleum supplies that became increasingly serious by the third quarter of 1972. Then tanker freight rates, refined product prices, and spot crude prices — the main market indicators — began to rise and continued to climb through 1973.

By the spring of 1973, then, the administration had put in place a mechanism which would enable Washington to exploit the coming crisis in the alliance that the Mideast war would precipitate. The crisis, it must be stressed, was coming in any event, as the United States and its allies competed more and more aggressively for international trade advantage and energy supplies. The war would advance the timing of the crisis, presumably before the allies were prepared to deal with it.

Moving to generalized floating, in which the international monetary system remained on a de facto dollar standard, left the United States in effective control of the level of financial liquidity yet in a position of exchange-rate flexibility. The fixed exchange-rate system of Bretton Woods did not possess sufficient flexibility to expand liquidity fast enough beyond that already present in the Eurodollar market. The "dollar overhang" in the Eurodollar market did contain sufficient liquidity to accommodate an initial spike in demand for greater liquidity — which a jump in oil prices would produce — but it was not adequate for the long run.[38]

Removal of capital controls by the end of 1974 would also facilitate the recycling of the very large petrodollar holdings the oil-producing countries would be accumulating. Theoretically, the float would cushion any exchange-rate disruption generated by rapid oil price increases, insulating the United States. It would also temper the inflationary impact of higher prices. The float would have other effects as well, such as derailing the move toward a European monetary system, even though at the outset it appeared to facilitate union. Finally, the float established an automatic adjustment mechanism for smoothing out exchange-rate differentials which the allies appeared to have manipulated to their advantage by artificially depressing their currencies in relation to the dollar.

The removal of oil import quotas enabled the United States to build a substantial position in the world petroleum market as an importer and gave Washington considerable leverage in placing upward pressure on price and/ or maintaining price levels. The larger United States market position reduced the availability of petroleum, the more so as supply tightened. Indeed, until the Arab oil embargo in October 1973, the United States imported 6.3 million barrels of oil per day, an increase of 1.6 million barrels per day over the 1972 rate of 4.7 million barrels.[39] Of the total, the United States imported 820,000 barrels per day from the Middle East, or roughly 13 percent of imports. The vast majority of imports, 3.9 million barrels per day, continued to come from the Western Hemisphere—Canada, Venezuela, and Mexico.[40]

Strangely, even as the market tightened, production increased. Aramco, for example, increased Saudi Arabian output from 6 million barrels per day in late 1972 to 9 million barrels per day in September 1973; and the Aramco board had approved plans to expand Saudi capacity to 13.4 million barrels per day by 1976 and to 20 million barrels per day by 1983.[41] Comparing the first three quarters of 1972 with the first three quarters of 1973, Saudi Arabia had increased its production by 36 percent, Qatar by 31 percent, and Abu Dhabi by 30 percent.[42] Even the non-Arab producers Iran and Nigeria increased output in 1973. In other words, correctly anticipating the outbreak of hostilities, the oil-producing countries—spurred on by the oil companies—increased their production rates sufficiently to offset the inevitable dislocation that would accompany another conflict.

Indeed, the word had already gotten around by early May. On May 3, King Faisal in a meeting with Frank Jungers, president of Aramco, urged the oil chief to exert pressure on the United States government to disavow Israel, whose policies "were on the verge of having American interests thrown out of the area." The king's adviser, Kamal Adham, was more to the point. Sadat, he said, "would have to 'embark on some sort of hostilities' in order to marshal American opinion to press for a Middle East settlement. 'I knew he meant war,' said Jungers later, 'the king liked to give signals.' Jungers quickly passed on the warning to Exxon and Co. in New York and California."[43] It would seem that the coming war in the Middle East was one of the worst-kept secrets in recent history.

CHAPTER

7

Toward October and Yom Kippur

Once the strategic decisions had been made, the task of diplomacy was to keep all parties on course. From the spring until the outbreak of the war, Kissinger personally strove to keep the Western allies, the Soviets, and the Israelis on track. Each presented a special problem. The Western allies were continuing to develop an independent position by pressing forward with plans for European unity; the Soviets were signaling increasing doubts about the benefits to be gained from supporting a limited conflict in the region and were seeking alternatives; and the top Israeli leadership was under growing pressure from its military to execute a preemptive attack against Egypt and Syria as they openly positioned forces for the battle.

Kissinger's tactics were (1) to keep the allies off balance by a formal effort to renegotiate the terms of the Atlantic alliance, (2) to turn a deaf ear to Soviet rumblings regarding the growing prospect for conflict and Moscow's interest in a superpower condominium, and (3) to sternly command the Israeli leadership to absorb the first blow. Kissinger was reported to have said in response to friends' queries about the American role in the coming conflict, "I can't do anything until I have all the strings in my hand, and I won't have them in my hand until there is a crisis."[1]

It was obvious that the impact of detente upon the Western alliance would be to accelerate already long-developing centrifugal tendencies propelled by the growth of allied economic power. As

Washington improved relations with Moscow, the allies, particularly Bonn, sought to do likewise. In an era of detente and nuclear parity the nations of Western Europe sought to enhance their security by improving relations with the East. As Kissinger saw it,

> Nuclear parity would erode the relevance of American protection and Europe's conventional inferiority would dictate a "political" solution — an elegant phrase for accommodation to Soviet power. This might be camouflaged as closer East-West economic relations, but insofar as these worked they would also increase Western Europe's dependence on Moscow.[2]

This was the self-evident and well-understood contradiction between the "tripolar" and "trilateral" concepts. It was also clear that mere pleas for Atlantic unity would not head off this development. Thus, in the context of the American strategic decision to employ the coming crisis in the Middle East as one means of reintegrating the Western alliance, the administration's — and particularly Kissinger's — efforts to promote the renegotiation of the Atlantic charter in a proposed "year of Europe" take on the character of a delaying action whose objective was to forestall any West European initiatives until the United States was ready to act. As Kissinger put it, "We sought to discourage the Europeans from unilateral initiatives to Moscow by demonstrating that in any competition for better relations with Moscow, America had the stronger hand."[3]

The administration's tactic was to attempt to delay the European movement toward unity as well as head off the indiscriminate rush to development of relations with the East — both of which Washington viewed as weakening the alliance — by proposing to renegotiate the Atlantic partnership. In the process, the United States hoped to play off one alliance partner against another to achieve the desired end, as it had done successfuly in the past. Though publicly proclaiming support for European unity, the United States had no interest — at least not yet — in promoting the actual emergence of a unified and independent Western Europe, which would simply be a major competitor on the global scene.

Kissinger initiated the United States plan with an address titled "1973: Year of Europe" before the annual meeting of the Associated Press editors in New York on April 23, 1973. Kissinger declared that the "era that was shaped by decisions of a generation ago is ending.

The success of those policies has produced new realities that require new approaches."[4] These new realities included Western Europe's recovery and movement toward "economic unification," as well as the shift in the strategic military balance from American preponderance to near equality, which demanded "a new understanding of the requirements of our common security."

Japan, too, had emerged as a major power center, which meant that in many ways "Atlantic" solutions "must include Japan." Although the world was entering a period of relaxation of tensions "new assertions of national identity and national rivalry" were becoming visible. Finally, he said, new problems were also arising which were unforeseen a generation ago, such as the need for "insuring the supply of energy for industrialized nations."

Kissinger proposed that the Atlantic partners work out an economic, military, and diplomatic blueprint of a new Atlantic charter "by the time the president travels to Europe toward the end of the year." Economically, he noted, there had been "a sense of rivalry in international monetary relations." In trade, the European nations seemed to be moving toward "a closed trading system embracing the European Community and a growing number of other nations in Europe, the Mediterranean, and Africa . . . at the expense of the United States and other nations which are excluded." And in agriculture, the United States was "particularly concerned that Community protective policies may restrict access for our products." In short, the secretary averred, "A new equilibrium must be achieved in trade and monetary relations."

Defense was another area of concern. Under conditions of nuclear parity the previous strategy of massive retaliation simply invited mutual suicide. Thus, flexible response had become "central to a rational strategy and crucial to the maintenance of peace." But the requirements of flexibility were "complex and expensive," and while the allies were committed to flexible response "in principle" a great deal remained to be accomplished "to give reality to the goal." The United States expected, he said, "from each ally a fair share of the common effort for the common defense."

Finally, it was crucial, he said, to establish common objectives and restore mutual confidence during the current period of transition. Once basic agreement on common goals was reached it would become possible to maintain the momentum of detente along the desired course. Coming to the heart of his speech, Kissinger referred to "America's contribution," declaring that the United States was prepared to work cooperatively on new common problems faced by the alliance, such as energy.

> Energy . . . raises the challenging issues of assurance of supply, impact of oil revenues on international currency stability, the nature of common political and strategic interests, and long-range relations of oil-consuming to oil-producing countries. This could be an area of competition; it should be an area of collaboration.[5]

In these few sentences, Kissinger had laid before his audience the stark outline of the crisis that would soon overtake and engulf United States-alliance relations.

The virtually universal response from Europe and Japan was to avoid any substantive reply, let alone subscription to Kissinger's proposals. Worse, as weeks passed, by mid-year the so-called Euro-American dialogue increasingly took on the character of an adversary proceeding.[6] In an unprecedented shift the EEC determined that the Community would deal with the United States on this matter through its chairman, curtailing Washington's leverage, rather than allowing the United States the traditional luxury of private negotiation with each member.

Furthermore, a dialogue with Washington would commence only after the European alliance partners had drafted a unified position. Thus, if Kissinger had hoped to utilize the "Year of Europe" speech to forestall movement toward European unity, initially at least it had the opposite effect, as the alliance partners moved closer together in an effort to deal with the United States with one voice—at least on this subject. At the same time they continued to develop cooperative ties with the Soviet Union.

While alliance relations curdled into acrimony, Kissinger was forced also to deal with a Soviet leader who was becoming increasingly restive. Brezhnev began to fear that the conflict he had agreed to underwrite would not bring the expected return, and might even boomerang. His discomfort, however, offered Kissinger an opportunity to take out insurance against the possibility that the coming conflict would spiral out of control. This was the Agreement on the Prevention of Nuclear War, which was signed on June 22, the next to last day of the Nixon-Brezhnev summit.

The agreement, which had been under negotiation since Kissinger's April 1972 trip to Moscow, was far more important at the time than the "bland set of principles" Kissinger called it in his memoirs.[7] It was certainly true that the Prevention of Nuclear War Agreement was far less than the agreement on no first use of nuclear weapons which Moscow wanted. But when analyzed in the context of mid-1973 and the secretary's preoccupation with the coming conflict in the Middle East, the Prevention of Nuclear War Agreement takes on an altogether different significance.

Indeed, if Kissinger had sought to gain prior Soviet agreement to ensure that the coming conflict would not escalate into a superpower confrontation, he could not have produced a better-worded document. The two countries agreed "to remove the danger of nuclear war and of the use of nuclear weapons"; "to prevent the development of situations capable of causing a dangerous exacerbation of their relations"; "to avoid military confrontations"; "to exclude the outbreak of nuclear war between them and between either of the Parties and other countries."[8]

Further, it was stipulated that if after all "the risk of a nuclear conflict" arose, then the two powers "shall immediately enter into urgent consultations with each other and make every effort to avert this risk." Finally, the two parties emphasized that nothing in the agreement impaired the right of individual or collective self-defense under the UN Charter's provisions, or the obligations of either party "toward its allies or other countries."

Despite the last caveat regarding each power's "obligations" to its allies, the agreement reeked of superpower condominium. Indeed, NATO allies, especially the French, immediately and persistently criticized the United States on these grounds. Nor were allied concerns mitigated by the fact that Kissinger turned for assistance in drafting the agreement to the British Foreign Office, rather than to the U.S. State Department, which was kept completely ignorant of the agreement until Brezhnev's arrival.[9]

But Kissinger was walking a fine line. Clearly, allied concerns were well founded. The agreement did smack of great-power condominium, despite all his attempts to deny it. The point was that Kissinger needed to build as close a relationship with Brezhnev as was feasible to avert any possibility that the coming war in the Middle East could escalate into a superpower crisis. Therefore he was willing to run the risk of allied criticism in order to achieve a larger, more important end.

Once the conflict was over and American objectives had been met, the agreement, having served its purpose, would be allowed to fade quietly like the Cheshire Cat's grin. This explains Kissinger's retrospective dismissal of it as not worth the effort. But the enormous amount of time, secrecy, and manipulation of the Soviet leadership over a period of many months all belie that evaluation.

Brezhnev's concerns about the Middle East (and China),[10] perhaps generated by Nixon's growing political troubles, led him to attempt an unprecedented maneuver on the last night of the summit during Brezhnev's stay at the Western White House in San Clemente. In a late-night meeting abruptly demanded by Brezhnev after both sides had retired for the night, the Soviet leader attempted to browbeat Nixon into accepting a "secret deal" which would be the basis for an imposed Middle East settlement.[11] But the terms of the proposed secret deal were the standard Arab fare of Israeli withdrawal from the canal to the 1967 borders in return for an end to the state of belligerency. Final peace, however, would not occur until completion of a satisfactory negotiation with the Palestinians.

Brezhnev, as Kissinger noted, in typical Russian fashion "wanted to bulldoze us into solving his dilemmas without paying any price. At a minimum he sought to build a record for shifting the onus of a deadlock onto us and to prevent further erosion of the Soviet position in the Arab world."[12] Did the Soviet leader also believe that Nixon was vulnerable to pressure because of his visibly weakening domestic position? Certainly, he understood that Israel was militarily stronger and that any Arab-Israeli conflict contained the high probability of Arab defeat, Soviet embarrassment, perhaps even geopolitical setback or superpower confrontation, despite the just-signed PNW Agreement. Or was Brezhnev suggesting that there was a price the United States would have to pay in advance? Whatever the deeper purposes behind the late-night harangue, part of the "price" soon became evident.

Moscow, too, had been preparing for the coming conflict by consolidating its positions along the northern tier. Guarding against the worst case of an Egyptian shift into the Western camp, Moscow was channeling a larger proportion of its military supplies to Syria and Iraq than to Egypt, so that regardless of the outcome the Soviet northern tier position in the region would remain intact. In that connection occurred the relatively bloodless overthrow of King Zahir in Afghanistan by his cousin, brother-in-law, and former prime minister (1953–1963), Prince Mohammed Daoud, on July 17, 1973.

Daoud, whom the king had ousted ten years earlier, had for over a year been discussing plans for a coup d'etat with various opposition elements, including the Afghan military (he had once commanded the central forces garrison) and members of the Afghan Communist party, the People's Democratic Party of Afghanistan, as it was officially known.[13] It was natural for Daoud to seek the support of the Soviet Union for his plans, since as prime minister in the fifties he had established the Soviet-Afghan relationship and had maintained close ties to Moscow ever since.

On an undertaking of a magnitude involving the overthrow of a monarchy it is inconceivable that Daoud would act entirely on his own with the meager resources at his disposal unless he could be assured of outside support. Soviet encouragement, if not subtle, covert support, was thus essential. In any case, Daoud received the full backing of the Afghan Communist party, whose leaders he rewarded immediately upon taking power with key posts in the newly proclaimed Republic of Afghanistan.[14] Moscow officially recognized the new regime two days after the coup and quickly established a large and active military assistance program.

From the Soviet perspective, the change of regime in Kabul offered the possibility of exercising leverage in two directions in the future — toward Pakistan and, of course, toward Iran. For the moment, the Soviet hold on the northern tier appeared sufficiently firm to withstand the shock of the approaching conflict. The Soviet leadership may well have calculated that the United States would not take any forceful counteraction over Afghanistan for fear of upsetting its larger Middle East prospects. There can be little question that the coup in Kabul was a blow to American intersts, for Washington had quietly supported the king's independent stance for the decade since Daoud's ouster in 1963.

For Kissinger finally there was the most difficult task of all — deterring Israel from taking preemptive action against the Arabs as they positioned their forces for the attack. The evidence that war was approaching was overwhelming, as all commentators have noted, but it does not follow that the failure to anticipate its outbreak was a political failure to properly evaluate accurate intelligence.[15] The evidence is that both American and Israeli political leaders interpreted the intelligence all too well, but they decided — on the insistence of the United States — that Israel must accept the first blow. After the outbreak of the war it was Henry Kissinger who set forth the interpretation that the failure to anticipate the Arab attack was a failure of the political leadership to evaluate the evidence correctly, a view that was accepted by the Meir government—after some initial confusion and an attempt to exculpate themselves.[16]

The Kissinger-Ismail "review" of late February made it plain to Sadat that there would be no American diplomatic initiative, and it was from that point that he commenced all-out preparations for war. His first step was to secure the necessary arms. Thus, immediately following Ismail's meeting with Kissinger, Sadat sent him directly to Moscow, where, during a week's stay from February 26 to March 2, Ismail concluded "the largest arms package ever negotiated for the Middle East."[17] Sadat described the arms deal as "a turning point"—a view which, then at any rate, Moscow appeared to share. The communiqué issued afterward noted Soviet support for the Arabs' "right to use 'any' means to liberate their lands," although as the year wore on the Soviet media vacillated between the "any means" formula and exhortations for a peaceful resolution. Moscow also supplied Egypt with every principal category of weapon requested (except for the MiG-23), including nuclear-capable SCUD surface-to-surface missiles, which were delivered only after the United States-Soviet June summit.[18]

Negotiation of the arms agreement, which was not a closely held secret, opened the way for the development of a war plan. On March 26, Sadat announced to the Egyptian National Assembly that "the stage of total confrontation has become inevitable, and we are entering it whether we like it or not. The military situation must be made to move, with all the sacrifices that this entails."[19] A few days later, in an interview with then *Newsweek* columnist Arnaud de Borchgrave, Sadat made essentially the same statement to the world.[20]

Planning with Syria began in early April, and within three months, on July 2, Syria's foreign minister announced while in Cairo that the two countries had "developed a joint Middle Eastern policy."[21] The Cairo-Damascus reconciliation (relations had been strained since the 1967 war) enabled rapid progress thereafter toward Arab unity and consensus on war aims, as Jordan and Iraq were brought into the planning process. In August, Saudi Arabia, which had pledged privately to underwrite Egyptian arms purchases earlier, now publicly backed Sadat while at the same time linking the "oil weapon" to any Middle East settlement.[22] In September, Egypt and Syria reestablished formal diplomatic relations with Jordan (broken since

March of the previous year over King Hussein's proposal for a plebiscite on the West Bank).

If the announcement in July of Egypt and Syria's decision to pursue a joint policy was not sufficiently alarming, the numerous tactical indicators signaling Arab intentions and increased capabilities could not have been, and were not, missed or ignored.[23] Most serious was intelligence relating to Soviet delivery in July and August of SAM 2, 3, and 6 systems to Syria and Egypt — the last a new mobile SAM which constituted 60 percent of the total force.[24] The SAM system, of course, was the crucial combat element enabling the decision to go to war, but Israeli planners had been evaluating the military tactic of using SAMs as a protective umbrella for ground force advance since the abortive 1970 attempt.[25]

As we have seen, the Israeli leadership was reluctant in the extreme to accept any change in the status quo, and it required the greatest pressure that Kissinger could exert to keep the Meir government from breaking the understanding to accept the first blow from the Arabs. Kissinger's efforts became particularly exhaustive in September as Arab war preparations intensified. Kissinger demanded — and the top Israeli leadership, specifically Meir and Dayan, eventually and very reluctantly acquiesced — that Israel would in fact accept the first blow in the coming war.

The Kalb brothers described a typical encounter in their biography of Kissinger:

> Kissinger's warning was not new. It had been his constant refrain for months. Shalev [Israel's chargé in Washington] knew it by heart. So did Ambassador Dinitz, who was then in Israel to attend his father's funeral. "Don't ever start the war," Kissinger would admonish them. "Don't ever preempt!" He would then forecast absolute disaster if Israel ignored his counsel. "If you fire the first shot, you won't have a dogcatcher in this country supporting you. You won't have presidential support. You'll be alone, all alone. We wouldn't be able to help you. Don't preempt." It was the kind of warning no Israeli leader could ignore. Shalev assured Kissinger that Israel was not planning any preemptive action. Mrs. Meir had given her word.[26]

The United States ambassador to Tel Aviv, Kenneth Keating, was also instructed to drive home the same point more explicitly. In discussion with Prime Minister Meir on the eve of the conflict, he declared: "If Israel refrained from a preemptive strike, allowing the Arabs to provide irrefutable proof that *they* were the aggressors . . . then America would feel morally obliged to help."[27] Despite great pressure from within the Israeli government, especially from Chief of Staff David Elazar and others in military intelligence who urged full mobilization and a preemptive strike, Prime Minister Meir held fast and braced for the attack.[28]

Yom Kippur: Soviet and American Objectives

Moscow knew that a war was coming in the Middle East because it had agreed to supply the hardware for it to happen and because Soviet military advisers were assisting in Arab preparations. The evidence is equally persuasive that the Soviet leadership did not know precisely when war would break out, because Sadat did not trust the Russians and feared that they would somehow attempt to spoil his plans. His fears were well grounded, for Moscow's interests were only partially congruent with Sadat's.

Clearly, the Soviet Union had little choice but to support the Arabs, if only to protect its own interests, once they had determined to embark upon another war. Moscow hoped to profit from the conflict by regaining access to the Suez Canal, which would serve larger ends; but it was also true that Arab success would very likely work to the disadvantage of the Soviet Union by establishing the basis for a negotiated settlement between Egypt and Israel, which Moscow obviously did not favor.

Soviet strategy was quite complex and probably unrealizable in its entirety because the larger trends in the region were negative and because Moscow's hand was not strong enough to turn the trends to advantage. Soviet leaders had assessed the subtle changes that were taking place in the region, the tenuousness of Moscow's relationship with Egypt, and the gradual United States diplomatic shift to a central position. The implications were plain. If the coming conflict opened the door to a negotiated settlement, the United States would use its broker position to realign the region, drawing Egypt into the Western camp and breaking the Arab encirclement of Israel.

Moreover, the signs that Sadat was willing if not determined to make such a shift were also clear. Thus, Moscow's main objective would be to attempt to play the coming crisis in such a way that the Middle East would remain polarized, an outcome which would defeat both Washington's and Cairo's plans (though, ironically, it would support Tel Aviv's). Fundamentally, Moscow sought to drive the United States off the middle position and block any avenue Egypt might have for shifting out of its orbit. This, of course, risked possible Egyptian defeat as well as confrontation with Washington and tends to explain, at least in part, Soviet tentativeness.

On the other hand, Moscow also hoped at a minimum to regain access to the Suez Canal. After all, this was a basic objective which Moscow had sought since the 1967 war and which was nearly attempted in 1970. But this required an Egyptian victory—at least to the extent of Egypt's being able to cross and maintain a force on the east bank of the canal. Moscow's dilemma was that a limited victory—besides being the minimum condition for the Soviet Union—would also open the door to a negotiated settlement with Israel, which the Soviets opposed.

The ideal solution from Moscow's point of view would be a limited Egyptian victory which recovered the canal but also repolarized Middle East politics (and brought Sadat's replacement by a more responsive leader), an outcome that could only be achieved by either demonstrating American duplicity à la 1967, or by prodding Washington prematurely into the full backing of Israel against the Arabs. Kissinger put it this way:

> The likelihood . . . is that the Kremlin believed that its interests were served whatever happened. If the Arabs did well, the credit would go to Soviet arms and Soviet support. If they did poorly, Moscow thought it could emerge, as in 1967, the champion of the Arab cause; the consequent radicalization of the Arabs would strengthen Soviet friends and perhaps even get rid of Egypt's troublesome Sadat. . . .[29]

As it turned out, of course, Moscow would fail to repolarize the region, though it would regain access to the canal; but the search for both results explains the course of Soviet policy during and indeed prior to the conflict.

American strategy, too, was to use the conflict for larger purposes, to bring about a fundamental restructuring of the region based on an Egyptian-Israeli settlement and to begin the process of reintegrating the Western alliance. Any negotiated settlement between Egypt and Israel required that Cairo shed the image of the defeated party by achieving at least a limited victory against Israel, which, however, would be impossible if Israel preempted and destroyed Egypt's forces before they could mount a credible challenge. It was thus absolutely necessary that Israel accept the first blow to give Cairo the opportunity to cross the canal — an achievement which could be represented as both a military victory and a basis for negotiation of an equitable political settlement.

A negotiated settlement, in turn, was dependent upon Washington's maintenance of a position of credibility to both sides in order to act as broker. The optimum outcome for Washington therefore was one in which Israel carried on the conflict without any major infusion of military assistance from the United States. If resupply became necessary it could only begin after the Soviet Union had begun to resupply the Arabs and thus occur in the context of both superpowers' providing aid to their respective clients. Nevertheless, even then, resupply had to remain limited and delayed as long as possible to prevent an outright Egyptian defeat, an event which would only have defeated United States objectives, too. That is why Washington's major resupply of Israeli forces came after and not during the war.[30]

To maintain the appearance of impartiality, the United States could not be seen to be providing Israel with the weapons necessary to bring about the outright defeat of Egypt. Obviously, the identification with Israel as a function of full and early resupply would seriously compromise any credibility the United States could hope to have with the Arabs, but it also worked the other way around. The same reasoning applied to the other extreme possibility, a major Israeli defeat. The United States would not allow an Israeli defeat by Soviet arms in any case, but this was the least likely outcome. Kissinger puts it succinctly:

> Once war had started, it was plain that the diplomatic stalemate would be broken. But it would not be easy. If Israel won overwhelmingly — as we first expected — we had to avoid becoming the focal point of all Arab resentments. We had to keep the Soviet Union from emerging as the Arabs' savior, which it could do either by pretending that its bluster stopped the Israeli advance or by involving itself directly in the war. If the

unexpected happened and Israel was in difficulty, we would have to do what was necessary to save it. We could not permit Soviet clients to defeat a traditional friend. But once having demonstrated the futility of the military option, we would then have to use this to give impetus to the search for peace. In sum, we had the opportunity to dominate events; but we ran the risk of becoming the butt of every controversy.[31]

Sadat's suspicions of both Moscow and Damascus led him to adopt unusually strict security precautions, whereby all preparations including the positioning of forces would be completed without divulging to anyone the precise date on which the attack would begin—not even to his war partner, Hafez Asad of Syria. Although two general periods had been agreed upon, September 7–11 and October 5–10, Sadat kept the actual choice of date and time secret until some seventy-two hours before the conflict was to begin.[32] Apart from the obvious need for secrecy, Sadat evidently assumed that Asad was in collusion with Moscow, which may explain why he refused until the last possible moment to inform the Syrian leader of the date the war would begin.

On October 1, Sadat called in Soviet ambassador Sergei Vinogradov to hint broadly that war would come soon, without much advance warning. "It may be," he said, "that we shall find ourselves obliged to move fast." He urged the ambassador to "tell Brezhnev . . . that the coming days will be a real and practical test for the Soviet-Egyptian treaty."[33] Two days later, in a disclosure procedure previously agreed upon with Asad, Sadat called Vinogradov in again to say that the outbreak of the war was imminent, still without informing him of the exact date. Fending off Vinogradov's importunate questions of when the war would begin, Sadat asked, "What will the Soviet attitude be?"[34] On the following day, October 4, Asad called in the Soviet ambassador to Syria, Mukhidinov, to inform him of the date, which he himself had only learned the day before when Sadat's minister of war, General Ahmed Ismail, visited Damascus to tell him. Reportedly, Asad was infuriated by the short notice, but went along with it.[35]

Moscow reacted in two ways to the gradually firming information regarding the date when the war would begin. First, the Soviet Union intensifed satellite reconnaissance coverage of the Middle East.[36] Following the Sadat-Asad meetings of late August the Soviet Union launched Cosmos 583 on August 30, Cosmos 584 on September 6, and Cosmos 587 on September 21 — each satellite remaining in orbit for the normal aloft time of thirteen days. Immediately after Sadat's meeting with Vinogradov on October 3, however, Moscow launched the first of seven reconnaissance satellites it would deploy to monitor the conflict (on October 3, 6, 10, 15, 16, 20, and 27). In five of the seven cases, Moscow launched and recovered the satellites in shorter than normal time intervals, six days instead of the usual thirteen, to provide as close as possible to real-time intelligence coverage of the rapidly changing battlefield situation.[37]

Once certain that the conflict was about to erupt, Moscow's second step, undoubtedly prepared in advance, was to attempt to provoke Israel into a preemptive attack by a series of moves which made plain to Israeli intelligence that war was indeed imminent. On the one hand, stories circulated in the communist press warning of an imminent Arab attack. For example, the day after the October 1 meeting between Sadat and Vinogradov, the Bulgarian news agency issued a story declaring that Egypt and Syria were about to attack Israel; and the day after the October 3 meeting between them the Czech news agency did likewise. The next two days saw several stories in the Western press forecasting the imminent outbreak of hostilities.[38] The Soviet press itself, of course, did not and could not report that the Arabs were about to attack Israel, but *Pravda, Izvestia*, and Tass did report that Israel was about to attack Egypt and Syria, making the same point that war was imminent.

On the other hand, the Soviets resorted to the unprecedented and provocative step of evacuating Soviet civilian dependents from both Egypt and Syria.[39] As soon as Asad informed Moscow of the date for the attack, the Soviets instructed Vinogradov to request permission from Sadat to allow the evacuation, a request which "dumbfounded" the Egyptian leader.

> On . . . Thursday the Soviet ambassador wanted to see me urgently. I thought he would give me a reply to my question [regarding the Soviet attitude], but instead, the moment he saw me, he said: "I have an urgent message from the Soviet leadership. Moscow asks you to allow four big aircraft to arrive in Egypt to fly the Soviet families out. . . . They want them to land at a military airfield . . . so as not to be seen at the international airport and to maintain secrecy."[40]

But of course there could be no secrecy from monitoring Israeli electronic and human intelligence. Landing at the military airport, furthermore, strongly suggested that the Soviets were flying in last-minute supplies for the attack, even though in reality the planes arrived empty. Finally, while the evacuation was under way, on October 5, Moscow also began to reposition its ships, moving them out of the ports of Alexandria and Port Said.

Israeli preemption, of course, would very likely result in the defeat of Arab plans and lead Sadat to the conclusion that he had been deceived by Washington, just as many Egyptians believed that Washington had deceived Nasser in 1967. Then (as now) the United States had played an important role in publicly assuming a mediator's stance, attempting to forestall a conflict, only to have Israel conduct a surprise attack with devastating results. But however closely the current situation seemed to resemble that of 1967, Moscow was not in a position to determine events. In fact, even though there were some in the Israeli leadership who did indeed press for preemptive attack, 1973 was not 1967, and Kissinger successfully forestalled Israeli action.

The Soviet attempt to provoke Israel into striking first implied that Moscow was willing to concede the objective of regaining access to the canal in return for repolarizing the region in order to reestablish Egyptian dependence. In the end a fundamentally feeble attempt to provoke Israeli action failed, and Moscow then strove to secure the minimum objective of access to the canal, even while persisting in efforts to deny Washington the broker's role by undermining American credibility with the Arabs.

Once the war began, Moscow sought to terminate the conflict at the point of maximum initial advance of Syrian and Egyptian armies. Time was on the side of the militarily superior Israel; the longer the battle, the more devastating the eventual defeat for the Arabs. A short war was the only profitable outcome for Moscow. Once that proved impossible, the Soviet leadership was faced with the highly difficult task of maintaining the battlefield momentum for both Syrian and Egyptian forces, for if either's offensive faltered, Israel would be able to concentrate forces against the other, thereby defeating both, one at a time.

Washington's preferred outcome, on the other hand, was the defeat of Syria—which otherwise would leave Israel in a vulnerable position in the north—and a cease-fire in place with Egyptian forces on the east bank of the canal. From Washington's perspective, therefore, the war had to continue long enough to enable Israel to reverse initial Syrian gains and to reestablish — at a minimum — the status quo ante bellum on the Golan Heights. The problem was, however, that once Israeli forces gained the upper hand against Syria it would prove difficult to restrain them from driving Egypt's forces back across the canal. Indeed, at the end, Israeli determination to create a strong bargaining position in terms of final military positions threatened not only the total defeat of Egypt, but also triggered a major crisis in United States-Soviet relations.

Superpower-Client Wartime Interaction

Within hours of the outbreak of the conflict, Kissinger proposed to Moscow that the two powers table "a joint cease-fire resolution advocating a return to the status quo ante," assuming that the Soviet leadership would not accept it.[41] The proposal put the United States on record as favoring a prompt termination of the conflict even though that was not Washington's intent, for a Soviet rejection would give Israel the time necessary to gain the upper hand. In a conversation with Ambassador Dobrynin Kissinger prophetically argued that unless the war was concluded quickly "the problem will be to get the Israelis back to the cease-fire line."[42]

The Soviet reply which arrived three hours later was a stall; it explained that Moscow was "considering . . . possible steps to be taken." Kissinger's response was to harass Dobrynin with the charge that "your message . . . either means you are confused or you are cooperating with them."[43] In fact, neither was true, for at that moment Moscow was attempting unsuccessfully to obtain President Sadat's agreement to an immediate cease-fire in place, its preferred even if unrealistic outcome.

Six hours after the war had begun, Soviet Ambassador Vinogradov met with Sadat bearing a message from Moscow which contained Syrian President Asad's wish to conclude a cease-fire "forty-eight hours at most from the start of military operations on the 6th," a position which he said Moscow, too, supported.[44] Expressing his "doubt" that Asad had "really demanded" an immediate cease-fire, Sadat declared that "even if Syria did demand it, I won't have a ceasefire until the main targets of my battle have been achieved."[45]

Sadat's position was understandable. Egyptian forces were in the process of putting a formidable force of over 1,000 tanks and 100,000 men across the canal onto the east bank.

Vinogradov, alarmed and exasperated, blurted out, "This is . . . an official message from the Soviet leaders; if you have any doubts you may get in touch with President al-Asad and talk it over with him."[46] Then he added: "I must officially inform you that President Hafiz al-Asad is our partner."[47] Now thoroughly aroused by what he was being told, Sadat concluded their meeting by saying that he would indeed consult with Asad since "no stipulations of this nature were part of our agreement."[48]

Sadat immediately cabled Asad, who replied twenty-four hours later — an unusually long delay considering the critical battlefield situation — to deny that he had requested an immediate cease-fire. To make matters more confusing, Vinogradov arrived shortly after Sadat had received Asad's reply to say that he had yet *a second request* from the Syrian leader for an immediate cease-fire![49] Sadat angrily closed off further discussion with the remark that Asad's cabled denial was good enough for him. There would be no cease-fire, he said, until their jointly agreed war aims were accomplished — that is, Syrian recapture of the Golan Heights and Egypt's seizure of the three Sinai passes, accomplishments which would destroy forever the Israeli security theory that peace could be imposed on the Arabs by force of arms.

What is to be made of this bizarre episode? There was deception here, to be sure, but whose? Asad's denial made it appear that Moscow was engaged in a crude attempt to deceive Sadat into accepting an immediate cease-fire. Although it was true that the Soviets frequently resorted to such crude ploys and although it was clearly in Moscow's interest to have an immediate cease-fire, there was virtually no chance that a bald lie could succeed.[50]

Moreover, afterwards it was learned — and confirmed by Sadat — that Asad in fact had made not two but *three* separate requests for a cease-fire, the first before the conflict had begun. But he had made them to Moscow and not directly to Sadat, which indicated cooperation if not collusion between Syria and the Soviet Union, at the very least.[51] Finally, it was decidedly in Asad's interest to have an early cease-fire when Syrian forces had reached the point of furthest advance and before Israel's counterattack had begun.[52]

There seems, in short, little doubt that both Asad and Moscow wanted an immediate cease-fire, but a cease-fire after only six hours of battle would invalidate the pre-war Egyptian-Syrian agreement on war aims. Asad could not acknowledge to Sadat that he wished a cease-fire when his objectives were as close to being fulfilled as they were ever going to be, while Sadat's drive to the passes had not yet begun. Yet all knew that once Israel's mobilization took effect, Syria would not be able to hold the position it had seized on the Golan Heights unless Egypt pressed its advance.[53]

It had become clear almost immediately that Israel's strategy was to concentrate on repulsing Syria in the north while trading space for time in the Sinai, thus avoiding the danger of fighting a two-front war simultaneously. Indeed, patched-together Israeli units commenced a counterattack (even though not yet large or well organized) against Syrian forces in the Golan Heights within forty-eight hours of the outbreak of the war, early on the morning of October 8.[54]

Syrian strategy was essentially a bold gamble and a hope. The gamble was that Damascus could deliver a single, massive, knockout blow on the Golan; and the hope was that Egypt's attack across the Suez would provide a sufficient diversion of Israeli forces. Syria's assault, spearheaded by 1,500 tanks, broke through Israeli defenses on the heights, causing disarray and consternation with a never-before-displayed night-fighting capability, which reduced further Tel Aviv's mobilization time and brought Syrian forces to within ten minutes' driving time of the Sea of Galilee.[55]

In the first day of battle the Syrian attack staggered the Israeli defenders but did not break them. During the second day, October 7, Syria's inability to mount a follow-up blow as powerful as the first proved to be Damascus' undoing as Israeli mobilization began to stiffen the defenses, then provide the basis for a coordinated counterattack. When the counterattack began at 0830 hours Monday, October 7, Soviet leaders faced a critical decision. Sadat's refusal to accept a cease-fire and his failure to press his advance toward the passes meant that there was no pressure on Israel from the Sinai, which enabled Israeli forces to concentrate against and ensure the defeat of Syria.

Moscow's response was to attempt to prod Egypt into action to relieve the pressure on Syria and to organize an immediate effort to prevent the possible collapse of Damascus. Tuesday evening, the eighth, Vinogradov informed Sadat that the Soviet airlift would begin shortly.[56] At the same time Asad and the Soviets appealed to the Egyptian leader to push his forces toward the passes, but Sadat demurred on the grounds that it had been agreed there would be an "operational pause" after crossing the canal and taking the Bar-Lev line.

The Syrians objected violently, maintaining that the agreement was to continue the attack until Egyptian forces reached the passes, at which time there could be a "pause."[57] Sadat's refusal to heed Syrian and Soviet appeals to press forward left Moscow with no alternative but to strengthen Syria's defenses, and beginning on the tenth (some accounts say the ninth) the Soviet airlift to Damascus began, and the next day to Cairo. Moscow intensified its ongoing seaborne aid to both countries and urged its Arab and non-Arab clients to assist.[58]

Meanwhile, by October 9, the Israeli leadership was deciding upon a course of action that would take optimum advantage of the successful counterattack against Syria. Fundamentally, the Israeli decision was to turn Soviet-Arab strategy against itself. If the imminent collapse of the Syrian front demanded that Egypt press its attack in the Sinai, then Israel would encourage the impression that such a course of action was indeed feasible and thereby lure Egypt into a trap. [59]

The fact was that Israel stood little chance of pushing Egyptian forces back across the canal as long as they remained ensconced behind their protected position within the SAM air-defense bubble. By the third day of the war Israel had already lost 50 of the 102 planes it would lose in the entire conflict, the vast majority the result of missile and anti-aircraft fire.[60] It was thus imperative that Egyptian forces be drawn out from under the security of their air-defense system before Israel could hope to defeat them.[61]

There were two basic components to the Israeli policy: The first was to induce Egypt to begin an offensive in the Sinai by undertaking a heavy push into Syria proper to threaten Damascus. The second was to press Washington for supplies on the grounds that Israeli forces were running low on war materiel. At the chief of staff's conference on the ninth, Elazar determined that

> pressing forward in Syria with the purpose of taking it out of the war was the first priority. Accordingly the policy on the Egyptian front must be to endeavour to improve the ratio of forces by allowing the Egyptians to attack and incur casualties against the Israeli defence. After breaking the major Egyptian attack *that had to come*, the possibilities of counter-attacks, including the crossing of the Canal in the area of Deversoir, would become viable.[62]

Israeli Air Force bombing attacks that day on Damascus and Homs (including the Soviet cultural center in Damascus) threatened the beginning of a major effort to take Syria out of the war. That evening Defense Minister Moshe Dayan sought to foster the same impression in the Israeli press. Addressing a group of editors, he emphasized that the first priority was to neutralize the Syrian front. Israeli forces, he said, "did not have the strength to throw the Egyptians back across the Canal; it would not be possible to carry out both operations — taking the Syrians out of the war and throwing the Egyptians back across the Canal — at the same time."[63]

He indicated that Israel would have to pull back to "new and shorter lines" in the Sinai somewhere "between the Canal and before the mountains."[64] The following day, October 10, the general staff convened to decide how far the counterattack should go, for by then Israeli forces had driven the Syrians back across the DMZ, or the "purple line," as it was called. Again, Elazar pressed the argument that "the Israelis had to achieve a penetration some 12 miles in depth . . . [to] neutralize Syria as an element in the war and bring pressure to bear on Egypt [to drive to the passes]."[65] Prime Minister Meir concurred in the chief of staff's view, deciding to continue the feint into Syria, an attack which was redoubled the next morning, October 11.

In Washington, meanwhile, early in the morning of the ninth, Israeli Ambassador Simcha Dinitz mounted the second part of the plan. In a meeting with Kissinger, Dinitz described Israeli military operations and made a pitch for immediate reinforcement.[66] Afterward, Dinitz took Kissinger aside to propose that Prime Minister Meir make a secret visit to Washington to plead personally for urgently needed arms aid. Recognizing the transparent attempt to place added pressure on the administration to take a public stand on Israel's behalf, the secretary fended off the request.

He knew full well that the visit of the Israeli prime minster "could not be kept secret" and would force the United States "to announce a massive supply policy, destroying any possibility of mediation. The Arab world would be inflamed against us. The Soviet Union would have a clear field."[67] On the other hand, Kissinger concluded that if Meir were willing to leave the country in the midst of the war with critical battles imminent, the leadership "must be close to panic."[68]

Throughout the crisis President Nixon had played no substantive role. The issue of the proposed Meir visit was no exception. Kissinger had rejected Dinitz' request "out of hand and without checking with

Nixon."[69] Nevertheless, the battlefield situation was now judged serious enough to call upon the president to lend the weight of his office to Kissinger's decision to accelerate the delivery of "consumables" (Sidewinder missiles and electronic countermeasures equipment) and aircraft. Heavy equipment like tanks could not be delivered in time for the coming battle; but the United States promised formally to "guarantee to replace Israel's losses, thus Israel would be freed of the need to maintain exorbitant reserve stocks during the battle."[70]

While conveying presidential assurances to the Israeli government, the United States nevertheless did not in fact begin an all-out supply effort for three more days, until October 13. The delay was not, as Kissinger claimed, because the administration bungled several alternate plans to transport the material so that United States government aircraft need not be used, or even because it was calculated that Israel had sufficient stocks to fight for two more weeks. It was because American and Israeli interests were divergent.

As Kissinger candidly acknowledged, "The best outcome was an Israeli victory that pushed back the Arabs without producing an Arab debacle."[71] Israel, of course, sought precisely "an Arab debacle," as later events would clearly show. Furthermore, as Kissinger also noted, the larger danger in beginning an unrestricted supply effort to Israel was in compromising Washington's position as middleman in the postwar diplomacy, ruining several years of patient diplomatic maneuver to bring about the "reversal of alliances" Kissinger believed was inherent in the strategic trends he saw in train.[72]

So Washington procrastinated. Secretary of Defense James Schlesinger later admitted that "there was a cover story . . . that the source of resistance [to the airlift] was to be the Pentagon. This story was basically to protect the realities of national policy."[73] Nor was this "story" misunderstood by Dinitz, who realized that the two countries' interests were not entirely coincident. Kissinger, in describing his relationship with the Israeli ambassador, all but says the delay in resupply was deliberate:

Like all experienced diplomats, we took great pains to keep our disagreements from becoming personal. One device is to blame — usually transparently — someone else for painful decisions. Dinitz was brilliant at mobilizing media and Congressional pressures but much too wise to make his process explicit. . . . In turn, when I had bad news for Dinitz, I was not above ascribing it to bureaucratic stalemates or unfortunate decisions by superiors. Neither of us fooled the other. . . .[74]

As the war approached the critical juncture, a perceptible edge of panic crept into the decisions of all the parties. The Soviets had repeatedly sought a cease-fire in place since the early hours of the war when both Syria and Egypt had made their initial thrusts, but were frustrated by Sadat's determination to continue the war — even though he did not advance his forces. Now Syria not only had lost the hope of regaining any of the territory it had lost in 1967 and held briefly on the first day, but the grim prospect grew that Damascus itself could fall.

Thus, Moscow began its airlift to Syria, placed three of its seven airborne divisions on alert, and made another démarche to Washington. Too subtle by half, on the morning of October 10 Moscow indicated that the Soviet Union would not block adoption of a cease-fire in place resolution in the UN Security Council if it were put forward. In other words, the Soviets themselves did not wish to put forward such a resolution publicly, since Sadat had already rejected it privately time and again, but hoped that if the United States proposed or sponsored a cease-fire through a third party, Sadat might comply.

However, Washington was not yet ready. To give Israel sufficient time to regain the initiative, Kissinger stalled. The secretary believed that a cease-fire in place would only be useful if Israel were winning; in fact, it might not be obtainable if it were not. He turned to Ambassador Dinitz to urge quick and decisive Israeli action:

> With resupply assured, Israel did not need to hoard reserves. . . . Everything depended upon the Israelis pushing back to the prewar lines as quickly as possible, or beyond them on at least one front. We could not stall a cease-fire proposal forever.[75]

Kissinger's conversations with Dinitz at noon on the tenth revealed yet another devious maneuver, which betrayed an edge of panic in his own thinking. The secretary knew that Israel's forces had aready driven Syria off the Golan Heights and were preparing to mount a drive toward Damascus.[76] His remark to Dinitz made increasingly clear the growing divergence between their two countries. Kissinger was urging an immediate attack on heavily fortified Egyptian positions on the east bank, while the Israeli leadership was gambling that the feint toward Damascus would persuade Sadat to attempt to relieve pressure on Syria, whereupon Israeli forces would then attack and destroy the Egyptian armies as soon as they left their protected positions but before they reached the Sinai passes.

Kissinger says that he urged immediate action simply because he could not stall the Soviets forever on their cease-fire proposal. But he certainly understood the political implications of the heavy losses Israeli forces would inevitably sustain in an assault on the fortified Egyptian positions on the east bank, as well as the political value of a military standoff in the postwar negotiations.

Whatever tactical differences there were soon became academic as it became apparent (that same day, in fact) that Sadat would press the battle. On October 10, news arrived that Sadat was urging King Hussein to enter the battle in support of Syria and that King Faisal would send a Saudi tank brigade.[77] (The Iraqis, Moroccans, and Kuwaitis had already committed tank brigades.) Sadat's plan was straightforward. He hoped to buttress the Syrian front against collapse, thus tying down Israeli units in continuous battle while he made an attempt to seize the Sinai passes.

Israel's advance on Damascus, begun on the morning of the eleventh, was completed within twenty-four hours, although fighting for favorable position would continue until the cease-fire of October 22 — mainly with Iraqi and Jordanian units. But Israel had no intention of capturing Damascus.[78] Israeli tank units penetrated the planned twelve miles into Syrian territory, up to the inner defense line some eighteen miles from the capital, and halted their advance.

At that point, on the twelfth, Israeli leaders communicated to Kissinger their willingness to accept a cease-fire in place, undoubtedly secure in the assumption that Sadat would reject it as he prepared his own attack.[79] In any case, Kissinger promptly contacted the British ambassador, Lord Cromer, who agreed to offer a cease-fire in place resolution to the UN Security Council the next day, the thirteenth. Moscow also approved, leaving Kissinger the impression, according to his memoirs,[80] that the Soviets expected Egypt to accept. But Sadat, for the reasons described above, peremptorily rejected the proposed British effort, which was quashed.

Endgame Crises: Superpower-Client Conflicts

Events were moving rapidly toward what would become a week and a half of protracted climax, culminating in superpower confrontation. The Israeli drive on Damascus prompted Moscow to alert four more airborne divisions, bringing the total to seven, and raised the decibel level of threats emanating from the Soviet capital warning of the dire consequences that would arise from the fall of a Soviet client.[81] With Syria effectively out of the war, the Soviets feared that Sadat was walking into a trap as Israel concentrated forces to thwart the drive to capture the passes.

To ensure that Egypt would not be driven back across the canal in total defeat whatever the outcome of the imminent offensive in the Sinai, Moscow stepped up the airlift, with the bulk of sixty-seven flights on October 13 alone going to Egypt.[82] Soviet caution was now in sharp contrast to Sadat's seeming tactical abandon, as he shifted his main strategic reserves, elements of two armored divisions — the 21st and a brigade of the 4th — across the canal on the twelfth and thirteenth to supporting positions on the east bank of the canal.[83]

The shift of 230 tanks of Egypt's strategic armored reserve to the east bank, leaving the west bank lightly defended with only one hundred tanks, was the signal both Washington and Tel Aviv were waiting for, but for quite different reasons. For Washington, the deployment meant that Sadat's major push was about to begin, prompting Kissinger to initiate the all-out airlift of supplies for which Israel had been clamoring since the war broke out. Delivery began on the afternoon of the thirteenth. Kissinger later noted:

> In the first full day of the airlift we had more than matched what the Soviet Union had put into all the Arab countries . . . combined in all of the four previous days.[84]

Indeed, the airlift coincided with Egypt's drive to capture the passes on the morning of October 14. Egypt had deployed over one thousand tanks to the Sinai front. Four hundred moved out from under their protective air-defense umbrella against a now refortified Israeli force in what became the largest tank battle since Kursk-Orel in World War II. The result — in a single day of fighting — was a military defeat of catastrophic proportions as Egypt lost 264 tanks to

Israel's 6, thanks to a combined-arms defense of armor, anti-tank, and air support.[85]

For the Israeli leadership, the shift of Egypt's strategic tank reserve opened the way, once the Sinai drive was blunted, for a crossing to the west bank of the canal, an operation that had been planned for some time but was decided upon only on October 12.[86] After the defeat in the Sinai, Sadat's decision was to regroup behind the protected positions along the east bank, where his armies would be secure within the still-functioning air-defense network. The Israeli leadership understood that it would be extremely difficult, perhaps impossible, to drive Egypt back across the canal in a frontal assault as long as the missile defense remained intact. The Israeli plan therefore was to deploy a tank force on the west bank to attack the SAM sites, crack the air-defense system, and make Egyptian forces on the east bank vulnerable to Israeli air power.[87]

The crossing was a daring but extremely risky gamble because Egyptian forces were lodged in strength along the east bank. The Israeli plan was to cross at the north end of Great Bitter Lake at Deversoir-Metzmed, between the lines of the Egyptian Second and Third Armies. The advance force, including a dozen or so tanks, began its crossing at approximately 1:30 a.m. October 16 and completed its move by 8 a.m., establishing a bridgehead some three miles in depth.[88]

The Israelis could not immediately secure the crossing point because Egyptian forces on the east bank of the canal detected and engaged them, while they themselves were unable to implace a large, prefabricated bridge, which had been damaged, across the canal. In retrospect, the resultant thirty-six-hour delay while the way was cleared and the bridge repaired was fortunate for it reinforced the initial Egyptian perception of the crossing as a small, diversionary raid and not the major division-sized operation it actually was.[89] The failure of the Egyptian command to respond quickly gave the Israelis the time needed to secure the bridgehead, although it was a close call.[90] Indeed, at one point the operation was nearly canceled.

By the time Egyptian forces were able to mount a counterattack it was too late. Israeli forces were across the canal in strength, with over 300 tanks, and fanning out toward Ismailia in the north and Suez in the south, knocking out SAM batteries and cutting supply lines to the Egyptian Second and Third Armies on the east bank. At this point, Moscow sent Politburo member Alexei Kosygin to Cairo to remonstrate once again with Sadat for a cease-fire. According to Sadat, he had received a message from Moscow on October 13 requesting permission for Kosygin to visit.[91]

The Soviets evidently wanted to be in position to exert maximum leverage on Sadat when the outcome of the coming offensive in the Sinai was clear. In any event, Kosygin's arrival on October 16 coincided with the Israeli crossing to the west bank, although it is doubtful that the Soviet leader was aware of it until after he arrived. His purpose was to press Sadat for a cease-fire in the wake of the failure of the Sinai offensive; the west bank crossing gave him added leverage. Indeed, Kosygin magnified the crossing into a threat to Cairo itself, which Sadat ridiculed as "sheer nonsense."[92]

Still, Sadat refused to countenance a cease-fire, probably assuming that the Israeli crossing had been contained, even when Kosygin offered Soviet (and, without authorization, American) guarantees that the cease-fire lines would be maintained.[93] Kosygin angrily left Cairo late on the evening of the eighteenth with only Sadat's agreement in principle for a cease-fire, and no decision to accept one. That would not come until after Kosygin had left.

Sadat made his decision for a cease-fire when he belatedly realized that the Israeli crossing had not in fact been contained and that, with the destruction of the missile sites, the threat to the security of his armies on the east bank was growing by the hour. Soon after midnight on the 19th, following a contentious meeting with his chief of staff, Said Hussein al-Shazli, Sadat cabled Asad of his decision to accept a cease-fire and also informed Moscow a short time later.[94]

Sadat's argument was that he decided upon a cease-fire because he refused to fight the United States, which was now fully in support of Israel, an interpretation which minimizes the significance of the west bank crossing and the threat to Egypt's Third Army, in particular. Yet there can be little doubt that the failure to contain the crossing was the critical factor determining the decision for the cease-fire.[95] Indeed, Sadat summarily dismissed Chief of Staff Shazli for failing to contain the Israelis at Deversoir, although the decision was not made public until December 12.[96]

As soon as Brezhnev received word from Sadat, he cabled Washington requesting that Kissinger come immediately to the Soviet capital to work out cease-fire arrangements, since "every hour counts."[97] Kissinger interpreted the Soviet cable as the step which "solved most of our problems."

We could not now confuse virtuosity with a long-range strategy. We had to avoid risking everything for marginal gains, for we had achieved our fundamental objectives: We had created the conditions for a diplomatic breakthrough.[98]

In short, the secretary believed that "we held the cards now. Our next challenge was to play our hand."

Playing the hand, however, required addressing the conflict of interests between Washington and Tel Aviv regarding the ultimate purpose of the war, which had thus far been subsumed in the question of logistics. However much Israeli leaders had declared their willingness to reach a negotiated settlement, now that the war was ending in their favor the fundamental predisposition toward a victor's peace manifested itself in the determination to encircle and hold hostage, if not destroy entirely, the Egyptian Third Army.

The Israeli armed forces' grip on the Third Army reflected more than the effort to obtain an advantageous bargaining position. It indicated a disdain for a truly negotiated solution and strong preference for the former structure of the region—encirclement by hostile but vanquished Arabs, with security guaranteed by exclusive American support for Israel. The danger here for American strategy was that Israel might do what the Soviet Union could not—edge the United States off center and deny Washington the opportunity to restructure the region on the basis of an Israeli-Egyptian settlement.

The American-Israeli conflict of interests focused on the fate of the Egyptian Third Army. Israel was determined to eliminate Egypt's position on the east bank, while Kissinger was equally determined to preserve it as the basis for a subsequent negotiated settlement. Later Israeli accounts of the war claim that Kissinger deceived his ally, while Kissinger himself denies such intent at length.[99] Both views are clearly smoke screens to obscure the truth. No careful reading of the record can leave any doubt that both sides understood that their interests and objectives were in conflict. The argument that Kissinger deceived the Israelis is fundamentally crafted to justify Israeli violation of the cease-fire to achieve their objectives; Kissinger's protests are intended to paper over very real differences.

The cease-fire resolution which Kissinger and Brezhnev drafted after relatively minor haggling in Moscow on October 21 called for an immediate cease-fire in place, implementation of Security Council Resolution 242, and immediate negotiations "between the parties concerned under appropriate auspices."[100] Kissinger suggests that it was Brezhnev's haste to relieve the position of the Third Army that led to early agreement, but it was also because he too sought that objective.

Continued Israeli action to encircle the Third Army would not only threaten Moscow's minimum objective — the only one attainable at this point — of regaining access to the canal, but Washington's, too, by removing Sadat's negotiating leverage. After further discussion, Kissinger and Brezhnev agreed to call the Security Council into session at 9:00 p.m., October 21, Washington time, with the cease-fire to take effect twelve hours after passage of the resolution. UN Security Council Resolution 338 went into effect at 6:52 p. m. local time, October 22, 1972.[101]

During the wrap-up in Moscow, exchanges with the Israeli government over the cease-fire resolution led to the request by Meir that Kissinger stop off in Israel on his way back to the United States. Kissinger agreed, thus committing what was probably the single most serious mistake he made in the course of the conflict, which led directly to superpower confrontation. Perhaps without realizing it, Kissinger allowed himself to be led into a compromising situation which enabled the Israeli leadership to justify further military action in violation of the cease-fire.

The Israelis knew that to defy a direct request from Washington to agree to a cease-fire would jeopardize needed United States support after the conflict. But in discussion with Kissinger they maneuvered him into agreeing that it would be permissible to defer immediate compliance with the cease-fire resolution on the grounds that "in Vietnam the cease-fire didn't go into effect at the exact time that was agreed on."[102]

In other words, Kissinger's discussion in Tel Aviv gave the Israeli leadership grounds for arguing plausible misunderstanding. Matti Golan described the Israeli position: "Perhaps it was only a chance remark, but Kissinger's hosts did not ask for further clarification. The words sounded to them like an indirect go-ahead for the continuation of the fighting. . . ."[103] Kissinger, in his memoirs, later concurred:

> I also had a sinking feeling that I might have emboldened them; in Israel, to gain their support, I had indicated that I would understand if there was a few hours "slippage" in the cease-fire while I was flying home. . . .[104]

In any event, Israeli forces immediately disregarded the cease-fire and moved to complete their encirclement of the Third Army. In Moscow suspicions were heightened that Kissinger and the Israeli leadership were colluding to outmaneuver and embarrass the Soviet Union.

Sadat also believed that he had been duped and publicly demanded that both Washington and Moscow intervene with military forces to guarantee the cease-fire.[105] When Israeli forces disregarded a second cease-fire resolution (no. 339) passed in the Security Council the next day—which called for a return of forces to the original cease-fire position—and when Washington still took no restraining action, Moscow faced a dilemma. To do nothing would not only lead to the loss of any hope of regaining access to the canal, it would also demonstrate the bankruptcy of Soviet policy in the region.

On the other hand, to react unilaterally in support of Sadat's demand that Moscow make good on its pledge to guarantee the cease-fire would provoke a confrontation with Washington. The Soviet decision was to escalate what had been up to this point a conflict between Arabs and Israelis, with the superpowers in the background, to a superpower confrontation. Hoping to snatch victory from the jaws of defeat and salvage at least a modicum of credibility in the Arab world, Brezhnev sent a message to President Nixon October 24, the relevant passages of which read:

> Let us together . . . urgently dispatch to Egypt the Soviet and American military contingents, to insure the implementation of the decision of the Security Council of October 22 and 23 concerning the cessation of fire and of all military activities and also of our understanding with you on the guarantee of the implementation of the decisions of the Security Council.

> It is necessary to adhere without delay. I will say it straight that if you find it impossible to act jointly with us in this matter, we should be faced with the necessity urgently to consider the question of taking appropriate steps unilaterally. We cannot allow arbitrariness on the part of Israel. . . .[106]

The message was not quite what it has since been portrayed as being. In reality the message represented Moscow's last-gasp attempt to push the United States off center and defeat the strategy of employing the conflict as the basis for a negotiated settlement beween Egypt and Israel. Moscow gambled that its *privately conveyed threat* would prod Washington into siding openly with Israel in response to a presumed Soviet deployment of forces on behalf of Egypt, thus repolarizing the region, as Kissinger immediately recognized.

> The strategy we had laboriously pursued in four years of diplomacy and two weeks of crisis would disintegrate: Egypt would be drawn back into the Soviet orbit, the Soviet Union and its radical allies would emerge as the dominant factor in the Middle East.[107]

While apprehending the political implications in the note, Kissinger understated the most likely military consequences of the failure to maintain the cease-fire. The more ominous threat was in fact less that of a Soviet military intervention than of a complete unraveling of the cease-fire and a resumption of the battle, perhaps including the use of tactical nuclear weapons. The Soviets could be under no illusions either that Washington would agree to any joint action plan, or that unilateral military intervention would succeed in enforcing a cease-fire. It is extremely doubtful that unilateral action was ever seriously contemplated, although all preparations were completed to make the threat credible.[108]

Whether understood or not, the Soviet threat to intervene actually provided Washington the opportunity to take the steps necessary to avoid repolarizing the region by freezing the battlefield situation and preventing the resumption of fighting. When the cease-fire had failed to hold initially, on October 22, Sadat had ordered the firing of two SCUD missiles (undoubtedly with Soviet concurrence since Soviet crews manned the missiles) at the Israeli positions at Deversoir,[109] clearly signaling his determination to employ deep strikes against Israel proper if the fighting continued.

The firing marked the first offensive involvement of the Soviet Union in the conflict other than in supply and air-defense roles. More ominously, a Soviet cargo ship carrying nuclear materiel—probably tactical nuclear warheads for the SCUDs—had been detected a week earlier passing through the Bosporus.[110] At the same time, Israeli nuclear forces, with an inventory of an estimated thirteen nuclear bombs, had been placed on alert, raising the grim possibility that a resumption of fighting might indeed lead to a tactical nuclear exchange.[111] Although it will probably never be known for certain, it would appear that it was the threat of losing control of the conflict and the possibility of its escalation to a tactical nuclear exchange, rather than the threat of Soviet military intervention, that prompted the United States nuclear alert of October 25.[112]

Washington's response was fourfold. In addition to counter-escalating by placing United States forces on DefCon III—a more visible state of readiness, but still substantially short of a war alert—Washington also communicated to each of the participants. To Moscow, Washington reemphasized its readiness to cooperate—with observers but not troops—in maintaining a cease-fire. To Cairo, Washington sought to persuade Sadat to withdraw his request for deployment of Soviet and American troops as guarantors of the cease-fire. And to Tel Aviv, Washington threatened the total withdrawal of support should Israel fail to comply with the cease-fire.

Both Moscow and Cairo responded affirmatively, but Israel still proved recalcitrant. Brezhnev sent a note in which he chose to interpret the United States offer to cooperate as complying with his ultimatum of the twenty-fourth. Moscow thus was able to back away from its threat to take unilateral action without loss of face.[113] Cairo, too, now "clarified" its earlier call for American-Soviet guarantees as meaning UN provision of an "international" force, which customarily excluded participation of permanent members of the Security Council.[114]

Israel, coming perilously close to precipitation of an enlarged conflict, refused to back off, more determined than ever to capture the Third Army, which produced extreme exasperation in Washington. In an oral message to Ambassador Dinitz, Kissinger issued what was in effect an ultimatum: "We cannot permit the destruction of the Egyptian army under conditions achieved after a cease-fire was reached in part by negotiations in which we participated."[115]

Secondly, he said, if Tel Aviv will not permit the resupply of non-military items to the Third Army, "we will have to support in the UN a resolution that will deal with the *enforcement* of [resolutions] 338 and 339."[116] Reportedly, he also conveyed what was the ultimate threat—abandonment: "Soviet airborne forces were prepared to intervene directly to save the Egyptian Second and Third Armies. Unless Israel accepted a ceasefire, the United States would not stand in the way of the Soviet Union."[117]

Through threat, cajolery, support, and denial of support, Kissinger managed to bring the conflict stage to a successful conclusion and initiate the negotiation stage which would begin the transformation of the regional geopolitical structure. Here, however, the pent-up frustration and animosity that had developed in the American-Israeli relationship would spew out into the refusal of the new Israeli leadership under Yitzhak Rabin (who replaced Golda Meir in the spring of 1974) to proceed beyond agreement on cease-fire to a broader political solution.

Nevertheless, by the end of 1973, Henry Kissinger had accomplished the first part of his larger strategic objective, to strengthen the Middle East regional balance. As the Arabs and Israelis entered the negotiating phase of their relations, Kissinger moved to deal with the issue of sharp increases in the price of oil, which already had had an impact on United States-Allied relations in the refusal of the allies to cooperate with the United States during the conflict and which afterward threatened to do irreparable harm to NATO.

CHAPTER

8

The Failure of Trilateralism: 1973–1976

The Yom Kippur War set in motion fundamental changes in Middle East politics. Washington began the restructuring of the greater Middle East as the administration moved to build an inner core of friendly states and Moscow, having little recourse, attempted to strengthen its position in states on the periphery. In the principal structural shift, Washington reestablished ties with Egypt (broken in 1967) and attempted to forge a double axis around Cairo-Tel Aviv rapprochement and Riyadh-Tehran cooperation, while Moscow developed ties with Libya, a former Anglo-American client. Although the United States was in the broker position, the forces of resistance made progress slow, and the new structure the administration sought to construct would not be completed during Kissinger's tenure in office. Only initial steps could be taken at this time.

Washington's shift from the Geneva forum initially agreed upon with Moscow to Kissinger's "step by step" approach was also a shift from a comprehensive to a bilateral concept, whose effect was to exclude Moscow from any substantive role in the Egyptian-Israeli settlement, although not in the Syrian-Israeli agreement, where Moscow's behind-the-scenes influence proved decisive. Indeed, Washington's move to broker an Egyptian-Israeli settlement spurred Moscow's shift toward Syria to ensure against the worst case, that there would be no broad settlement between Damascus and Tel Aviv, which would exclude Moscow from the region entirely.

The war enabled Washington to lay the cornerstone of a new structure for the region—rapprochement between Israel and Egypt—which removed Tel Aviv from a two-front to a one-front conflict situation. But progress beyond this vital first step was thwarted once again, as it had been before the war, by an Israeli leadership whose internal dissension and distrust of all outsiders proved impossible to overcome. The Israeli government refused to go beyond a disengagement-of-forces agreement to the broad political rapprochement urged by Washington. The freeze in the status of Israeli-Egyptian relations, a freeze marked by the transition from the Meir to the Rabin governments but begun before that, threw Israeli-American relations into an extended period of crisis lasting virtually until the end of the decade.

The consequences of the war for American policy were even more disastrous beyond the region. If Kissinger had anticipated using the war to generate political-economic pressure on America's alliance partners with a view to reestablishing American hegemony, it was a complete failure. The allies declined to cooperate with the United States during the conflict out of fear of Arab denial of energy supplies, and they remained politically distant afterward with the imposition of the Arab embargo. In fact, some sought to use the crisis as an opportunity to strengthen bilateral ties to the energy producers.

Even more serious, if possible, was the total miscalculation regarding the economic effect of sharply higher oil prices. The assumption that higher oil prices would place a brake on the rapidly growing economies of the allies proved to be disastrously wrong. In fact, the reverse occurred as the middle seventies witnessed a great acceleration of economic activity by the allies, generating intense competition with the United States in what is best described as a protracted economic war for wealth and power.

Yom Kippur and American-Israeli Relations

Postwar negotiations quickly brought to a head the basic divergence of interests between Washington and Tel Aviv over the desired structure of the region. Washington sought to parlay Egyptian-Israeli rapprochement into Cairo's shift to the Western camp and stronger regional defense (the Cairo-Riyadh-Tehran axis) against Soviet pressures. Both Egypt and Israel sought narrower objectives—in Cairo's case to facilitate its shift into the Western camp, and in Israel's to remove Egypt from the Arab encirclement. Even though both sides said that the disengagement agreement of January 18, 1974, was but "a step toward a final, just and durable peace,"[1] neither side was in fact willing to make the compromises necessary to reach that end. Indeed, Israeli refusal to go beyond the disengagement agreements with Egypt and Syria, or even to consider one with Jordan, produced a growing crisis in American-Israeli relations from mid-1974 onward.

Tactically, the Geneva conference concept had been instrumental in obtaining Soviet cooperation in bringing the conflict to an end, but once the war was over, Geneva was no longer useful from Washington's point of view.[2] As an instrument of American diplomacy the Geneva approach could only produce a settlement if all of the participants had the same objective — which was of course not now the case. Therefore its only function was to bring all of the participants together initially, after which each side would attempt to negotiate its own solutions. In other words, Geneva equated to stalemate.

Moscow understood the Geneva concept and its function in the same way but urged its use because stalemate was precisely the Soviet objective, for it would forestall Egypt's shift away from Moscow — or failing that, it would at least enable Moscow to generate maximum possible obstructive pressure. Finally, through the negotiating process the Geneva forum gave the Soviets access to Israel, which they would otherwise not possess. Thus, Washington's threats to return to Geneva when bilateral negotiations reached an impasse carried the implication of Soviet reentry into the negotiating process and a corresponding diminution of American support for Israel.

To achieve his objectives, Kissinger maneuvered to cut Moscow out of any role even as preparations were being made for the Geneva conference.[3] This was the "step by step" diplomacy the secretary undertook over the ensuing six months, which produced the disengagement agreement between Israel and Egypt of January 18, 1974, but which encountered increasing difficulty afterward even though Kissinger managed to conclude a disengagement-of-forces agreement between Israel and Syria on May 31. In truth, "step by step" succeeded only to the extent that the participants permitted it to succeed. It was successful in Egypt's case, since it was Anwar Sadat who sought to extricate his country from its relationship with Moscow. "Step by step" had no comparable success with Syria's Hafez Asad, who, in fact, strengthened relations with Moscow even while agreeing to reestablish diplomatic relations with Washington. In any case, contrary to Kissinger's assertion, Moscow was not "excluded to the fringes of Middle Eastern diplomacy," although there can be little doubt that the Soviet Union suffered a major reversal in Egypt.

The centerpiece of Washington's efforts was Egyptian-Israeli rapprochement, a policy Kissinger devised based upon the Israeli leadership's publicly avowed willingness to negotiate "permanent peace with defensible borders" with Egypt.[4] Indeed, as he himself put it:

> My idea was to use an interim agreement to break the impasse. Once achieved, such a step would ease the way to further advances. But I also parted company with those in Israel who regarded an interim disengagement as a way to avoid any further withdrawals. On the contrary, the chief utility of a disengagement along the Canal in my view was to launch a process of negotiation that might ultimately lead to peace with some or all of the Arab states. (This was, of course, the concept of "step by step" progress, which unlocked the peace process in 1974.)[5]

There were irreconcilable differences between "those in Israel" who saw the disengagement agreements as the last step and Kissinger, who saw them as the first step "that might ultimately lead to peace." That this was a grave miscalculation on Kissinger's part soon became apparent. When the time came to translate the principle of "permanent peace with defensible borders" into reality, the Israeli leadership shrank from the implications of its position, using every available political subterfuge to avoid a genuine peace with Egypt and with Jordan, preferring, in varying degrees, a condition of "no war, no peace" with its neighbors.

There were at least two reasons for Israeli intransigence aside from congenital insecurity. The first was the growing weakness of the American administration as President Nixon's political fortunes dissolved in the Watergate crisis. It was already clear by the spring of 1974 that the president would not be able to serve out the rest of his term of office. The Israeli leadership calculated that the erosion of Nixon's authority would make it impossible for the United States to generate political pressure on Tel Aviv and probably drew the same conclusion with regard to his successor, Gerald Ford.

The second was the impact of modern weapons upon Israeli security calculations, intensifying deep-rooted fears. The Israeli leadership had concluded from their analysis of the conflict that modern military technology made a territorial buffer more important than ever. The grim irony here was that the Israeli conclusion cut across the strategic rationale which underlay both Henry Kissinger's purpose in precipitating the conflict and Anwar Sadat's decision to conduct it. Kissinger had envisaged the conflict as establishing the basis for a negotiated settlement, a settlement that required an Israeli withdrawal from most if not all of the Sinai, while Sadat's purpose was to destroy Israel's "theory of security" — that is, of peace imposed by force of arms based upon acquisition of a territorial buffer.

Thus, there existed a basic divergence of objectives between Washington and Tel Aviv in yet another sense, which, however, did not become apparent until the spring of 1974 during the negotiations for the disengagement-of-forces agreement on the Syrian front. It developed into an impasse over the question of an agreement with Jordan regarding the West Bank. In short, Kissinger's miscalculation regarding Israel lay in his assumption that the Israelis wished to go beyond disengagement to genuine peace with Egypt and to reach agreement with Jordan to strengthen King Hussein's hand against the radical Palestinians.[6]

The Egyptian-Israeli disengagement-of-forces agreement established a new borderline between the two countries. The new boundary roughly represented the farthest point of advance established by Cairo's forces during the conflict and gave Egypt a position on the east bank of the canal for the first time since 1967. Separated by a United Nations disengagement zone, the two countries agreed to limited deployment of arms and forces in the area contiguous to the UN zone. The agreement was specifically "not regarded by Egypt and Israel as a final peace agreement," but as "a first step toward a final, just and durable peace. . . ."[7]

The Egyptian-Israeli disengagement-of-forces agreement was a crucial first step in Washington's postwar diplomacy, but its very accomplishment became an obstacle to further progress. Both Moscow and Tel Aviv, for different reasons, moved quickly to contain Washington's diplomatic momentum. On February 4, in a meeting with Kissinger, Soviet Foreign Minister Gromyko accused him of "systematically violating" their understanding that Middle East negotiations would proceed under joint American-Soviet "auspices."[8] The Soviet Union insisted that the Syrian disengagement be negotiated in Geneva under the "auspices" of Soviet-American cochairmanship. To ensure against any possible Syrian defection to Kissinger's blandishments, Moscow also agreed to a major new arms package for Syria. In the communiqué announcing the deal on April 16 the two sides stipulated that "any disengagement 'must be part and parcel' of an overall Middle East peace settlement."[9]

Kissinger asserts in his book that Asad was in reality on his side, citing a note from the Syrian leader following announcement of the Soviet arms deal that he "would stick with the plan that excluded the Soviets."[10] He claims that this demonstrated the "weakness of the Soviet position," but events soon demonstrated otherwise. While it was literally correct to say that Asad wished to negotiate without a direct Soviet role, it did not imply that he was in agreement with Washington.

If Kissinger actually believed that Asad would cooperate with the United States in reaching an agreement with Israel, it was a self-deception. Shortly after the announcement of the Soviet-Syrian arms agreement came the beginning of heavy Syrian artillery bombardment of Israeli positions on the Golan Heights. The attacks continued throughout the negotiations and ceased only with the signing of the disengagement accord on May 31. The artillery fire was less an act of terror than it was of desperation, although Israeli defenders on the Golan undoubtedly viewed it as the former. But for Asad, having lost territory in a conflict he initiated, the shelling was essential. Except for sixty-five prisoners of war, he possessed no negotiating leverage with which to bargain a return to the original demarcation line of October 6. Whatever agreement would be reached would involve essentially an Israeli withdrawal from advanced positions twenty miles from Damascus. But in return for what? Asad's artillery "war of attrition" was in reality his attempt to develop a bargaining position in which Israeli withdrawal could be (and was) exchanged for a cessation of the shelling and a return of prisoners.

Asad was in a fundamentally losing bargaining position. He demanded an *advance* over the position from which he had begun the war, as well as recovery of the territory he had lost in the conflict. He knew, however, that he had no alternative but to settle on the best terms he could obtain. Bargain hard to be sure, but settle nonetheless, for to reach no settlement would leave him literally and figuratively with Israeli guns pointed down his throat—a condition which would severely undercut his domestic political position. But there was never any possibility that Asad would go beyond a disengagement-of-forces agreement with Israel.

If Kissinger understood Asad's fundamentally weak position he gave no sign of it. He appeared only slightly less confused by Asad's tough bargaining stance than he was by the sequence of musical political chairs preceding the collapse of the Meir government (masking a major change in Israeli strategy) just before the Syrian disengagement negotiations got under way.

Following the December 31 elections in which the Labor-Alignment coalition emerged victorious but weakened, Prime Minister Meir attempted to form her third government. Increasing criticism of her government's conduct before and during the war, particularly of Defense Minister Moshe Dayan's role, prompted the defense minister to decline participation in the new government. Meir's replacement for Dayan was Yitzhak Rabin, a political independent with no factional loyalties but an excellent record of government service both as chief of staff of the armed forces during the Six Day War and as ambassador to the United States afterward.[11] Moreover, he was untainted by the recent conflict, having played no decision-making role.

If the prime minister thought that Rabin's appointment would quell criticism of the government she was mistaken. When she presented the new cabinet list to the Knesset on March 3, the resounding criticism triggered her immediate resignation. When Knesset members pleaded with the prime minister to reconsider, she agreed, but only on the condition that Moshe Dayan be reinstated as defense minister.[12] Dayan thereupon publicly declared his willingness to return to government service, displacing Rabin; and to justify his turnabout he adduced the flimsy pretext of intelligence reports warning against the danger of renewed hostilities on the Syrian front.

The third Meir government did not last five weeks. The prime minister had agreed the previous fall to the formation of a commission under Supreme Court Justice Shimon Agranat to investigate the government's conduct before and during the Yom Kippur War. The publication of the Agranat Commission's report in early April precipitated a new crisis, which brought down the government and led to Golda Meir's retirement from public life. Its main conclusion exonerated the political leadership of Meir and Dayan while blaming the military leadership, specifically the chief of staff of the armed forces, David Elazar, for negligence and intelligence failures in the months leading up to the war. The report was immediately denounced amid a renewed public outcry demanding the resignation of Moshe Dayan, the responsible civilian official. Before Dayan could respond, however, the prime minister brought the matter to a head by tendering her own resignation on April 11, bringing the entire government down.

At this juncture, Yitzhak Rabin was chosen (over Shimon Peres in a close vote) to head the new government. While he was attempting to form it, according to custom, the Meir government continued to function in a caretaker capacity. It was agreed that the Meir leadership would see to conclusion the negotiations for a disengagement-of-forces agreement with Syria, at which point the Rabin government would assume office.

The change of leadership in reality meant a change of strategy, although this was not immediately evident. Whether by design or chance, the Israeli leadership had immobilized itself. Neither the caretaker Meir government nor the successor Rabin government could undertake any new initiatives, the former because it was not empowered to do so and the latter by virtue of its composition. The Rabin government was in fact a troika, the prime minister, who had no political power base of his own, being flanked by Dayan protege Shimon Peres on one side and Yigal Allon on the other. The positions of the three men on the key issues of the current negotiations with Syria, the West Bank, and relations with Jordan, cancelled each other out, despite an initial and misleading indication toward compromise.

Rabin's position seemed quite flexible — or perhaps it is better to say ambiguous. He had articulated a "peace plan" the previous January, which in part called for no concessions on the Golan Heights and retention of sovereign control of Jerusalem — a non-negotiable stand taken by all Israeli leaders. Civil administration of the rest of the West Bank was to be turned over to Jordan, with Israeli troops remaining in control until "true peace" arrived at some undetermined time in the future.[13] Rabin had subsequently hinted at greater flexibility, however, in a remark to the effect that he would not mind visiting the Jewish settlements in the West Bank "on a tourist visa."[14] Shimon Peres' position was tougher, opposing any military withdrawal from the West Bank, although he, too, was willing to turn over civil authority to Jordan. Allon was most open to compromise, having also proposed a plan, the "Allon Plan," whereby Israel would make a substantial, but not complete, military withdrawal from the West Bank in a negotiated peace with Jordan.[15]

At any rate, it is evident that with the change of government the Israeli position was beginning to harden on the Golan Heights issue, yet it appeared to be open to compromise on the West Bank question. Undoubtedly, the fact that the successor to the Meir government was known to be tougher on the Golan Heights question but seemingly flexible on the West Bank affected both Asad's attitude toward what was ultimately attainable in the disengagement-of-forces negotiations and Kissinger's view toward what was feasible on the West Bank.

The Syrian-Israeli disengagement-of-forces agreement, signed on May 31, 1974, was similar in construction to the Sinai accord, but with some subtle differences.[16] In brief, it included the readjustment of military lines back to the October 6 starting point, with a United Nations buffer zone in between. Syria gained a small symbolic advance in Israel's acquiescence to Damascus' civil administration of the traditionally Syrian town of Kuneitra, which was placed within the UN buffer zone. The agreement specified limited forces sectors on either side of the UN buffer and exchange provisions for prisoners of war. Finally, just as in the Sinai accord, it was stipulated that it was "not a peace agreement"; but whereas the Sinai accord declared that the disengagement agreement was "a step toward a final, just and durable peace," the Syrian agreement left out the word "final."

Impasse Over the "Jordanian Option"

Kissinger's difficulties with the Meir government—and they were substantial—paled by comparison to those he shortly faced with the successor Rabin government. It soon became apparent, in fact, that the United States and Israel were moving in opposite directions regarding the structure of the region. Having produced disengagement agreements on Israel's northern and southern fronts, Kissinger now sought to tackle the Palestinian question. His efforts and the Rabin government's response precipitated a protracted crisis pushing Israeli-American relations to a new level of acrimony.

The crisis broke during President Nixon's unprecedented Middle East tour in mid-June. The trip itself was an event of major significance to American diplomacy, despite the reaction of some domestic critics who viewed it as an attempt to deflect criticism from

Watergate. The trip not only symbolized the increase in American influence in the Middle East, as the first sitting American president since Franklin Roosevelt visited the major capitals of the region, it was also the vehicle for a second step forward in the attempt to build what in later years would be termed a strategic consensus in the region.

The core of Kissinger's approach was the attempt to establish the basis for a resolution of the Palestinian problem. As the secretary put it, much less grandly, after its failure:

> I had thought that everybody's interest would be served best by establishing as rapidly as possible a Jordanian presence on the West Bank. This would make moderate Jordan the negotiator for the Palestinian phase of the peace process.[17]

In short, what Kissinger believed he could do and what he was led to believe he could do by the Israeli leadership was to shift the negotiation "into one . . . between the Jordanians and the Palestinians, rather than between the Palestinians and the Israelis."[18]

The opportunity seemed ripe. There was a new government in Israel headed by a "new" leader who appeared to be flexible on the key issues and who was, moreover, untainted by the war policy of the Meir government. The United States, too, seemed positioned to make a major move. Not only had the war been brought to an end with a demonstration of American might in facing down a Soviet "ultimatum," Washington had deftly maneuvered Egypt safely into the Western camp while also translating the cease-fires on both fronts into at least middle-term disengagement-of-forces agreements which carried clear political overtones.

Washington appeared to be in position to exert maximum influence over Israeli decision making as Tel Aviv was now isolated internationally and totally dependent upon the United States for political, economic, and military support. The move made at this time was not simply an attempt to "keep the momentum of the negotiations going" as one commentator has concluded;[19] it was an effort to lay the foundation for a long-range solution.

Nor did the American démarche take the Israeli leadership by surprise. At least two weeks before the president's trip Kissinger had told the Senate Foreign Relations Committee that a move toward Jordan would be "the sensible next step,"[20] and he said the same thing both to American Jewish leaders and to Moshe Dayan himself. Indeed, to the outgoing defense minister, Kissinger prophetically made the alternatives plain: either "bring the Jordanians into the West Bank, or . . . stonewall with Jordan and sooner or later all hell will break loose with the Palestinians."[21]

The American proposal fell upon deaf ears in Israel. The Israeli leadership would not be budged from its preferred strategic position, which it believed it had already attained with the two disengagement-of-forces agreements. Until this point, Prime Minister Rabin had taken no formal commitment one way or another on the question of the West Bank.[22] Now, while President Nixon and Secretary Kissinger were still in Israel, he announced that he would adhere to the Meir government's pledge to take any proposed solution of the West Bank to the voters in a general election. Taking this step locked the Rabin government into the same position as its predecessor, which barred any settlement and was a sharp rebuff to Washington. The Israeli leadership chose to "stonewall." It was willing to agree to administrative, but not military, disengagement on the West Bank.

Both Kissinger and Matti Golan, who have recounted the events from their respective sides, attempt to cover up the divergence that occurred at this time in different, but nevertheless transparent, ways. Yet both assign the responsibility for it to the Rabin leadership. Golan, for instance, observes that "Rabin had trapped himself with his pledge of general elections over any movement on the west bank [sic]," then explains it unconvincingly with the remark: "Perhaps it was his lack of experience, perhaps his sense of insecurity, perhaps it was just an inexplicable impulse."[23]

Kissinger also attempts to explain away the crisis with the comment that "conditions did not exist for such a step" inside Israel.[24] But the two negative "conditions" he cites quite literally were not responsible for the impasse. His first point was former Prime Minister Meir's commitment to take the West Bank issue to general elections, and his second the argument that Rabin's cabinet held only a one-vote majority, which "was too narrow a base to sustain a negotiation as divisive as disengagement on the West Bank."[25]

The problem with Kissinger's explanation is that it was factually incorrect, but only a reader familiar with Israeli politics would know this. On the first point, while it was true that Meir had vowed to take the West Bank issue to the general electorate, this was not the case for the successor Rabin government—at least, not until the moment

Nixon and Kissinger raised the issue during their trip. It was then and only then, in response to the American proposal, that Rabin reaffirmed the Meir government's commitment. Up to that point it had been an open issue, pointedly made so by Rabin himself. Indeed, that was partly why Washington had felt it politically feasible to raise it.

Kissinger's second point, that Rabin's cabinet held only a one-vote majority and was thus too narrowly based, rested upon more dubious ground. The secretary argued that the National Religious Party (NRP) would bring the Rabin government down "at the first sign of a West Bank negotiation."[26] The only problem with his explanation was that the NRP was not in the government at that time and thus could not bring it down over the West Bank issue.[27] Rabin's one-vote majority was achieved without the support of the NRP, which entered the government only later in October.

Clearly, the accounts of both men conceal the break point in United States-Israeli relations. Kissinger rather magnanimously concludes that the upshot of the Nixon visit to Israel was "to submerge the strategic question in a process of consultation," a result which "suited the necessities of *both* sides at that moment."[28] Golan, on the other hand, says simply that "Kissinger had not reckoned with the Byzantine intricacies of Israeli internal politics."[29]

If Kissinger had miscalculated his ability to persuade the Israeli leadership, he did not miscalculate the consequence of Israel's refusal. "When on October 28, 1974, an Arab summit in Rabat designated the PLO as the sole Arab representative and spokesman for the West Bank and removed Jordan from the diplomacy, the Israeli dilemma and the Palestinian negotiating stalemate that I predicted—and did not head off—both became inevitable."[30] The impasse of mid-June 1974 would shape the structure of United States-Israeli relations from then up to the present. Neither trivial nor transitory, the conflict of June 1974 also placed a major stumbling block in the path of American Middle East strategy.

United States-Israeli Strategic Crisis

Precisely because the conflict was strategic, long-term, and structural, it did not end with the June impasse. Kissinger continued to press the issue in different ways until it became impossible to push it any further—that is, until the Rabin government closed off all openings. Over the following month Washington suggested that unless Israel agreed to the Jordanian option the United States would attempt to deal with the Palestinians at Geneva, and to emphasize the point Washington slowed down arms deliveries.[31] Obdurate, the Israeli government responded with a July 21 cabinet decision agreeing to hold "negotiations for a peace agreement with Jordan." Adoption of a position calling for a final resolution to the problem, "a peace agreement," was in reality a decision to seek no resolution, for in private negotiations several months earlier King Hussein had already turned down such an offer based on the Allon plan. Thus, the Israeli leadership knew that a peace agreement was unlikely in the extreme when they proposed it. In fact, the Israeli decision was yet another repudiation of Secretary Kissinger, who was urging the Rabin government to agree to an "interim accord."[32]

Kissinger made one last half-hearted effort to reopen the Jordanian issue during Yigal Allon's visit to Washington in July, but when he was rebuffed, the secretary shifted to negotiation of a second disengagement agreement with Egypt, which the Rabin government had earlier proffered in lieu of an agreement with Jordan. But here, too, Israel now "stonewalled." Following Rabin's visit to Washington in September and Kissinger's trip to Israel the following month, Israel refused in addition further negotiations with Egypt. The Israeli leadership undoubtedly believed that it could refuse cooperation with impunity given the political malaise which settled over Washington in the summer of 1974. President Nixon's resignation on August 8 and the assumption of the presidency by Gerald Ford simply reinforced this conclusion. Ford was viewed as a caretaker president with little leverage, so the Israelis continued to stall, now defiantly.

Kissinger's November trip to the Middle East had produced a renewed willingness by Sadat to negotiate a second agreement with Israel, despite the Rabat injunction against separate agreements. Sadat wanted the return of the Sinai passes and the Abu Rudeis oilfields. In a bow to Rabat he insisted that the agreement be purely military in appearance, with no overt political concessions to Israel, although there would be obvious political implications to it.

It was in response to renewed pressure for a second Sinai agreement that the Israeli leadership, having closed off the Jordanian option, adopted a deliberate policy stance of defiance and disarray on the Sinai question, hoping to dissuade both Washington and Cairo of the desirability of further negotiations, or, if pressed, to agree only

on its own terms. First came the prime minister's remarkable interview of December 3, 1974, with the newspaper *Haaretz*.[33] In it he
offered a rather simplistic geostrategic analysis of the consequences
of the Yom Kippur War as the basis for a policy of inaction. The Arab
world's "ascent" due to ownership of oil, Europe's "descent" due to
dependency on it, and continued "sharp" contradictions between the
United States and the Soviet Union "in everything concerning the
Middle East, detente notwithstanding," boded ill for Israel's immediate future.

Under these circumstances "the central aim of Israel should be to
gain time," by which he meant "up to seven years, . . . seven lean
years." At this point the prime minister made a succession of utteran-
ces for which he was later heavily criticized as "giving away" Israel's
negotiating strategy, but which were carefully designed to provoke
Egypt into refusing to enter the talks.[34] "Our immediate practical
interest must be . . . to prevent Egypt's return to Soviet influence"
and Egypt's cooperation with Syria. The price Israel was willing to
pay to accomplish this was "another partial settlement." Israel, he
said, was willing to dispense with its demand for an Egyptian "non-
belligerency declaration" and enter into a military agreement which
had political implications.

However, the agreement must result in "no substantial change" in
Israel's military situation. Egypt must agree not to advance with its
forces into any area from which Israel withdrew. In any case territorial
concessions would not include the Sinai passes, which "[would]
remain in our hands." Rabin hinted at some flexibility with the remark
that territorial concessions would be "a little to the north and a little
to the south" of the passes, which implied a willingness to negotiate
return of the Abu Rudeis oilfields located near the southern tip of the
Sinai peninsula. The prime minister had omitted any mention of the
oilfields in his interview.

He went on to say that "tension between Israel and the United
States is likely to increase over the form this settlement should take."
This meant that Israel must pass the next year of its relations with
the United States "on the tips of our toes." Then in obvious reference
to the coming presidential elections he said: "If we pass 1975 in peace
and make it to 1976 we will gain not one year, but two." Finally, Rabin
boasted that the PLO "does not worry" him. In a slap at the Rabat
summit decision, which deprived King Hussein of his negotiating
authority on the Palestinian question, Rabin declared: "We must

prove that there is nothing to talk about with the PLO, and we will not talk with the PLO. This is likely in one year to restore Husayn as a partner in a positive move toward progress through talks."[35]

In a single brief interview Rabin managed to convey Israel's decision to freeze its position for "seven lean years," tough terms for a partial agreement on Sinai, disdain for the PLO, and readiness to resist all pressure from Washington. Israel was determined to hold out until election-year politics would undercut administration efforts to promote further compromise.

Kissinger's public reaction was, "Has Rabin gone mad?" Privately, however, he understood precisely what had happened. Indeed, it would appear that it was about this time that Kissinger decided enough was enough and began to engage in a test of strength with the Rabin leadership, which had evidently made a similar decision. Yigal Allon arrived in Washington a few days later. His meeting with Kissinger would mark the beginning of a six-month-long descent of American-Israeli relations to arguably the most serious conflict in an already crisis-studded relationship.

Allon had come with even tougher terms than those offered by Rabin in his interview, initiating a pattern in which Israel would publicly offer conciliatory terms but privately repudiate them.[36] This was the case now. The main points of Allon's negotiating brief centered around the reinstatement of the non-belligerency demand, contradicting what Rabin had said only a few days before. Similarly, where Rabin had been willing to sign an "interim agreement" with military content and only political implications, Allon demanded that negotiations result in an "agreement," not an "interim agreement," and that Egypt commit itself in advance to enter into a "peace agreement" of twelve years' duration. In return, Israel would pull back between thirty and fifty kilometers from its present positions but would relinquish neither the passes nor the oilfields.[37]

Both President Ford and Secretary Kissinger flatly rejected Allon's demands, pointedly noting the disparity between his and Rabin's positions. Allon's clearly inadequate reply was to claim that Rabin had been misquoted. In any case, when Sadat was informed of the Israeli position, he too rejected it outright. American-Israeli relations entered the new year at impasse, as the Israeli leadership sought to buttress its bargaining position by seeking to improve relations with Moscow.

Rabin inaugurated the campaign to improve relations with the Soviet Union during a speech January 27. Following his statement issued a few days earlier that Israel would be willing to return to the Geneva conference, he now called upon the Soviet Union to resume diplomatic relations with Israel if Moscow hoped "to play a meaningful role in the Middle East."[38] The Soviets, he said, "have to learn from the Americans that they cannot have an influence in the area unless they are able to talk to both sides." Rabin's diplomatic probe produced the desired result. As would be revealed in April, Soviet and Israeli officials held discreet talks.[39] But if the Rabin leadership thought that such talks would influence either the Soviet Union or the United States toward a softer line, they were mistaken. Moscow offered to guarantee Israel's borders "if it withdrew from occupied Arab lands," and Washington declared that "if Israel wants to go back to the 1967 borders with a Soviet guarantee, this is the way to do it."[40]

In the meantime, as Kissinger was preparing to visit the Middle East on an "exploratory trip" to determine the feasibility of resuming negotiations for a Sinai II agreement, Rabin once again took a publicly conciliatory position. In an interview on February 7 with an ABC correspondent, he offered to exchange both the passes and the oilfields "for an Egyptian commitment not to go to war, not to depend on threats of use of force, and an effort to reach true peace."[41] Although Golan viewed Rabin's offer as "the worst Israeli error during the whole lengthy negotiations," prompted by his running battle with Defense Minister Peres, and Kissinger said that Rabin was "destroying the negotiations even before they start," the prime minister's comment was contrived to put Israel on record as favoring the resumption of negotiations, as well as to lay the groundwork for blaming Egypt for their failure, as Rabin himself privately admitted.[42]

Three days later, on February 10, Kissinger embarked upon his "exploratory" trip, visiting Cairo, Jerusalem, Damascus, Amman, and Riyadh before meeting Soviet Foreign Minister Gromyko in Geneva on the sixteenth and the shah of Iran in Zurich the day after. His talks in Cairo and Jerusalem persuaded the secretary that conditions were ripe for a second shuttle, and his discussions with Gromyko appeared to clear up apparent Soviet objections. After their meeting Gromyko and Kissinger issued a joint statement affirming that the Geneva conference played an "important part" in the peace process and "should resume its work at an early date."[43] The following day Kissinger met with the shah in Zurich to arrange a secure oil supply for Israel to compensate for the anticipated loss of the Abu Rudeis oilfields. In a news conference on the eighteenth the shah offered an inducement, declaring that "Iran would send Israel *additional* oil if it returned the Abu Rudeis oilfields as part of a peace settlement with Egypt."[44]

With everything seemingly in place Kissinger returned to the Middle East on March 8 for what he believed would be the final negotiations of a Sinai II agreement. By March 19, after eleven days of shuttling between Cairo and Jerusalem, Kissinger had put together a compromise package which he recommended to the Israelis. Essentially, it included the following: In return for Israel's withdrawal from the passes and the oilfields, Egypt would agree to a "non-use of force" in their relations, thereby finessing the non-belligerency demand. The agreement would remain in effect until superseded by another agreement, also finessing the demand that Egypt commit itself in advance to a follow-on peace agreement. The central portion of the passes would be under UN control, while Egypt and Israel would occupy the western and eastern approaches, respectively. The UN peacekeeping mandate would be renewed every year instead of every six months.[45]

The Rabin leadership would have none of it, refusing Kissinger's compromise package. And Kissinger, attempting to influence the Israeli cabinet's deliberations, compounded the problem by resorting to his oft-used device of a threatening "presidential message."[46] In yet another in a litany of misjudgments, Kissinger's use of the "presidential threat" backfired, precipitating what was coming anyway—a crisis over conflicting strategy between the two countries, which in this case also was a bitter personal confrontation between Rabin and Kissinger.[47]

Hoping to forestall a rupture, Kissinger chose the "shock tactic" of threatening a break to bring about compliance and move around the impasse between Israel and the United States which threatened to destroy his larger plan of building a strategic consensus in the region. He hoped that maximum pressure applied at the last moment with a message from President Ford, which he evidently worded, would bring the Israelis around.[48] President Ford's March 21 message read, in part:

> I wish to express my profound disappointment over Israel's attitude. . . . Kissinger's mission, encouraged by your government, expresses vital United States' interests in the region. Failure of

the negotiations will have a far-reaching impact on the region and on our relations. I have given instructions for a reassessment of United States' policy in the region, including our relations with Israel. . . . You will be notified of our decision.[49]

The Rabin leadership would not buckle; it rejected Kissinger's package and ended the secretary's March shuttle in public and ig-nominious failure the next day. Rabin claimed in his memoirs that Kissinger's package did not satisfactorily resolve three key issues: the two countries' respective positions in the passes, continuation of Israel's early warning station in the Gidi Pass at Umm Hashiba, and the duration of the agreement.[50] Kissinger, however, denied that these were crucial issues. As he observed just prior to his departure: "An agreement would have allowed the United States to remain in control of the diplomatic process. Compared to that, the location of the line eight kilometers one way or the other does not seem very important."[51] The Israeli leadership had successfully defied the United States, its principal and perhaps only ally of significance, delivering to Washington a major setback at a time when, as Kissinger put it, "we look weak—in Vietnam, Turkey, Portugal, in a whole range of things."

But the glow of defiance faded quickly with Washington's ensuing "reassessment," which was accompanied by a continuation of pres-sure through materiel deprivation. Over the next two months, United States military and economic assistance to Israel was sharply curtailed and formal relations strained to the utmost, as Washington's "reassessment" looked more and more like retribu-tion. Both sides assiduously attempted to mobilize support within the United States Congress and among members of the foreign policy establishment. Kissinger blamed Israel for the breakdown of the negotiations, while the Rabin government held its ground. Calling upon its friends in Congress, the Israeli government managed to gain the endorsement of seventy-six senators for its position. The senators addressed a public letter to President Ford on May 21 calling for greater aid to Israel and supporting Israel's insistence upon "defensible" borders.[52]

But when the furor died down Israel had prevailed for the simple reason that the consequences of failure were greater for the United States than for Israel—at least in the short run. Indeed, during the two months following the breakdown of the shuttle, a reevaluation had been undertaken by both sides. Even though Kissinger's dire predictions regarding the failure to reach agreement had not materialized, the Israeli leadership had decided to return to the bargaining table for other reasons. Kissinger had warned that the failure to reach a second agreement would unite the Arabs, let the Soviets back in, and increase the danger of war.[53]

But Sadat knew that the war option was no longer realistic. To keep open the possibility for another settlement, he took Egypt out of a potential united Arab front Moscow was attempting to piece together with Syria and the PLO, buttressed by Libya. Sadat renewed the UN mandate in the buffer zone and announced that the Suez Canal would reopen on schedule, June 5. The mark of Moscow's failure to capitalize on the crisis in American-Israeli relations was the cancellation of Brezhnev's already once-postponed trip to Cairo. Moscow failed both to mend the break with Egypt and to reforge Arab unity. The Soviets did, however, establish relations with Libya, concluding a major arms arrangement in mid-May that was valued at between $1 billion (by United States intelligence) and $12 billion (by Sadat).[54] In a very real sense, Moscow and Washington had exchanged clients.

Even so, the Rabin leadership had decided that continued defiance of Washington was against its long-term interests. Israel would reach agreement with Egypt on a Sinai II accord but would go no further. If satisfactory assurances for Israeli security could not be obtained from Egypt directly, then the United States itself should compensate Israel by increasing its security commitment. Kissinger and President Ford, in a converging analysis, had come to the conclusion that continued pressure on Israel had become counterproductive and decided to shift approaches. Kissinger would now seek to purchase agreement through increased American support for Israel.

In what can only be interpreted as a major setback, the United States decided to accept the Israeli strategic choice of a "structural freeze" and forgo for the time being any further attempts to construct a strategic consensus. In return for the Sinai II accord, Washington agreed that the next round of negotiations with both Egypt and Jordan would be for the purpose of reaching final peace agreements— a bargain that was tantamount to saying that there would be no further negotiations, at least not under the current American leadership. Washington also agreed that it would neither recognize nor negotiate with the PLO as long as that organization did not recognize the state of Israel's right to existence.[55] Further negotiations with Syria were, of course, out of the question.

The Sinai II accords, signed September 4, 1975, pushed the United States into a greater commitment to Israel than to perhaps any other single state. With the Sinai II accord, the United States became a "virtual guarantor of the Middle East peace," turning the United States-Israeli relationship into an unwritten alliance.[56] The price was exorbitant but deemed worthwhile in terms of overall American strategy. The financial cost of obtaining Israel's agreement exceeded $2 billion. Washington obligated itself to supply the latest in American weapons technology — the F-16 aircraft and the Pershing IA missile (with conventional warheads) — and to see to it that Israel's current and reserve petroleum needs were met for five years. Finally, Washington agreed to deploy "technicians" to man the electronic monitoring stations in the passes.

Washington all but committed itself to come to Israel's defense if threatened by a major power — that is, the Soviet Union.[57] Worse, Kissinger agreed to Israeli demands that the Ford administration agree "to coordinate with Israel any future U.S. peace proposals and to refrain from recognizing or negotiating with the PLO until it acknowledged Israel's right to exist."[58] In other words, Kissinger gave the Israeli government a veto over American policy and made it virtually impossible to deal with the PLO.

In summary, the Sinai II accord represented a major failure of American Middle East strategy and a corresponding victory for Israel, however short-sighted that victory might appear in retrospect. Kissinger had sought to strengthen the Middle East *including Israel* against Soviet pressures by restructuring the region. The core of the strategy was Egyptian-Israeli rapprochement, which would break the Arab encirclement of Israel, bring Egypt into the Western camp, and enable Israel to concentrate its defense energies northward against Syria without concern for two-front engagement against Egypt as well. This much was in fact accomplished, but Kissinger had sought more than this minimum structural change. He had hoped to carry "step by step" diplomacy forward to a final peace agreement between Egypt and Israel and to neutralize the Palestinian issue through the reestablishment of Jordanian sovereignty over the West Bank.

Here his strategy failed in the face of determined Israeli refusal to withdraw from the territorial conquests of 1967. In what was a brilliantly conceived and masterfully executed rearguard negotiating campaign with the United States, the Israeli leadership—first under Meir and Dayan and then under Rabin, Peres, and Allon—made the minimum number of concessions necessary to maintain American support. The Israelis saw little benefit to their security in total withdrawal. Despite growing pressure from Washington—which at one point threatened the destruction of relations between the two countries—Israel refused to negotiate beyond the initial, partial withdrawal agreements. The second Sinai accord was literally a product of American coercion and bribery, for which Israel extracted an unprecedented price.

Aside from the issue of security, which was enormously important, there was the question of strategy. The success of Kissinger's strategy to build a structure capable of sustaining Soviet pressures implied a *reduced* United States commitment to Israel by virtue of broader American relations with the Arab nations. In Israeli eyes, if Washington succeeded in establishing a Tehran-Cairo-Riyadh axis there would be reduced reliance upon Israel to express American interests in the region. Although it appears to this author that this was an incorrect assessment of American strategic objectives, it nevertheless formed the basis for policy. Israel appeared to prefer a condition of maximum crisis requiring constant American commitment to a condition of reduced threat, which implied a concomitant reduction of commitment.

In brief, Kissinger committed a miscalculation born of *hubris* in assuming that he could realign Israel in a new structural-political relationship with the Arabs. His error lay in assuming that the Israelis would see, or could be persuaded to see, their strategic options in the same way that Washington saw them. The fact that Kissinger was required to purchase Israeli acquiescence at enormous cost would actually mean less, not more, influence over Israeli strategy and politics in the future. Ironically, in the end Kissinger adopted the approach that Nixon had advocated—direct political pressure combined with military and economic inducements—but only after the damage had been done. The failure to resolve the Palestinian-West Bank issue immediately shifted the conflict between the PLO and Israel to a new battleground in Lebanon. That error in judgment, serious as it was, however, was comparatively small beside the postwar miscalculations regarding the larger issues of oil, trade, and the dollar, to which we now turn.

Intensification of Intra-allied Political Contention

The Yom Kippur War and the accompanying energy crisis must be seen as an integrated, preemptive policy response by the United States to the multiple, intractable problems of Middle East deadlock; West European movement toward monetary, energy, and ultimately political unity; and West German and Japanese surges to economic superpower status. It was obvious that a politically unified and economically powerful Western Europe would lead to a restructuring of the global order, establishing a political bloc important enough to function as an independent entity between the United States and the Soviet Union and powerful enough to negotiate independent energy arrangements with the oil-producing nations. Within such a political grouping would be an economically, and to some extent militarily, resurgent West Germany—strong enough to shape the politics of continental union. Finally, Japan's parallel rise to economic superpower would become self-sustaining once Tokyo established independent access to crude oil supplies, presenting Washington with a similar problem in the Pacific. In other words, the rise to economic superpower status of West Germany and Japan threatened a return to the global structure of pre–World War II politics in which a strong Germany sought to control Europe and a powerful Japan attempted to dominate Asia.

The United States policy response was to employ the energy crisis in an attempt to derail the West European move toward political unity, which in practice meant undercutting EEC monetary and energy plans. Washington also sought to brake the economic growth surges of West Germany and Japan while at the same time siphoning off some portion of the wealth the two states had accumulated. Washington's strategic objective was to reestablish a political-economic balance within the alliance through a change in the terms of trade between Washington and its increasingly powerful allies by raising their basic costs of production.[59]

Washington was only partly successful over the succeeding five-year period through 1978. The movement toward West European unity was clearly forestalled, particularly the efforts to construct a monetary union and a common energy policy (which collapsed in early 1974 under the impact of the energy crisis);[60] but the objectives of containing the economic growth of West Germany and Japan and favorably altering the terms of trade in America's favor were not met.

In fact, much the opposite occurred as Washington's two allies—West Germany followed by Japan—produced an accelerated burst of export-led growth to overcome higher energy costs. Indeed, it is difficult to avoid the conclusion that the Kissingerian "strategic gamble" was largely responsible for the global crisis that followed, as much of the industrialized world was unable to respond successfully to the challenge.

The energy crisis began during the Yom Kippur War but was only peripherally related to it. OPEC and oil company representatives met October 8–12, 1973, in Kuwait for a negotiating session scheduled several months earlier. The oil company representatives refused to accept proposals for a 100 percent price increase, offering instead first an 8 percent, then a 15 percent rise in posted prices.[61] The failure to reach agreement resulted in a breakdown of the negotiations and on October 16 the unilateral announcement by the six Gulf ministers of OPEC of a 70 percent increase in the price of Arabian light marker crude to $5.12 per barrel, up from the previous marker price of $3.01 per barrel. Other OPEC members quickly followed suit.

The next day, October 17, the ten Arab members of OPEC, or OAPEC,[62] met in an attempt to employ the "oil weapon" as previously promised against Israel and its allies. Their decision, proposed by Saudi Arabia, was to cut production by 5 percent per month until Israel had withdrawn totally from the territories occupied in the 1967 war and the "legitimate rights of the Palestinian people are restored." Secondly, they decided to place an embargo against the United States, the Netherlands, Portugal, and South Africa, Israel's main supporters, while allowing "friendly" countries to continue to import the same volume of oil received prior to the cutback. Although an elaborate list grading various countries into categories of "most favored," "preferred," "neutral," and "embargoed" was drawn up, by January 1974 *all* countries except the four on the embargoed list had been moved to the "most favored" or "preferred" list,[63] which enabled them to import at levels reached before the war.

The peak of the Arab cutback occurred during November–December 1973 when 4.5 million barrels per day were withdrawn from the market. This represented a 14 percent reduction in OPEC output and a 10 percent reduction in total non-communist world output. While this was a real loss that created shortages for a brief period throughout the industrialized world, it was a cutback from the artificially high level of output of the second and third quarters of

1973 (see chapter 6 above). Indeed, the entire year's output was well within the industry's projected 9.5 percent historical growth rate.[64] (Remarkably, fourth-quarter 1974 output would be virtually the same as that of 1973, and the concern at that time would be about a potential *surplus*, not shortfall.)

Nevertheless, on the basis of the cutback in the fourth quarter 1973, in late December the price of oil was raised again sharply from $5.12 to $11.65, effective January 1, 1974—a price level which would remain more or less constant until the second oil shock in 1979. The December price increase was the direct result of the surge in spot market prices in response to the fourth-quarter market shortfall and triggered a split between Saudi Arabia and Iran, the two largest producers, over the advisability of a large price increase.

Although the Saudis had been the prime movers behind the political use of the "oil weapon" in support of the Arab cause against Israel, they now sought to limit its economic consequences. On December 16 the Iranian National Oil Company had for the first time conducted an auction of some of its oil, bringing unexpectedly high bids, the highest being $17.30 per barrel.[65] Saudi Foreign Minister Ahmed Zaki Yamani argued that the $17 per barrel price obtained at the December 16 auction "should not be taken as the basis for determining the new posted prices for Gulf crudes."[66] The high spot price, he said, was simply a reflection of the effect of the "oil embargo and cutback measures" which were of a political nature and "should not have an economic effect."

But this was precisely the aim of the shah of Iran, who, ironically, was neither Arab nor anti-Israeli and who had never been a proponent of high prices, either. In an abrupt turnabout, the shah now demanded a major price increase, to $23 per barrel, which he said was more than justified by the $17 spot price. Yamani countered with a proposal for $8 per barrel. After intense argument a compromise was reached on the price of $11.65, but the split between the Saudis and the Iranians which emerged at the meeting would persist (indeed, it continues to the present).[67]

The abrupt reversal in the shah's position and the obvious benefit to the United States and to the multinational oil companies of the price rise prompted immediate and persistent rumors of conspiracy.[68] In his zeal to refute charges that the shah and Washington were in collusion, Kissinger's account of the December price hike raises more questions than it answers. Apart from the counteraccusation that the collusion argument is "demagogic ignorance," he asserts incorrectly that there was "unanimous" agreement in OPEC for the price rise, conveniently ignoring Saudi objections.[69] Of course, to acknowledge a split within OPEC would open the door to breaking the price, which was not Kissinger's intention. If there was no collusion, there was certainly a coincidence of interest between Washington and Tehran.

Kissinger's attempt to explain why the shah pressed for ultra-high prices is unsatisfactory. "Perhaps," he offers, it was his nationalism; "surely," ego played its part; "very likely" the shah desired to show solidarity with the Arab cause.[70] The last was a particularly peculiar argument to make in view of the facts that Tehran continued to supply American and Israeli petroleum needs and that Iran's relations with the Arabs were not close.[71] Finally, Kissinger claims that "the record sketched in these pages leaves no doubt that neither we nor our industrial allies were informed of the plan for a colossal price increase until it was nearly upon us—too late to affect it—and that we then reacted strenuously." The fact is, however, that Kissinger's "record" addresses none of these issues, focusing overwhelmingly on his efforts to lift the embargo, but not to fight the price increase.[72]

On December 25, two days after the shah announced the price hike to $11.65, OAPEC removed virtually all of the oil sanctions from all but the four embargoed importers and then, cancelling the scheduled 5 percent cutback for January, announced a 10 percent production increase, thus marking the beginning of the end of the oil shortage. (So much for the Arab vow that the cutbacks would continue until Israel had withdrawn completely from the occupied territories and the Palestinian people's legitimate rights had been restored. At this point, not even the first Israeli-Egyptian partial settlement had been concluded.)

But whether there was collusion between the United States and one of its closest allies, or merely a happy coincidence of interest, Kissinger moved quickly to take advantage of the crisis before the moment for action was lost. By this time, the Europeans and the Japanese were assiduously separating themselves from Washington's position on the Middle East while intensifying their attempts to establish independent links to the oil producers.

During the October war, Washington's allies, with the exception of the Netherlands and Portugal, refused to allow the United States the use of NATO facilities for the transport of military supplies to

Israel, or even to permit the overflight of their territory for that purpose. Their stated rationale was to remain neutral in the conflict, but their obvious interest was in using the opportunity afforded by the conflict to develop independent relations with the oil producers. This aloof attitude naturally became more pronounced after the Arab imposition of the embargo and production cutbacks, and it did not abate when restrictions were removed toward the end of the year. This was the state of affairs when Kissinger moved to play Washington's cards in the energy game with the Western allies.

Prodding the Allies into Disarray

The energy crisis obscured the changes that were continuing to take place in the global petroleum market, particularly regarding the position of the once-dominant multinational oil companies. In the few years since 1970, the producing countries had regained owner-ship of their oil either through negotiation with, or expropriation of, the oil companies. Gradually they began to venture into the world market through their own national oil companies. Left to run its course unimpeded, this trend would have eventually led to the withering away of the American companies' control of world oil. Having relinquished control of in-country production operations, the oil companies were now threatened with loss of control of the distribution and allocation system, too, since the producing countries were no longer bound to market all of their oil through the inter-nationals.[73]

A second factor threatening to undercut the majors' positions further was the imminent influx onto the world petroleum market of several new sources of oil, an influx that would be accelerated by the rise in oil prices. The new sources, all outside of OPEC, were North Sea oil, which would eliminate both Great Britain's and Norway's former dependence on imports and make them net exporters; Alaskan oil, which would provide an important supplement to American crude needs; and Mexican oil, where new discoveries in 1972 promised to make Mexico a major player in the market again, as it had been earlier in the century.

Production trends within OPEC itself were disquieting. Only in 1970 had Nigeria begun to produce oil in prodigious quantities, and in 1973 it produced over two million b/d.[74] The United Arab

Emirates occupied a similar position. From 1971 the UAE had begun to produce in excess of one million b/d, reaching 1.5 million b/d in 1973.[75] When one adds to this the eventual release for sale of the million and a half barrels of oil per day being held back by Libya's Gadhafi, the prospect for an inundation of the petroleum market was quite high.

The gradual loss of control of the world petroleum system combined with the near-term inevitability of excess supply led American strategists to several inescapable conclusions. First and foremost, it would mean the end of American ability to control European and Japanese independent access to petroleum and the beginning of the end of American hegemony in the Western alliance as it had existed after World War II. The less West Germany and Japan had to pay for oil in dollars, or to rely upon American goodwill and protection to obtain oil, the stronger would become centrifugal tendencies against the dollar bloc—that is, the current, non-communist global system of multilateral trade and currency exchange.[76] Secondly, independent access to inexpensive energy would greatly enhance the low production costs that had enabled the allies to make the export-led trade gains achieved to date, placing the United States at even greater disadvantage. The net result would facilitate the emergence of de facto deutschemark and yen blocs, which would be the foundation stones for emerging political independence.

American policy from early 1974 would be to maintain a high world oil price regime, lock the allies into it to the extent possible by establishment of a consumers cartel, and preserve the key distribution role of the American multinational oil companies. The Washington Energy Conference, convened in mid-February 1974, was the starting point. Kissinger averred that establishment of a consumers cartel would "strengthen the bargaining position of the consumers vis-à-vis the producers," but went on to add defensively:

> Some participants would deny that this was the purpose and even believe it in their fear of the moment. But reality transcends what people say about it, and the reality of what came to be known as the International Energy Agency (formally established later in the year) was to promote the cohesion of the industrial democracies in the field of energy, which in turn made a major contribution to improving the bargaining position of the consumers.[77]

If by strengthening consumers against producers Kissinger meant that IEA gave the consuming nations *price* leverage against the producers, he was incorrect—even from the vantage point of eight years afterward when he published his memoirs. The reality was that the dollar price of oil did not change appreciably between 1974 and 1978.[78] The IEA did, however, strengthen the position of the United States vis-à-vis the Western allies, precisely by promoting the stabilization of high prices and institutionalizing the role of the multinational oil companies as primary distributors.

When Kissinger issued formal invitations on January 9 for the Washington conference, the allied response was decidedly unenthusiastic, for they were themselves individually attempting to establish direct ties to the producers. The French made European (and undoubtedly Japanese) concerns explicit. Hoping to avoid convocation of a Washington-sponsored gathering, Pompidou proposed on January 24 that producers and consumers "meet bilaterally at the European level."[79] And to reinforce his point he sent his foreign minister, Michel Jobert, on a tour of the Middle East in search of barter deals during the days prior to the opening of the conference. Jobert's trip offered a glimpse of what would soon be termed the "Euro-Arab dialogue."

In retrospect, what appeared to be a crude policy play by the United States to restrict allied efforts to enter into private arrangements with the oil-producing countries was actually its opposite. In this instance perhaps more than most, it is necessary to have a clear perception of actual as opposed to stated American objectives. Although the stated objective was to strengthen consumers vis-à-vis producers, the actual United States objective was to disorganize the European powers, forcing national as opposed to supranational responses to the crisis, thereby blocking progress toward West European unity, whose foundation stones were monetary and energy union. Since oil was bought and sold in dollars and not in other currencies, the role of the dollar remained central in the international monetary order. Thus, the sharp hike in oil prices had dealt a staggering blow to European monetary union. In fact, the just-established European monetary arrangements would atrophy in the succeeding five years, not to be revived until 1979.[80]

The energy crisis in general and the Washington Conference in particular also functioned as instruments to block efforts toward creation of European energy unity. For example, although the EEC had been in the process of forming a common energy policy since 1970, the Yom Kippur War overtook and undermined those efforts. When the Netherlands, one of the embargoed nations, on October 30 requested EEC agreement to pool and share supplies, the EEC, with the British and French in the forefront, rejected the request, on the grounds that since no common energy policy had yet been formulated, there was no requirement to share.[81] The lesson was clear and undoubtedly not lost upon American leaders. Energy needs took precedence over political unity.

Thus, although the declared intent of the Washington Conference was to organize the consumers and thereby—as interpreted by the allies—deny them flexibility in oil supply arrangements, it had the opposite effect. Kissinger made a great spectacle of refusing to countenance any suggestions that consuming countries meet with producing countries before the consumers were "united," for they would then be free to reach any arrangement they wished, bypassing Washington and the multinationals. In a January 8 meeting with the NSC staff he was reported to have railed against the Europeans and vowed that the United States would not

> give them a free field for bilateral deals. And if they will not work multilaterally, we will force them by going bilateral ourselves. If we go bilateral, we can preempt them, I think, in most areas. We will in no circumstances turn over the field to them bilaterally.[82]

This accounted for Kissinger's insistence upon convening the conference first. But the simple fact was that despite bluster and threat from Washington—and there was quite a bit of it—there was precious little that the United States could do to "force them" to cooperate, or to prevent the allies from making whatever arrangements they considered necessary. But Washington could attempt to affect the *timing* of those arrangements. Indeed, the very declaration of intent to organize the allies spurred them into a frenzy of bilateral deals.

In other words, the elaborate American posturing ostensibly designed to head off allied efforts to make bilateral agreements with the oil producers was actually contrived to prod them into striking hastily arranged, long-term supply contracts while the prices were at a peak, thus reinforcing the price level. The allies in this way would saddle themselves with increased energy costs in their zeal to ensure security of supply.[83] The fact that Washington was even then renegotiating its own relationships with both Saudi Arabia and Iran (which would be consummated in the spring of 1974) sharply reinforced allied bilateral tendencies, severely undercutting the move toward European union.

The Washington Conference itself, as Kissinger has noted, was "a strange event." A meeting of allies, "it had something of the character of a clash of adversaries."[84] Although the allies reluctantly agreed to establish the International Energy Agency (except for France and briefly Norway), the establishment of a consumers cartel gave no leverage to the oil-importing nations. In fact, the very act of forging a buyers cartel to deal with OPEC tended to reinforce the oil producers' organization.

There were from Washington's point of view two principal achievements at the conference.[85] The first was acceptance of an American-proposed oil-sharing plan whereby in case of a subsequent shortage of supply an emergency allocation scheme would be put into effect. The emergency plan would be triggered automatically whenever a member nation experienced a 7 percent shortfall in supplies. The plan, however, was never activated — not even during the second oil shock of 1979. The IEA itself became essentially an information collection body for the multinational oil companies on the plans and capabilities of member countries.

The second "achievement" was the agreement to institutionalize the multinational oil companies as a quasi-cartel in their own right. Their status change would occur formally in November when the International Energy Agency would be established. Based upon their impartial, competent allocation of short supplies during the crisis, the oil companies were assigned the responsibility of executing the emergency allocation program, a decision which had the effect of strengthening their middleman role as distributors. This, too, reinforced the overall bloc-like structure of producers and consumers, with the multinational oil companies as go-between.

High Oil Prices, Trade, and the Dollar

Aside from a plethora of public declarations deploring the high price of oil and "inadvertent" disclosure of "contingency plans" regarding seizure of the oilfields, the United States took no substantive action to bring down prices. The Saudis quickly perceived Washington's disinclination to seek a price reduction. Their reasoning was that if the United States actually desired to bring down prices Washington would have exerted pressure upon the shah of Iran, who clearly held the key to lowering prices. The Saudis were already convinced that prices were too high. Thus, they reasoned, if the United States were able to convince the shah to lower prices, "nothing could have prevented a combined effort by Iran and Saudi Arabia to bring this about."[86]

The United States not only did not exert any pressure on the shah, its principal spokesman and policymaker, Henry Kissinger, did exactly the opposite. When Kissinger visited Tehran in the fall of 1974, the Saudis expected him to remonstrate with the shah on the issue of oil prices. Instead, according to Iranian accounts afterward, Kissinger "expressed general satisfaction with the prevailing oil price level."[87] The same was true for Saudi Arabia. According to the recollection of Saudi Foreign Minister Yamani:

> The real interest for the United States is in higher oil prices. I do not recall that Dr. Henry Kissinger ever raised the subject of oil prices with us although he talks to us frequently. These are well-known facts. Their whole interest is in raising the price of oil. This is a political decision in the first instance, then an economic one.[88]

In fact, Kissinger sought to convey the impression that any attempt to lower prices would create instability while maintaining the fiction that the Saudis and the Iranians held a common price position. In an interview in Business Week in early 1975, he declared: "The only chance to bring oil prices down immediately would be massive political warfare against countries like Saudi Arabia and Iran to make them risk their political stability and maybe their security if they do not cooperate. That is too high a price to pay even for an immediate reduction in oil prices."[89]

What made Kissinger's behavior doubly transparent was that his efforts to prop up oil prices came during a period when price was weakening and there was widespread expectation that the end of high prices was in sight. By the fall of 1974 the effects of the energy crisis began to be felt economically in a worldwide recession which resulted in a sharp reduction in world trade volume, the first since

World War II.[90] There occurred a commensurate decline in demand for petroleum as well as greater conservation. Moreover, since the price of oil remained high and did not respond to the drop in demand, the high price continued to attract additional oil to the marketplace. Not only was OPEC having increasing difficulty controlling the production of member countries, which had oil to sell and now their own national oil companies through which to sell it, non-OPEC oil began coming on the market as well from Mexico, Alaska,[91] and the North Sea.

In auctions held by Iran and Kuwait to market spot crude in the fall, bids ranged between $10.10 and $10.25, substantially below the official OPEC price of $11.65.[92] In their efforts to firm up prices OPEC cut production by 3.6 million b/ d, from 30.7 million b/ d to 27.1 million b/ d. Two American oil companies in Indonesia, Texaco and Standard Oil of California, also reduced production by 200,000 b/ d,[93] while the United States continued to import ever larger amounts. Both of these actions, of course, had the same effect, firming prices by reducing surplus.

At this juncture, in early 1975, Kissinger proposed the establishment of a price floor of an incredible $6.00 to $8.00 per barrel on the grounds that a reduction in price would make it increasingly difficult to justify investment in alternative energy sources.[94] The allies, particularly Japan, immediately rejected Washington's proposal. Kissinger persisted, however, and in December of 1975 the International Energy Agency adopted a $7.00 per barrel price floor, saddling consumers with high energy costs indefinitely. The price floor plan was eventually included as part of the IEA's "Long Term Energy Cooperation Program" in 1976, making clear the United States' interest in maintaining a high oil price regime indefinitely.

How well did the high oil price strategy work? The energy crisis clearly stopped the momentum toward European unity as the individual member states scrambled to ensure stable sources of supply. Movement toward monetary union was also halted. But success depended greatly upon braking the growth surges of West Germany and Japan, siphoning off a portion of the wealth they had accumulated, and reestablishing a political-economic balance among the three powers that would entail relatively similar rates of growth. Thus harnessed, alliance stability would be reinforced.

Here, American strategists miscalculated badly. They expected that the rise in energy costs would bring closer if not equalize the costs of production between the United States and its allies, making American products more competitive and improving Washington's trading position. They also anticipated, as computer simulations would have indicated, that the higher energy costs would be a drain on reserves which Germany and Japan would have to use to pay for oil. Finally, they calculated that the overall effect would be to slow down the rates of growth of Washington's two allies.

But American strategy backfired. Although production costs increased, Germany responded immediately and vigorously to the challenge posed by the United States, and Japan reacted only slightly less strenuously after a year's delay. The result was that not only did American policy fail to brake German and Japanese growth in any long-lasting sense, it also failed utterly to equalize the terms of trade among them. Worse, the ensuing "struggle for the world product,"[95] as German Chancellor Helmut Schmidt aptly described it, accelerated the fragmentation of the very international economic system the United States sought to strengthen.

Clearly, the cost of oil as a percentage of gross national product increased for all nations and was higher for West Germany and Japan than it was for the United States, but it was not an excessively heavy burden for them.

Cost of Oil
As a Percentage of GNP

	U.S.	West Germany	Japan
1972	0.36	1.29	1.50
1974	1.72	3.26	4.66
increase	1.36	1.97	3.16

Source: Gisselquist, *Oil Prices and Trade Deficits*[96]

The increased energy costs posed a subtle dilemma for the allies. If they *appreciated* their currency to reduce energy cost they would raise the cost of their exports through exchange-rate adjustment; if they *depreciated* their currency to increase exports, energy costs would rise, increasing the cost of production. Either course of action theoretically would lead to an automatic adjustment of imports and exports, which would over time gradually equalize the trade positions among the three powers. In addition, the allies would be forced to use a portion of their accumulated reserves to help defray the increased cost of energy. The overall effect would be to siphon off some of their wealth, rein in their previously high rates of growth, and enable the United States to reestablish a preeminent position within the alliance, or at a minimum prevent the erosion of the American position—at least, so went the theory.

Unfortunately for the United States, events did not follow theory. American strategy failed in the central purpose of checking its principal allies. Both West Germany and Japan, virtually alone among industrialized countries, solved the dilemma of high energy prices, albeit in different ways. It was Bonn's response to allow the deutschemark to appreciate to reduce energy costs, while Japan, initially at least, chose the depreciation approach, hoping to offset higher energy costs through increased trade revenue.

West Germany under Willy Brandt, somehow anticipating the energy crisis, had begun an energy conservation program in September 1973 prior to the outbreak of the Yom Kippur War. By December, Bonn had cut energy consumption by 20 percent and was well positioned to respond to the energy challenge.[97] Over the next five years through 1978, Bonn would gradually allow the mark to appreciate against the dollar, from DM2.40 in 1974 to DM1.82 in 1978.[98]

According to the theory, this should have meant a reduction in West Germany's trade surplus as a result of the increased price of German goods, but it did not. West Germany achieved the unprecedentedly large trade surplus in 1974 of $19.6 billion, compared to $11.7 billion in 1973.[99] And it would continue. Bonn ran large surpluses each year; in 1975 it was $15.2 billion, in 1976 it was $13.8 billion, in 1977 it grew to $16.6 billion, and in 1978 it reached $20.4 billion.[100] Nor was there any drain on West German reserve holdings, which, including gold, increased progressively except for a slight dip during the global recession in 1975, from $33.1 billion in 1974 to a remarkable $57.8 billion in 1978.[101]

Japan's strategists performed equally well, lagging only slightly behind the West German performance. Tokyo's initial approach was to depreciate the yen, possibly calculating that they would be able to hold down production costs sufficiently to pay the additional energy cost. In any case, the yen/dollar exchange rate went from Y280 in 1973 to Y300 in 1974 and Y305 in 1975, but produced no significant increase in exports.[102] The global recession hurt the Japanese badly. Exports stagnated between 1974 and 1975 at $55.5 billion and $55.7 billion. In 1975 Japan cut back on imports to reduce a $6.5 billion deficit to $2.1 billion in 1976, beginning a rebound that, as it turned out, would continue to the present.

Part of the recovery involved a shift from depreciating the yen to appreciating it, beginning in 1976 and continuing through the period.[103] The yen went to Y292 in 1976, Y240 in 1977, and Y194 in 1978. The result was a sharp turnaround in both the trade and reserve positions. From 1976 to 1978 Japan's trade surplus increased dramatically, from $2.5 billion to $9.8 billion to $18.5 billion.[104] Similarly, reserve holdings (including gold) moved from $12.8 billion in 1975 to $33.4 billion in 1978 — an astonishing increase.

The global recession had hindered Japan much more than West Germany, but by the end of 1975, when it was ending, both nations had resumed their strong performances. Indeed, recovery by America's two powerful allies turned the tables on Washington and presented the United States with a painful dilemma. The high oil price strategy now began to work against American interests, for while West Germany and Japan had begun to recover from the recession, almost none of the rest of the industrialized world (not to mention the less industrialized nations) had done so.

In truth, high oil prices were beginning to undermine the entire world system. If the United States continued its struggle with West Germany and Japan, the system would be threatened. On the other hand, if Washington gave up the struggle in order to save the system, West Germany and Japan would move further ahead. Washington's choice, made in late 1976, was a tentative attempt to accomplish both the recovery of the industrialized and less industrialized nations, and the placement of restraints upon the Germans and the Japanese. On the one hand, Washington began to increase its imports to enable other countries to export more and to thus facilitate their recoveries. On the other hand, Washington pressed Bonn and Tokyo to reflate — that is, to import more themselves, expanding their domestic economies while holding back somewhat on exports. In 1979, Under Secretary of State for Economic Affairs Richard Cooper explained the United States policy decision:

> By late 1976, the world economy was in a very precarious situation. Unemployment was high in the United States; it was high

and rising in Europe. Many countries, including some of the large industrialized countries as well as many developing countries, found themselves with a very large burden of external indebtedness. Those countries had to engage in economic and financial retrenchment. Yet that alone would have aggravated and prolonged the world recession, making corrective actions in all countries more difficult. Under these circumstances, *for both domestic and foreign policy reasons*, the United States undertook a program of economic expansion to end the recession.[105]

In terms of international economic policy, President Ford's legacy to the incoming Carter administration was one chiefly of hope — hope that West Germany and Japan would cooperate in holding together what was now a rapidly disintegrating global economic system. The stark inadequacy of this policy would soon become apparent. While the United States struggled vainly with its allies to maintain the integrity of the Western alliance system, the Soviet Union moved to exploit the opportunities unfolding before it under the rubric of "detente."

CHAPTER

9

Detente and Tripolar Politics, 1973–1976

Central to Henry Kissinger's effort to construct a new international order were Washington's relationships with Moscow and Beijing. Toward the former, he hoped through "detente" to draw the Soviet Union into a beneficial, but not irreversible, network of political and economic relationships with the West including increased trade, credit, technology transfer, and arms control. His assumption was that with a larger stake in the existing order Moscow would be less inclined to employ growing strategic weapons power to alter the geopolitical balance of forces—at least for the time being. Meanwhile, Kissinger sought to use the time gained during the period of peaceful relations to attempt to adjust United States positions around the Soviet periphery—the first steps of disengagement—in Western Europe, the Middle East, Southwest Asia, and the Far East.

Toward Beijing, Kissinger initiated a complex diplomatic maneuver designed on the one hand to reinforce the Sino-Soviet adversary relationship and on the other hand to increase Beijing's dependence upon the United States for support against Moscow. Here, too, Kissinger sought to draw China into a fruitful set of political-economic relationships, while moving to shape the geopolitical order around China's periphery. Thus, in addition to improving economic relations with Beijing, Washington maneuvered to place China in a geopolitical vise between the Soviet Union in the north and a unified Vietnam in the south.

The policy designed to achieve this objective was the abrupt and complete abandonment of the Paris Peace Accords formula of continued maintenance of the fragmented structure of Indochina and the withdrawal of American presence and influence from the Southeast Asian mainland. The result was not only the establishment of a unified Vietnam under Hanoi, but also the extension of Sino-Soviet adversary relations to Cambodia and elsewhere. At the same time, Washington appeared to promote an American-Japanese-Chinese entente to strengthen the Northeast Asian theater against Soviet pressures.

Key parts of Kissinger's finely crafted geopolitical scheme began to fail almost as soon as he attempted to put them into place. He badly miscalculated the effect on the Maoist leadership of Washington's policy shift in Vietnam, which had an immediate adverse impact on Sino-American relations. Nor did he anticipate correctly the Soviet reaction to detente as Moscow surprised American leaders with a sweeping strategic weapons advance and then sought to take advantage of unfolding geopolitical opportunities in precisely those areas in Asia, the Middle East, Southwest Asia, Europe, and even Africa (in the wake of Portugal's imperial collapse) that Kissinger had hoped to strengthen. With his strategy failing, Kissinger attempted to exacerbate Sino-Soviet hostility in Angola; and when this, too, failed, he denounced Soviet expansionism as incompatible with detente.

By 1976, President Ford would declare detente dead, American-Soviet relations would be on rocky ground, and the United States-China relationship would be stillborn. Both the tripolar and trilateral initiatives that comprised the new American strategy, even though they produced small successes in each area that moved the United States incrementally toward the desired structural position, were failures in a larger sense, for they left the nation far worse off than at the inception of the new strategy.

The Economic Web of Detente

In endeavoring to develop its economic relationship with the Soviet Union, the administration proceeded unilaterally without advice or consent from the U.S. Congress, which was constitutionally responsible for the regulation of American trade.[1] Whether by design or ignorance, this course of action guaranteed an eventual congressional response — even backlash — which would severely limit, perhaps even scuttle, the administration's policy. But a congressional response would be some time in coming, long enough, perhaps, for the administration to accomplish its objectives. The legislative record of Washington's efforts to extend most-favored-nation (MFN) status and long-term credit to Moscow suggests that Kissinger never intended to lock the United States into a fixed and inflexible trade relationship with the Soviet Union, but used the prospect of one as a means of immobilizing Moscow while moving to adjust the United States position around the Soviet periphery.[2]

Washington had carefully nurtured Soviet expectations regarding the economic benefits of a cooperative relationship with the United States. Trips to Moscow by Secretary of Commerce Maurice Stans in November 1971 and Secretary of Agriculture Earl Butz in April 1972 stimulated a revival of American-Soviet trade. For example, in the first significant commercial transaction between the two countries in the Nixon administration, on February 16, 1972, the Department of Commerce announced that the U.S. government had approved fifty-one licenses for the export of $367 million in truck manufacturing equipment for the Kama River plant.[3]

Then, at the Moscow summit in May, the two countries agreed to establish a joint commercial commission whose tasks would be to negotiate a trade agreement, which would include most-favored-nation status for the Soviet Union, establish long-term credit arrange-ments, facilitate the opening of offices in both countries to promote trade, and conclude an arbitration mechanism for settling commercial disputes.[4] The joint commercial commission was something of a disappointment for the Soviets, who had been pressing for conclusion of a trade agreement between the two countries to accompany the arms control measures agreed to at the time; but Washington made clear that full development of trade relations must await settlement of outstanding issues between the two countries, particularly the war in Vietnam and a World War II lend-lease settlement.

If the failure to conclude a trade agreement during the summit was disappointing to the Soviets, two other developments were very encouraging. First, on July 8, 1972, the United States and the Soviet Union signed a three-year grain agreement, according to which the Soviet Union would purchase more than $750 million worth of wheat and other grain from the United States. The agreement was the single largest commercial transaction in the history of trade between the two countries.[5] It was accompanied by the an-nouncement that the United States Commodity Credit Corporation would provide credit for the huge Soviet grain purchase.

Second came the report of Secretary of Commerce Peter G. Peterson, "U.S.-Soviet Commercial Relationships in a New Era," released in August following his return from the first meeting of the joint commercial commission. Stressing the "natural fit" of the Soviet and American economies, Peterson called for a *$10 billion* expansion of the U.S. Export-Import Bank's credit authority to facilitate the extension of long-term government credits to Moscow, particularly for the development of two gigantic Siberian natural gas projects, "North Star" and Yakutia. Proposing a vast expansion of American-Soviet trade, Peterson offered to include high technology in the bargain on the grounds that "the increased availability of high technology products elsewhere rendered some of our original curbs on exports to the Soviet Union increasingly anachronistic."[6]

Progress in the negotiations between Washington and Hanoi during the first week of October quickly brought agreement on the American-Soviet trade front, suggesting that there was indeed a degree of linkage involved. On October 14 the two sides signed a maritime agreement which opened forty ports in each country to the vessels of the other for shipping and access for replenishment and repairs. Four days later Washington and Moscow signed a three-year trade agreement and an agreement settling World War II lend-lease claims.[7] Moscow agreed to repay $722 million on its original war debt of $11 billion,[8] while Washington agreed to most-favored-nation status for the Soviet Union and extension of Export-Import Bank credits for Soviet purchases in the United States. The trade agreement contained the explicit expectation that American-Soviet trade would "at least triple" over the next three years compared to the 1969–1971 period.

The trade agreement appeared to establish the foundation for a greatly expanded economic relationship. However, while American-Soviet trade more than tripled between 1972 and 1975 (from $542 million to $1.83 billion), the content of the trade relationship — mostly agricultural goods — fell far short of Soviet expectations. Even as the administration implemented the agreement, congressional opponents of detente and expanded economic relations with Moscow, led by Senator Henry Jackson of Washington state, all but gutted any possibility of the development of a major trade relationship involving the transfer of American capital goods and technology between the United States and the Soviet Union.

Three key amendments attached to pending trade and Export-

Import Bank legislation severely limited the nature of any future trade relationship. The Jackson-Vanick amendment, introduced on October 4, 1972, tied the expansion of trade to relaxation of Soviet emigration laws for Jewish citizens. It required specific congressional approval to extend most-favored-nation status and financial credits to the Soviet Union beyond a period of twelve to eighteen months and congressional approval of a presidential determination that the emigration requirements of the Trade Act were being followed. A second amendment, sponsored by Senator Adlai Stevenson III of Illinois, on June 17, 1974, placed a $300 million ceiling on loans to the Soviet Union by all government agencies and a presidential determination that any sale over $50 million was in the national interest. Finally, Senator Frank Church of Idaho gained passage of an amendment which specifically proscribed United States credits for the two large, long-term energy projects in Siberia.

While this legislation was pending, the administration continued to promote trade relations on both a governmental and private basis.[9] On November 16, 1972, less than a month following the signing of the trade agreement, Pepsi Cola Corporation concluded an agreement whereby in exchange for the right to make and sell Pepsi in the Soviet Union, the company would market Soviet vodka and wine in the United States. The next day Chase Manhattan Bank announced Soviet approval of its proposal to establish a branch office in Moscow.

On March 20, 1973, the Ex-Im Bank signed the first loan agreement with the Soviet Union, granting $101.2 million in direct government loans and another $101.2 million in guaranteed commercial bank loans for the purchase of industrial equipment in the United States. On April 12, 1973, Armand Hammer's Occidental Petroleum Corporation contracted to supply technology and equipment for a fertilizer manufacturing complex in return for Soviet shipments of ammonia, urea, and potash for twenty years. And in June, Occidental and El Paso Natural Gas Corporation reached agreement with the Soviet government to participate in exploration and development of gas fields in the Yakutsk region of Siberia. There were also several smaller deals during this period involving the establishment of American business and banking offices in the Soviet Union.

But the anticipated bonanza of American credit and MFN status never materialized. Only one other extension of Ex-Im Bank credit was approved before blocking legislation was passed later in the year. This was a $180 million credit in May of 1974 to help finance the fertilizer plant, contracted through Occidental Petroleum, as well as the purchase of chemical storage facilities, pumping station and pipeline equipment, and railroad tank cars.

The passage of the Trade Act on December 18, 1974 — including the Jackson amendment — and the Ex-Im Bank bill the next day extinguished any possibility of a full-blown trade relationship with Moscow. President Ford signed the bills on January 3 and 4, 1975. The Soviet government, which had in the meantime reaffirmed and stiffened its emigration stance, acknowledged the final outcome when it notified the United States a few days later, on January 10, 1975, that it would not "put into force the 1972 trade agreement."

The Political-Economic Quid Pro Quo

There is considerable irony in the nearly universal assessment of Kissinger's detente policy as a failure. This evaluation is based upon the assumption that the United States sought to improve economic ties to the Soviet Union as an end in itself. If only Kissinger had been more attentive to the workings of Congress, particularly to Senator Jackson, or if he had pursued the correct legislative procedure, it is said, he would have succeeded in expanding the economic relationship. [10] But expanded economic relations with Moscow were decidedly not an objective sought for its own sake, however much some within the United States leadership and American business community may have desired it. There was from the beginning a clearly posited quid pro quo, which was that improved economic ties would be accompanied by Soviet strategic weapons and geopolitical "restraint."

Explaining American policy to Congress following the Moscow summit, Henry Kissinger plainly conveyed the quid pro quo which Washington had put to Soviet leaders.

> The SALT agreement does not stand alone, isolated and incongruous in the relationship of hostility, vulnerable at any moment to the shock of some sudden crisis. It stands, rather, linked organically to a chain of agreements and to a broad understanding about international conduct appropriate to the dangers of the nuclear age. . . . We hoped that the Soviet Union would acquire a stake in a wide spectrum of negotiations and that it would become convinced that its interests would be best served if the

entire process unfolded. We have sought, in short, to create a vested interest in mutual restraint.[11]

In other words, improved economic relations between the United States and the Soviet Union would depend upon Soviet strategic weapons and geopolitical "restraint." What appeared to be an administration blunder in failing to manage safe passage of the trade and Ex-Im Bank bills through Congress was in actuality the desired outcome because Moscow sought to pocket American economic concessions without reciprocal "restraint." Indeed, Kissinger delayed congressional action for as long as he could to give Moscow an opportunity to demonstrate its sincerity, to no avail. From mid-1973 onward, first in the testing of four new MIRVed ICBMs and then in what appeared to be extensive direct and indirect support for a multi-pronged geopolitical offensive against the United States in Afghanistan, Angola, Vietnam, and Southwestern Europe, Moscow demonstrated its unwillingness to accept the status quo. Under these circumstances, the administration was no longer willing to keep its side of an obviously one-sided bargain and allowed congressional opposition to prevail.

From the beginning there was an inherent disadvantage for the United States in the proposed political-economic arrangement. American economic concessions would be extended in the near term, while the political benefits arising from Soviet restraint would only become apparent over the long term. An approach was needed, therefore, that would enable the United States to drag out final commitments on economic concessions to the extent necessary to ensure that reciprocal political restraint was forthcoming from the Soviet side. Whether wittingly or unwittingly, this was in fact the role that Senator Jackson played.

The best perspective for an analysis of the legislative history and the Jackson-Stevenson-Church amendments which denied American credit and technology to the Soviet Union would therefore appear to be not the relationship between that legislation and Soviet emigration policy, but that between the legislative process and the demonstration of Soviet "restraint." This would be especially pertinent in the realm of strategic weapons, which ostensibly had just been placed in check by SALT I.

If Moscow had wished to cooperate with the United States in maintaining a stable international environment, it would soon have become apparent, and the economic side of detente would have been allowed to go forward. (Soviet emigration policy would be one barometer of Soviet intent.) But it would also soon have become apparent if Moscow simply sought to use detente as a means of exploiting American wealth and technology even while proceeding to challenge its position. Then, of course, there would have been no point in a flourishing economic relationship, which, realistically speaking in any case, would amount to an extension of advanced technology in return for raw materials.

In the deepest sense, it would seem, the failure of detente was due primarily to the profoundly mistaken Soviet belief that America's "capitalists" would put greed above principle, that they would disregard the changing "correlation of forces" and not only sell the wood and the rope but also build the scaffold and fit the noose for their own execution. Thus it was that Soviet leaders eagerly awaited the distribution of American largess, while brazenly moving forward with policies designed to accelerate the shift in the correlation of forces to bring about America's demise.

Kissinger's choice of legislative path and his management of the issue supports the quid pro quo thesis. This is not to say that there was any collusion between the secretary and Henry Jackson; by all accounts the two men were on opposite sides.[12] The senator would go as far as he could to derail what he viewed as "phony detente." (There may well have been a degree of collusion between the president and the senator, however, for reasons which derive from the argument presented on Watergate in chapter 4 above; but this lies outside the scope of the present analysis.) It is to say that Senator Jackson's well-known opposition to detente could be channeled to a useful end by the resourceful Kissinger.

The first task was to establish parallel legislative paths for both the trade agreement and Jackson's amendment. This was also Jackson's intent. The administration chose to delay signing the trade agreement until later in the fall — until Soviet support for the Paris peace negotiations became evident. Indeed, had the trade agreement been signed at the Moscow summit and presented to Congress at that time, the euphoria over detente might well have been sufficient to overcome Senator Jackson's or anyone else's objections.[13]

On September 30, after the White House ceremony during which he signed the SALT agreement, the president and Senator Jackson struck a deal during a private forty-five-minute "stroll" in the Rose Garden. In return for Nixon's agreement to release fifteen to eighteen

Senate loyalists to support Jackson's amendment, the senator agreed to delay a vote on it until after the election.[14] Thus, Senator Jackson introduced his amendment tying trade to Soviet emigration policy on October 4, and the administration delayed signing the United States-Soviet trade agreement until October 18, only a few hours before Congress adjourned for the pre-election recess.

The next task was to link the trade agreement to comprehensive trade legislation then being prepared for presentation to Congress to replace the expiring Trade Act of 1962. The special trade representative argued that splitting the United States-Soviet trade agreement and MFN status away from the Omnibus Trade Bill would ensure its passage, but Kissinger rejected that view in favor of linking the two in one package. Jackson's staff interpreted this decision as "playing into our hands,"[15] as indeed it was, but intentionally so. It meant that Kissinger would retain control. In effect, from Kissinger's point of view, the Jackson amendment was insurance that no groundswell of congressional sentiment in favor of passage would occur to take control out of the administration's hands. Passage of any trade legislation would require prior compromise between the administration and Jackson.[16]

It was therefore appropriate that Kissinger "isolated himself from those in Congress who might have helped to counter the Jackson amendment."[17] Kissinger would not support at least three substantive offers for substitute amendments which would have undercut Jackson. Senator Jacob Javits offered to propose a substitute amendment but was turned down. In the House Ways and Means Committee, California Representatives James C. Corman and Jerry L. Pettis found no support from the administration for their compromise amendment. Finally, Senators Allan Cranston and Adlai Stevenson III could stir no interest from Kissinger in offers to "help get around Jackson." [18]

Yet, he was careful to steer Congress in the direction he wished. Thus, in June of 1974, when Senator Stevenson was formulating an amendment which would limit the amount of Ex-Im Bank credit that could be extended to the Soviet Union, Kissinger held as many as six meetings with the senator and "seemed receptive" to the $300 million limit being proposed.[19] It seems hardly likely that, as Kissinger put it in his memoirs, "the administration was caught flat-footed" by the Stevenson amendment.[20] Indeed, the relationship between the trade and Ex-Im Bank bills was explicit for months. In January, ninety-one House members had co-sponsored a resolution stating that the Ex-Im

Bank "should not lend to the Soviet Union until the Senate had resolved the Jackson amendment," and that same resolution was adopted in the Senate on March 11.[21] Finally, at no time did Kissinger make *any* effort to remove the $300 million ceiling from the Ex-Im Bank Bill.[22]

Meanwhile, Kissinger and other members of the administration repeatedly assured Soviet leaders that the Jackson amendment was of "little concern."[23] Indeed, initially at least, Soviet leaders were quite ready to accept Kissinger's assurances. It seemed incredible to them that a fundamental state decision on MFN status and enormous credits involving potentially billions of dollars could rest on what was by comparison a seemingly trivial Soviet internal matter, involving a relatively small number of Jews wishing to leave the country.

Kissinger, astutely playing on Soviet unfamiliarity with congressional procedures and powers, restricted executive branch contact with Soviet representatives. According to the recollection of a high-ranking trade official, the secretary had reached an understanding with Soviet Ambassador Dobrynin whereby "there would be no channels of conversation except when they designate. . . . Trade discussions with Russia are not handled by trade people. . . . And when trade negotiators do talk, then others come along and tell the Russians to ignore the previous discussions because they don't count."[24]

It was late in the game before Moscow realized just how potentially devastating the Jackson amendment could be and at once attempted to undercut it. On March 30, little more than a week before the trade bill would be sent to Congress, Brezhnev sent a message to the president informing him that the Soviet Union was lifting the punitive education tax that had been levied on all emigres.[25] Rather than removing the remaining objection, the Soviet shift simply encouraged Senator Jackson to increase his demands, now asking that the Soviet Union guarantee a minimum number of emigres annually and permit emigration by all nationalities, not just Jews. And later, when Moscow got into the numbers game by agreeing to allow an annual number of emigres, Jackson simply raised the number.[26]

Perhaps in frustration, Moscow reprimanded "the Soviet embassy and Dobrynin personally . . . for not having reported the threat of the Jackson amendment in Congress early enough and accurately enough."[27] Indeed, in April there were published reports that Dobrynin would be reassigned following Brezhnev's trip to Washington in June, but he was kept on, possibly to save face or to avoid acknowledging that the Soviets had been deceived.[28] Later, in

November, Moscow posted Anatoly Gromyko, an expert on American affairs and son of the Soviet foreign minister, to Washington in an effort to establish both a check on Dobrynin and a separate line of communication. But this arrangement did not last, and in a few months Gromyko returned to Moscow.

Moscow's Missile Breakout and the United States Quandary

While the issue of American-Soviet economic relations was being deliberated in the Congress, during 1973 Moscow initiated a major strategic weapons démarche. Despite strenuous efforts by Henry Kissinger to forestall and gain control of it, the Soviet Union began extensive and intensive testing of the second, or MIRV, stage of its ballistic missile program.[29] The tests made clear that Moscow sought counterforce superiority over the United States rather than mutual deterrence at the countervalue level. It was this development above all—although there were subsequent geopolitical moves which also raised concern—that destroyed any possibility for a major improvement in economic relations between the two countries. Kissinger's assumption that Moscow could be drawn into a cooperative relationship and dissuaded from seeking strategic superiority was a major miscalculation. The Soviet counterforce decision forced Washington to make the same choice, producing the so-called "Schlesinger Doctrine." Despite the Vladivostok agreement of December 1974, the United States was still left vulnerable to the emergence of a future first-strike threat—a threat which in fact appeared during the Carter administration.

Having achieved its principal strategic weapons objectives in the SALT I accords—stopping further development of American defensive and offensive systems—Moscow was disinclined as before to accept any constraints upon its own offensive weaponry. Despite the provision in the Interim Agreement that both sides would immediately begin follow-on negotiations and the threat (incorporated as part of the Interim Agreement[30]) that failure to conclude a second accord within five years would constitute grounds for withdrawal of the United States from the Anti-Ballistic Missile Treaty, Moscow stalled on arms control while pressing forward with its MIRV program, testing four new ICBMs from mid-1973 onward.

The first of the follow-on meetings occurred in November–December 1972, but negotiations did not resume until late March of the following year, when the Soviet Union proposed a ban on any new strategic weapons during the period of a new agreement, while allowing for modernization of existing weapons.[31] This seemed at first to be a feasible proposition, until it was explained that the term "new" applied only to United States systems, especially Trident and B-1, not to Soviet weapons, which were only being "modernized."

Although Kissinger described the Soviet gambit as "a proposal so one-sided that one wonders how any serious person could ever have believed that it might be discussed, much less negotiated,"[32] he shortly understood its purpose. Moscow wanted no agreement that would restrict full development of its ICBM force, particularly its MIRV stage, which was just getting under way. So Soviet negotiators put forth an unacceptable proposal, which included the demand once again to count American forward-based systems in any agreement. Soviet negotiators would hold to this position throughout the next eighteen months (presumably until completion of MIRV testing).

United States intelligence had for some time expected that the Soviet Union would develop new or modified ICBMs as a follow-on to the SS-9. These were the SS-11 and SS-13. The original estimate, based on observations of silo construction in 1971, had been *two* new missiles.[33] Discovery that Moscow was about to begin testing *four* new missiles, the SS-16, SS-17, SS-18, and SS-19, each with a MIRV capability, came as a grimly unpleasant surprise. Secretary of Defense Schlesinger would describe the Soviet effort as "an ICBM development program which was unprecedented in its breadth and depth."[34] The formulation of a new United States arms control position, "hastily decided upon,"[35] just prior to Kissinger's early May departure for Moscow to prepare for Brezhnev's June trip to the United States, suggests that the discovery came toward the end of April.

In Moscow, Kissinger put forth Washington's new position, the heart of which was a proposal to freeze deployment of land-based MIRVs and to ban any further testing. It also included provision for equal aggregates with a ceiling of 2,350 delivery vehicles. Although Kissinger spoke disparagingly of this move as another of many "one-sided proposals by which each side pleased its bureaucracy" and as "fairy-tale diplomacy,"[36] it is obvious that Kissinger himself was responsible for its final contents. Nor should the reader accept the secretary's assertion that he was not surprised by its quick rejection, for he went to considerable lengths to stop Soviet MIRV testing and would hold to the core of this position for over a year.

What appears to have happened is that the United States, taken by surprise by Moscow's missile maneuver, sought to derail it at the last moment with an offer for a ceiling of 2,350 delivery vehicles, some 732 higher than the SALT I ceiling of 1,618 agreed upon the previous year, in return for a MIRV ban. Kissinger's estimated ceiling was not far off the mark. The Vladivostok agreement of November 1974 would contain a ceiling of 2,400, only fifty more than the current offer. Kissinger was in fact gradually moving toward a position within the concept of equal aggregates that would later be termed "counter-balancing asymmetries," whereby the United States would retain a small MIRVed land-based force (the United States had already MIRVed 400 Minuteman III missiles, each with three warheads) and the Soviet Union a larger, non-MIRVed force with each side having roughly the same number of warheads.[37]

When Brezhnev would hear nothing of any proposition that sought to block Moscow from MIRVing its ICBM force, Kissinger then offered tentatively to trade the non-deployment of the long-range cruise missile for a Soviet agreement to ban MIRVs, with equal lack of success.[38] Brezhnev would not agree to accept a "pig in a poke," so to speak, for the United States had not yet developed the weapon and, indeed, Soviet leaders appear not to have understood the significance of what was being proposed. (Later, *after* Vladivostok, when the United States began to develop the long-range cruise missile in air, land, and sea configurations, Moscow would strain mightily to close off this most promising avenue of weapons technology.)

In effect, Kissinger had offered the Soviet leadership an opportunity to demonstrate the kind of restraint expected in detente. Moscow declined to show any restraint at all and indicated that the Soviet Union's objective was not equality but superiority. MIRVing the heavy SS-9/18 force of 308 missiles would alone be sufficient to threaten Minuteman, once terminal guidance systems were perfected. Moscow would in fact test the SS-17 and the SS-19 in addition to the SS-18, portending an extremely threatening force.[39] As Kissinger remarked:

> Sometime in the Eighties our land-based missiles would become vulnerable, depending on the rapidity with which the Soviets placed multiple warheads on their land-based missile launchers and improved their accuracy. . . . Sooner or later, *even if the overall number of warheads were equal,* the Soviets would combine their growing counterforce capability with their traditional

conventional superiority to bring about changes in the geopolitical balance.[40]

Kissinger's May attempt to stop the Soviet MIRV program through negotiation was admittedly a long shot, following as it did the intelligence failure to anticipate that Moscow was well along in preparations for testing an entire new generation of missiles. In this sense, it was not a total surprise that the Soviet Union rejected what was an eleventh-hour proposition. Once testing got under way, however, following the Washington summit, in late July the Soviet Union indicated its willingness to discuss limitation but not proscription of land- and sea-based MIRV weapons, raising hopes that some restraints could still be negotiated.[41] Thus began a series of fruitless exchanges along the lines of "after you, my dear Alphonse," over the next year as Moscow dangled the prospect of arms reductions in return for American credits and technology and Washington held out the prospect of credits and technology in return for an arms control agreement.

If one assumes that Soviet leaders sought genuine detente, their position was self-defeating and confusing, for it was contradictory. The Soviets were essentially demanding the extension of American wealth and technology in exchange for the *promise* of arms control, or something for nothing. Moscow had only to agree to compromise on arms control to reap the benefits of American wealth. That this was not done made plain Soviet lack of interest in any long-term cooperative relationship with its main enemy. The fall and winter of 1973 thus passed at impasse with the United States holding to its so-called "fairy-tale"[42] position of May on the proscription of MIRVs, and the Soviet Union to its position of March to ban all "new" American weapons while permitting the "modernization" of Moscow's.

By the fall of 1973 the grim facts were that the United States had failed to slow down, let alone stop, the Soviet Union's strategic weapons program in either the launcher or MIRV stages. Under these circumstances there could be no genuine detente unless it were to amount to disguised surrender, and it would be only a matter of time before the United States-Soviet trade agreement would be quashed. The Soviet MIRV démarche shattered all prospects for detente, which had lasted all of two years since the decision was made to seek an improved relationship in December 1971. Indeed, the House Ways and Means Committee voted on September 28 to deny MFN status to those countries restricting emigration.

Detente was in fact dead, but for the time being appearances would have to be kept up for several reasons. First, Kissinger hoped to squeeze as much operating room as possible out of detente, to put as much of his new international order into place as he could. Secondly, delaying public recognition of failure until the 1976 election campaign would theoretically give some political advantages to the Republican candidate. Finally, it was in Kissinger's personal interest to cover up this immense failure for as long as he could. Indeed, it is difficult to discern here which took precedence — the secretary's personal reputation or the national interest — so preoccupied was he with fear of failure.

Thus, for example, in his relations with the national security bureaucracy, Kissinger encouraged proposals of diverse negotiating schemes in the knowledge that what was in fact occurring was a bureaucratic exercise in a strategic deadlock. In his memoirs, Kissinger artlessly attempted to lay the responsibility for the failure of his strategy at the feet of the national security bureaucracy, especially the military leadership, contending: "So we came up with a position that gave everybody what he wanted — usually the best proof that consensus was replacing a coherent strategy."[43]

Meanwhile, American leaders quietly and without public fanfare were making the decision to match Moscow in the acquisition of counterforce capability for its ICBM force. On January 17, 1974, the administration issued top-secret National Security Decision Memorandum (NSDM) 242, several months before the celebrated "debate" on the subject between Kissinger and Secretary of Defense Schlesinger conveyed the decision to the people.[44] Earlier, in yet another miscalculation, the Nixon administration had deliberately declined to develop a counterforce capability in hopes of eliciting the same decision from Moscow. Now it was in the position of having to catch up by improving the accuracy of American missiles.[45]

Then, over the course of the next month, United States leaders also decided upon a new SALT position, NSDM 245, which was issued on February 19. It called for equal aggregates of missiles and bombers, a ceiling of 2,350 delivery vehicles and equal throwweight for MIRVs. Although this is the position that Kissinger described as giving "everybody what he wanted," it is better understood as recognizing the futility of further attempts to limit Soviet programs and requiring equality for both American and Soviet systems in future negotiations.[46] Thus, NSDM 245 was a fallback position designed at a minimum to make it theoretically impossible for the Soviet Union to achieve strategic weapons superiority. (In fact, the Vladivostok accord in November 1974 would incorporate the essence of this position.)

But Kissinger decided to make one more sustained attempt to place restraints upon the Soviet program. His trip to Moscow in late March to prepare for the president's visit in June provided the occasion. Based upon his conception of "counterbalancing asymmetries," the secretary put forth a convoluted formula designed to gain Soviet acceptance of "the principle of unequal aggregates for MIRVs."[47] Kissinger proposed to Brezhnev that since by current count the Soviet Union had 280 more land-based missiles than the United States, Moscow should agree to forgo that numerical difference to the American land-based MIRVs. Since the United States proposed to MIRV a total of 550 Minuteman III, that would mean that the Soviet Union would be allowed to MIRV only 270 missiles.

Prior to his departure for Moscow Kissinger had publicly predicted a "conceptual breakthrough" based in part on an encouraging reaction from Dobrynin.[48] Privately, he admitted "there was no realistic prospect that they would confine themselves to 270 land-based MIRVed ICBMs." What he apparently believed he could do was talk the Soviets into a compromise. He declared that if Moscow "accepted the principle of unequal aggregates for MIRVs . . . I hoped to shape an outcome that would delay the Soviets' achievement of a first-strike capability."[49]

But Brezhnev would not bite. He quickly saw through this transparent scheme and put forth a counterproposal that was as insulting as it was unacceptable. Brezhnev proposed equal limits on MIRVed missiles of 1,000 for each side, a limit almost quadruple that of Kissinger's 270. Kissinger's explanation of "our difficulties" with the proposal resembled nothing so much as a personal plea to Brezhnev to change his mind about the high limits. Explaining what Brezhnev already knew, that acceptance of a 1,000 limit was no limit at all, Kissinger concluded by saying, "You would be able to destroy our Minuteman."[50]

Of course, Brezhnev immediately and "strenuously" denied any such intent but just as firmly refused to countenance a limit of 270. To accept such a limit, he said, would mean that "I will be destroyed." At an impasse, they agreed to resume negotiations two days later on Kissinger's last day in Moscow, setting the stage for the bargain that Kissinger believed he could shape somewhere between 270 and 1,000. When they met again on March 27, Brezhnev offered to extend the Interim Agreement to 1980, accepted the principle of unequal aggregates, and then proposed MIRV limits of 1,100 for the United States and 1,000 for the Soviet Union.[51]

Even though the proposal was openly derisory, Kissinger attempted to put the best possible face on it, describing the proposal as "a major step forward." Indeed, he boasted that "once the principle of unequal MIRV aggregates in our favor had been conceded, the gap would almost certainly be subject to improvement through negotiations." But there was no "give" at all in the Soviet leader's position, as he peremptorily rejected Kissinger's counterproposal to establish a "sublimit on land-based missiles," prompting the terse conclusion:

> The concept of an inequality of MIRVs in our favor was extremely important. The particular application of it was preposterous; I turned it down without even checking with Washington.[52]

Indeed, Kissinger's March meeting with the Soviet leadership was a major setback as Moscow's general position began to harden—not only on the MIRV issue, but on the Middle East as well.[53] Here Brezhnev "bristled," accusing the United States of violating their agreement to act jointly and instead proceeding unilaterally. In response to Kissinger's attempted explanation, the Soviet leader remarked that "never before . . . had he heard such an open statement of the American intention to exclude Soviet participation."[54] The one area where Brezhnev showed any flexibility at all was Jewish emigration, and this apparently was in order to string the United States along in the rapidly diminishing hope of obtaining economic concessions on the still-pending trade agreement.

At this point there could be no misunderstanding of the Soviet leadership's position. They wanted no restriction of any kind on their MIRV program; hence the "preposterous" proposal to set their MIRV limit at 1,000. Yet Kissinger professed to believe that, despite the unambiguous Soviet stance, "we were basically heading in the right direction." [55] Therefore he persisted in attempting to reach agreement on MIRV limits. Indeed, in discussions with Soviet Foreign Minister Gromyko the following month, April 28–29, Kissinger made an offer which, if accepted, would have *sanctioned* the attainment of a Soviet first-strike capability against Minuteman.

Kissinger offered a MIRV agreement with limits of 1,000 for the United States and 850 for the Soviet Union. His reasoning was that

United States intelligence believed Moscow would place some 200 MIRVed weapons on submarines. Since these would be counted against any MIRV limit, it would allow Moscow to MIRV only 600 or so land-based missiles, reducing the threat to Minuteman.[56] The reasoning was fallacious and contradictory, at best. Since it had been determined long before, during the SALT I negotiations, that the 308 sublimit for the SS-9 was already sufficient to present a threat to Minuteman once the system was MIRVed and made accurate, it was ludicrous to argue that doubling that limit now would somehow reduce the threat.[57]

Kissinger's April discussions with Gromyko were the penultimate attempt to reach MIRV limits based on the concept of unequal asymmetries. With the exception of negotiations at Summit III, henceforth the United States would seek "reduced, equal aggregates." The public signal of the change of position came in early June when Secretary of Defense Schlesinger replied to a letter by Senator Jackson (dated April 22, presumably just after discovery of Moscow's intent to begin missile tests). Jackson had called for overall reductions and equality in missile force levels, a position which Schlesinger, too, now supported. As Kissinger noted, ". . . in practice, this meant the end of the scheme we were negotiating."[58]

Although both Kissinger and Nixon attempt to blame the Pentagon for impeding any progress (Kissinger also blames Nixon's "galloping weakness"[59]), the fact is there was no possibility of an agreement on the Soviet side. It may have been true that Brezhnev was a "detentist," but if so his definition of the term was decidedly not the same as the American definition. In any case, while profuse in his profession of cooperation, the Soviet leader would not agree to any scheme which limited Soviet force levels in any substantive manner. This was finally and decisively demonstrated to the American leadership during Summit III, June 27 to July 3, 1974.

During the discussions in Moscow, Kissinger made yet another effort to gain Soviet compliance for MIRV limits based on his formula — despite the fact that it had been overruled — to no avail. During a lengthy exchange with Brezhnev in Nixon's presence, the Soviet leader interrupted Kissinger to say to the president that if this represented the last position of the administration, then there was ". . . no basis for an agreement."[60] At this point in his memoirs, Nixon made the observation that Kissinger, rather than to go home empty-handed, was willing to accept "even a controversial SALT agreement . . . convinced that we would have been able to educate public opinion to accept it."[61] By "controversial" the president meant "disadvantageous."

Perhaps the unwillingness to go home empty-handed partly explains the decision to enter into a decidedly disadvantageous agreement amending the ABM treaty. Proposed by the Soviet Union, this was the agreement to forgo the option of building a second ABM site in addition to one protecting the national capital. It meant that the United States, having already rejected the option of protecting its capital the year before, now gave up the option of defending its missile fields. Even Kissinger, who was responsible for negotiating the agreement, later questioned its value. "Leaving fixed ICBM silos totally undefended reduces an attack on them into a mere engineering problem; as accuracy improves and the number of attacking warheads expands, it is not irrational to consider ABM defense of missile fields as a possible protection if the requisite technology is available."[62]

Soviet refusal to succumb to Kissinger's forensic skills may have been partly responsible for the secretary's incontinent outburst during a news conference on July 4 when he declared in the context of the failure to achieve any agreement limiting MIRVs: "What in the name of God is strategic superiority? What is the significance of it, politically, militarily, operationally, at these levels of numbers? What do you do with it?" But, as he noted in his memoirs, the notion that "strategic superiority had lost all significance . . . was not really my view."[63] It was nevertheless a telling remark testifying to the failure of his strategy at the time.

On the crucial issues dealing with nuclear weapons Summit III was a failure, as it was foredoomed to be. One wonders why the meeting was held at all. But as in all such cases where no agreement is reached on the main issue, the two sides signed several secondary pacts. Among these were: the Threshold Test Ban Treaty, which prohibited underground nuclear testing above 150 kilotons (which was not ratified); an agreement to negotiate a ban on environmental warfare (which led to formulation of an international convention signed by the United States, the Soviet Union, and thirty other countries in 1977); agreement to attend a summit conference on European security (which was held in Helsinki in 1975); cooperation in energy matters; and agreement to open several more consulates in both countries. [64]

Two proposals by the American side kept alive hope for further progress on arms control, such as it was. The first was Kissinger's suggestion to Gromyko that the two sides agree to negotiate a new framework, a ten-year agreement spanning the decade 1975–1985. It was thought that a longer-term agreement would make it easier and less risky to reduce weaponry in a balanced manner without either side's becoming vulnerable in the process.[65] The second was Nixon's proposal to Brezhnev while en route to the airport after the summit that they meet again in a "mini-summit" sometime between October and December of that year at a "halfway house."[66] Thus, the framework for a follow-on arms agreement and a meeting time were agreed upon. The place, Vladivostok, would not be decided upon until later, after President Nixon had resigned and had been succeeded by Gerald R. Ford.

Chinese Expectations and American Policy in Asia

The earliest manifestation of Kissinger's strategy in Asia surrounded United States inaction in Indochina and its impact on domestic Chinese politics. From the beginning, the issue of the Vietnam settlement contained within it implications for the future structure of Asia and for Washington's relations with both Moscow and Beijing.[67] First-term policy as President Nixon had developed it was to work toward a resolution of the conflict in Vietnam that would reestablish the status quo ante bellum in Indochina. This outcome would be structurally similar to that achieved in Korea twenty years before and would reestablish the Southeast Asian sector of America's traditional containment structure.

Restoration of the status quo ante bellum would also be consistent with Beijing's long-term objective to perpetuate the fragmentation of the region and thus forestall the emergence of any threat from the south. Continuation of the first-term policy, therefore, would involve extended cooperation between Washington and Beijing along the lines which had evolved since 1969 to maintain the fragmented structure of Indochina. It would mean the defeat of long-term Soviet strategy to build a strong counterweight on China's southern flank and minimize Soviet presence and influence in Southeast Asia. Most important, it would mean victory for the United States in its longest war.

These were the undisguised assumptions upon which both Mao Zedong and Zhou Enlai based their arguments to Henry Kissinger when he traveled to Beijing in mid-February 1973. The Chinese leadership clearly hoped that the impetus which had driven the two countries together in the first place — the menacing growth of Soviet power and the problem of Vietnam — would continue to infuse American policy. At the same time they sought reassurance now that the Paris accords had been signed that the United States would maintain continuity of policy. Just below the surface of their remarks could be glimpsed the concern that the United States was poised for a change in strategy. Zhou Enlai expressed it in a series of questions during his conversation with Kissinger:

> Would we emphasize containment even in Asia? Or would we seek our security in the mutual exhaustion of the two Communist giants? With the war in Vietnam over, were we prepared to face Soviet expansionism head-on? Or was the West going to try to conciliate the Soviets in the desire to "push the ill waters of the Soviet Union . . . eastward."[68]

Zhou's own views were unambiguous and emphatic. He "derided the very thought of negotiating with the Soviet Union," which Kissinger had explained was necessary for the United States to gain "the freedom of maneuver we need to resist in those places which are the most likely points of attack or pressure." Instead of conciliating Moscow the Chinese premier called on the United States to organize an anti-Soviet coalition which "should stretch from Japan through China, Pakistan, Iran, and Turkey to Western Europe."[69]

And in this context, Zhou eagerly seized upon Kissinger's suggestion that the two countries establish a "permanent point of contact." Confounding the assumption that "Peking's envoys would never appear where Taiwan's representatives were established," Zhou insisted that liaison offices be set up in Beijing and Washington headed by chiefs with ambassadorial rank.[70] Each side would have the same privileges conferred by formal diplomatic recognition — diplomatic immunity, secure communications, and the power to conduct all exchanges between the two countries. In short, the liaison offices would be embassies in all but name. Here, with unvarnished simplicity, Zhou offered China's inclusion in the Western camp.

On the subject of Southeast Asia, Zhou expressed his complete support for the Paris agreement, which, of course, served China's interests perfectly as long as it held. He conveyed his concern that the collapse of the agreement would present China with a painful dilemma.

Either the war would resume, and with it the Chinese dilemma of having to run risks in its relations with us on behalf of North Vietnam. . . . Or, even worse from Peking's point of view, Hanoi would achieve hegemony in Indochina without a fight, discredit the United States internationally as a paper tiger, and create on China's southern border a powerful Vietnamese state, with a long tradition of anti-Chinese feeling, dependent for its military supplies entirely on the Soviet Union.[71]

Kissinger observed laconically, "A unified Communist Vietnam dominant in Indochina was a strategic nightmare for China. . . ."

These same themes were pursued relentlessly by Mao Zedong himself when he met with Kissinger late on the night of February 17. The purpose of meeting with the American envoy was to underline Sino-American friendship and Mao's personal commitment to improving relations. After the obligatory picture-taking session, Mao wasted little time getting to the strategic heart of the matter.

In Mao's view the Soviet threat was real and growing. He warned against a fake detente that would sap resistance to Soviet expansionism and confuse the peoples of the West. The United States and Europe should resist the temptation to "push the ill waters eastward." It was a futile strategy, for in time the West, too, would be engulfed. The United States and China must cooperate. This required institutionalizing our relationship. Setting up the liaison offices in each other's capitals was a good decision. He urged an expansion of contacts and even trade, calling the present level "pitiful."

In Mao's view the United States would serve the common interest best by taking a leading role in world affairs, by which he meant constructing an anti-Soviet alliance. . . . As had Zhou, Mao stressed the importance of close American cooperation also with Western Europe, Japan, Pakistan, Iran, and Turkey.[72]

Both Mao and Zhou conceived of China's role fully within the construct of a bipolar global order. As such, Mao's proposed strategy was the obverse of the one he had put forth in 1957. Then, Mao had sought to prod Moscow to lead the communist camp in an anti-American crusade. Now, having switched sides, he proposed that the

United States head "an anti-Soviet alliance" in which China would take part. Indeed, Mao went much farther than Zhou had gone in suggesting an "alliance" with the United States. Zhou had called for a more ambiguous "anti-Soviet coalition." Nevertheless, in both cases, Mao's proposed role for China was to support one superpower against the other. There was no inkling that he saw China capable of assuming an independent stance at this stage in its history, although that is obviously what he hoped would evolve in the long run.

This, of course, was not what Kissinger had in mind. His strategy required the establishment of detente and arms control with the Soviet Union before consolidation of positions around the Soviet periphery. This applied with particular force to China. Despite the exhortations of the Chinese leaders to move forward on normalization of relations to maintain an anti-Soviet containment posture and to uphold the fragmentation of Indochina — as represented by the Paris accords — in early 1973 the United States shifted off this course.[73] As Kissinger himself observed, the Chinese "like many other nations — could not believe that the United States would accept military defeat, *much less engineer it*."[74] The precipitate and largely unanticipated complete American withdrawal from Vietnam expressed in the refusal to enforce the Paris accords against immediate, gross, and repeated North Vietnamese violations brought into reality the structural outcome the Chinese most feared. Regardless of the public justifications given to explain American inaction, and they were many, the refusal to sustain the South Vietnamese government meant that following a "decent interval"[75] there would emerge on China's southern flank a Vietnam unified under the control of Hanoi. In theory, as described in chapter 4, this would lock Beijing between the Soviet Union in the north and a hostile and powerful Soviet client state in the south, leaving China with no alternative but to rely upon the United States for support against the Soviet-Vietnamese nutcracker.

This outcome would presumably serve to perpetuate the Sino-Soviet conflict and put the United States in position to balance one communist power off against the other. In fact, Kissinger made the new approach explicit in a message to Nixon as he was returning home from Beijing.

> With conscientious attention to both capitals we should be able to continue to have our mao tai and drink our vodka too. Peking, after all, assuming continued hostility with the USSR,

has no real alternative to us as a counterweight (despite its recent reaching out to Japan and Western Europe as insurance). And Moscow needs us in such areas as Europe and economics.[76]

Of course, to create these conditions meant to promote the success of Soviet strategy against Beijing's and to accept defeat in Vietnam, for the collapse of South Vietnam would be an American defeat no matter how it was disguised or papered over with explanations of presidential weakness or congressional culpability. But the unpredictable variable in this calculation was China.

The decision to restructure Asia by maneuvering China into a position of dependence upon the United States and perpetually adversarial relations with the Soviet Union was based in part upon the assumption that Mao Zedong was above serious challenge from within, an assumption which was very easy to make at the time. Mao had after all silenced his opponents both in the opposing faction of Liu Shaoqi and Deng Xiaoping and within his own group after the mysterious demise of Lin Biao. Mao appeared to have a firmer grip on the reins of power than at any other time in his long and tumultuous career, with no challengers in sight. Nevertheless, the assumption that he was above challenge was a complete misreading of Chinese politics, a fact that soon became evident.

As American inaction made Beijing's "strategic nightmare" of a big Vietnam an imminent reality, that looming specter quickly induced a bitter and prolonged policy and leadership struggle in the Chinese capital. Beijing's internal crisis, in turn, had an immediate and disastrous effect upon the nascent Sino-American relationship, crippling Kissinger's tripolar strategy from the outset and freezing further improvement until well into the Carter administration. Was it in fact true, as Kissinger claimed, that the Chinese had "no real alternative to us as a counterweight" to Moscow? Was it realistic to presume that the United States could maintain close relations with Beijing even while removing one of the major components of the relationship? Or did it really matter what transpired in Sino-American relations, short of the worst-case of Sino-Soviet rapprochement, so long as the United States accomplished the structural reorganization of the region it sought?

The crisis in the Chinese leadership surfaced quickly in the spring of 1973. Mao's strategy of employing the United States to counterbalance Soviet pressure as well as to assist in reestabishing a dominant position in Southeast Asia began to fail as the precipitous American shift off the mainland got under way. Those Chinese leaders, led by Deng Xiaoping (Liu Shaoqi had died during internment in 1968), who had opposed Mao's strategic course and had been purged as a result during the Cultural Revolution were quick to respond. And Mao, unable to refute the criticism that his strategy was failing, was forced to retreat politically in a manner reminiscent of his setback in 1958 following the fiasco of the Great Leap Forward. He was forced to relinquish a portion of his political power once again and to acquiesce in the return of those "capitalist roaders" and "revisionists" he had so recently purged. Beginning in mid-April with the reinstatement of Deng Xiaoping himself, the Chinese leadership became embroiled in debate over the wisdom of Mao's strategy in general and over the question of how to counter the immediate and longer-term problems posed by the United States shift off the Southeast Asian mainland.

Deng's reappearance came on the occasion of a state dinner for the deposed Cambodian chief of state, Prince Norodom Sihanouk, suggesting that the Indochina question was closely related to his rehabilitation. In the party debate that followed, the familiar pre–Cultural Revolution policy antagonism between Mao and Deng resurfaced. Questions were raised in the Chinese press regarding China's geopolitical orientation, Washington's value as a "trustworthy partner," as well as United States "violations" of the Vietnam cease-fire agreement.[77] The upshot was that further improvement in relations with the United States was blocked from the spring of 1973, while the reorganized Chinese leadership determined upon a policy response to the problems posed by the now inevitable North Vietnamese conquest of South Vietnam. As the Chinese deliberated, both Soviet and American leaders attempted to influence the outcome, but in different ways.

Moscow Probes for an Opening in Beijing

The Soviets, too, had been taken by surprise by the American refusal to enforce the Paris accords, but, perceiving the policy crisis in Beijing, they began a sustained effort to reestablish friendly relations with the People's Republic. In short, Soviet leaders inferred that

Deng Xiaoping's return to power raised the possibility of a strategy reversal. To signal receptivity to such a change, Moscow made a major readjustment in policies being pursued since the Twenty-fourth Party Congress of 1971, not only toward China, but also toward Japan. In the two years since the congress, Soviet-Japanese economic negotiations had entered a new stage, specifically focusing on several very large development projects in Siberia, including Tyumen oil and Yakutia natural gas and coal. By early 1973 the principal obstacles to completion of negotiations were the territorial problem (four islands of the Kurile chain off the northern coast of Hokkaido that the Soviet Union had seized following World War II and that Japan still claimed) and Japanese reluctance to provide long-term, low-interest loans to finance the projects.

In January 1973, however, perhaps in response to American prompting to generate greater East-West trade with the Soviet Union, Japan's Prime Minister Kakuei Tanaka undertook a major new initiative, for the first time specifically separating the Kurile islands issue from economic relations.[78] Tanaka rationalized his action on the premise that goodwill built through economic cooperation would eventually lead to resolution of the territorial question. The initial Soviet response was receptive but incredulous, and Moscow sought reassurances on the availability of long-term, low-interest loans. A letter from Tanaka to Brezhnev on March 8 reaffirming the Japanese proposal and suggesting a visit to Moscow, produced an enthusiastic Soviet response. The Soviet press acclaimed the Tanaka initiative as a breakthrough in Soviet-Japanese relations, and Brezhnev extended an invitation to the Japanese prime minister to visit Moscow later in the year for substantive deliberations.[79] In other words, by the spring of 1973, immediately prior to the outbreak of the policy crisis in Beijing, Soviet hopes for establishing a major new economic relationship with Japan appeared on the verge of realization.

But Moscow declined to follow through on the Japanese initiative. Having perceived the leadership change in Beijing, the Soviet Union in early June reversed its position toward Japan and now actively *dis*couraged further progress in negotiations for the next several months. On June 6, the Soviet ambassador to Tokyo, Oleg Troyanovsky, postponed the Tanaka visit on the grounds that the date originally set for late August would be "inconvenient," the conventional diplomatic term used to indicate a change of plans. Making

plain the reversal, Moscow then moved to discourage Japanese interest in the energy projects by increasing the cost of Japanese participation and reducing the projected return. For example, the maximum
amount of crude oil Japan was to obtain from the Tyumen oil project
was reduced from between forty and fifty million tons annually to
twenty-five million tons.

The change in Soviet policy toward Japan was clearly not a function
of their bilateral relationship, which had just then entered into a most
promising stage, nor was it some clever communist negotiating tactic.
What persuaded Moscow to forsake an objective so long and eagerly
sought was the evident turmoil in Beijing. The Soviets viewed the
growing policy debate in the Chinese capital as a potentially great
opportunity—the first genuine opportunity in many years—to bring
the rancorous relationship with their erstwhile ally to an end and to
resolve their most serious security problem. The turnabout in Soviet
policy, although confusing to the Japanese, was fully consistent with
the decision to seek an improvement in relations with China. Timing
was the key to Soviet actions. A strong move toward Japan would be
read in Beijing as an effort to contain China (which it was originally
intended to do). The Soviets now wanted to avoid conveying that
impression, which would only provide Mao Zedong and his supporters
with ammunition for their expected efforts to thwart any reconciliation
scheme. Therefore, Moscow put off negotiations on the economic
issue, instead pressing Japan to sign a peace treaty and to declare
adherence to the Asian Collective Security System, two steps the
Soviets knew the Japanese simply would not take.

While shifting policy toward Tokyo but before making a move
toward Beijing, the Soviet leadership carefully and elliptically probed
the attitude of the American leadership. The Soviet concern was that
what was perceived as an opportunity might actually have been a
smoke screen behind which the United States and China were making
another secret maneuver. Having in mind to offer Beijing a mutual
non-aggression pact, Soviet leaders intently probed the prospects for
United States military assistance to China, which of course would
rule out any Soviet offer. Thus, during Kissinger's May 4–9 visit to
Moscow to prepare for Brezhnev's summit trip to the United States
the following month, the Soviet leader grilled the American emissary,
who evidently missed the point.

While on a boar-hunting outing, Brezhnev suddenly shifted from
congenial small talk to a vituperative denunciation of China. Reviling

the Chinese as "treacherous, arrogant, beyond the human pale . . .," the Soviet leader bemoaned the fact that China was acquiring a nuclear arsenal. "The Soviet Union could not accept this passively," he asserted, "something would have to be done."[80] Kissinger correctly interpreted Brezhnev's remark as "fishing for some hint" but incorrectly surmised that it was for "American acquiescence in a Soviet pre-emptive attack" on China, which he discouraged. Then, making his point, Brezhnev declared that the United States must not provide any military assistance to China. "Any military assistance . . . by the United States would lead to war." That this was no mere spontaneous reaction by the Soviet leader became clear the next day when Dobrynin took Kissinger aside to "stress that the China portion of the discussion . . . was not to be treated as social. Brezhnev had meant every word of it."

Evidently reassured that the United States was not going to provide military assistance, Moscow offered the Chinese a mutual non-aggression pact sometime in mid-June. The failure of Beijing to respond generated considerable anxiety within the Soviet leadership, anxiety that was clearly manifested during the Nixon-Brezhnev summit in San Clemente in late June. On June 23, the last full day of what was an otherwise routine set of meetings, Brezhnev unexpectedly began another tirade against the Chinese.[81] "The Chinese were perfidious and . . . sly in concealing their aims" and "Mao had a treacherous character."[82] Warning that in a decade China's nuclear program would be where the Soviet program was now (which was an extraordinary exaggeration), Brezhnev "proposed a secret exchange of views on China through the Presidential Channel." Then, professing his intent "to expose China's bellicosity to the world," he revealed the Soviet offer of a non-aggression pact, adding quickly his certainty that the Chinese would rebuff it. However, Brezhnev described the Soviet offer as one Moscow *would soon make*, rather than as one it had already made.

At this point, Brezhnev discussed with Nixon the same Soviet concerns regarding China that he had covered with Kissinger the previous month—and in virtually the same words. Moscow, he said, had "no objection to state-to-state relations between Washington and Peking. Military arrangements would be another matter." Nixon reassured the Soviet leader that the United States "had never had any military discussions with China," but neither he nor Kissinger offered any reassurance about future American policy.

Satisfied, Brezhnev dropped the matter as abruptly as he had raised it, but later that evening Gromyko took Kissinger aside (just as Dobrynin had in May) to reemphasize the same Soviet threat: "Any military agreement between China and the United States would lead to war."

Perhaps encouraged by the American leadership's denials, Moscow attempted to sweeten the offer to Beijng by modifying the Asian Collective Security concept to make it more palatable. Two new principles were added — the right of each member country to control the disposition of its natural resources and the right of each nation to determine its own social and economic systems.[83] On August 24, the day the Tenth Party Congress secretly convened in Beijing, *Pravda* and *Izvestia* both carried front-page editorials extolling the benefits of the system. Brezhnev himself, in major speeches delivered in Alma Ata in August and in Tashkent in September, prominently linked the twin themes of Sino-Soviet relations and the Asian Collective Security system. The major reversal of Soviet policy toward Japan combined with the carefully crafted offer to improve relations with China left little doubt about Soviet priorities.

The Chinese response, given by Zhou Enlai in his speech to the Tenth Party Congress, was skeptical but not unreceptive. Castigating the Soviet revisionist clique, Zhou noted: "Recently, the Brezhnev renegade clique have talked a lot of nonsense on Sino-Soviet relations. It alleges that China is against relaxation of world tension and unwilling to improve Sino-Soviet relations."[84] Rejecting this allegation, Zhou went on to suggest what Moscow could do if it were sincere:

Why don't you show your good faith by doing a thing or two — for instance, withdraw your armed forces from Czechoslovakia or the People's Republic of Mongolia and return the four northern islands to Japan? . . . Must China give away all the territory north of the Great Wall to the Soviet revisionists in order to show that we favour relaxation of world tension and are willing to improve Sino-Soviet relations? . . . The Sino-Soviet controversy on matters of principle should not hinder the normalization of relations between the two states on the basis of the five principles of peaceful coexistence. The Sino-Soviet boundary question should be settled peacefully through negotiations free from any threat.[85]

While Zhou's remarks did not close the door to improvement in state-to-state relations, afterward he made it plain that any Soviet hope for a dramatic improvement was at best premature. In an interview with *New York Times* reporter C. L. Sulzberger in late October, he implied that the Chinese had explored the Soviet offer but rejected it. He declared that "there was no point in" the Soviet offer of a non-aggression pact, as the very definition of such a pact included avoiding the threat of force as well as the actual use of force. "Since the Russians didn't agree on that, what would be the point of a . . . non-aggression pact?"[86]

Despite the Chinese leadership's substantial realignment as Deng Xiaoping and many of his supporters were returned to posts in the party, state, and military hierarchies, it was clear that it was too early to expect any fundamental change in Chinese policy. Deng himself, undoubtedly required to profess support for Mao's policies as a condition of further political advance, began to take a pro-American stand, declaring that there was positive value in a continued American presence in Asia, supporting Japan on the northern islands issue and on the temporary necessity for continued United States-Japan security ties, and taking a stand critical of the Soviet Union.[87] Since Deng Xiaoping was the leader in whom the Soviets had placed their hopes, his public shift to a position of support for Mao's policies persuaded Moscow that there was little possibility for an improvement in relations in the near term.

When it became obvious that there was no hope for an improvement in relations with Beijing, Moscow began to criticize Deng Xiaoping by name in the press and reversed its policy toward Japan once again. The Soviet Union now returned to the course pursued before Deng had returned to power — the attempt to establish strong economic ties with Japan. Thus, in early 1974, the Soviet Union began to deemphasize the need for a peace treaty with Japan and Japan's adherence to the Asian Collective Security system, instead stressing once again the need for immediately expanding practical economic cooperation. The policy reversal succeeded. In April 1974 the Japanese government agreed to extend $1.05 billion in Export-Import Bank credits for the exploitation of Yakutia coal and natural gas and Siberian forestry development. Moscow's initial probe regarding the significance of Deng's return to power was over for the time being.

American Inaction in Vietnam and Beijing's Response

Meanwhile, by the time that the Tenth Party Congress had concluded its deliberations in late August 1973, the Chinese leadership had decided upon its policy response to American inaction in Vietnam. Faced with the imminent collapse of its entire southern security zone, Beijing moved to contain and to counter the inevitable emergence of a unified Vietnam under Hanoi. Paradoxically, Beijing's first decision was to resume large-scale military and technical assistance to Hanoi. Chinese aid tended to focus Hanoi's efforts on the final conquest of South Vietnam and to some extent also inured the North Vietnamese to Chinese actions to which they would ordinarily be expected to object. The net effect of the policy change was to give Beijing the time and the opportunity to take action in the Paracels, in Cambodia, toward Thailand, and elsewhere with little initial overt resistance from Hanoi.

Immediately after the congress, Beijing began preparations for the invasion of the Paracel Islands, establishing a secret training base at Leizhou Bay in Guangxi province.[88] It would be there that the entire assault plan for the Paracels would be developed and practiced. The attack itself would occur January 19–20, 1974. Even though the Paracels were at this time claimed by Saigon and not Hanoi, which confused contemporary observers regarding Chinese motives, it was the prospect of a unified Vietnam under Hanoi that prompted Beijing's preemptive action.[89] The further high probability of a long-term adversary relationship with a militarily powerful Soviet client state was no doubt decisive in the Chinese leadership's calculations in resolving to settle by force a jurisdictional dispute of almost two centuries.

Another equally important reason for acting immediately against a fatally weakened Saigon regime rather than waiting to confront what would undoubtedly be a far stronger unified Vietnam was the desire to establish as quickly as possible a claim to the petroleum reserves which lay beneath the South China Sea. Ongoing exploration by Western petroleum companies had established the presence of vast reserves all along the shallow waters of the broad continental shelf. Control of the Paracels, in particular, would establish Chinese legal and physical access to the seabed surrounding the archipelago and, using the islands as a base-point, between them and the mainland. There was every expectation that Vietnam once unified would seek its share of access to the undersea petroleum and would contest Chinese claims. Curiously, when China attacked and took control of the Paracels, Hanoi made no objection. It was perhaps out of concern to not jeopardize Chinese aid for the coming campaign in South Vietnam that the North Vietnamese remained conspicuously silent, even though the implications of Chinese control over the islands must not have been lost on them.[90]

The centerpiece of the Chinese effort to contain a future reunified Vietnam and to prevent Hanoi's domination of all of Indochina was the decision to establish a Chinese client state in Cambodia, the only place remaining in the region where Beijing could hope to maintain some degree of leverage. This effort would preoccupy the Chinese for the next two years. By the time Hanoi had completed its conquest of South Vietnam in the spring of 1975, Beijing had helped to establish the Kampuchean People's Republic under Pol Pot in Phnom Penh. The consequence of American withdrawal from mainland Southeast Asia was to extend Sino-Soviet adversary relations to the region, and specifically to Cambodia itself as Beijing supported Pol Pot and Sihanouk while Moscow now supported Lon Nol.[91]

With regard to Thailand, Beijing moved to improve state-to-state relations with Bangkok, which had become increasingly interested in improving relations with Beijing in the wake of United States withdrawal. Thus, Beijing gradually squeezed off support for the Communist party of Thailand over the period 1973–1975, while slowly opening the door to Bangkok. By mid-1975, Mao Zedong could say to the visiting Thai premier, Kukrit Pramoj: "You don't have to worry about the communist party of Thailand. . . . It has existed for more than ten years, but not a single Thai communist has [ever] come to see me."[92]

As Sino-American relations began to congeal, Mao made another strong effort to shift China into the United States camp; it came during Kissinger's November 1973 trip. In a two-and-a-half-hour session with the secretary, Mao went over the same strategic arguments he had raised early in February regarding the containment of the Soviet Union, but this time he did not suggest an alliance. What he did do, however, was to make it plain that China would normalize relations with the United States whenever Washington wished and that Taiwan would not be an obstacle. While declaring that, of course, the United States would be required to sever diplomatic relations with Taiwan before establishing them with Beijing, he said that "Taiwan was not an important issue. . . . The issue of the overall international situation is an important one."[93] Mao went on: "We can do without Taiwan for the time being, and let it come after one hundred years. Do not take matters on this world so rapidly. Why is there need to be in such great haste?" But in his next breath, he said: "As for your relations with us, I think they need not take a hundred years. . . . But that is to be decided by you. We will not rush you." Clearly, Mao was offering the normalization of relations and clearing away the main obstacle—Taiwan.

Kissinger professed not to comprehend the point, musing:

> What did all this mean? Was it another hint that normalization could be separated from the issue of Taiwan? And that the rate of normalizing relations was up to us?[94]

Mao had placed the full weight of his authority behind the offer to normalize relations with the United States. He now sweetened it by expressing his willingness to move forward on other aspects of the relationship. He agreed to settle all outstanding claims between the two countries, pending some technical details, expand trade and exchanges, and also enlarge the scope of the recently established liaison offices. The final communiqué contained language suggesting Sino-American unity on a broad front, extending their "joint opposition to hegemony" from the Asia-Pacific region to the global plane, and made specific reference to "the normalization of relations" based upon the confirmation of the principle of one China.

Mao Zedong's opening led nowhere. For whatever reasons (Kissinger suggested Watergate), the United States declined to take up Mao's offer. The result:

> The claims-assets talks were broken off by the Chinese under transparent pretexts. Exchanges languished. The overall orientation of the policy was maintained but its substance was substantially frozen. Subsequent trips in 1974 and 1975 either were downright chilly or were holding actions—though relations never went backward.[95]

The consequence was that American inaction had a significant impact on internal Chinese deliberations regarding the "overall international situation," which was resolved more along lines espoused by Deng Xiaoping than by Mao. Indeed, it would be Deng himself who would announce Beijing's new course in a speech delivered at the United Nations in early April 1974. There, Deng set forth China's new approach within the context of "the theory of three worlds." In it, the United States and the Soviet Union occupied the First World; the developed nations of Europe and Asia, the Second World; and the developing nations of Asia, Africa, and Latin America, the Third World, which included China.

The new strategy permitted China to assume a position roughly equidistant between Washington and Moscow, which in practice meant drawing away somewhat from the recent rapprochement with the United States. Indeed, this was a clear step back from Mao's positions of February and November 1973 when he exhorted Kissinger to accept a Sino-American alliance against the Soviet Union and offered to settle all outstanding differences with Washington. The new conception also allowed China to establish closer relations with Europe and Japan quite independently of any relationship with the United States and with the developing nations of the Third World as well. The effect of the new strategy was to immobilize Chinese relations with the United States, despite strong efforts by Washington to forestall the standstill.

Washington's reaction to the rise of Deng Xiaoping was to attempt to win him over to support of American policy, even while denying that any substantive change had occurred in the Chinese leadership. Kissinger acknowledged that a "domestic power struggle over the value of the rapprochement with the United States" was occurring at this time, but he identified Mao and Zhou as the main combatants.[96] The issue, of course, was Mao's strategy of rapprochement, but the principal dissenter was not Mao's long-time ally Zhou Enlai, toward whom the criticism was directed, but Deng Xiaoping. In any case, the failure to identify Deng's role in the domestic power struggle was either a further misunderstanding of Chinese politics, which is improbable at this point, or an effort to cover up the failure to anticipate the negative impact of earlier United States policy on the Chinese domestic political scene.

Deng Xiaoping's return to power confounded Kissinger's quixotic strategy of attempting "to have our mao tai and drink our vodka too." Instead of the United States moving into position to balance off Moscow against Beijing, it was Beijing that was playing Washington off against Moscow. At any rate, the upshot of the Chinese policy shift was to freeze Sino-American relations while reversing what had been a promising economic relationship. United States-China trade plummeted during the 1974–1976 period from a high of $922 million in 1974 to a low of $337 million in 1976.[97] Even this picture was misleading, for the $337 million figure was due mainly to American imports of Chinese goods. Chinese imports from the United States better illustrate the shift, moving from a 1974 high of $807 million to a 1976 low of $135 million, an 85 percent decline!

PRC Trade with the United States

	1971	1972	1973	1974	1975	1976
PRC Imports	-	64	689	807	304	135
PRC Exports	5	32	64	115	158	202

In retrospect, the basic pattern of American relations with China began to emerge in 1973 and 1974. This was nothing less than implied acceptance of Beijing's stated strategy of maintaining a position of equidistance between the two big powers. Thus, with the significant exception of the succession period, 1976–1979, about which more will be said in another volume, American policy toward China became "active" only when it appeared that the Chinese were attempting to edge away from the middle position and toward the other superpower.[98]

The immobilization of the American-Chinese relationship was not offset by the superficially compatible geopolitical positions that both took. If United States policy could be interpreted as attempting to draw China into adversarial positions with the Soviet Union, one could just as easily argue that China, in at least a few cases, was acting in its own interests, however newly defined. Cambodia was one case in which Chinese national interest clearly drove policy irrespective of the state of the internal political balance or of American policy. Pakistan was a similar case where policy would be essentially the same no matter who was in power in Beijing, but Angola was another matter. Here, Deng's return to power had a dramatic impact on policy (as will be discussed in the next chapter).

In sum, the new American strategy of attempting to cement China into a position between Moscow in the north and a Hanoi-controlled

Vietnam in the south and dependent upon the United States for support had only partially succeeded through 1976. Kissinger had made a serious miscalculation in assuming that the decision not to sustain South Vietnam would have no serious consequences in internal Chinese politics. The result was to breathe new life into Mao's opposition led by Deng Xiaoping, who, returning to power, soon moved into position to block further improvement in Sino-American relations, despite strenuous efforts by Henry Kissinger to win him over.

In fact, Deng would set forth a Chinese strategy that was in some ways the mirror image of Kissinger's own, as each power attempted to move to the center position between the other two in the tripolar structure. Indeed, had Mao's position remained unimpaired, the management of American policy would have been far simpler, for there would have been no prospect of an improvement in Sino-Soviet relations. On the other hand, with Deng in command there was no impediment to improvement of Sino-Soviet relations, giving Beijing greater leverage in its relations with Washington. Overall, American Asian strategy was a mixture of success and failure. Kissinger had succeeded in establishing the desired geopolitical structure for the mainland but failed to maintain a positive relationship with Beijing, a failure which immobilized America's relations with China until well into the administration of President Jimmy Carter.

10

Angola and Detente:
The Politics of Desperation

By mid-April of 1974 Kissinger's tripolar initiatives toward both Moscow and Beijing had in fact collapsed. He had failed utterly in the attempt to place *any* restraints upon Soviet MIRVs as Moscow refused to negotiate limits on its unexpectedly ambitious and threatening fourth-generation ICBM program.[1] The conclusion was now inescapable that Moscow was striving for strategic weapons superiority. From the administration's internal point of view, therefore, detente was expiring fast, although the public facade was maintained. Following the resignation of Richard Nixon, Kissinger strove to maintain some semblance of detente momentum in the arms control accord negotiated at Vladivostok on November 24, 1974. The accord itself set no meaningful limits on the Soviet missile buildup; instead, it constituted an attempt to leave open an American option to match it.[2] What Kissinger searched for through 1975 was some sort of leverage or bargaining chip which he could employ to steer Moscow back on a more restrained course. It was a measure of his desperation to salvage his failing strategy that he chose Angola to serve that purpose.

Kissinger's Asian strategy had also foundered upon the failure to anticipate the impact of withdrawal from Vietnam on Mao's domestic political position. After his reemergence, Deng Xiaoping gradually had reversed the direction of Sino-American relations, although here, too, public perception lagged behind private reality. Worse, Deng had pushed through a major shift in Chinese strategy, the Three Worlds concept, which he had unveiled in a speech to the United Nations on April 7, abandoning the long-held two-camp thesis.[3] The practical effect of the strategic shift was to unlock the door to the improvement of Sino-Soviet relations, a door that had been held firmly shut by Mao Zedong for over a decade and a half. Although the door would not in any case open very quickly, it was now unlocked.

Moscow had perceived the possibility of repairing the relationship with Beijing when Deng first reappeared, thus the offer for a non-aggression pact in 1973, which the Chinese had refused. But with Deng's alteration of Beijing's strategy it could be anticipated that Moscow would try again, and the result might well be different. In any case, it was evident to the secretary that his tripolar initiatives had failed.[4] Instead of building an adversary relationship between Moscow and Beijing, his policies had had, if anything, the opposite effect.

Kissinger attempted to do two things in Angola. First, he aimed to reinforce Sino-Soviet adversary relations through the promotion of a proxy conflict in an effort to close off any possibility (however remote) of reconciliation between the two communist powers. This phase lasted from July 1974 until June 1975. When that ploy failed with the Chinese withdrawal from Angola, he injected American power in Beijing's place in an effort to build leverage for a negotiated solution which would serve to reinforce detente. Here Moscow would not cooperate, and the result was the end of detente and with it all hope of restraining Soviet arms, the Soviet acquisition of Angola as a client state, and the establishment of a strong Soviet position in Africa.

Kissinger's Angolan Gamble

The months of April and May 1974 were a time of anguish for Kissinger as he searched desperately for some way to rescue policies collapsing on all fronts. It was the military coup in Portugal on April 25 — and specifically, direct Chinese involvement in Angola — which fortuitously offered an immediate opportunity to reverse his disastrous policies. Kissinger gambled that he could successfully instigate a Sino-Soviet proxy conflict while keeping the United States on the sidelines and in the process possibly develop some negotiating leverage which might help in resurrecting detente, the cornerstone of his strategy.

The collapse of the Portuguese dictatorship of Marcello Caetano had come as no surprise, although the precise means and timing of its demise may have been unexpected. By the early seventies there were already numerous indicators of decay—economic decline at home and disaffection with empire abroad.[5] After taking power the new regime under General Antonio Spinola immediately moved to bring about divestiture of the world's oldest empire. Spinola initially planned to hold a referendum in Angola to determine the nature of the colony's future relationship with Portugal, but his government was divided. He himself favored federation,[6] but more radical members of his government, particularly General Vasco Goncalves, who would become prime minister in July, argued for the granting of independence. In an effort to effect a peaceful transition to self-rule, the new regime in Lisbon offered a general cease-fire, began releasing political prisoners, and encouraged the formation of political parties and competition through the electoral process, in hopes of diverting liberation movements from continuation of the "resistance" war that had plagued the colony sporadically since 1961.

The prospect of even limited self-rule was sufficient to spur all of the resistance groups in Angola to establish offices in the capital at Luanda. Indeed, within a month of the coup there were some thirty "parties" and splinter groups vying for sanction from Lisbon, producing an extraordinarily chaotic situation. Three groups were of consequence: the MPLA (Popular Movement for the Liberation of Angola) led by Augustino Neto, FNLA (National Front for the Liberation of Angola) led by Holden Roberto, and UNITA (National Union for the Total Independence of Angola) led by Jonas Savimbi. It is in the context of the various resistance groups' scramble to establish legitimate political organizations and outside powers' attempts to influence the resulting competition that Kissinger's Angolan gamble must be understood.

At the time of the Portuguese coup the outside power in the strongest position to influence events in Angola was the People's Republic of China. Beijing maintained friendly relations with Zaire, Zambia, and Tanzania; was active in the Congo (despite Soviet involvement there), Botswana (with which it would establish diplomatic relations in January 1975), and Mozambique (where its position was stronger than Moscow's); and was aiding resistance movements in Namibia, Rhodesia, and Angola. Indeed, in December 1973, Beijing had reached agreement with President Mobuto Sese

Seko of Zaire and Holden Roberto of FNLA to build an Angolan resistance army of fifteen thousand men, with China providing two-thirds of the technical assistance and equipment and Zaire one-third.[7]

Neither Moscow's nor Washington's position in southern Africa was comparable to Beijing's. By the early seventies the Soviet Union maintained state-to-state relations with the Congo (Brazzaville), Nigeria, Algeria, Tunisia, Egypt, and Somalia, but provided only token support for liberation movements in sub-Saharan Africa, particularly in the Portuguese colonies of Guinea-Bissau, Mozambique, and Angola.[8] In Angola, Moscow had nominally supported the MPLA under Augustino Neto since the beginning of the guerrilla resistance in 1961. But the MPLA was never a very cohesive, disciplined organization, and the Soviet Union suspended aid in the early seventies as the MPLA fell into disarray once again following successive offensives undertaken against it by Portuguese forces.[9] At this point, it would be difficult to conclude that Moscow was engaged in a serious competitive struggle with Beijing for influence anywhere in southern Africa.

At the time of the coup in Lisbon, Washington was perhaps in the worst position of the three outside powers to influence events in Angola. American interests in the Azores Islands base and the lease arrangements that secured it tended to dominate the United States attitude toward Lisbon, especially after the Yom Kippur War, during which Portugal proved to be the only European nation to permit the United States to use its bases in transshipping materiel to Israel. Although the United States did not support Portugal's colonial rule, Washington exhibited an "understanding" attitude toward Lisbon's colonial difficulties, which resulted in a relaxation of restrictions on arms exports.[10] Washington's understanding attitude extended to Angola. From 1962 until 1970, the CIA had provided "program assistance" to Holden Roberto of from $10,000 to $20,000 per year.[11] In 1970 Washington cut off CIA funding for the FNLA and closed the CIA station in Angola.

Kissinger Rolls the Dice

The specific opportunity for Kissinger's "Angolan gamble" came on May 29, 1974, with the arrival in Kinkuza, Zaire, of the initial contingent of what would eventually total at least 120 Chinese

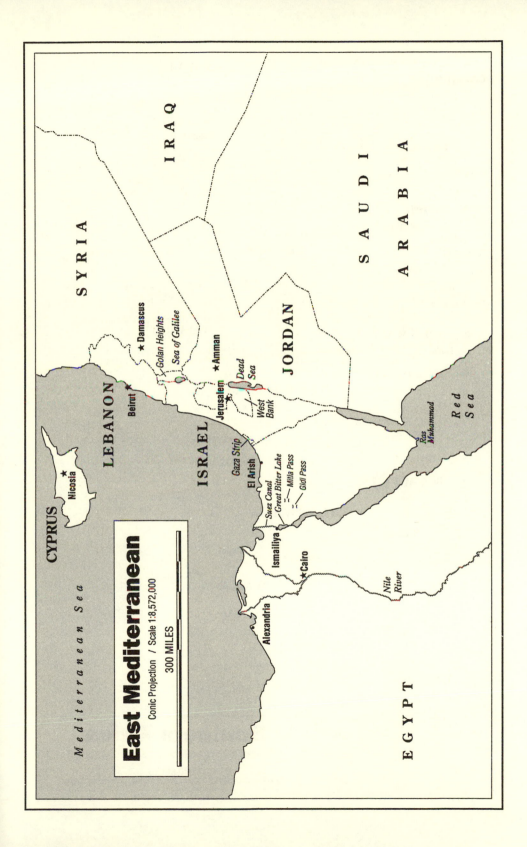

CYPRUS

*Nicosia

Mediterranean Sea

LEBANON

Beirut*

ISRAEL

*Damascus

Golan Heights

Sea of Galilee

*Amman

Dead Sea

Jerusalem*

West Bank

Gaza Strip

El Arish*

Suez Canal

Great Bitter Lake

Mitla Pass

Gidi Pass

Ismailiya*

*Cairo

Alexandria*

SYRIA

I R A Q

JORDAN

SAUDI

ARABIA

Ras Muhammad

Red Sea

Nile River

EGYPT

East Mediterranean

Conic Projection / Scale 1:8,572,000

300 MILES

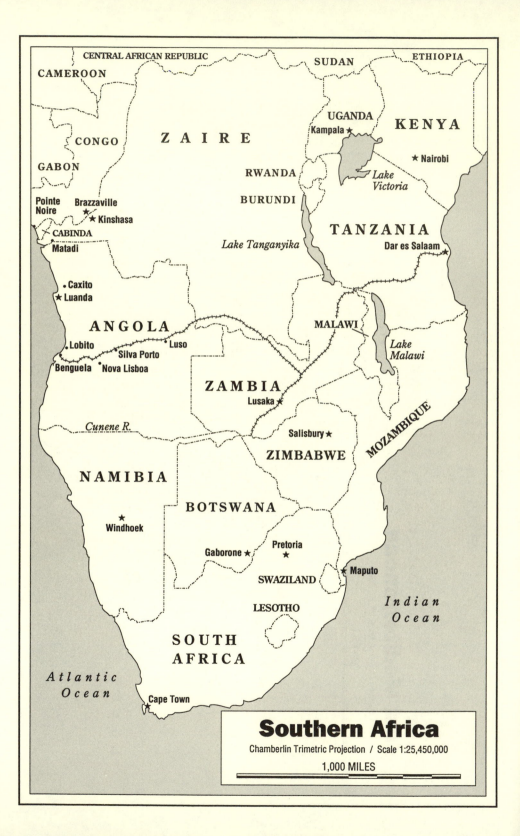

CENTRAL AFRICAN REPUBLIC

SUDAN

ETHIOPIA

CAMEROON

CONGO

ZAIRE

UGANDA
Kampala ★

KENYA

GABON

★ Nairobi

RWANDA

Pointe
Noire

Brazzaville
★
★ Kinshasa

BURUNDI

Lake
Victoria

CABINDA

Matadi

Lake Tanganyika

TANZANIA

Dar es Salaam ★

● Caxito
★ Luanda

ANGOLA

● Lobito
Benguela
● Silva Porto
● Nova Lisboa

● Luso

MALAWI

Lake
Malawi

ZAMBIA

Lusaka ★

Cunene R.

Salisbury ★

MOZAMBIQUE

ZIMBABWE

NAMIBIA

BOTSWANA

★
Windhoek

Gaborone ★

Pretoria
★

Maputo

SWAZILAND

★

Indian
Ocean

LESOTHO

SOUTH
AFRICA

Atlantic
Ocean

Cape Town

Southern Africa

Chamberlin Trimetric Projection / Scale 1:25,450,000

1,000 MILES

"advisers" to begin training Holden Roberto's FNLA army.[12] Kissinger's gamble was deceptively simple. He sought to align the United States with the People's Republic of China in support of the FNLA in hopes of eliciting a countermove from Moscow through the MPLA. If successful, he would at one stroke have accomplished both the aggravation of Sino-Soviet differences and the stabilization of the tripolar balance. The gamble was that the Chinese would not back off, having just announced the new policy of even-handed treatment of the superpowers, or that the Soviets would decline to be drawn into a situation that would have obvious negative ramifications regarding "detente." Barring external interference, the Soviets could expect that the leftward orientation of the Portuguese government would lead to the victory of the MPLA in Angola without excessive Soviet involvement there.

Kissinger's policy would therefore have to be executed with the utmost precision, secrecy, and caution. He had to do enough to draw in Moscow, but not so much that he would scare off Beijing. His first step, in early July, was to instruct the CIA to resume support for Roberto from its private funds—"small amounts at first, but enough for word to get around that the CIA was dealing itself into the race."[13] This activity took place in Kinshasa, Zaire, where Roberto had his headquarters and spent most of his time. Zaire, under President Mobutu Sese Seko, became the conduit through which virtually all CIA support for the FNLA was channeled.[14]

Moscow was attentive and responded cautiously. In August the Soviet Union announced that it viewed the MPLA as the "true spokesman of the Angolan people." Keeping a low profile, the Soviets "began flying arms to Dar-es-Salaam."[15] The arms were publicly ticketed for support of "African liberation movements," which made it initially unclear who the actual recipient or recipients were; but by October 1974, CIA intelligence reports confirmed that the Soviet Union was "filtering limited amounts of arms to the MPLA."[16] Later, when the level of involvement rose, Moscow would arrange to ship material to the MPLA through Brazzaville, Congo, across the river from the CIA operation in Kinshasa.

Meanwhile, on September 10 the FNLA had acknowledged publicly the arrival of 450 tons of Chinese supplies (presumably the first of several shipments which included AK-47s, machine guns, light mortars, and grenade launchers) and the rest of Beijing's advisory team.[17] The CIA also continued its funding of Roberto and "the flagrant, semiovert activities of the CIA station in Kinshasa ensured that American support of the FNLA would be widely known."[18] Kissinger had succeeded in creating the impression that the United States and China were cooperating in support of Holden Roberto's FNLA where no cooperation in fact existed.[19] But Moscow had nibbled at the bait and cautiously responded to Kissinger's move with a similarly guarded one of its own.[20]

At this point, American and Soviet interests meshed in a curious way over China as each sought to forestall movement by the other toward Beijing. To keep Moscow and Beijing apart, Kissinger now approached Moscow with an arms control proposition that the Soviets found too tempting to refuse. The Soviet leadership, in turn, saw Kissinger's proposition as a major step toward their larger objectives vis-à-vis the United States, as well as a potential roadblock against the apparently growing American-Chinese cooperation in Angola.

In discussions with the Soviet leadership during his Moscow trip in October, Kissinger privately proposed, and the Soviets accepted, resumption of the arms control talks on the condition that the United States agree to exclude Moscow's newly deployed Backfire bomber from any agreement.[21] In his zeal to tie Moscow into an agreement, which might coincidentally aid President Ford's coming electoral campaign, Kissinger offered this concession secretly and on his own initiative. There had been no authorization from or even consultation with President Ford or the relevant officials charged with responsibility for arms control.[22]

Indeed, after the Vladivostok talks in December, when the two sides were composing the aide-mémoire formally detailing the extent and nature of the accord, Kissinger made yet another concession — on cruise missiles. Although the two sides had not discussed the specific issue of cruise missiles at Vladivostok, Moscow insisted afterward in preparing the aide-mémoire that the reference to "air-launched missiles" included cruise missiles as well as ballistic missiles, while Washington insisted that the phrase meant only ballistic missiles. Finally, after several weeks of wrangling, Kissinger agreed to omit the word "ballistic" from the aide-mémoire, although he sent a note declaring that the American understanding of the phrase "air-launched missiles" excluded cruise missiles.[23] Nevertheless, Kissinger had yielded to Moscow's view on both issues in the final document. The Vladivostok accord referred only to "missiles" and to "bombers" without further specification. (Brezhnev had sent a note to Ford declaring that the Backfire was not a strategic weapon, which Ford accepted.) This may have facilitated agreement at the time, but it would create major stumbling blocks to final agreement once the concessions became known.

In all seriousness, Kissinger had to have known that his concessions would in fact bar any final agreement because they were unacceptable to the American side. He was too experienced a negotiator not to have also known that once concessions were made, Moscow would be most reluctant to relinquish them. In any case, with the framework of an arms control agreement completed, the stage was now set for the next step in the scheme to deepen Sino-Soviet hostility. It came in the wake of Portuguese efforts to forge an agreement among the three Angolan movements to pursue a peaceful and cooperative approach to independence.

On July 27, following the appointment of General Goncalves as prime minister, President Spinola declared that Portugal would give independence to the colonies and two weeks later announced a transition plan for Angola.[24] Lisbon's plan called for the establishment of a provisional government to effect what was anticipated to be a two- to three-year transition to independence. The provisional government, which would be composed of representatives of the main liberation movements, the ethnic groups, and the white population, would prepare a draft constitution, write an electoral law, oversee national elections prior to independence, and define Angola's future relationship to the mother country.

The announcement, however, had the opposite of its intended settling effect. Virtually all parties opposed Lisbon's plans as conditions worsened. The local white hierarchy's objections culminated in an unsuccessful plot to seize power in Luanda. The MPLA and FNLA continued to fight each other while objecting to the inclusion of ethnics and whites in the provisional government and to the electoral timetable. In addition, the MPLA had split into three groups—one under Neto; another under Vice-chairman Daniel Chipenda, whose forces were deployed on the Zambian front (hence their designation as the "eastern faction"); and a third group under Father Joaquim Pinto de Andrade which had no armed forces and consisted mainly of intellectuals.

By the end of July both the MPLA and UNITA had reached cease-fire agreements with Portugal, but the FNLA had not. Roberto's forces instead moved from their base camps in Zaire into the bordering Angolan province of Uiga to build a military presence in-country. By late September the FNLA had established an occupied zone through the center of the province. Only then, when the FNLA could command a strong position on Angolan territory, did Roberto agree to a cease-fire, which he negotiated on October 12.[25]

The splintering of Angolan politics was matched by growing polarization in Lisbon. In late September, Spinola, attempting to reverse the growing pro-Neto orientation of the radicals in the government, signed an agreement with Zaire's President Mobutu designed to exclude Neto by recognizing MPLA dissident leader Daniel Chipenda as the "legitimate" head of the MPLA.[26] Spinola's resignation on September 28 and his replacement by General Francisco da Costa Gomez brought an end to this plan, but not to the growing dissension within the Portuguese ruling group. The removal of Spinola strengthened the hand of the radical elements urging recognition of the Neto faction of the MPLA as the sole legitimate authority in Angola, and it undoubtedly influenced both the FNLA and UNITA to come to terms.

Against the backdrop of continuing clashes in Luanda as each of the major factions sought to strengthen its position, leaders of the MPLA, FNLA, and UNITA met in Mombasa, Kenya, on January 4 and reached agreement to maintain a common front in negotiations with Lisbon. Negotiations with the Portuguese government were conducted January 10–15, 1975, in southern Portugal (at Alvor, which gave its name to the resulting agreement). The Alvor accord established the three groups as the "sole legitimate representatives of the people of Angola" (thereby excluding Chipenda entirely), proclaimed Cabinda province "an undeniable component part of Angola," and set an early date for independence, November 11, 1975.[27] The three groups agreed to establish a provisional government which would draft a constitution and conduct elections prior to independence. They also consented to a step-by-step plan for the merger of their respective forces into a national army and the gradual withdrawal of Portuguese forces, which would be completed by February 19, 1976.

The Secretary Raises the Stakes

Moscow immediately praised the Alvor accord as "an important step along the path to decolonization."[28] This was the logical position for

Moscow to take since, despite cautious resumption of support to the MPLA, Neto's organization was still in disarray and needed time to build strength. In terms of military forces at this time, the balance was heavily in favor of the FNLA.[29] Furthermore, the political viability of the Alvor agreement aside, since whichever group was in possession of the capital on independence day would win de facto control of the government, and since the MPLA was then dominant in Luanda, the avoidance of open conflict—and thus support for Alvor—was in its best interest. Finally, the predisposition of the Portuguese government—as it was then constituted—toward the MPLA made cooperation the obvious course.

Once the FNLA had been granted recognition in the Alvor accord, this same appreciation of the forces at play in Luanda and Lisbon led Roberto to the opposite conclusion. It was in his interest to use his military advantage as soon as possible to attempt to gain control of the capital—if he could be confident of continued support from Washington and Beijing. The Chinese had already demonstrated good faith with the shipment of weapons and advisers and showed every indication of continuing to fulfill their commitment to arm and train his army. Roberto would hear from Washington in one week.

In Washington on January 22, Kissinger summoned the Forty Committee, the government's designated authorizing body for covert operations, to discuss the situation in Angola. Having for six months surreptitiously encouraged factional strife through clandestine CIA support for the FNLA which bypassed the Forty Committee, Kissinger now urged it to authorize continued support for a cause he termed "compelling."[30] This, of course, would also shift responsibility from himself to the committee. Clearly, an FNLA drive against the MPLA in Luanda would force Moscow to respond by increasing its support to Neto, and the situation would be moved one step farther along the path Kissinger had charted.[31] This explains why he was eager to allocate $300,000 for the FNLA, which, while small in terms of CIA programs elsewhere, was some thirty times the amount ever given to Roberto. It also explains why the secretary rejected a proposal to provide any support for UNITA. Even though Savimbi had an office in Luanda, his base of operations was small and in the south—and therefore irrelevant, for the time being, to the immediate objective.

But Kissinger had another equally urgent reason to move rapidly, which derived from Beijing's recent and sudden warming to Moscow.

In late 1974, in a move consistent with the Three Worlds concept, Beijing indicated its willingness to reconsider Moscow's earlier offer of a non-aggression pact.[32] Acceptance was contingent upon unlikely Soviet willingness to make certain concessions on Chinese border claims and to withdraw substantial numbers of troops from the border area. The discreet Sino-Soviet exchange was under way in November when Kissinger visited Beijing, where he received a decidedly cool reception. The secretary, sensitive to the ongoing exchange, was prepared to offer concessions to the Chinese to keep them from edging closer to Moscow, including unspecified concessions on the Taiwan issue.

But the Chinese stunned and, at least publicly, confused him by declining to negotiate. Moreover, perhaps as a sign of his displeasure, Mao did not receive him at all; and his visit with Zhou Enlai, who had entered the hospital for treatment of the illness that would take his life in January 1976, was terminated after only half an hour, even though the ailing premier appeared to be in good condition. Indeed, Zhou would only engage in small talk, brushing aside Kissinger's attempt at serious discussion with the remark that his doctors would not permit it. Kissinger in turn professed to be at a loss "why political problems impaired his health more than small talk. . . ."[33] The final communiqué issued at the end of his visit was no better. The brief (four-sentence) document pointedly marked the low point to which the new relationship had fallen.

Thus, there was renewed urgency in Kissinger's attempt to provoke a Soviet response in Angola.[34] It was, as former NSC staffer Roger Morris notes, "never doubted" that Soviet intelligence would "register" the new infusion of funds.[35] Indeed, it could hardly have been missed. The effect of American aid was "swift and highly visible." Almost immediately the rumor mills of Luanda passed the word of "heavy continuing CIA support for the FNLA," and the rumors were quickly substantiated.[36] "Suddenly Roberto had all this money . . . and he began throwing it around for guns, uniforms and anything he wanted. You can't hide that sort of thing in a poor country."[37] Nor did Roberto attempt to hide his newly acquired largess. Instead, he flaunted it by taking over a Luanda television station and the city's leading daily newspaper in an effort to improve the image of the FNLA.

Bolstered by what for him was a strong show of CIA financial support, reinforcements from Zaire's army, and the decision of Daniel

Chipenda to join his ranks, Roberto was emboldened to strike.[38] Following the installation of the provisional government in Luanda on January 31, minor clashes occurred between the factions as Roberto began to move large numbers of troops into Luanda from bases in Zaire and in Uiga province north of the capital. The first major clash took place on March 23, when FNLA units attacked MPLA installations in Luanda in an attempt to drive Neto's forces from the city.[39] Three days later, at Caxito, thirty miles north of Luanda, FNLA troops reportedly massacred fifty-one MPLA recruits. Over the next two months, despite three cease-fires—on March 28, April 8, and May 12—fighting spread north and south of the capital. In May, however, the battlefield initiative began to shift away from the FNLA toward the MPLA as a large infusion of Soviet arms and Cuban advisers began to have a telling effect.

Moscow had indeed "registered" Washington's decision to support the FNLA and responded quickly. It must be emphasized that not much "provocation" was necessary; Moscow was more than prepared to support its side in Angola, although at this point still somewhat circumspectly. Nor is there much ground for the argument that Moscow's involvement was primarily to counter Beijing's. Had that been true, Soviet support would have been much more in evidence earlier, following and perhaps matching the 450-ton Chinese shipment to the FNLA the previous fall. Moreover, the "counter Peking argument" ignores the Sino-Soviet dialogue at that time over Moscow's offer for a non-aggression pact.[40] It would have been contradictory to have taken an openly hostile position in Angola while simultaneously attempting to reach a reconciliation.

In any case, from March onward the Soviet Union did mount a substantial air- and seaborne logistics effort to support the MPLA. Moscow airlifted equipment to the Congo (Brazzaville) in AN-12 and AN-22 transports. There, short-haul aircraft and small ships "filtered the weapons to MPLA units near Luanda."[41] In April, May, and June, eight cargo ships (four Soviet, two East German, and two Yugoslav), unhindered by ostensibly neutral Portuguese port authorities, delivered extensive stocks of ammunition and weapons, including small numbers of armored vehicles, tanks, and artillery, to the MPLA.[42] By late May, following negotiations begun as early as the first week in April, 480 Cuban advisers had also arrived to assist and train MPLA forces in operating the tanks and artillery Moscow had supplied.[43] Soviet-Cuban assistance enabled the MPLA to seize the initiative, forcing FNLA and UNITA troops out of the Luanda suburbs in early June.

Then occurred the event which upset Kissinger's carefully laid plans. "By early June intelligence sources had revealed that China was giving up on the FNLA and had told Roberto not to expect more than $100,000 in aid by the end of 1975, at which time all help would cease."[44] In other words, Beijing was shifting to a position favoring "tripartite unity, not FNLA hegemony, though the Chinese were not yet prepared to withdraw their military instructors."[45] The Chinese decision reflected the recognition that as the conflict escalated Beijing would be locked into an adversary relationship vis-à-vis Moscow. It was also consistent with the earlier shift to the Three Worlds strategy requiring a position of equidistance between the superpowers. The announcement of Beijing's disengagement from Angola meant that Kissinger's gamble of drawing Moscow and Beijing into proxy conflict had failed.[46]

Kissinger Throws Craps and Changes the Game

Initially the secretary had hoped to use Beijing's involvement in Angola to accomplish a double purpose: to create an impediment to improvement in Moscow-Beijing relations and to prod Moscow into making a strong countermove. No excessive American involvement, aside from the provision of funds and propaganda support, had been part of his original plan. News of Beijing's withdrawal foiled one part of his scheme, and Moscow's cautious support for the MPLA was ruining the other part. Moscow had shipped in sufficient materiel, which, combined with Cuban advisers, was tipping the scales in favor of the MPLA. But so far there was no visible Soviet presence in Angola itself, Soviet supplies and advisers being shipped to neighboring Brazzaville. By mid-1975, there were several hundred Cubans in Angola, but few if any Russians.[47]

The question facing Kissinger in early June 1975 was, with the Chinese on the way out (all military instructors would depart on October 27) and the MPLA in the ascendancy, should he accept defeat of his scheme through a face-saving "diplomatic solution"? Or, now that Moscow at least was engaged, should he use the developing conflict for another purpose? That the Chinese announcement upset and forced a reconsideration of his plans is apparent in Kissinger's procrastination through June and half of July as he moved to recast his policy. His decision was to substitute the United States for the role initially envisaged for Beijing, attempt to promote a stalemate on the battlefield, and bring the conflict to an end through a cooperative effort with Moscow, thus demonstrating American — and Soviet — restraint.

There was never any question of providing enough support to ensure victory for the FNLA. Victory was understood to be unattainable.[48] The objective was to parlay a successful resolution of the conflict into a resurrection of detente, perhaps leading to the conclusion of a successful arms control agreement. What had begun as a low-cost, high-return operation with the United States on the sidelines was turning into an ambitious, potentially risky move that contained the seeds of future confrontation between Washington and Moscow. In his desperation, however, Kissinger was prepared to run risks.

The Forty Committee met in June after Kissinger had learned of Beijing's decision. Although it favored increased support for the FNLA, Kissinger set aside a CIA proposal for a $30 million program and "insisted that the issue be given a formal airing by way of a National Security Council study."[49] To the officials involved, the "transfer of a nominally covert policy into the wider, less secure forum of the NSC study seemed an obvious bureaucratic sign . . . that Kissinger expected the policy to become public."[50] Some of those involved believed that "he commissioned the NSC review, hoping for a leak." This view is reinforced by Kissinger's assignment of Ambassador Nathaniel Davis to chair the interagency NSC task force study.[51] A month after being sworn in, on May 1, Davis had produced a status report on Angola. In it he cautioned against a covert aid program, which he believed would lead to "probable disclosure." Thus, Kissinger knew that the individual he was appointing to head an interagency study would produce a strong dissenting view of his own covert program.

Kissinger had initially selected Davis for the post of assistant secretary of state for African affairs for the impact his reputation in Chile would have in prodding Moscow. Kissinger had appointed him on January 8 and neither involved him in, nor informed him of, the Forty Committee's January 22 funding decision. Davis only learned of the $300,000 allocation six weeks later, after his March 11 confirmation by the Senate. It was information which "came as a surprise." While ambassador to Chile, Davis was widely but erroneously believed to have engaged in covert efforts to subvert the government of Salvador Allende, [52] and his nomination prompted an immediate outcry by African leaders. On February 21, the Organization of African Unity (OAU) passed a consensus resolution questioning what Davis' appointment might bring in light of what was termed "the U.S. policy of 'political destabilization' in Latin America."[53]

The change in Kissinger's policy required a change in Davis' role. Where previously he sought to use Davis' reputation provocatively, he would now use his actual views to serve a new purpose — which explains why he assigned the ambassador to chair the interagency NSC task force on Angola. There is little doubt that Kissinger had the power to keep a covert program going without recourse to an NSC task force "review." Why chart a course of action that he knew would produce a policy conflict? The answer is that he wanted word to get out that the United States government was divided over whether to commit itself to a major aid program to the FNLA and UNITA. Once the dispute was leaked and the decision taken to go forward with the program, it would give greater visibility to the United States role. It would also carry greater credibility in Moscow and presumably elicit a similarly visible Soviet countermove.

Ambassador Davis' group submitted its completed study on June 13. As expected, the "great majority" of the task force favored the "diplomatic option," the advantage of which was that "the factional competition within Angola might be shifted back toward the political arena, thereby improving FNLA and UNITA prospects and reducing the likelihood of Soviet arms determining the outcome. We believed that such an effort might [also] reduce the danger of big-power confrontation and might further our policy of supporting peaceful solutions on that continent."[54] The report also noted that "U.S. military intervention might contribute to increased involvement by the Soviet Union and other foreign powers." The day after submitting his report, Ambassador Davis departed on a fifteen-day official African tour.

Meanwhile, having digested Davis' report, Kissinger called a National Security Council meeting on Angola for the twenty-seventh, two days before Davis' scheduled return.[55] At the meeting, the secretary ordered the CIA to prepare an "options paper" for consideration by the Forty Committee. The CIA's Africa Division produced an options paper which circulated among the concerned parties for over a week prior to the Forty Committee meeting of July 14.[56] Although the CIA paper offered four options, they were for varied degrees of involvement; no option proposed staying out of the conflict altogether. The options ranged from limited financial support for political activity only, to a $40 million program "to sustain Roberto's and Savimbi's armies for a year." Although the paper asserted that the last option "would likely match any Soviet escalation," there was no explanation of how Soviet capabilities or intentions had been estimated.[57]

On July 12, having returned from his African trip, Ambassador Davis submitted a memorandum to Kissinger criticizing the CIA options paper and strongly opposing any covert intervention.[58] Two days later, before the Forty Committee met, he sent a second memorandum summarizing the first and emphasizing that the diplomatic option was the proposal "favored by most of the agencies participating."[59] But the ambassador was not given a hearing. He "had asked for the opportunity to attend" that day's Forty Committee meeting "but was not invited."[60] The July 14 Forty Committee meeting reached a decision to proceed with a $14 million option (option number three of the four presented) and instructed the CIA to draft "a covert action plan for the Angolan operation" within forty-eight hours.[61]

On the sixteenth the ambassador sent the secretary his third memo in four days. He now objected to the covert plan on the grounds that the situation had "importantly changed." The MPLA had expelled the FNLA from Luanda, the Soviets were introducing "more, heavier and more sophisticated weapons," and there was evidence of "some support" from South Africa to the FNLA.[62] The next day, reflecting an urgency bordering on desperation, Davis sent his fourth memo arguing against intervention. Although Kissinger "assured me afterward that he had described my views fully and clearly to the President and had given the President a copy of my memorandum of July 12 to read," Davis was not permitted to participate in the decisive meeting on that day.[63]

The situation in Angola was indeed changing rapidly. Despite a meeting of Neto, Roberto, and Savimbi at Nakuru, Kenya, June 16–21, under Jomo Kenyatta's chairmanship, in which they reaffirmed respect for the provisional government, it had no effect. On July 9, the MPLA initiated heavy attacks in Luanda that quickly spread throughout the country. Within a week—by mid-July—the MPLA had driven both the FNLA and UNITA from the capital and made a shambles of the provisional government. Civil war was now unavoidable, and political control of Angola would be determined on the battlefield.

Under these circumstances, the Forty Committee met on the seventeenth to consider the CIA action plan, again pointedly excluding Ambassador Davis. The committee approved a $14 million outlay to Roberto and Savimbi, in two installments of $6 million and $8 million.[64] In addition, $16 million was ticketed to reimburse Zaire and Zambia for equipment and services already expended. It was only at this point that the CIA began to set up an organization to manage the utilization of American money and materiel for the FNLA and UNITA. Nothing had been done following the January decision—which reinforces the view that no involvement was initially intended. Moreover, the CIA's Angola task force was formed hastily, run (according to its chief, John Stockwell) amateurishly, and was clearly ad hoc.[65]

It also seems evident that Kissinger never seriously contemplated a diplomatic alternative and that the entire exercise of an NSC task force study was what some believed at the time—a way of leaking to the Soviet Union that the United States was about to make a major move into Angola.[66] This would ensure that Moscow would continue to support its side, the MPLA, which was now in the ascendancy. He may also have been hoping that a larger American commitment would persuade the Chinese to remain, but that seems less likely. A few days earlier, in mid-July, Beijing had authorized Mobutu to release what was left of the 450-ton shipment to the FNLA;[67] but this was designed to close down the aid program, not to signal greater Chinese involvement. Nor was there any coordination with the CIA, despite the fact that CIA covert arms shipments got under way in late July.

Washington Intervenes and Tips the Balance

Pursuant to the authorization of the Forty Committee decision by President Ford, on July 29 the CIA sent the first C-141 planeload of equipment to Kinshasa, Zaire.[68] Two more followed within a week. The C-141 could transport twenty-five tons of equipment; thus by early August, in an effort to blunt the MPLA drive, the United States had quickly injected some seventy-five tons of military equipment for its side in the rapidly escalating civil war. The CIA also began preparations to send a shipload of equipment on the cargo ship

American Champion. The *Champion* would set sail from Charleston, South Carolina, on August 30 and arrive at Matadi, Kinshasa's port located at the mouth of the Congo River, two weeks later, on September 12.[69] The United States would ultimately accumulate at Kinshasa a 1,500-ton stockpile of arms and materiel, which was distributed to FNLA forces in Angola at a rate of ten tons per day.

Paralleling Washington's supply effort, which had a rapid effect in stiffening FNLA resistance in the north, South Africa began to provide a small amount of covert assistance (troops in mufti), first to Chipenda's wing of the FNLA in July and then to Savimbi's small force in August.[70] At the same time, mid-July, South African units were deployed, ostensibly to guard the hydroelectric installation on the Cunene River that supplied water and electric power to Namibia, but also, it seems, to attack SWAPO (South West Africa People's Organization) guerrilla base camps. At first, South African forces skirmished with Savimbi's units as well as Neto's; later, arrangements were made to support UNITA.[71]

From the middle of August a combination of events occurred which prompted Moscow to become more decisively involved. Before it began to stall, the MPLA surge had encompassed twelve of Angola's fifteen provinces. Part of the reason for the MPLA's success was due to their ability to keep their opponents separate, but the very success of Neto's forces built pressure for cooperation among the MPLA's adversaries. American and to some extent South African support clearly facilitated further cooperation. The key to whether Moscow would become involved on a greater scale was how well MPLA forces could maintain the battlefield initiative; two key factors here were the growing cohesion and capabilities of their enemies.

The MPLA had been holding talks with UNITA with regard to establishing an alliance against the FNLA, but the talks broke down on August 15, and Savimbi promptly moved five days later (on August 20) to align UNITA with the FNLA. The failure of Neto to reach an accord with Savimbi meant that the MPLA would be faced with a two-front conflict, which at this point dimmed any prospect for victory. That same day the Forty Committee decided to increase United States support by $10.7 million.[72] Total funds authorized by the Forty Committee since January were now $25 million, but the military impact of the funds was greater due to accounting and bookkeeping procedures which undervalued the cost of equipment provided by the United States.

Whatever the true value of American equipment by the end of August, not only had the MPLA's drive stalled, the FNLA and UNITA, now aligned, began to make headway against Neto's forces. Finally, after two weeks of increasing tension, on August 28 pro-MPLA Prime Minister Goncalves fell from power in Lisbon, and Portuguese government policy reverted once again to support for a true coalition of the three factions. Certainly toward the end of August, and probably sooner, as the impact of American support became evident on the battlefield, Moscow began to establish a logistical network which would enable the Soviet Union and its allies to engage in any contest of escalation and ensure that the Soviet-supported side would not be outgunned regardless of the scale of Washington's future involvement.

The problem was how to go into an African conflict on a large scale without appearing to be the external aggressor and without providing a pretext for counterinvolvement by Washington. Up to this time, it should be recalled, there was little if any Western perception of foreign involvement in Angola.[73] Kissinger, in particular, had played a deft hand and kept Washington's role barely discernible to the outside world. The only publicly committed foreign power was the People's Republic of China, and the Chinese had already informed Roberto that they were disengaging, a fact which Moscow "must have known."[74]

Nevertheless, resolving one part of Moscow's quandary, the Soviet press commenced in mid-August an intensive propaganda campaign criticizing Beijing for its involvement on the side of American imperialism in Angola.[75] Moscow's decision was to publicize the decreasingly relevant Chinese presence in Angola as the pretext for greater involvement against the United States, but the nature of that involvement was as yet undisclosed. It was, of course, to arrange for the deployment of Cuban combat forces on a scale never before undertaken by Havana—Moscow's trump.[76]

It is as pointless to argue that Moscow "used" Castro as a proxy in Angola as it is to say that Castro took "independent" action without regard to Soviet views. There can be little doubt that Moscow and Havana had been in close consultation over the requirements of the MPLA as the military situation evolved from the spring. Cuban involvement in Africa was long-standing, dating back to 1961, and to the MPLA since 1965, albeit primarily as a supplier of military advisers.[77] An expansion of Cuban involvement in Angola was as natural as it was necessary from both Moscow's and Havana's points of view. Their side was losing.

In the previous fifteen years of Cuban involvement in Africa, with a single exception, Cuban military presence never exceeded four hundred men. Cuban military missions were invited to Ghana (1961), Algeria (1963), Congo-Brazzaville (1965), Zaire (1965), Guinea-Bissau (1966), Sierra Leone (1972), Equatorial Guinea (1973), and Somalia (1974). The missions were of varying length and generally provided training and organization for guerrillas, popular militia, and security forces such as "palace guards," all of which involved various forms of weapons instruction from tanks to light arms.

The single African exception to this experience occurred in the Congo in mid-1966 during a test of strength between the ruling party and the army, which culminated in an army revolt. During the period of tension before the revolt and afterward, the Cuban presence expanded to about one thousand men and was evidently instrumental in maintaining then-President Massamba-Debat in power. Even so, the "adviser" level was sharply reduced in 1968 when Marien Ngouabi took over. Outside Africa, Cuba sent elements of two armored brigades, between five hundred and seven hundred fifty tank troops, to Syria during the Yom Kippur War. And Castro sent a two hundred–man military mission to South Yemen earlier that same year, which expanded to some six hundred men in Iran's support for Oman during the Dhofari rebellion in December.

None of this prepared Washington for what was to come in Angola. In mid-August Cuban authorities had begun to assemble volunteers from regular units as well as from Castro's special independent armored division for dispatch to Angola.[78] In early September three ships departed Cuban shores, arriving off the West African coast at the end of the month. On October 7 and 11, two of the ships, *El Coral Island* and *La Plata*, docked at Pointe Noir, Congo, where troops were disembarked.[79] Some of the troops were sent by coastal craft to Angola and some overland to Cabinda.[80] The third ship, *El Vietnam Heróico*, sailed directly to Porto Amboim, south of Luanda, where on October 4 it discharged its cargo of heavy equipment and seven hundred Cuban troops, which evidently included another contingent of advisers.[81] The advisers went to the Cuban training camp at Benguela, while the troops joined MPLA forces moving south to Nova Lisboa.[82] Although the Cubans were combat troops, the first deployed to Angola, they were not complete units. They were mostly tank troops, *tanquistas*, who were inserted into MPLA units for needed expertise. (No separate Cuban military units as such were identified prior to November.)

After several weeks of desultory fighting, in mid-September the United States-supported side first stemmed MPLA drives and then gained the initiative. In the north, Mobutu's insertion of two of his best commando battalions (1,200–1,500 troops) tipped the balance in favor of the FNLA, whose mixed force of Angolan, Zairian, and former Portuguese troops retook Caxito on September 17 and then began a cautious advance on Luanda.[83] In the south, at this same time, Savimbi's forces were reeling from attacks on two flanks—from a Cuban-led MPLA force moving eastward from Lobito along the Benguela railroad toward Nova Lisboa, and from a Katangan mercenary force which had driven them back at Luso.[84] To relieve pressure on Savimbi, South Africa sent a thousand-man armored column supported by armored helicopters across the border into southern Angola. The twenty-five-mile penetration was explained as a defensive reaction to SWAPO "terrorist attacks," but advisers were also sent to the UNITA camp at Silva Porto.[85]

Meanwhile, in early October, after the initial appearance of Cuban troops, the Angolan task force working group met to discuss the implications. The working group viewed the Cuban deployment as a "worrisome escalation," but not one which would decisively tip the balance against Roberto.[86] So far, including the new development of the Cubans, it was a "gentleman's war," with "no surprises." John Stockwell presented the lone dissenting view, arguing that since momentum now lay with "our side," Moscow would not allow its large and now highly visible program to be crushed cheaply. Moreover, Cuba had stated publicly an intention to intervene. He anticipated a strong Soviet countermove on the order of "ten to fifteen thousand Cuban soldiers, a squadron of MIGs, and a hundred or so tanks."[87] His warning was dismissed.

Independence day was now less than a month away, and it appeared that the combined if somewhat ragtag forces of FNLA-UNITA with the support of Zaire, South Africa, and the United States would be more than enough to offset the Soviet-supported and Cuban-augmented MPLA—even though Cuban advisers and *tanquistas* now numbered approximately fifteen hundred men.[88] From the middle of October, in a broad pincer-like advance, the FNLA from the north and UNITA from the south retook most of the territory lost since

July, leaving MPLA forces with a narrow strip of territory including just three provinces from the coast around Luanda and eastward.[89]

On October 14 a UNITA force of 1,500 to 2,000 men, including white mercenaries, some of Chipenda's FNLA troops, and a few South African soldiers, began a drive northward.[90] This was followed nine days later, on the twenty-third, by a major South African intervention. Pretoria invaded Angola with what appeared to be a two-battalion-size force (1,200–1,500 men), including Portuguese mercenaries and more of Chipenda's troops. Supported by ground-based armor and helicopter gunships, one column of this combined force drove 600 miles northward along the coast, taking Benguela and Lobito and halting some 150 miles from Luanda.[91] A second column drove toward the railroad town of Texeira da Sousa on the Angolan-Zairian border but could not seize it from the MPLA. By November 7, only a few days before independence, this South African-UNITA force was poised for a march on Luanda.

Meanwhile, in the north, combined FNLA-Zaire forces under-took two operations, a diversionary thrust into Cabinda province on November 2, which was quickly repulsed by MPLA-Cuban forces, and a march on Luanda begun on the eighth. By independence day, the eleventh, Mobutu had deployed 1,500 additional Zairian troops on the Cabindan border for a second try at capturing the oil-rich province,[92] and the march on Luanda had brought the FNLA to within twelve miles of the capital. A state of panic had existed in the MPLA leadership for weeks. At one point, Neto was on the verge of proclaiming the People's Republic of Angola on November 5, rather than waiting until the eleventh, to be able to establish a "legitimate" basis for Soviet assistance.[93] As it was, he would establish his regime a day early.

Moscow Plays a Trump: the Cuban Card

On the eve of independence, it appeared that the United States-supported side was on the verge of victory. The closing pincer of FNLA-Zaire from the north and UNITA-South Africa from the south seemed to be superior to the MPLA troops holding Luanda. But Kissinger understood that while the United States-supported side might seize control of the capital, it could not hold it in the face of a major Soviet counterescalation. This was the limitation built into the covert operation that he had been managing these past several months; if Moscow mounted a massive escalation, Washington would be unable to match it solely through covert means. Kissinger's objective, therefore, was not to seek victory but to create the basis for a negotiated settlement—a stalemate—which he hoped Moscow would cooperate in arranging. The secretary would repeatedly take this position during November and December until it was foreclosed by Moscow's trump—large-scale Cuban intervention.

Kissinger had begun to set the stage for a settlement in Angola toward the end of October with the signing of a United States-Soviet long-term (five years) grain agreement. Earlier in the year the Soviet Union had experienced its most disastrous harvest in the Brezhnev era—140 million metric tons, which was less than two-thirds of the target figure.[94] Unable to make up the shortfall, Moscow began to purchase large amounts of American grain, reaching a total of 9.8 million metric tons, or 375 million bushels, before President Ford placed a hold on further sales on August 11.[95] A month later the president extended the moratorium on sales while announcing his intention to seek a long-term agreement, which was subsequently negotiated during October and signed on the twentieth. The grain agreement demonstrated American responsiveness to Soviet need and kept alive prospects for cooperation on other matters.

Then, on Angolan independence day, November 11, in answer to questions following his address to the Pittsburgh World Affairs Council, Kissinger stated that the "United States has no national interest in Angola" and that Washington preferred a political compromise without foreign intervention. "We favor a negotiation among the three major groups there to attempt to create a transitional government that would permit the popular will to be consulted. . . . We would support any move that keeps outside powers out of Angola, and we would participate in such a move." The secretary concluded: "But we cannot recognize one group that seized the capital with foreign assistance."[96]

The preference for a political compromise and the assumption that the United States side held the advantage would appear to explain why Kissinger prevailed upon South Africa to halt on November 11 the advance of the UNITA-South Africa column before Novo Redondo, still some three days' march from Luanda, while it was clearly able to proceed, and to permit Roberto's forces to advance on the capital alone.[97] Perhaps Kissinger assumed that the forces of the

MPLA and the FNLA would fight to a standoff and enable him to hold the South African-UNITA force in reserve as a decisive factor. But if that was his belief he had miscalculated once again, this time fatally, both as far as the FNLA was concerned and for the success of his stalemate scheme, because the status of the MPLA's forces had been sharply and secretly improved a few days earlier, decisively changing the battlefield equation.

On November 5, undoubtedly in consultation and in cooperation with the Soviet Union, Castro decided to send additional troops. Commencing on the seventh and continuing until the twentieth, Havana secretly airlifted a 650-man battalion to Luanda for defense of the capital until major reinforcements could arrive by sea later in the month.[98] Termed "Operation Carlota," troops on the first several flights were transported under the "cover of civilian holiday-makers." Gabriel Garcia-Marquez describes it:

> Dressed in holiday clothing with nonmilitary insignia, and carrying briefcases and their own ordinary passports, they had the look of healthy tourists roasted by the Caribbean sun. . . . But inside their cases were machine-guns; and the cargo hold of the aircraft was filled not with holiday gear but with a fine load of light artillery, personal firearms, three 75mm guns and three 82mm mortars.[99]

The first two flights (of a probable total of eight) of this secret, emergency deployment departed Havana at 4 p.m. November 7 and, after refueling stops in Barbados, Guinea-Bissau, and Brazzaville, arrived under cover of darkness at 10 p.m. on November 8 in Luanda airport. The 160-odd troops aboard the first two flights of turboprop Bristol Brittannia 218 aircraft "were convinced that they were already too late, and their sole remaining hope was to save Cabinda."[100] But thanks to the halt of the southern column, not only were they in time to support the defense of Luanda, they could concentrate on the single advancing column of Roberto's forces, who did not know of their arrival. Thus, on November 11 Roberto's forces began their advance on Luanda, not suspecting what lay before them. In recent weeks they had repeatedly bested MPLA troops in battle and were eager to administer the final blow. Morale was understandably high as Roberto's forces, some 1,500 strong, began to move through the Quifangondo valley toward Luanda.[101]

Armed with the full complement of equipment which Moscow had supplied (Cuba sent only a few pieces of equipment in the airlift), particularly the most feared 122m multiple-rocket launcher, the "Stalin organ," Cuban forces struck at the advancing FNLA column when it was most exposed on the open valley floor with no available protection. It was a massacre. As CIA and South African observers watched from an adjacent ridge,

> two thousand rockets rained on the task force as it broke and fled in panic, scattering across the valley in aimless flight, abandoning weapons, vehicles, and wounded comrades alike. Survivors would call it Nshila wa lufu—Death Road.[102]

The successful Cuban-led defense of Luanda destroyed the northern pincer, despite Washington's attempts to rebuild it using mercenaries.[103] The FNLA-Zaire combination was knocked out of the war, and thereafter, for all intents and purposes, it was no longer able to mount an effective fighting force. Belatedly, Kissinger recognized that the quick and surreptitious insertion of a Cuban "special forces battalion" had foiled his scheme. Resumption of the UNITA-South African advance north[104] and the addition of some three thousand additional South African troops in the second half of November and early December[105] greatly strengthened the UNITA challenge to MPLA rule, keeping hope alive that a stalemate could still be retrieved. Indeed, according to Garcia-Marquez, "in the first week of December, the situation was so desperate that serious consideration was given to the possibility of retrenchment in the Cabinda enclave and evacuation from a secure beachhead near Luanda."[106] Nevertheless, from mid-November until its conclusion the war was essentially a one-front conflict, as the northern front was never revived.

The timely arrival of more Cuban regular army units in late November enabled the MPLA to stabilize the southern front. On November 27 three Cuban ships unloaded an artillery regiment, a battalion of motorized troops, and "a number of rocket-launcher crews."[107] These troops were joined by the Cuban chief of staff, who arrived in Angola at this time. Thus by early December both South Africa and Cuba had deployed roughly five thousand troops in Angola; and despite Kissinger's earlier miscalculations, he appeared to believe that a stalemate would evolve after all—if the United States side could match the Cuban escalation, which he believed had reached its limits.[108]

That Kissinger hoped to move toward a negotiated settlement sometime in January at the latest emerges clearly from his actions and statements at the time and afterward. Thus, on November 24, in a speech in Detroit, he declared that the "United States cannot be indifferent while an outside power embarks upon an interventionist policy—so distant from its homeland and so removed from traditional Russian interests."[109] The secretary then offered the olive branch as well as the stick, saying that the United States would be happy to cooperate in "a policy of restraint which permits Angolans to resolve their own differences without outside intervention." But, he warned, "time is running out; continuation of an interventionist policy must inevitably threaten other relationships."

Four days later Kissinger put to rest any fears that his statement implied direct military intervention by the United States in Angola. In response to a question during a news conference regarding any foreseeable set of circumstances under which the United States might intervene, Kissinger answered, "The United States has no plans to intervene militarily in Angola."[110] To a follow-up query whether this included "sending military arms there," he replied evasively: "The United States cannot be indifferent to what is going on, but the United States will not intervene militarily in Angola."

In the first week of December, after word had leaked out that the United States was indeed involved in sending military arms to Angola, the questions became more insistent. At a news conference on December 9, Kissinger was asked, "Isn't it about time that you told us roughly what the United States has done in the way of helping forces in Angola, and since when?" In his response Kissinger made the first official, even though elliptical, admission that the United States had been providing assistance to forces in Angola when he said, "Whatever we have done was started long after massive Soviet involvement became evident. . . . The Soviet Union has been active there . . . since March."[111]

When at the end of November it became apparent that a major Soviet-Cuban escalation was under way, Kissinger strove mightily to match it. He instructed the CIA to prepare a plan that could win the conflict—even though his actual objective was to build a "bargaining chip" for future negotiations.[112] Africa Division quickly produced three more options, of $30 million, $60 million, and $100 million. He chose the smallest of the three and cut that by an additional $2 million, to $28 million. He did this apparently because, having exhausted the CIA's contingency reserve fund, he was forced to gain congressional approval to expend additional money.

Kissinger, Angola, and Detente

Kissinger's scheme to gain congressional approval for continuing his covert operation while simultaneously establishing a limit to it and thus demonstrating American "restraint" to Moscow was too clever by half. The secretary was clearly acting on the assumption that a demonstration of American "restraint" would be reciprocated by Moscow. He also assumed that agreement to future limitations would be sufficient to persuade Congress to support him in building a stalemate in Angola. But he failed to reckon with rising dissatisfaction in the Senate led by liberal Senators John Tunney, Hubert Humphrey, and Jacob Javits, among others, who foiled his scheme. Nor did Moscow respond to Kissinger's increasingly incredible propositions, as the Soviet Union continued to pour materiel, Cuban troops, and Soviet advisers into Angola, providing the MPLA with a decisive edge. By mid-December administration estimates were that Moscow had sent twenty-seven shiploads of materiel and flown thirty to forty flights to Angola, deploying close to five thousand Cuban troops and two hundred Soviet advisers, although there was a momentary lull in the Soviet supply effort at this time.[113]

Amid daily revelations of CIA covert involvement in Angola, on December 15 the Senate postponed action on the defense appropriations bill and scheduled a closed session on December 17 "to determine whether the appropriations bill would allow the United States to spend more money on covert operations."[114] The day after the postponement, December 16, the Senate Foreign Relations Subcommittee on Security Assistance voted unanimously for an amendment to the security assistance bill proposed by Senator Dick Clark "that would eliminate covert military assistance for any party in the Angolan conflict. However, the language of the amendment would not immediately cut off covert assistance since it is related to the $4.7 billion security assistance bill which does not reach the floor until January."[115]

Senate aides noted that "it leaves a breathing space until the Organization of African Unity meets in January and votes on the Angolan issue. . . . It is drafted to make sure we preserve the African options before they meet."[116] The amendment also stipulated that future American involvement should be open — "no more covert aid" — and that "any assistance sought by the Administration would require Congressional approval in 30 days." Indeed, the point of the Clark amendment to the Security Assistance Act was that since it was an authorization bill, Kissinger would be free to "reprogram" or divert funds from one account to another to obtain his needed $28 million.

As Kissinger's testimony in January before the Senate Foreign Relations Subcommittee on African Affairs makes clear, the Clark amendment was very close to, if not precisely, what the secretary wished to see emerge from the Congress. It contained a limitation on future covert funds, thus demonstrating United States "restraint," while simultaneously continuing current funding through January to enable establishment of a standoff in Angola. In his testimony Kissinger said:

> For example, Mr. Chairman, the amendment that you offered was not one which we found incompatible with our purposes.... Once the additional sums that we were then attempting to reprogram, that is to say, once these $28 million were expended, if any additional funds were required, it was my personal belief that we had come to the end of the covert phase of our action and we would then have to request additional funds in some overt manner. And, therefore, your amendment, Mr. Chairman, was not one that I found incompatible with our policies, because either what we were then doing would lead to a negotiation, which, on the whole, I expected, or it would demonstrate that the Soviet Union and Cuba were engaged in a degree of massive intervention that would require a widespread American public decision before we proceeded in opposing it.... Our concern was that events in December, in the middle of an attempted effort to crystalize the negotiations, terminated abruptly something that had been developing over a period of months. Our disagreement is not with the proposition that there must be a limit beyond which covert action cannot be made compatible with congressional oversight, it was rather with the methods that were chosen in December that were not actually the ones that you had recommended in your own amendment, which we, as you know, had not actively opposed.[117]

The methods to which Kissinger referred, of course, were those devised by Senator John Tunney, cutting off all money for Angola immediately. In closed sessions on December 17 and 18, Tunney planned to introduce an amendment which would prohibit the use of any funds in the defense appropriations bill "for any activities involving Angola directly or indirectly."[118] When Kissinger learned of Tunney's proposed amendment, he immediately offered a "compromise," whereby in return for the Senate's willingness to appropriate $10 million for Angola, "the Administration would have to obtain regular Senate approval of any further funding."[119] An informal counteroffer for $9 million "was rejected by President Ford in a telephone conversation but picked up and accepted later by Secretary Kissinger."[120] It was too late. The next day, December 19, the Senate voted 54–22 in favor of the Tunney amendment immediately prohibiting expenditure of any funds for Angola.

Deprived of all leverage, Kissinger now resorted to bluff. During a news conference on December 23, four days after the Senate vote, he alternately threatened and pleaded with Moscow. On the one hand, he asserted that although the Senate vote "seriously complicated" the administration's efforts to provide assistance to its side in Angola, he would utilize the $9 million remaining in the foreign military aid budget to oppose "Soviet expansion"—even at the cost of a setback in United States-Soviet relations.[121] Unless Moscow showed some "restraint," overall relations would inevitably suffer, he said, hinting that both grain sales and the strategic arms limitation talks could be affected. He raised the possibility that his coming trip to Moscow, already postponed once, might be canceled, and because of Angola he declared that the administration would "do nothing" to revive efforts in Congress to grant the Soviet Union trade concessions.

The secretary went on at great length to plead with Moscow to accept a negotiated solution.

What is happening in Angola has nothing to do with the local situation in Angola. We were prepared to accept any outcome in Angola before massive arms shipments by the Soviet Union and the introduction of Cuban forces occurred. We are not opposed to the MPLA as such. We make a distinction between the factions in Angola and the outside intervention. We can live with any of the factions in Angola, and we would never have given assistance to any of the other factions if other great powers had stayed out of it.[122]

It was our belief, and it remains our belief, that this is a situation that can be solved by negotiation; and if we have the minimum degree of unity . . . it will be resolved.

We have to make a decision whether, with an emerging super-power, we should conduct our foreign policy entirely on the basis of unbridgeable hostility or whether, through a combination of moderation, or creating incentives for moderation, and firmness when challenged, channel the inevitable competition into a direction which prevents what has generally happened when a new superpower emerged—namely, a war.[123]

In response to a question about the SALT negotiations and detente following his remarks, Kissinger took a softer, "clarifying" position. "SALT and what I described as detente is in our common interest," he said. "It is not a favor we grant to the Soviet Union. It is an inherent necessity of the present period."[124]

Soviet leaders answered Kissinger's pleas for restraint, moderation, and negotiations the next day, December 24, by resuming the air and sea delivery of arms, Cuban troops, and Soviet advisers on an even larger scale than before.[125] Over the course of the next month, Moscow more than doubled the size of the Cuban "expeditionary force" to over 11,000 men, essentially division size, and provided it with a full complement of equipment, including a squadron of MiGs, helicopter gunships, and tanks, and reinforced its naval screen deployed off the Angolan coast. Moscow had called Kissinger's bluff.

Remarkably, in the face of the blatant Soviet arms buildup in Angola and even while trumpeting Washington's refusal to accept Soviet "expansionism," Kissinger and Ford publicly marked an ignominious retreat from all of the "threats" uttered in December. President Ford began the retreat on January 5 in a speech to the American Farm Bureau Federation. Noting approvingly the conclusion of the American-Soviet long-term grain agreement the previous October, he said that the "United States must be a reliable supplier." Therefore, he concluded, it would be "a serious mistake to assume that linking our export of grain to the situation in Angola would serve any useful purpose whatsoever."[126]

On the same day, in a taped interview for NBC, the president was asked, "As a result of the Soviet role in Angola, the fact that the SALT talks now have bogged down somewhat, the fact that the spirit and the letter of the Helsinki agreement have not been fully carried out by Russia, are you now less enthusiastic about the prospects for detente?" The president answered,

> I am not at all, and I think it would be unwise for a President — me or anyone else — to abandon detente. I think detente is in the best interest of this country. It is in the best interest of world stability, world peace. . . . Politically, I think any candidate who says "abandon detente" will be the loser. . . .[127]

Kissinger, too, was forced to eat his words. There would be no cancellation of his trip to Moscow for SALT negotiations, no "linkage" of Angola and SALT, but no agreement either. On January 14, in announcing that he would make the trip, the secretary declared that he would not pressure the Soviets on Angola in order to obtain an agreement on SALT. A few days later he told a closed meeting of American diplomats assigned to African posts that he expected a "diplomatic rather than a military solution" there.[128] During a news conference on the eve of his departure, he also sounded an optimistic note on the arms control negotiations, saying, "We have been given a clear promise that there would be a significant modification in the Soviet position. Under these conditions, we are prepared to put forward a modification of our position."[129]

Whatever Kissinger professed in Washington, when he arrived in Moscow on January 20 his beliefs were rudely shattered. During a joint press conference prior to their first meeting, Brezhnev declared that Angola was not his country, and he had no intention of discussing it with Kissinger. To Kissinger's retort that "it certainly will be discussed," Brezhnev shot back, "You discuss it with Sonnenfeld," referring to Kissinger's aide.[130] Consistent with that public exchange, Soviet leaders remained adamant on Angola and similarly intransigent on SALT. There would be no negotiated solution over Angola, nor any agreement on SALT, despite the earlier "promise" of a "significant modification."

Why did Moscow embark upon such a massive and openly defiant effort to install its faction in power in Angola? Certainly, the belief that it could be done with impunity carried important weight in the decision. This would involve both a perception of a favorable balance of strategic forces as well as the political incapacitation of the United States. The fact that Moscow possessed the capability of injecting that amount of power had to have been a key consideration. The Soviets had never before demonstrated the ability to project division-size power vast distances from their borders, coordinating what was in essence a worldwide airlift and pre-positioning equipment for use by Cuban troops transported from thousands of miles away.

There were local and regional considerations. Angola was an opportunity to build a strong position on the Atlantic coast of southern Africa, demonstrating to other states Soviet capability and willingness to act in support of its clients. Kissinger estimated the cost of the Soviet Angolan program at $300 million in February 1976, which was a tripling of estimates made in December.[131] This seems to have been a conservative estimate counting equipment value but not troop costs.

But what of detente? The United States made every effort to reach a solution acceptable to Moscow within the context of detente, which Moscow rejected. If detente was the two-way street American leaders insisted it had to be to work, then Moscow's Angolan "demonstration" was an intended roadblock which froze existing positions. The conclusion seems unavoidable that Moscow chose as deliberate policy a course which openly demonstrated Soviet superiority and American weakness in defiance of detente. Indeed, by early spring of 1976, the strategy of detente lay in shambles. It was therefore not surprising that President Ford did in early March precisely what in early January he had vowed he would never do, and that was to "abandon detente." Despite fitful attempts by Henry Kissinger during the remainder of 1976 to reestablish substantive contact with the Soviets, Moscow declined, choosing to await the outcome of the presidential election campaign.

Conclusion

The period 1968-1976 was a watershed in the history of post-World War II American foreign policy. The rise to military power by the Soviet Union and to economic power by Germany and Japan effectively compromised the American strategy of containment that had been pursued since the war. Containment after all was a double-edged strategy which sought not only to block Soviet expansion but also to forestall the resurgence of the former Axis powers — Germany and Japan.

By the late sixties containment had failed in both of its intended missions, and a crisis of strategy had arrived for the American leadership. The crisis led to an acrimonious internal debate over the viability of containment that veered far outside American constitutional processes. Its outcome saw the political defeat of Richard Nixon and the rise to power of Henry Kissinger, an unelected government official, who through extralegal processes gained control and set the nation on a course toward construction of a new international order.

Kissinger attempted to reshape the international order to facilitate the withdrawal of the United States from forward, vulnerable positions around the Soviet periphery. His scheme involved the creation of stable political-economic structures in Europe and Asia and the relocation of American power to more secure positions. His ultimate purpose was to reconstruct the international order to remove the risk of thermonuclear war with the Soviet Union while enabling the

United States to contend with the growing political-economic challenges of West Germany and Japan.

But the first attempt to recast American strategy — as detailed in this volume — failed utterly to achieve the central objectives of detente and arms control with the Soviet Union, and the reequilibration of economic relationships with Germany and Japan. Indeed, Kissinger engineered defeat in Vietnam, leaving a permanent scar on the national psyche, turned a promising rapprochement with China into a stillborn relationship, promoted war in the Middle East, badly mishandled relations with Israel, and turned Angola into a battleground. It would be hard to find a less successful period of American foreign policy than the Kissinger shogunate.

Notes

Introduction

1. See Robert S. McNamara, *The Essence of Security, Reflections in Office* (New York: Harper and Row, 1968), p. 58.
2. Lawrence Freedman, *U.S. Intelligence and the Soviet Strategic Threat* (Boulder: Westview Press, 1976), p. 132.
3. For an illuminating treatment, see F. Charles Parker, *Vietnam, Strategy for a Stalemate* (New York: Paragon House, 1989).
4. See the author's "South Asia: Imbalance on the Subcontinent," *Orbis*, Fall 1975.
5. See the author's *China: A Political History, 1917–1980* (Boulder: Westview Press, 1982).
6. See C. Fred Bergsten, *The Dilemmas of the Dollar: The Economics and Politics of United States International Monetary Policy* (New York: New York University Press, 1975).
7. See Peter R. O'Dell, *Oil and World Power* (New York: Penguin Books, 1980), pp. 56–57.
8. Bergsten, *Dilemmas of the Dollar*, pp. 83ff.

Chapter One

1. "The President's toast to the acting president of India," New Delhi, July 31, 1969, in Richard Nixon, *U.S. Foreign Policy For The 1970's, A New Strategy For Peace*, February 18, 1970 (Washington: Government Printing Office, 1970), pp. 156–60.
2. Henry Kissinger, *White House Years* (Boston: Little, Brown and Co, 1979), p. 426.
3. David Gisselquist, *Oil Prices and Trade Deficits: U.S. Conflicts with Japan and West Germany* (New York: Praeger Books, 1979), p. 29.

4. Kissinger describes these negotiations in *White House Years:* on EEC, pp. 425–29; on Berlin, pp. 389–91; on Okinawa, pp. 325–40.

5. For in-depth analysis of these events, see the author's *China: A Political History, 1917–1980.*

6. For an excellent military analysis of this period, see Harvey W. Nelsen, *The Chinese Military System* (Boulder: Westview Press, 1977).

7. Lawrence L. Whetten, *The Canal War, Four-Power Conflict in the Middle East* (Cambridge, Massachusetts: MIT Press, 1974), p. 168.

8. Richard M. Nixon, *The Memoirs of Richard Nixon* (New York: Grosset and Dunlop, 1978), p. 369–70.

9. Joseph Whelan, *World Communism, 1967–1969: Soviet Efforts to Reestablish Control*, a study prepared for the Internal Security Subcommittee of the Senate Judiciary Committee, June 11, 1970 (Washington: Government Printing Office, 1970), p. 127.

10. *Izvestia*, December 2, 1968, p. 2, quoted General Losik, the newly appointed commander of the Soviet Far Eastern Military Region as saying that "military maneuvers have taken place in the east of the Soviet Union." The Chinese government sent a protest note to the Soviet Embassy on September 16 claiming that between August 9 and 29 alone Soviet forces had "intruded" on twenty-nine occasions into Heilungchiang province. See "Sino-Soviet Border Developments 1967–1969," *China Topics*, May 1, 1969, p. 9.

11. Yao Ming-le (pseud.), *The Conspiracy and Death of Lin Biao* (New York: A. Knopf, 1983), p. 63. An important but most unusual source. A collective account written following Deng Xiaoping's ascendancy for Western consumption, it offers new details on the rise and fall of Lin Biao. Much is consistent with known material, but much remains to be corroborated.

12. Ibid. Lin Biao evidently ordered the strike in hopes of strengthening his claim as Mao's successor, a position he was formally accorded at the Ninth Party Congress in April.

13. Kissinger says that the Sinkiang clashes convinced him that the Soviets were the initiators. While implying that he came to that conclusion in late May, the accompanying map in his book dates clashes in Sinkiang as early as April 16. See *White House Years*, pp. 174–75, for a map depicting the location and dates of the clashes.

14. Nixon, *Memoirs*, p. 380. The president claimed that Sihanouk secretly "had asked the United States to retaliate against the North Vietnamese, either with 'hot pursuit' on the ground or by bombing the sanctuaries" the previous year, p. 382.

15. Kissinger, *White House Years*, pp. 246–47.

16. "China Said to Bar Soviets' Hanoi Aid," *New York Times*, March 15, 1969, p. 1.

17. *Foreign Broadcast Information Service-Soviet Union*, May 6, 1969, pp. A11–12. (Hereafter referred to as FBIS-SU).

18. Nixon, *Memoirs*, p. 383. Seymour Hersh, *The Price of Power, Kissinger in the Nixon White House* (New York: Summit Books, 1983), pp. 69–70, argues unconvincingly and without citation that previously undisclosed National Security Agency intercepts showed that "there was no evidence" the North Korean government knew of the attack in advance and that it had been "a

command and control error involving a single North Korean airplane." He also acknowledges that no such intelligence ever reached the president.

19. Nixon, *Memoirs*, p. 383.

20. Ibid., p. 384.

21. "Transcript of the President's News Conference on Foreign and Domestic Affairs," *New York Times*, April 19, 1969, p. 14.

22. Hersh, *Price of Power*, p. 74, termed Nixon's intelligence breach a "blunder," particularly since there had been an intelligence briefing just before his press conference to set forth what the president "could say publicly about the radar intercepts."

23. *Background Information Relating to Southeast Asia and Vietnam*, U.S. Senate Committee on Foreign Relations, June 1970 (Washington: Government Printing Office, 1970), pp. 295–302. (Hereafter referred to as Vietnam Background.)

24. Kissinger, *White House Years*, p. 261.

25. Vietnam Background, p. 296.

26. Tad Szulc, *The Illusion of Peace: Foreign Policy in the Nixon Years* (New York: Viking Press, 1978), p. 116.

27. Whetten, *Canal War*, p. 73.

28. Nixon insisted on the withdrawal of actual combat troops instead of support troops as recommended by his military commanders, but the president was intent upon conveying a genuine message to the Chinese, who would note the difference, as opposed to the American public, which would not.

29. Kissinger, *White House Years*, p. 145.

30. Nixon, *Memoirs*, p. 393.

31. Ibid. and Vietnam Background, p. 325.

32. Kissinger, *White House Years*, pp. 280–82.

33. Vietnam Background, pp. 319–20.

34. Ibid., p. 315.

35. Whelan, *World Communism, 1967–1969*, pp. 127f.

36. Ibid., p. 152.

37. Ian Stewart, "Peking Is Said to Expect a Soviet War by October," *New York Times*, July 6, 1969, p. 2.

38. Vietnam Background, pp. 315, and Szulc, pp. 133–4.

39. Richard Halloran, "China Labor Units Are Believed Out of North Vietnam," *New York Times*, September 3, 1969, p. 1.

40. *New York Times*, September 7, 1969.

41. Robert B. Semple, "Nixon Announces New Vietnam Cut of About 35,000," *New York Times*, September 17, 1969, p. 1.

42. H.R. Haldeman, the president's chief of staff, asserts in his book *The Ends of Power* (New York: New York Times Books, 1978), pp. 88–94, that the United States decision to support Beijing against Moscow was decisive in preventing the outbreak of war, but he is not precise about the timing of United States actions. Although both President Nixon and Henry Kissinger have denied the Haldeman account, the circumstantial evidence in their own memoirs suggests that the United States did indeed communicate to Moscow that the United States would not be a party—even by implication—to any Soviet attack on China. Kissinger, *White House Years*, pp. 185–86, says that China backed down

before the United States could do anything but admits that in mid-September he advised the president to make it clear that the United States would not play along with Soviet tactics. Nixon, *Memoirs*, p. 399, in the context of discussion of Vietnam, says that in late September "we continued to keep up the diplomatic pressure on the Soviets." At the very least, for whatever reason, it seems clear that the United States was applying diplomatic pressure on Moscow in late September 1969.

43. Hersh, *Price of Power*, p. 124, while the first to uncover the alert, completely misses the relationship between it and the Sino-Soviet crisis.

44. "Text of Chinese Statement Agreeing to Discuss Border Issue With Soviet Union, *New York Times*, October 8, 1969, p. 10.

45. Nixon, *Memoirs*, p. 405.

46. Hersh, *Price of Power*, p. 124, notes that it remained in effect for twenty-nine days from sometime in early October.

47. Vietnam Background, p. 326.

48. Ibid. (emphasis added).

49. The best example of this line of argument can be found in Raymond L. Garthoff, *Detente and Confrontation, American-Soviet Relations from Nixon to Reagan* (Washington: Brookings Institution, 1985).

50. Hersh, *Price of Power*, p. 78, notes of 1969 that "Kissinger's role throughout this early period was that of the tactician dutifully executing orders from the strategist."

51. Kissinger, *White House Years*, pp. 1480–82, n.11.

52. Ibid. pp. 559–60.

53. For an analysis, see the author's "Soviet Strategy and the Vietnam War," *Asian Affairs* (April–May, 1974), pp. 205–28.

54. Nixon, *Memoirs*, p. 477.

55. Ibid., p. 478.

56. Ibid., pp. 480–81.

57. Whetten, *Canal War*, p. 68.

58. Hedrick Smith, "Surprise Voiced in Washington at Sharpness of Cairo Reaction to U.S. Note," *New York Times*, January 21, 1969, p. 14.

59. Whetten, *Canal War*, p. 73.

60. Ibid., p. 83.

61. Ibid., pp. 75–77.

62. For an analysis of the shift in Soviet policy at this time, see John M. Miller, *Soviet Strategy in Indochina, January 1969 through January 1973* (unpublished doctoral dissertation, George Washington University, 1982), pp. 45–54.

63. Thomas Wolfe, *Soviet Power and Europe, 1945–1970* (Baltimore: Johns Hopkins Press, 1970), p. 425.

64. Kissinger, referring to this period, noted that "the Kremlin had no clear line. It was trying pressure and accommodation simultaneously. It opened subjects it did not pursue and provoked a confrontation in the Middle East without definable purposes." *White House Years*, p. 526.

65. Nixon, *Memoirs*, p. 400. Singapore also complied with the United States request, but Nixon cut off United States foreign aid programs to Cyprus and Malta when they refused to comply.

66. See Colin Legum and John Drysdale, eds., *Africa Contemporary Record, 1969–1970* (New York: Africana Publishing Co, 1970), p. B175.

67. See Gary D. Payton, "Soviet Military Presence Abroad: The Lessons of Somalia," *Military Review* (January 1977), pp. 67–77.

68. Nixon, *Memoirs*, p. 479.

69. "Dayan Says Raids Are Curb on Cairo," *New York Times*, January 25, 1970, p. 19.

70. Nixon, *Memoirs*, p. 479 and *Pravda*, February 13, 1970.

71. Nixon, *Memoirs*, p. 479.

72. Kissinger, *White House Years*, p. 570–71.

73. Nixon, *Memoirs*, p. 480.

74. Whetten, *Canal War*, p. 94–95.

75. Kissinger, *White House Years*, p. 571.

76. See Hersh, *Price of Power*, esp. Ch. 16.

77. Frank Snepp, *Decent Interval* (New York: Random House, 1977), pp. 19–20. Early in the war a running controversy had developed within the intelligence community over the issue of Sihanoukville as a supply corridor for Hanoi. Army intelligence insisted that it was a vital logistics avenue, while the CIA, disputing field reports, viewed it as being of marginal value.

78. General William C. Westmoreland, *A Soldier Reports* (New York: Doubleday and Co., 1976), p. 182. Hersh, *Price of Power*, p. 200n., observes that after the United States-South Vietnamese incursion in May 1970 "captured documents showed that an estimated 23,000 tons of military supplies had been funneled through the port from 1966 to 1970, far higher than the 6,000 tons officially estimated by the CIA." Kissinger, *White House Years*, pp. 241–42, declared that the captured documents from the incursion "indicated that shipments through Cambodia far exceeded even the military's highest estimates." William Shawcross, *Sideshow, Kissinger, Nixon and the Destruction of Cambodia* (New York: Simon and Shuster, 1979), p. 64, comes to the same conclusion.

79. Craig Etcheson, *The Rise and Demise of Democratic Kampuchea* (Boulder: Westview Press, 1984), p. 85.

80. Ben Kiernan, *How Pol Pot Came to Power, A History of Communism in Kampuchea, 1930–1975* (London: Verso Books, 1985), p. 251.

81. Ibid., p. 251.

82. Ibid., pp. 251–52.

83. Ibid.

84. Ibid., pp. 255, 262–65.

85. Ibid., pp. 284–85.

86. Kissinger, *White House Years*, p. 241.

87. Hersh, *Price of Power*, pp. 179–80, says that there was also high-level approval of coup plans, which included the assassination of Sihanouk. The assassination plan was reportedly scrapped on Lon Nol's violent objection and request for "only overt United States military support."

88. Westmoreland, *A Soldier Reports*, pp. 180–82, chafed from the beginning (1965) at Washington's refusal to permit interdiction of communist supplies entering through Sihanoukville.

89. William Shawcross, *Sideshow*, pp. 113, 116.

90. Douglas Pike, *Cambodia's War* (New York: American Friends of Vietnam, 1971), p. 19.

91. Etcheson, *Rise and Demise of Democratic Kampuchea*, p. 85.

92. Shawcross, *Sideshow*, p. 114.

93. Milton Osborne, "Effacing the 'God-King'— Internal Developments in Cambodia Since March 1970," in Joseph Zasloff and Allan Goodman, eds., *Indochina in Conflict, A Political Assessment* (Lexington: D.C. Heath, 1972), p. 61.

94. See Etcheson, *Rise and Demise of Democratic Kampuchea*, p. 86.

95. Shawcross' discussion of the coup and events surrounding it contains much useful information. Unfortunately, the author's extremely accusatory approach mars the book's overall value. The interpretation presented here is an attempt to provide a balanced perspective on what is admittedly a murky subject, but the truth is elusive.

96. Shawcross, *Sideshow*, p. 116. Norodom Sihanouk, *My War with the CIA* (New York: Pantheon Books, 1972) p. 24, specifically disavows this argument, claiming that he went "to negotiate a military aid agreement."

97. Shawcross, *Sideshow*, p. 116.

98. Osborne, "Effacing the 'God-King,'" p. 62.

99. Shawcross, *Sideshow*, p. 118.

100. Sihanouk, *My War with the CIA*, p. 22.

101. Shawcross, *Sideshow*, pp. 118, 120.

102. Ibid., p. 119.

103. A few days after the coup, Lon Nol gave this rationale for his action to the London *Times*. See Shawcross, *Sideshow*, p. 119.

104. Ibid., p. 123, contrasts sharply with Sihanouk's account of his meetings in Moscow. Sihanouk, *My War With the CIA*, p. 25, claims that "the Russians agreed to supply everything we needed. But by then it was too late." However, Moscow would neither withdraw its diplomats from Phnom Penh after the coup, nor recognize Sihanouk's government in exile in Beijing.

105. Hersh, *Price of Power*, pp. 176–79, and Shawcross, *Sideshow*, pp. 114–16, detail some of these contacts, as does Sihanouk, *My War With the CIA*, p. 55. The Sihanouk volume, although reputedly a memoir written with Wilfred Burchett, closely follows the interpretation of the coup set forth by T.D. Allman in three articles in the *Guardian*, August 14 and 18 and September 18, 1971.

106. Kiernan, *How Pol Pot Came to Power*, p. 302.

107. Ibid., pp. 299–300.

108. Kissinger, *White House Years*, p. 451.

109. For purposes of convenience, Sihanoukville will be the name used throughout.

110. Kissinger's remark, *White House Years*, p. 463, that "we did not even grasp its [the coup's] significance for many weeks" is hardly credible unless it was meant to describe his distance from the president. It was more likely simply dissemblance.

111. Ibid., p. 465.

112. Ibid., p. 469.

113. See Tran Dinh Tho, *The Cambodian Incursion* (Washington, D.C.: U.S. Army Center for Military History, 1979), pp. 13–14.

114. Kissinger, *White House Years*, pp. 473–74.

115. See Ibid., p. 471, for a map of operations.
116. Quoted in Szulc, *Illusion of Peace*, pp. 243–44.
117. Ibid., p. 246.
118. Ibid., p. 259.
119. Kissinger, *White House Years*, p. 554.
120. Ibid., pp. 410–12, 424.
121. Nixon, *Memoirs*, p. 450. See Kissinger, *White House Years*, p. 1484, for the president's action memo and pp. 483–505 for discussion of the decision-making process.
122. Kissinger, *White House Years*, pp. 505–6.
123. See Tran Dinh Tho, *The Cambodian Incursion*, pp. 13–14 et passim.
124. *New York Times*, October 8, 1970, p. 1.

Chapter Two

1. Kissinger, *White House Years*, p. 805, puts it this way: "By the end of 1970 I had worked with Nixon for nearly two years; we had talked at length almost every day; we had gone through all crises in closest cooperation. He tended more and more to delegate the tactical management of foreign policy to me. During the first year or so I would submit for Nixon's approval an outline of what I proposed to say. . . . By the end of 1970 Nixon no longer required these memoranda. He would approve the strategy, usually orally. . . ."
2. Yitzhak Rabin, *The Rabin Memoirs*, (Boston: Little, Brown and Co., 1979), p. 176.
3. Whetten, *Canal War*, p. 108.
4. Rabin, *Memoirs*, p. 178.
5. Mohammed Heikal, *The Road to Ramadan* (New York: Ballantine Books, 1975), pp. 79–94, makes this point several times.
6. *Foreign Broadcast Information Service–Middle East Affairs*, May 4,1970, p. G15 (hereafter referred to as FBIS-MEA).
7. Rabin, *Memoirs*, pp. 176–82, describes these "consultations" in lively detail.
8. Heikal, *Road to Ramadan*, pp. 88–91, claims that it was Nasser's idea to accept the Rogers Plan to obtain "a breathing space so that we can finish our missile sites." Alvin Z. Rubinstein, *Red Star over the Nile* (Princeton: Princeton University Press, 1977), pp. 123–25, says that it was Moscow's idea to move the missiles forward under cover of the cease-fire. Anwar Sadat, *In Search of Identity* (New York: Harper and Row, 1977), p. 198, suggests that Nasser accepted the American plan when the Soviets refused to provide a "deterrent" weapon.
9. Whetten, *Canal War*, p. 112.
10. Ibid., p. 113.
11. See John Newhouse, *Cold Dawn, The Story of SALT* (New York: Holt, Rinehart and Winston, 1973), pp. 176–85, for discussion of these options.
12. Gerard Smith, *Doubletalk, The Story of SALT I* (New York: Doubleday and Co., 1980), pp. 125, 477.

13. Ibid., p. 153, noted that "the August 4 proposal was the first U.S. major move in SALT."
14. *Aviation Week*, August 21, 1970, and Whetten, *Canal War*, p. 130.
15. Whetten, *Canal War*, p. 132.
16. Ibid., p. 131.
17. Szulc, *Illusion of Peace*, p. 320.
18. Rabin, *Memoirs*, pp. 174–75.
19. Szulc, *Illusion of Peace*, p. 322.
20. Compare Hersh, *Price of Power*, p. 237, who asserts that "the Popular Front's continuing terrorist activities in September had little to do, in fact, with the Soviet Union's foreign policy. . . ."
21. Whetten, *Canal War*, pp. 135–36. Deployment of SAM–3s in combination with the SAM–2 was a significant development as each weapon covered a different spectrum of potential targets.
22. Kissinger, *White House Years*, p. 614.
23. Ibid., p. 609.
24. Ibid., p. 614.
25 Ibid., p. 614. Nixon, *Memoirs*, p. 485, states that one hundred tanks crossed into Jordan on September 18 and withdrew on the nineteenth. Then several hundred crossed on the twenty-first.
26. Kissinger, *White House Years*, p. 620.
27. Rabin, *Memoirs*, p. 187. Kissinger, *White House Years*, p. 623, claims that he asked only that Israel fly a reconnaissance mission to assess the situation.
28. Rabin, *Memoirs*, p. 188.
29. Kissinger, *White House Years*, p. 620.
30. Ibid., p. 623, Kissinger claims that he also said "we would do our utmost to prevent Soviet interference."
31. Szulc, *Illusion of Peace*, p. 330, says that on September 22 Nixon agreed to protect Israel against Soviet intervention and that it was knowledge of this decision that persuaded Hussein to move.
32. Hersh, *Price of Power*, p. 247, claims Asad reassured Hussein that Syria's air force would not intervene. Whatever the reason for Asad's decision, the disastrously unsuccessful Syrian adventure led to a crisis of the regime whose outcome was the assumption to power of Hafez Asad in November.
33. Sadat, *In Search of Identity*, p. 198.
34. Szulc, *Illusion of Peace*, pp. 326, 329, notes that Soviet advisers were attached to Syrian tank units.
35. Kissinger, *White House Years*, p. 582.
36. Ibid., p. 591.
37. Szulc, *Illusion of Peace*, p. 328.
38. Ibid., p. 330.
39. Ibid., p. 365, and Kissinger, *White House Years*, p. 638.
40. Kissinger, *White House Years*, p. 632.
41. Ibid., p. 634.
42. Robert F. Kennedy, *Thirteen Days* (New York: W.W. Norton and Co., 1969), pp. 216–18.
43. Kissinger, *White House Years*, p. 635.

44. Henry Brandon, *The Retreat of American Power* (New York: Doubleday and Co., 1973), p. 281.
45. Kissinger, *White House Years*, p. 643.
46. Ibid., p. 646.
47. Ibid., p. 647.
48. Ibid., p. 649.
49. Ibid., p. 650.
50. Ibid., p. 801.
51. Ibid., p. 389.
52. *Documentation Relating to the Federal Government's Policy of Detente* (Bonn,1978), p. 18.
53. Peter R. O'Dell, *Oil and World Power* (New York: Penguin Books, 1980), pp. 140–41.
54. Ibid., pp. 148–49.
55. Ian Seymour, *OPEC, Instrument of Change* (New York: St. Martin's Press, 1981), p. 67.
56. The well-known story of Exxon's refusal to support Occidental can be found in several sources. See, for example, Anthony Sampson, *The Seven Sisters* (New York: Viking Press, 1975), p. 212f.
57. *Multinational Oil Corporations and U.S. Foreign Policy*, Report to the Committee on Foreign Relations, United States Senate, (Washington, D.C.: Government Printing Office, 1975), p. 124. (Hereafter referred to as MNC Report).
58. Seymour, *OPEC, Instrument of Change*, p. 74.
59. Ibid.
60. Ibid., pp. 75–76.
61. Sampson, *Seven Sisters*, pp. 217–18.
62. Sidney E. Rolfe and James L. Burtle, *The Great Wheel, The World Monetary System* (New York: McGraw-Hill, 1973), p. 98.
63. Ibid., p. 100.
64. Kissinger, *White House Years*, p. 537.
65. Lawrence Freedman, *U.S. Intelligence and the Soviet Strategic Threat* (Boulder: Westview Press, 1977), pp. 156–57.
66. Smith, *Doubletalk*, p. 207 and Raymond Garthoff, "SALT and the Soviet Military," *Problems of Communism* (January–February, 1975), p. 30, both thought so. For an informative but extremely contentious interpretation of the SALT negotiations, see also Raymond Garthoff, *Detente and Confrontation*, pp. 127–98.
67. Newhouse, *Cold Dawn*, p. 189.
68. Kissinger, *White House Years*, p. 801.
69. Ibid., pp. 815–16.
70. Ibid., p. 815.
71. Ibid., pp. 814–23.
72. Ibid., p. 820.
73. Initially, the figure was thought to be 313, until it became clear that five holes were designated as command and control centers, not missile silos.
74. Freedman, *U.S. Intelligence and the Soviet Strategic Threat*, pp. 164–66. The timing of the May 20 agreement may also have been related to the public

indication of improved United States–China ties following Beijing's invitation of the United States ping-pong team to China the previous month; but it would seem that the decisive consideration was Soviet missile construction.

75. Kissinger, *White House Years*, p. 820.

76. Henry Kissinger, *Years of Upheaval*, (Boston: Little, Brown and Co.,1982), p. 863.

77. John M. Blair, *The Control of Oil* (New York: Vintage Books, 1978), p. 212.

78. Ibid., p. 238.

79. For this interpretation, see *MNC Report*, pp. 128–35; Sampson, *Seven Sisters*, pp. 212–29; and Seymour, *OPEC, Instrument of Change*, pp. 78–85.

80. Blair, *Control of Oil*, p. 227. See also, M.A. Adelman, *The World Petroleum Market* (Baltimore: Johns Hopkins Press, 1972), pp. 250–53.

81. Adelman, *World Petroleum Market*, pp. 250–53.

82. Competition would drive prices up only when demand was greater than supply. Under conditions of excess supply and an enormous price-cost differential, competition had the opposite effect, as in 1984–1986.

83. For an interpretation along the lines presented here, see V. H. Oppenheim, "The Past: We Pushed Them," *Foreign Policy* (Winter 1976–1977), pp. 24–57.

84. *MNC Report*, p. 128.

85. Ibid., pp. 124–25.

86. Ibid. and Blair, *Control of Oil*, p. 221.

87. James E. Akins, "The Oil Crisis: This Time The Wolf is Here," *Foreign Affairs* (April 1973), p. 471.

88. *MNC Report*, p. 125.

89. Seymour, *OPEC, Instrument of Change*, p. 67.

90. Adelman, *World Petroleum Market*, p. 254.

91. *MNC Report*, p. 125.

92. Ibid., p. 128.

93. Ibid.

94. Ibid, p. 129.

95. Adelman, *World Petroleum Market*, p. 254.

96. *MNC Report*, pp. 128–29.

97. Ibid.

98. Blair, *Control of Oil*, p. 225.

99. *MNC Report*, p. 131.

100. Blair, *Control of Oil*, p. 227.

101. *MNC Report*, p. 131.

102. Ibid., pp. 131–32.

103. Blair, *Control of Oil*, p. 225.

104. Adelman, *World Petroleum Market*, pp. 254–55 (emphasis supplied).

105. *MNC Report*, p. 133.

106. Seymour, *OPEC, Instrument of Change*, p. 92.

107. Sampson, *Seven Sisters*, p. 228.

108. M.A. Adelman, "The World Oil Market," in E. Erickson and L. Waverman, eds., *The Energy Question* (Toronto: University of Toronto Press, 1974), vol. I, p. 17.

109. See Blair, *Control of Oil*, chapter 9, "The Evisceration of the Libyan Independents," pp. 211–34.

110. In testimony before the Senate, hearings on multinational corporations, on June 5, 1974, the assistant attorney general for anti-trust matters from the Department of Justice, Thomas E. Kauper, in the context of discussion regarding the continuing validity of the Business Review Letters extended in January of 1971, declared that "our continuing study of the records of the London Policy Group indicates that what was to be an ad hoc organization has become a quasi-permanent institution for oil company cooperation, and that the discussions and studies within it tend to approach sensitive competitive areas of supply, cost, demand, control of downstream distribution and possible exclusion of independents by means of exclusive buy-back arrangements." See *MNC Hearings*, Part 9, p. 48.

111. Blair, *Control of Oil*, pp. 227–29.

112. Ibid., pp. 233–34.

113. See the useful article by Henry Bradsher, "Iran Pinched, Weighs Step Back From Arms Buildup," *Washington Star*, January 29, 1976.

114. David J. Meiselman, "Worldwide Inflation: A Monetarist View," in Patrick Boarman and David Teurk, eds., *World Monetary Disorder* (New York: Praeger, 1976), pp. 50–51.

115. *Statistical Abstract of the United States, 1980* (Washington, D.C.: Department of Commerce, 1981), p. 862.

116. D.C. Kruse, *Monetary Integration in Western Europe: EMU, EMS and Beyond* (London: Butterworth Scientific, 1980), p. 77, and Peter Coffey, *The World Monetary Crisis* (New York: Macmillan and Co., 1974), p. 24.

117. Kissinger, *White House Years*, pp. 951–62.

Chapter Three

1. See the author's "Soviet Strategy and the Vietnam War," *Asian Affairs* (March–April 1974), pp. 205–28.

2. William T. Lee, *Soviet Strategic and Tactical Strategy*, vol. I, *Viability of the ABM Treaty in the 1980s* (November 30, 1978, a report prepared for the Defense Nuclear Agency, Washington, D.C.).

3. Former director of Defense Advance Research Projects Agency (DARPA), Dr. Robert S. Cooper, in testimony before the Defense Policy Panel and the Research and Development Subcommittee of the House Armed Services Committee on March 26, 1987, noted that in 1972 the Safeguard "system concept was deemed suitable to defend the top 30 U.S. cities against a total attack level of, perhaps, several hundred re-entry vehicles. . . . Most responsible ABM system engineers of that era believed that large scale deployment of such a system could have limited the damage from an uncoordinated Soviet attack . . . to that of a few bursts on a few cities." The system was deemed not to be cost-effective at the margin — that is, that it could not be expanded as quickly as Moscow could deploy a MIRVed force to overwhelm it.

4. Kissinger, *White House Years*, p. 812. Curiously, on March 25, Kissinger sent an oral note to Moscow clarifying that construction would cease not when negotia-

tions began, but when the freeze went into effect, widening the loophole further. Ibid., p. 816.

5. Freedman, *U.S. Intelligence and the Soviet Strategic Threat*, p. 165. See also Garthoff, *Detente and Confrontation*, p. 183, who says that the number of silos was eighty.

6. The treaty would permit deployment of one hundred ABM launchers at a specified site or sites, enough to justify continued research and development but not to provide an effective defense.

7. Soviet Premier Kosygin made a strong call for increased energy cooperation during the Twenty-Fourth Party Congress. See his speech in *Pravda*, April 7, 1971.

8. Keith W. Nolan, *Into Laos, The Story of Dewey Canyon II/ Lam Son 719, Vietnam 1971* (New York: Dell Publishing Co., 1986), pp. 31–32. Nolan's book is a detailed analysis of the conflict from the perspective of those who fought it. For a succinct account from the perspective of JCS, see General Bruce Palmer, *The 25-Year War: America's Military Role in Vietnam* (New York: Simon and Schuster, 1984), pp. 106–16. See also Kissinger, *White House Years*, pp. 987–1010.

9. Vietcong documents confirmed that Lam Son 719 forced postponement of the timetable for resuming the strategic offensive and making 1971 the "year of decision." See study document, COSVN resolution 10, translated in *Vietnam Documents and Research Notes*, no. 99 (October 1971), Saigon, U.S. Military Assistance Command, Vietnam.

10. Nolan, *Into Laos*, p. 359.

11. North Vietnamese fortifications in the Tchepone area included nineteen anti-aircraft battalions, twelve infantry regiments, a tank regiment, an artillery regiment and elements of five divisions. Moreover, Hanoi could draw upon additional reinforcements from nearby units in Laos and North Vietnam. In the view of one analyst, "PAVN was close to home, in absolute control of terrain it could not afford to lose, and in a country where U.S. troops were prohibited by Congress from going." See William S. Turley, *The Second Indochina War, A Short Political and Military History, 1954–1975* (New York: New American Library, 1986), pp. 141–42.

12. Nolan, *Into Laos*, pp. 358–59.

13. Palmer, *25-Year War*, p. 112.

14. Turley, *Second Indochina War*, p. 142.

15. Kissinger, *White House Years*, p. 1004.

16. Palmer, *25-Year War*, p. 113, and Kissinger, *White House Years*, p. 1008.

17. Nixon, *Memoirs*, p. 499.

18. Nolan, *Into Laos*, pp. 366–68.

19. Remarkably, although helicopter losses were high, the loss rate was less than one percent per thousand sorties. See John J. Tolson, *Air Mobility, 1961–1971* (Washington, D.C.: Department of the Army, 1973), pp. 251–52.

20. *FBIS-SU*, February 10, 1971, p. A1.

21. Ibid., February 12, 1971, "New Times" commentary, p. A5, and ibid., Nikolayev "commentary," accusing the United States of "turning Indochina into another Korea" by occupying "South Vietnam, Cambodia and southern Laos," p. A6.

22. *Izvestia*, February 11, 1971, p. 1, and Radio Moscow to South Asia, February 14, 1971, in *FBIS-SU*, February 16, 1971, p. A25.

23. *Izvestia*, May 16, 1976, p. 2.
24. *FBIS-PRC*, February 16, 1971, p. A8.
25. Ibid., February 16, 1971, pp. A1–2.
26. Ibid., pp. A2–3.
27. Ibid., February 20, 1971, pp. A1–2.
28. *FBIS-Trends*, February 24, 1971, p. 11.
29. *FBIS-A&P*, March 10, 1971, pp. K22–27.
30. Ibid., p. K24.
31. Ibid., March 12, 1971, p. B1. Beijing's initial hostile reaction to the events in Laos may have been related to Lin Biao's growing political strength. At precisely the moment of the incursion, Lin was reaching the pinnacle of his political fortunes in the contest with Mao for control of the party provincial committees which were in the final stages of reconstruction following their collapse during the cultural revolution. See the author's *China: A Political History*, pp. 347–355.
32. Whetten, *Canal War*, pp. 143–44.
33. Ibid., p. 146.
34. Sadat, *In Search of Identity*, p. 220.
35. Ibid., p. 221. Sadat denied that the Soviet Union sent any aircraft, but evidently the shipments included a handful of improved MiG-21s. See Edward H. Kolcum, "Soviets Spur Arms Flow to Egypt," *Aviation Week and Space Technology*, April 19, 1971, pp. 14–16.
36. Whetten, *Canal War*, pp. 178–79.
37. Sadat, *In Search of Identity*, p. 218.
38. Ibid., p. 222.
39. For an analysis of events from February to May, see Raymond Anderson, "Egypt Asks Death Penalty for Sabry and 8 Others," *New York Times*, September 5, 1971, p. 2.
40. See Rubinstein, *Red Star Over the Nile*, pp. 144–53, and Whetten, *Canal War*, pp. 189–90.
41. See the useful article by Anthony Sylvester, "Mohammed vs Lenin in Revolutionary Sudan," *New Middle East*, July 1971, pp. 26–28.
42. Whetten, *Canal War*, pp. 316–17.
43. For a discussion of Soviet initiatives from 1969 through the signing of the treaty in August 1971 and Gandhi's reticence, see Sydney Schanberg, "Pact Said to Bury India's Nonalignment," *New York Times*, August 14, 1971, p. 6.
44. See the author's "South Asia: Imbalance on the Subcontinent," *Orbis*, Fall 1975, pp. 864–66.
45. See International Institute for Strategic Studies, *The Military Balance: 1972–1973*, London, pp. 48–49, 53.
46. *Aviation Week and Space Technology*, December 13, 1971, p. 9.
47. See *New York Times*, April 13, 1971, p. 1, for Zhou Enlai's pledge of support.
48. Kissinger, *White House Years*, p. 855.
49. Ibid., p. 860.
50. For the treaty text, see *FBIS-SU*, August 9, 1971, pp. B4–7.
51. See Kissinger, *White House Years*, pp. 857 and 869, for President Nixon's letters

to Yahya urging a peaceful resolution of the crisis and the establishment of East Pakistani autonomy.

52. Ibid., p. 875.

53. Nixon, *Memoirs*, p. 531, believed Gandhi to have been "hypocritical" and "duplicitous," having "made up her mind to attack Pakistan at the time she saw me in Washington" yet she "assured me she would not."

54. For early reports of the Indian attack, see "Big Indian Force Reported Going Into East Pakistan; Fighter Aircraft in Clash," *New York Times*, November 24, 1971, p. A1.

55. Ibid.

56. Charles Mohr, "Rail Line is Cut, New Delhi Says," *New York Times*, December 1, 1971, p. A8. The United States quietly agreed to allow Jordan and Saudi Arabia to transfer a few jet fighters to Pakistan, but with little effect.

57. For the text, see Kissinger, *White House Years*, p. 1488 n. 7.

58. Ibid., p. 905.

59. Ibid., pp. 894–95.

60. Brandon, *Retreat of American Power*, p. 261.

61. As a way of obviating the United States secret pledge, some former State Department officers have attempted to make the argument that India did not attack East Pakistan on November 21, 1971, but that the outbreak of the war occurred with the West Pakistani air strike in Kashmir on December 3. If Pakistan were the aggressor, of course, then the secret American pledge to aid Pakistan in case of Indian aggression would not apply. For examples of this convoluted and specious interpretation, see Christopher Van Hollen, "The Tilt Policy Revisited: Nixon-Kissinger Geopolitics and South Asia," *Asian Survey*, April 1980, pp. 339–61, and Garthoff, *Detente and Confrontation*, pp. 263–66, who follows him.

62. Kissinger, *White House Years*, pp. 900–901.

63. See the author's *China: A Political History*, pp. 350–55, and Yao, *Conspiracy and Death of Lin Biao*, pp. 156–85.

64. Hedrick Smith, "Soviets and Chinese Accuse Each Other on Fighting," *New York Times*, December 6, 1971, p. 16.

65. Jack Anderson, "U.S. Task Force Didn't Frighten India," *Washington Post*, December 21, 1971, p. E15. The *Times of India* first leaked the Soviet pledge on December 14.

66. Thomas Powers, *The Man Who Kept the Secrets*, (New York: A. Knopf, 1979), p. 206.

67. Kissinger, *White House Years*, pp. 900–901.

68. James M. McConnell and Ann H. Kelly, "Super-Power Naval Diplomacy: Lessons of the Indo-Pakistani Crisis of 1971," *Survival*, November–December 1973, p. 289.

69. Kissinger, *White House Years*, p. 905. The public United States treaty commitment was to support Pakistan against Communist aggression, which, of course, did not apply. This was the first revelation of a specific written commitment to assist Pakistan in case of Indian attack.

70. "India Sending High Official to Moscow for Consultation," *New York Times*, December 11, 1971, p. A13, and Hedrick Smith, "High Level Soviet

Delegation Leaves for Talks in New Delhi," *New York Times*, December 12, 1971, p. A27.

71. McConnell and Kelly, "Super-Power Naval Diplomacy," p. 289.

72. Kissinger, *White House Years*, p. 905.

73. A second Soviet task force of four ships was sighted passing through the Tsushima Strait on December 15, having departed from Vladivostok around the tenth.

74. Hedrick Smith, "Moscow Assails U.S. Step," *New York Times*, December 14, 1971, p. 17.

75. Mulatov Commentary in Mandarin, "Liberation Struggle Ignored," *FBIS-SU*, December 8, 1971, p. D4.

76. Charles Mohr, "Indians Closer to Dacca; Land Paratroop Brigade; Report 3,000 Prisoners," *New York Times*, December 12, 1971, p. A1.

77. Kissinger, *White House Years*, p. 909.

78. *FBIS-MENA*, December 13, 1971, p. O2.

79. Nixon, *Memoirs*, pp. 525–31.

80. Kissinger, *White House Years*, p. 911.

81. Fox Butterfield, "Mrs. Gandhi Writes President: U.S. Could Have Averted War," *New York Times*, December 17, 1971, p. 1.

82. David K. Hall, "The Laotian War of 1962 and the Indo-Pakistani War of 1971," in Barry M. Blechman and Stephen S. Kaplan, eds., *Force Without War* (Washington: Brookings Institution, 1978), p. 198.

83. Fox Butterfield, "A 3-Pronged Drive," *New York Times*, December 14, 1971, p. A16.

84. Jack Anderson, *The Anderson Papers* (New York: Ballantine Books, 1974), p. 266.

85. Ibid., p. 233.

86. Anderson, "U.S. Task Force," p. E15. Kuznetsov's remark removed any doubt about Soviet complicity in the Indian war plan.

87. Henry Tanner, "Third Soviet Veto Bars Truce Plan," *New York Times*, December 15, 1971, p. 1.

88. Kissinger, *White House Years*, p. 912.

89. Ibid.

90. Indeed, it was his indiscretion of making public what the president sought to maintain a private matter that damaged Kissinger's relations with the president for a time thereafter, as Kissinger acknowledges. See ibid., p. 918.

91. Ibid., p. 916.

92. Nixon, *Memoirs*, p. 530.

93. For the text of the seven-point proposal, see Kissinger, *White House Years*, pp. 1488–89 (n. 11).

94. Ibid., p. 1018.

95. Jean Lacouture, "Toward an End to the Indochina War?" *Pacific Community*, January 1972, p. 330, argues that at most one NVA main force unit remained inside South Vietnam by the end of 1971.

96. Turley, *Second Indochina War*, p. 144, also concludes that the "communists . . . needed to reverse the deterioration of revolutionary strength at the local level inside South Vietnam to establish a position of strength for whatever was to follow, whether a negotiated settlement or more war."

97. Kissinger, *White House Years*, p. 1018.
98. Ian Ward, "North Vietnam's Blitzkrieg," *Conflict Studies*, October 1972, p. 5
99. See *FBIS-Trends*, September 29, 1971.
100. *FBIS-Trends*, November 24, 1971.
101. Ward, "Blitzkrieg," p. 1.
102. See Miller, *Soviet Strategy in Indochina*, appendix I, pp. 255–57, for a list of all public meetings between Soviet and North Vietnamese leaders between 1969 and 1973.
103. *FBIS-Trends*, October 6, 1971.
104. Ibid.
105. Kenneth Landon, "The Impact of the Sino-American Detente on the Indochina Conflict," in Gene T. Hsiao, *Sino-American Detente and its Policy Implications* (New York: Praeger Books, 1974), p. 210.
106. *Pravda*, March 28, 1972. There were many others. In late February a delegation from the Merchant Marine Ministry went to Hanoi, and in early March the Soviet minister of communications went, to name only two. Their responsibilities were self-evident.
107. Kosygin's meetings were on February 1, 11, and 14; Kirilenko's on February 7 and 25; Katushev's on February 19 and 25. See Miller, *Soviet Strategy in Indochina*, pp. 255–57.
108. Kissinger, *White House Years*, p. 1102. Kissinger's account of the Vietnam negotiations clearly shows intimate Soviet involvement in the process, although he interprets it differently.
109. Ibid., p. 1099.
110. For the text of the communiqué, see ibid., pp. 1491–92.
111. Turley, *Second Indochina War*, p. 145.
112. Sir Robert Thompson, *Peace Is Not At Hand* (New York: McKay, 1974), says fourteen; see pp. 114, 121.
113. Ten divisions were committed in the initial assault, see Turley, *Second Indochina War*, pp. 144–35.
114. Ward, "Blitzkrieg," p. 5.
115. According to Kissinger, *White House Years*, pp. 1114–24, they met on April 3, 6, 9, 10, 12, 15, 16, and 20.
116. Ibid., p. 1182.
117. Ibid., p. 1120.
118. Ibid., p. 1121.
119. Ibid.
120. Ibid., p. 1122.
121. Ibid., p. 1126.
122. Ibid., p. 1144.
123. Ibid., p. 1144–50.
124. Ibid., pp. 1149–52.
125. Nixon, *Memoirs*, p. 605.
126. Ibid. The president believed that this "new peace proposal . . . became the reference point for the terms of the final settlement the following January."
127. Ward, "Blitzkrieg," p. 7.

128. Admiral Moorer, during congressional testimony in June 1972, noted resumption of "heavy resupply of war materials," cited in Gareth Porter, *Peace Denied* (Bloomington: Indiana University Press, 1975), p. 114.

129. Following the signing of the "Paris Peace Accords," the former U.S. ambassador to the Philippines, William Sullivan, appearing on "Meet the Press," January 28, 1973, was asked what role China had played in the settlement. His reply was that "China has had a great deal to do with the way in which this situation has worked out. When President Nixon decided to put the mines into the harbors of North Vietnam May 8th, he produced a situation in which North Vietnam became one hundred per cent dependent upon China for the provision of its equipment. Everything coming from the Soviet Union had to transit Chinese territory. Nothing could go through the waters and come into Haiphong overseas. This means that China's preoccupation with Soviet encirclement came into play. This means that China's feeling that it would rather have four Balkanized states in Indochina rather than an Indochina that was dominated by Hanoi and possibly susceptible to Moscow, came into play."

130. See Raymond L. Garthoff, "SALT I: An Evaluation," *World Politics*, October 1978, p. 5.

131. For a concise discussion of United States arms control strategy, see the author's article written in collaboration with William H. Lewis, "Arms Control and Heavy Missiles," *Naval War College Review*, January–February 1984, pp. 93–107.

132. Kissinger, *White House Years*, p. 1251.

133. Ibid.

134. Snepp, *Decent Interval*, p. 23–24.

135. Kissinger, *White House Years*, p. 1306.

136. Ibid., p. 1374.

137. Thompson, *Peace Is Not at Hand*, pp. 110–11.

138. Porter, *Peace Denied*, p. 108.

139. Kissinger, *White House Years*, p. 1333. Snepp, in *Decent Interval*, pp. 25–27, at variance with Kissinger, argues that Hanoi had floated the trial balloon on National Day, September 1, that a settlement could be reached without Thieu's prior overthrow, that Brezhnev confirmed this change when Kissinger traveled to Moscow during the second week of September, and that Le Duc Tho reconfirmed this during his meeting with Kissinger in Paris on September 26–27.

140. In *White House Years*, pp. 1329–30, Kissinger does not share this view, believing that congressional pressures after the election would actually leave the president in a weaker, not stronger position; but he does not disclose how he knew in advance what the electoral results would be.

141. Ibid., pp. 1343f.

142. Ibid, p. 1365 and Nixon, *Memoirs*, p. 692.

143. Nixon, *Memoirs*, p. 697, and Kissinger, *White House Years*, p. 1382.

144. Nguyen Tien Hung and Jerrold L. Schecter, *Palace File*, (New York: Harper and Row, 1986), pp. 83–84. Captured Vietcong documents disclosed the land-grab plan on October 17.

145. Kissinger, *White House Years*, p. 1382.

146. Porter, *Peace Denied*, pp. 153f, a sympathetic supporter of Hanoi's position,

details the reversion to a tough stance as of course does Kissinger in *White House Years*, pp. 1415f.

147. Ibid., p. 1435.
148. Ibid., p. 1458.
149. Porter, *Peace Denied*, p. 163.
150. For the changes, see Kissinger, *White House Years*, pp. 1466–67.
151. *United States–Vietnam Relations, 1945–1967* (Washington: Government Printing Office, 1971), Book I, part III, "Summary of the Final Declaration, p. D–23.
152. Thompson, *Peace Is Not at Hand*, p. 137.
153. Porter, *Peace Denied*, pp. 166f.
154. Nguyen and Schecter, *Palace File*, p. 148.
155. *Pravda*, January 28, 1973, p. 1.

Chapter Four

1. Kissinger, *Years of Upheaval*, p. 258.
2. Robert Solomon, *The International Monetary System*, 1945–1981 (New York: Harper and Row, 1982), pp. 243f.
3. Ibid.
4. Rolfe and Burtle, *Great Wheel*, p. 110.
5. MNC Report, p. 135.
6. Ibid.
7. Amin Saikal, *The Rise and Fall of the Shah* (Princeton: Princeton University Press, 1980), pp. 119–20.
8. Blair, *Control of Oil*, p. 293.
9. Although I characterize the strategic debate as being between Nixon and Kissinger, the reader should understand this as a literary convention. While the president and national security adviser were the main protagonists, they in effect represented opposing views within the top American leadership.
10. Haldeman, *Ends of Power*, pp. 167f, believes that Nixon's plan to purge the executive branch of government was the underlying motive for Watergate.
11. Legally, a conversation and/or overt act whose intent is to impede or hamper a criminal investigation is an obstruction of justice.
12. As the president himself noted, "I gave them a sword. And they stuck it in. And they twisted it with relish. And, I guess, if I'd been in their position I'd have done the same thing." David Frost, "I Gave Them a Sword," *Behind the Scenes of the Nixon Interviews* (New York: William Morrow and Co., 1978), p. 269.
13. For an extremely thought-provoking excursion through several subterranean tunnels on the subject, see Carl Oglesby, *The Yankee and Cowboy War, Conspiracies from Dallas to Watergate and Beyond* (New York: Berkely Medallion, 1976).
14. Those tapped were NSC aides Morton Halperin, Helmut Sonnenfeld, Daniel Davidson, Richard Moose, Richard Sneider, Anthony Lake, Winston Lord; White House staffers John Sears, William Safire, James McLane; reporters Henry Brandon, Hedrick Smith, Henry Beecher, Marvin Kalb; State

Department officers William H. Sullivan and Richard F. Pederson; and Department of Defense Col. Robert E. Pursley.

15. J. Anthony Lukas, *Nightmare, The Underside of the Nixon Years* (New York: Viking Press, 1976), p. 60.

16. Ibid, p. 375.

17. Haldeman, *Ends of Power*, p. 195. Lukas, *Nightmare*, pp. 375f, is perplexed by the reasons given for the taping system. Nixon had dismantled Lyndon Johnson's system upon entering office, declaring that no one should be bugged in the president's office. Yet, if "history" were the purpose, then why not retain LBJ's system, or replace it with a new one immediately, instead of waiting for two years? Lukas' answer, missing the point completely, is that the president installed the taping system for tax purposes, to evade the provisions of the Tax Reform Act of 1969 which eliminated deductions for gifts of professional papers, but allowed deductions for presidential tapes.

18. Hersh, *Price of Power*, p. 81.

19. *United States-Vietnam Relations, 1945–1967*, see especially Book 1, III. A.1–3.

20. Lukas, *Nightmare*, p. 70.

21. Hersh, *Price of Power*, p. 390.

22. Ibid., p. 391, and Kissinger, *Years of Upheaval*, pp. 118f. Kissinger was "displeased that Ehrlichman had recruited one of my staff members without consulting me and while I was out of the country."

23. Hersh, *Price of Power*, pp. 394–95.

24. See Lukas, *Nightmare*, pp. 86f.

25. Jim Hougan, *Secret Agenda, Watergate, Deep Throat and the CIA* (New York: Random House, 1984), whose book is indispensable reading for anyone seeking an accurate factual recounting of the events, p. xviii, reaches the same conclusion.

26. Lukas, *Nightmare*, pp. 78f; Hougan, *Secret Agenda*, pp. 32f; See E. Howard Hunt, *Undercover: Memoirs of an American Secret Agent* (New York: Putnam, 1974), pp. 141–45.

27. See the memo to Thomas Karamessines, "Subject: E. Howard Hunt — Utilization by Central Cover Staff," October 14, 1970, cited in Hougan, *Secret Agenda*, p. 7, n.11.

28. Lukas, *Nightmare*, p. 79.

29. Ibid. and Hougan, *Secret Agenda*, p. 33.

30. Colson's zeal in first inserting Hunt into the White House and then moving him into sensitive positions strikes the observer as having a larger purpose beyond responsiveness to mere college ties. His role is at best unclear.

31. Hersh, *Price of Power*, p. 391.

32. Hougan, *Secret Agenda*, p. 29, and Eugenio Martinez, "Mission Impossible," *Harper's*, October 1974, p. 51.

33. Lukas, *Nightmare*, p. 97.

34. Hougan, *Secret Agenda*, p. 108, in what otherwise is a brilliant account, exonerates Mitchell almost completely, describing his role as "most aptly comparable to that of a latter-day Pontius Pilate." Nixon himself, *Memoirs*, pp. 625–87, found it difficult to believe that Mitchell had done him in, but circles close to this possibility in his account.

35. This was "operation sandwedge" proposed by private investigator Jack Caulfield. See Lukas, *Nightmare*, pp. 106–7, and Hougan, *Secret Agenda*, p. 96.

36. Jeb Stuart Magruder, *An American Life, One Man's Road to Watergate* (New York: Atheneum, 1974), pp. 169–71, and Lukas, *Nightmare*, p. 108.

37. For discussion of McCord's brilliant career, see Hougan, *Secret Agenda*, pp. 3–26.

38. Lukas, *Nightmare*, p. 171.

39. G. Gordon Liddy, *Will, The Autobiography of G. Gordon Liddy* (New York: St. Martins Press, 1980), p. 217.

40. Lukas, *Nightmare*, p. 190.

41. Hougan, *Secret Agenda*, pp. 17–19.

42. Liddy, *Will*, p. 243.

43. Lukas, *Nightmare*, pp. 169–70.

44. Liddy, *Will*, p. 217, and Lukas, *Nightmare*, p. 170–72.

45. Magruder, *An American Life*, p. 178. See also John Dean, *Blind Ambition, The White House Years* (New York: Simon and Schuster, 1976), pp. 79–85.

46. Magruder, *An American Life*, p. 178, and Dean, *Blind Ambition*, p. 85, whose version is similar.

47. Lukas, *Nightmare*, p. 173. Neither Dean nor Liddy makes reference to this conversation in his account.

48. Dean, *Blind Ambition*, p. 86.

49. Magruder, *An American Life*, p. 180.

50. Liddy, *Will*, p. 203.

51. Magruder, *An American Life*, p. 180.

52. Lukas, *Nightmare*, pp. 174f.

53. Dean, *Blind Ambition*, p. 86.

54. Liddy, *Will*, p. 203.

55. Magruder, *An American Life*, p. 180.

56. Dean, *Blind Ambition*, pp. 86–88. Dean's recollection on this matter is quite vague as well as being self-exculpatory.

57. Liddy, *Will*, p. 203.

58. Magruder, *An American Life*, p. 195.

59. Lukas, *Nightmare*, p. 189.

60. Magruder, *An American Life*, pp. 198–99.

61. Liddy, *Will*, p. 217.

62. For the curious circumstances surrounding McCord's choice of Baldwin, see Hougan, *Secret Agenda*, pp. 135–36, who suggests that a prior acquaintanceship explains McCord's selection, but offers no firm evidence.

63. For Baldwin's curious role in these events, see Fred D. Thompson, *At That Point in Time, The Inside Story of the Senate Watergate Committee* (New York: Quadrangle Books, 1975), pp. 208–12.

64. Liddy, *Will*, pp. 219–20.

65. See Hougan, *Secret Agenda*, pp. 139–57, for an authoritative, detailed, minute-by-minute account.

66. FBI and Chesapeake and Potomac Telephone Company technicians examined the DNC premises immediately following the June 17 break-in and confirmed that no electronic devices had been implanted. See Hougan, *Secret Agenda*, pp. 217–18.

67. Ibid., pp. 308f. McCord and Baldwin were monitoring and recording the activities of two brothels, one located in the Columbia Plaza apartment complex across from the Department of State and the other in a motel on Columbia Pike in Arlington. The brothels were evidenty being run at the behest of a foreign power seeking to build influence on American foreign policy by compromising high officials. Since domestic surveillance was outside the CIA's charter, its employees "retired" in order to perform their duties as private citizens.

68. Ibid., p. 152.

69. Liddy, *Will*, pp. 234–46, having heard nothing from McCord for several days following the May 28 entry, went over to the Howard Johnson's listening post to inquire. McCord proceeded to spin Liddy a tall tale, explaining that he was able to pick up only one of the implanted bugs. Though Liddy accepted this explanation, he became upset when he discovered that the bug McCord said he had not been able to pick up was not what it was supposed to be. Liddy had given McCord $30,000 to purchase a "room bug," which would relay anything said in the room; but McCord had, he said, installed a telephone bug instead. McCord also gave Liddy several pages of typed logs when Liddy noticed that there was a recording machine in the room. When Liddy asked why he did not simply record everything picked up, McCord declared that the recorders could not be plugged into the receiver because of mismatched electrical resistance. This seemed particularly odd in light of the fact that McCord had just purchased all-new equipment for this operation. When Liddy suggested that he buy compatible equipment, McCord assured him that when he read the typed transcripts he would see that the "system was working well" and no other equipment would be required. McCord explained that the advantage of his system was that it allowed him to "edit out the junk," which prompted Liddy to reply that he "wanted it all," and would do his own editing. Nevertheless, the only material Liddy received from McCord were edited and typed transcript logs.

70. Ibid., p. 236.

71. Ibid., p. 237.

72. Although Magruder, *An American Life*, pp. 209–10, speaks of photographed correspondence in the initial batch, both Liddy, *Will*, p. 238, and Hunt, *Undercover*, p. 231, say that the film was not developed until June 10.

73. Liddy, *Will*, p. 238.

74. Lukas, *Nightmare*, p. 203.

75. See Hougan, *Secret Agenda*, pp. 308f.

76. Lukas, *Nightmare*, p. 266.

77. For a good summary of CIA involvement, see Thompson, *That Point in Time*, pp. 145–82.

78. See Vernon Walters, *Silent Mission* (New York: Doubleday and Co., 1978), p. 604, for Helms' shocked expression upon his return to Langley after the meeting, and Powers, *Man Who Kept the Secrets*, pp. 244 and 363, n.5.

79. Dean, *Blind Ambition*, p. 123. John Ehrlichman, *Witness to Power, The Nixon Years* (New York: Simon and Schuster, 1982), p. 346, believes that "Mitchell and Dean inspired the cover-up idea." He refers to the June 23, 1972, tape of

a conversation in the president's office in which Haldeman says to Nixon, "Mitchell came up with [a plan] yesterday, and John Dean analyzed [it] very carefully last night and . . . concurs now with Mitchell's recommendation that the only way to solve this . . . is for us to have Walters [of the CIA] call Pat Gray [director of the FBI] and just say, 'stay the hell out of this. . . .'"

80. Dean, *Blind Ambition*, pp. 124, 140.
81. Powers, *Man Who Kept the Secrets*, p. 240, and Dean, *Blind Ambition*, p. 138.
82. Dean, *Blind Ambition*, p. 140.
83. Ibid., p. 146.
84. Hunt, *Undercover*, p. 275.
85. Dean, *Blind Ambition*, p. 162.
86. Ibid., pp. 157, 160.
87. Ibid., p. 162.
88. Ibid., pp. 163–64.
89. Ibid., p. 164.
90. Ibid., p. 165. Haldeman, *Ends of Power*, p. 223, tells a different and unconvincing story about the money, claiming that he told Dean "to transfer it to CRP and after that it wasn't my concern." He then exploded when he learned that "instead of transferring it as directed, he [Dean] sent over $40,000 for the defendants." Haldeman then says simply that "the rest of the money went to CRP in a bizarre way: a man wearing gloves furtively receiving the briefcase full of cash and handing over no receipt. Why did grown people act that way?" But this makes no sense. Haldeman acknowledges that the "man wearing gloves" was Fred LaRue and knew that LaRue was Mitchell's man and did not work for CRP.
91. Lukas, *Nightmare*, p. 259, and Dean, *Blind Ambition*, p. 166.
92. Lukas, *Nightmare*, p. 259.
93. Haldeman, *Ends of Power*, p. 223.
94. Dean, *Blind Ambition*, p. 167.
95. Ibid., p. 168.

Chapter Five

1. Nixon, *Memoirs*, p. 592.
2. Cf. Hersh, *Price of Power*, pp. 508f. Hersh's account, while highly critical of Kissinger, at the same time legitimizes his role.
3. Nixon, *Memoirs*, p. 592, emphasis added.
4. Kissinger, *White House Years*, p. 1156.
5. Ibid., p. 1154.
6. Ibid., p. 1144, emphasis supplied.
7. Ibid., p. 1146.
8. Ibid., p. 1147.
9. Szulc, *Illusion of Peace*, pp. 544–45, charged that this was the first administration offer of a cease-fire in place, which Kissinger rebutted by pointing out that the cease-fire in place formula was first broached in October 1970 and reiterated

May 3, 1971. Szulc, of course, could not have known that this was a deviation from presidential instructions, or that in any case it was never declared that the *final peace agreement* would allow Hanoi to keep troops in the South, *until* Kissinger went to Moscow in April of 1972.

10. Kissinger, *White House Years*, pp. 1146–7.
11. Ibid., p. 1158.
12. Ibid., pp. 1148, 1158.
13. Ibid., p. 1148.
14. Ibid., pp. 1160, 1163.
15. Ibid., p. 1160.
16. Ibid., p. 1162, and Nixon, *Memoirs*, p. 592.
17. Hersh, *Price of Power*, pp. 637–38.
18. Nixon, *Memoirs*, p. 689.
19. Ibid., p. 690.
20. Ibid., p. 692.
21. Kissinger, *White House Years*, p. 1347, and Nixon, *Memoirs*, p. 691.
22. Nixon, *Memoirs*, p. 693, and Kissinger, *White House Years*, p. 1361.
23. Ibid., p. 1348.
24. Ibid., p. 1361.
25. Hersh, *Price of Power*, pp. 589f, discusses these angles.
26. Ibid., p. 591.
27. Ibid.
28. Kissinger, *White House Years*, p. 1365.
29. Hersh, *Price of Power*, p. 595.
30. Kissinger, *White House Years*, p. 1361. Kissinger's claim is off the point, for he himself notes elsewhere in his memoir, p. 1438n., that he had often sent messages in the president's name that Nixon never saw "until afterward."
31. Hersh, *Price of Power*, p. 595.
32. Ibid., p. 597.
33. Kissinger, *White House Years*, p. 1377.
34. Ibid., p. 1381; Nixon, *Memoirs*, pp. 702–3; and Hersh, *Price of Power*, pp. 598–602.
35. Kissinger, *White House Years*, pp. 1388–89, and Hersh, *Price of Power*, p. 599.
36. Kissinger, *White House Years*, p. 1388.
37. Both Kissinger, ibid., p. 1389, and Nixon, *Memoirs*, p. 703, claim to have sent this message.
38. Kissinger, *White House Years*, p. 1496 n.4.
39. Hersh, *Price of Power*, p. 600.
40. Cf. Kissinger, *White House Years*, p. 1392, and Nixon, *Memoirs*, p. 703.
41. Kissinger, *White House Years*, p. 1394.
42. Nixon, *Memoirs*, p. 705.
43. Kissinger, *White House Years*, p. 1445. Kissinger audaciously asserts that his statement "prevented our being stampeded!"
44. Hersh, *Price of Power*, p. 605.
45. Nixon, *Memoirs*, p. 706.
46. Hersh, *Price of Power*, p. 608.
47. Nixon, *Memoirs*, pp. 706–7.

48. Hersh, *Price of Power*, p. 612.

49. Kissinger, *White House Years*, p. 1415. See also chapter 3.

50. Nixon, *Memoirs*, p. 707.

51. Porter, *Peace Denied*, pp. 145–47.

52. Kissinger, *White House Years*, p. 1417.

53. Nixon, *Memoirs*, p. 720.

54. Kissinger, *White House Years*, p. 1417.

55. Ibid.

56. Nixon, *Memoirs*, p. 720

57. Kissinger, *White House Years*, p. 1418.

58. Porter, *Peace Denied*, p. 149.

59. Kissinger, *White House Years*, p. 1418.

60. Ibid., pp. 1418–19.

61. Nixon, *Memoirs*, pp. 720–21, and Kissinger, *White House Years*, pp. 1419–20, who twice denies that it was "a directive."

62. Kissinger, *White House Years*, p. 1419.

63. Nixon, *Memoirs*, p. 720.

64. Kissinger, *White House Years*, p. 1446. Indeed, Kissinger acknowledges that while he "frequently received bellicose-sounding instructions intended to be read to the North Vietnamese, operational recommendations were much softer. I was told to keep on negotiating. . . . "

65. Ibid., p. 1420.

66. Ibid.

67. Ibid., and Nixon, *Memoirs*, p. 721.

68. Nixon, *Memoirs*, p. 721.

69. Ibid., p. 722, and Kissinger, *White House Years*, p. 1421.

70. Nixon, *Memoirs*, p. 722, emphasis added.

71. Kissinger, *White House Years*, p. 1421.

72. Ibid., p. 1422.

73. Nixon, *Memoirs*, p. 722.

74. Kissinger, *White House Years*, p. 1422.

75. Nixon, *Memoirs*, p. 723.

76. Kissinger, *White House Years*, p. 1422.

77. Nixon, *Memoirs*, p. 723, emphasis supplied.

78. Ibid., p. 697.

79. Kissinger, *White House Years*, p. 1402.

80. The "Christmas bombing" strikes went on for twelve days.

81. Nixon, *Memoirs*, p. 724, emphasis supplied.

82. Elmo Zumwalt, *On Watch*, pp. 412f. Zumwalt was "distressed at Nixon's duplicity," a remark which raises questions about the admiral's understanding of international affairs in general and the course of the negotiations in particular. Szulc, *Illusion of Power*, pp. 637–39, also notes "top secret plans" for the establishment of a post-cease-fire Defense Attache's Office (DAO), which would become "a permanent minicommand" in Saigon staffed by fifteen military officers and 1,345 DOD civilians. The DAO's main function would be to provide support for ARVN, including coordination of strike planning with Thailand-based B-52s.

83. Kissinger, *White House Years*, pp. 1427–28. The suspicion, unprovable, is that Kissinger put forth terms which Hanoi found very difficult to accept.

84. Ibid., p. 1430.

85. Ibid., p. 1429

86. Ibid.

87. Nixon, *Memoirs*, p. 725.

88. Kissinger, *White House Years*, p. 1430.

89. Nixon, *Memoirs*, p. 727. In his account, *White House Years*, pp. 1430–33, Kissinger carefully omits all specific reference to his recommendation that the United States adopt the policy of massive bombing. Chuck Colson first revealed that Kissinger advocated that course in early 1975. See Douglas Watson, "Colson Allegation, Links Kissinger to Bombing," *Washington Post*, February 8, 1975, p. 1. Kissinger said: "Start the bombing immediately. These madmen have double-crossed us." Later, in his book *Life Sentence* (1979), Colson also revealed that Kissinger had immediately called Nixon, who, in turn, called Colson to suggest that he lay off criticism because "you know we only have one President now. One Secretary of State. So we need to support them, you know, Chuck. They are all we have. I mean, you and I know Henry's faults, but as Americans we support our leaders and our country, right?"

90. Nixon, *Memoirs*, pp. 727–28, emphasis supplied.

91. Ibid., p. 728, emphasis supplied.

92. Kissinger, *White House Years*, pp. 1431–32. The "one more effort" to which Kissinger referred was the six-month-long bombing campaign he was urging.

93. Ibid.

94. Ibid.

95. Ibid., p. 1433.

96. Nixon, *Memoirs*, p. 729.

97. John Ehrlichman, *Witness to Power*, pp. 313–14, emphasis in original.

98. Nixon, *Memoirs*, p. 729.

99. Ibid., p. 730.

100. Kissinger, *White House Years*, p. 1433.

101. Ibid., p. 1434.

102. Nixon, *Memoirs* , p. 731.

103. Kissinger, *White House Years*, p. 1435.

104. Nixon, *Memoirs*, p. 731.

105. Ibid., p. 732.

106. Kissinger, *White House Years*, p. 1439.

107. Ibid., emphasis supplied.

108. Ibid., p. 1440.

109. Ibid., emphasis supplied.

110. Ibid., p. 1441.

111. Ibid.

112. Nixon had been trapped in an obstruction of justice situation when White House money began to go to Hunt and the others. Indeed, Oglesby, *Yankee and Cowboy War*, p. 264, says that Dorothy Hunt's luggage, recovered from the crash of United Airlines flight 553 on December 8, 1972, in which she perished, contained "as much as $2 million in securities." It is sufficient to explain Nixon's

turnaround in mid-December. But as argued here, Nixon saw this as a setback and not a defeat and hoped to recoup later in 1973 when he completed his reorganization and purge of the executive branch. The *final coup* occurred when the Eastern wing obtained copies of the Nixon tapes, probably sometime before McCord's March 19 letter to Judge Sirica accusing the president of a cover-up. That Nixon's opponents obtained copies of the tapes is suggested in the following item from *Newsweek*, September 23, 1974: "While former White House Chief of Staff H.R. Haldeman awaits trial for his part in Watergate, the Secret Service chief he ousted from the White House last year has landed a plum job. Robert H. Taylor, 49, who tangled with Haldeman over Nixon security procedures, is now head of the private security forces of all the far-flung Rockefeller family enterprises." The inference is that Taylor was rewarded for delivery of the tapes.

113. Kissinger, *White House Years*, p. 1447.
114. Hersh, *Price of Power*, p. 632.
115. Ibid., p. 636.

Chapter Six

1. *U.S. Department of State*, "Secretary Kissinger's Year-End Review," December 27, 1973, no. 472, Washington, D.C.
2. Ibid.
3. The cost of this strategy would eventually amount to something on the order of $80 billion in East-bloc debt to the West, most of which would be held by West Germany and Japan, making them increasingly willing to accommodate to Soviet plans.
4. Sadat, *In Search of Identity*, p. 225.
5. Kissinger, *Years of Upheaval*, p. 220.
6. Whetten, *Canal War*, p. 200.
7. Lt. Gen. Said el Shazly, *The Crossing of the Suez* (San Francisco: American Mideast Research, 1980), p. 126. The former chief of staff disputes Sadat's assertion, and says that the Soviet Union did, in fact, deliver weapons according to an October 1971 agreement but delivered them too late for action in 1971.
8. See Alvin Z. Rubinstein, *Red Star over the Nile*, p. 241–44, for a lucid discussion of Sadat's courtship of King Faisal.
9. Kissinger, *Years of Upheaval*, p. 196.
10. Sadat, *In Search of Identity*, p. 237–38.
11. Kissinger's treatment of Nixon's position on the Middle East is as contradictory as it is on Vietnam. He claimed that "Nixon was prepared to engage the United States diplomatically in an exploratory way now and fully after the Israeli election scheduled in October." (*Years of Upheaval*, p. 211.) This was in fact Kissinger's own position, not the president's. Nixon's view, as expressed in his diary entry of February 3, 1973, was: "I hit Henry hard on the Mideast thing. He now wants to push it past the Israeli elections in October, but I told him unless we did it this year we wouldn't get it done at all in the

four-year term. The Egyptian [Hafez Ismail, adviser to President Sadat] is coming over. What he works out I don't know, but I feel that some way we have got to get the Israelis moved off of their intransigent position. . . . The interim settlement is, of course, the only thing we can talk about—that's the only thing the Israelis will ever go for—and the Egyptians are just simply going to have to take a settlement of that sort. . . . I spoke to Henry about the need to get going on the Mideast. I am pressing him hard here . . . with regard to the need to make a settlement this year. . . . On the other hand, Henry has constantly put off moving on it each time, suggesting that the political problems were too difficult. . . . (Nixon, *Memoirs*, p. 706–7) Clearly the president also wanted to work toward an interim settlement immediately, yet Kissinger claimed that he favored "secret talks aiming at an overall settlement." Kissinger then professed to have been "astonished" when in his talk with Ismail, Nixon spoke in favor of an interim settlement. His astonishment can only have been after the fact, for it is obvious that Kissinger misrepresented Nixon's positon to blur the *real* difference between them, which was whether or not to compel Israel to agree to a settlement.

12. Kissinger, *White House Years*, p. 1300.
13. Kissinger, *Years of Upheaval*, p. 205.
14. Ibid., p. 206.
15. Ibid., p. 209.
16. Ibid., pp. 208–9.
17. Sadat, *In Search of Identity*, p. 238.
18. Moscow was already experiencing this pressure. In late 1972 the incidence of Syrian-Israeli border clashes rose sharply, prompting Moscow to commence shipment of large quantities of weapons to Syria *and* to Egypt to maintain the two-front threat to Israel.
19. Kissinger, *Years of Upheaval*, pp. 209–10.
20. Ibid., p. 210.
21. Sadat, *In Search of Identity*, p. 264, says as much. In a cable to Asad on October 19 during the height of the war, he declared: "I am willing to fight Israel no matter how long, but never the U.S.A."
22. Matti Golan, *The Secret Conversations of Henry Kissinger* (New York: Bantam Books, 1976), pp. 144–45.
23. Sadat, *In Search of Identity*, p. 238.
24. Israeli Prime Minister Golda Meir had arrived in Washington for a state visit on March 1, immediately after the departure of Hafez Ismail. In return for an increase in plane deliveries and an agreement to permit co-production of certain aircraft in Israel, Meir altered her earlier position in favor of the status quo to acceptance of "an interim disengagement agreement along the Suez Canal as a first step towards a final settlement." See Kissinger, *Years of Upheaval*, p. 221.
25. Solomon, *International Monetary System*, p. 226.
26. Coffey, *World Monetary Crisis*, p. 35.
27. Ibid.
28. Solomon, *International Monetary System*, p. 229.
29. Ibid., pp. 228–29.

30. Ibid., p. 230.
31. Ibid., p. 231.
32. Ibid., p. 232.
33. *Congressional Quarterly Almanac*, 1974, p. 555.
34. Ibid.
35. Ibid., p. 558.
36. Congressional Quarterly, *Energy Policy*, 2d ed. (Washington, D.C.: Government Printing Office, 1981), pp. 30–31.
37. Seymour, *OPEC, Instrument of Change*, pp. 99–100.
38. Brian Tew, *The Evolution of the International Monetary System, 1945–1977* (London: Wiley, 1977), pp. 198–99.
39. Gisselquist, *Oil Prices and Trade Deficits*, p. 61.
40. Stockholm International Peace Research Institute, *Oil and Security* (New York: Humanities Press, 1974), p. 71.
41. MNC report, pp. 136, 145.
42. Blair, *Control of Oil*, p. 267.
43. Sampson, *Seven Sisters*, pp. 244–45.

Chapter Seven

1. Ray Maghouri and Stephen Gorman, *The Yom Kippur War: A Case Study in Crisis Decision-Making in American Foreign Policy* (Washington, D.C.: University Press of America, 1981), p. 9.
2. Kissinger, *Years of Upheaval*, p. 148.
3. Ibid., p. 136.
4. Henry A. Kissinger, "1973: Year of Europe," Department of State, no. 8710, Washington, D.C., 1973.
5. Ibid.; for the chronicle of the European response, see Kissinger, *Years of Upheaval*, pp. 177f.
6. Kissinger, *Years of Upheaval*, p. 179.
7. Kissinger, *White House Years*, p. 1152.
8. For the agreement, see *The Washington Summit: General Secretary Brezhnev's Visit to the United States, June 18–25, 1973*, no. 8733, Department of State, Washington D.C., 1973. Cf. Garthoff, *Detente and Confrontation*, pp. 334–44, who argues that the agreement had little effect on the behavior of either party.
9. Garthoff, *Detente and Confrontation*, pp. 337–68.
10. See Chapter 9 in this volume.
11. Kissinger, *Years of Upheaval*, pp. 279f.
12. Ibid., p. 298.
13. Thomas T. Hammond, *Red Flag over Afghanistan*, (Boulder: Westview Press, 1984), p. 36.
14. Ibid., p. 37.
15. See the excellent article by Janice Stein, "Military Deception, Strategic Surprise, and Conventional Deterrence: A Political Analysis of Egypt and Israel, 1971–73," *Journal of Strategic Studies*, March 1982, pp. 94–120.

16. See "Kissinger: 'The Crisis for Us Started at 6 A.M. Oct. 6,' " *Washington Post*, October 26, 1973, pp. A8–9, and Kissinger, *Years of Upheaval*, p. 459. Mrs. Meir's cryptic comment to Kissinger just after the war broke out is also of interest, p. 477. On October 7, she sent a message to him saying: "You know the reasons why we took no preemptive action. Our failure to take such action is the reason for our situation now. If I had given the chief of staff authority to preempt, as he had recommended, some hours before the attacks began, there is no doubt that our situation would now be different."

17. Ibid., p. 209, and Galia Golan, *Yom Kippur and After* (New York: Cambridge University Press, 1977), p. 39.

18. Stein, "Military Deception," p. 104.

19. *Sunday Times* (London), October 14, 1973.

20. Anwar el-Sadat, interview with Arnaud de Borchgrave, *Newsweek*, April 9, 1973.

21. Whetten, *Canal War*, p. 237.

22. Rubinstein, *Red Star over the Nile*, p. 243.

23. Ibid., pp. 250–51, n.12. Rubinstein notes, for example, that "Israeli journalists were pressed by the military and the government to minimize the seriousness of the Arab military moves and refrain from drawing attention to them." See also Stein, "Military Deception," pp. 107–14.

24. Chaim Herzog, *The Arab-Israeli Wars* (New York: Random House, 1982), p. 254. Shazly, *Crossing of the Suez*, p. 207, says that the Soviet Union had delivered one SAM-6 brigade and one SCUD brigade in the third quarter of 1973.

25. Stein, "Military Deception," p. 113. See also Chapter 1 in this volume.

26. Marvin and Bernard Kalb, *Kissinger* (New York: Dell Publishing Co., 1975), p. 520.

27. Ibid., p. 521.

28. Chaim Herzog, *The War of Atonement* (Boston: Little, Brown, and Co., 1975), pp. 52–53.

29. Kissinger, *Years of Upheaval*, p. 469–70.

30. Herzog, *War of Atonement*, p. 277, notes that the United States airlifted 22,000 tons of war materiel between October 14 and November 14. Kissinger, *Years of Upheaval*, p. 525, declares that during the conflict the United States airlifted 1,000 tons per day. Presumably, then, between October 14 and the first cease-fire on October 22, the United States delivered 8,000 tons of equipment, with 14,000 coming during the course of the next three weeks. More, of course, came later by air and still more later by sea, for a total of some 56,000 tons.

31. Kissinger, *Years of Upheaval*, p. 468.

32. Heikal, *Road to Ramadan*, p. 4. Although Sadat, *In Search of Identity*, p. 242, declares that he and Asad had agreed to October 6 during their meeting in late August, what they evidently agreed to at that time was the October rather than the September period and not the exact date.

33. Heikal, *Road to Ramadan*, p. 15.

34. Sadat, *In Search of Identity*, p. 246.

35. Golan, *Yom Kippur and After*, p. 69.

36. See *World Armaments and Disarmament, Yearbook 1974*, Stockholm Peace Research Institute (Cambridge: MIT Press, 1974), p. 300, for launch times, dates, places, and orbital inclinations.

37. American satellite coverage was far more advanced. A Big Bird satellite went into orbit on the evening of July 13 and remained in position for ninety-one days. A "close-look" satellite was launched on September 27 and hovered over the Middle East area for thirty-one days, providing policymakers with real-time information on the course of events. Ibid., pp. 290–91, 299. For additional discussion of the satellite television technology employed during the conflict, see Sandra Hochman, *Satellite Spies* (New York: Bobbs-Merrill Co., 1976), pp. 110–12.

38. See Golan, *Yom Kippur and After*, pp. 70f, and Rubinstein, *Red Star over the Nile*, pp. 255f.

39. Rubinstein, *Red Star over the Nile*, p. 260, notes that this was "the first time that the Soviet leadership ever removed its citizens from danger *before* the actual outbreak of fighting in a Third World setting."

40. Sadat, *In Search of Identity*, p. 247.

41. Kissinger, *Years of Upheaval*, p. 472.

42. Ibid.

43. Ibid., p. 473.

44. Sadat, *In Search of Identity*, p. 252.

45. Ibid., pp. 252–53.

46. Ibid.

47. *FBIS-MEA*, September 16, 1975, p. D5.

48. Ibid.

49. Sadat, *In Search of Identity*, p. 253.

50. For the Soviet view as expressed by Ambassador Vinogradov, see *FBIS-MEA*, April 24, 1974, pp. D11–13.

51. *FBIS-MEA*, September 29, 1975, p. D27.

52. In retrospect, it probably was also in Sadat's interest to have agreed to an early cease-fire. See Herzog, *War of Atonement*, p. 77, who concurs.

53. Shazly, *Crossing of the Suez*, p. 111, discloses that Sadat's plans included some deceptive options, too, involving a secret plan within a secret plan. The first was Operation 41, "the drive to cross the canal and seize the Sinai passes in a single operation, to be drawn up in collaboration with our Soviet advisors." The second was code-named "High Minarets." It was to hold a bridgehead across the canal and go no further. If true, these plans contained a doublecross of both Syria and the Soviet Union from the outset!

54. Herzog, *War of Atonement*, p. 118.

55. Ibid., p. 117.

56. Heikal, *Road to Ramadan*, p. 218.

57. Ibid., pp. 218–20.

58. For example, Moscow offered to replace all equipment expended by Iraq if it would provide help and offered to mediate between Iraq and Iran to relieve pressure on Baghdad's flank. According to Sadat, *In Search of Identity*, pp. 254–55, Brezhnev also pressed Tito to prevail upon Sadat to accept a cease-fire, but the Yugoslav leader declined, offering to send tanks to the Syrian front instead.

59. Jon D. Glassman, *Arms for the Arabs, The Soviet Union and War in the Middle East*, (Baltimore: Johns Hopkins University Press, 1978), pp. 131–32, also notes the Israeli trap plan.

60. Herzog, *War of Atonement*, p. 260.
61. The air-defense system was based upon the mobile SAM-6, ZSU-23 radar-controlled anti-aircraft gun and SAM-7 hand-held short-range missile and the fixed SAM-2 and SAM-3. Together these weapons produced an integrated and extremely effective defense sytem over the canal area.
62. Herzog, *War of Atonement*, p. 195 (emphasis supplied).
63. Ibid.
64. Ibid., pp. 195–96.
65. Ibid., p. 129.
66. Kissinger, *Years of Upheaval*, p. 492.
67. Ibid., p. 493.
68. Ibid., p. 495.
69. Ibid., p. 493.
70. Ibid., p. 495.
71. Ibid., p. 494.
72. Kissinger, *White House Years*, p. 1300.
73. Edward Sheehan, *The Arabs, Israelis and Kissinger: A Secret History of American Diplomacy in the Middle East* (New York: Readers' Digest Press, 1976), p. 33.
74. Kissinger, *Years of Upheaval*, p. 485.
75. Ibid., p. 499.
76. Herzog, *War of Atonement*, p. 127.
77. Kissinger, *Years of Upheaval*, p. 500.
78. Herzog, *War of Atonement*, p. 136.
79. Kissinger, *Years of Upheaval*, p. 509.
80. Ibid., p. 511.
81. See Golan, *Yom Kippur and After*, pp. 94–95, for a survey of Soviet press accounts.
82. Kissinger, *Years of Upheaval*, p. 512, and William Quandt, "Soviet Policy in the October Middle East War—II," *International Affairs*, October 1977, p. 588.
83. Sadat, *In Search of Identity*, p. 259, claims that he shifted these units in response to Asad's demands to relieve the pressure on Damascus.
84. Kissinger, *Years of Upheaval*, p. 525.
85. Herzog, *War of Atonement*, p. 206. Shazly, *Crossing of the Suez*, p. 244, says 250 tanks were lost.
86. Herzog, *War of Atonement*, p. 208.
87. Ibid., pp. 223, 235.
88. Ibid., pp. 220–23.
89. Shazly, *Crossing of the Suez*, pp. 253–55, notes that the crossing was not detected until mid-morning of the sixteenth, but "even so, those first reports gave no reason to panic. Second Army said it was coping. We still had the 250 tanks of our strategic reserve. . . . I alerted the reserve units we had in the Cairo area to be ready to move if Second Army lost control of the situation." By midday "news was still confused. Some of our rear SAM units, stationed almost ten miles behind the canal, began to report attacks by enemy tanks. Nobody seemed to know where the tanks had come from."
90. Sadat, *In Search of Identity*, pp. 261–62, says that "on October 16 I ordered Chief of Staff Said Hussein al-Shazli [Shazly] to go to Deversoir to handle the

counterattack on the spot. It wouldn't have been difficult on that day to deal with the infiltrating forces; it was a race against time. If he had carried out the orders that both Marshal Ali and I had given him, and at the times fixed by me — to besiege the area around the Bitter Lake and so stop the advance of the trickle of men that had already crossed and confine them to the narrow strip they had captured — it would have been easy to destroy them." Herzog, *War of Atonement*, pp. 231–34, concurs.

91. Sadat, *In Search of Identity*, p. 258.
92. *FBIS-MEA*, September 16, 1975, p. D6.
93. Galia Golan, *Yom Kippur and After*, pp. 106–7.
94. Even having decided to accept a cease-fire, Sadat informed his chief of staff that "we will not withdraw a single soldier from the east to the west," a decision which the chief of staff saw as "a combination of madness, ignorance and treason." Shazly, *Crossing of the Suez*, p. 266. Shazly says he wanted to transfer four armored brigades back to the west bank to deal with the large force Israel then had there, which still would have left ample forces to hold the east bank. Sadat, *In Search of Identity*, pp. 261–62, is vague, probably deliberately, on the precise chronology of his cease-fire decision. In one place he says his decision was made "at 1:30 a.m. on October 19" and in another that it was made at "midnight on October 19/ 20," two times roughly twenty-four hours apart. In a later speech (see *FBIS-MEA*, September 16, 1975, p. D8), he says "the 19th at 0200." The 0130–0200 timeframe on the nineteenth is undoubtedly correct.
95. Reinforcing this view is Heikal's claim, *Road to Ramadan*, p. 252, that Kosygin showed Sadat satellite photographs on the eighteenth which depicted Israel's position on the west bank, including some 270 tanks and armored vehicles. Sadat, *In Search of Identity*, p. 260, claims to the contrary that "we received nothing at all from the Soviet satellite. . . ."
96. Sadat, *In Search of Identity*, pp. 262–63.
97. Kissinger, *Years of Upheaval*, p. 542.
98. Ibid., p. 544.
99. For the deception charge, see Matti Golan, *Secret Conversations*, pp. 77f. For Kissinger's views, see *Years of Upheaval*, pp. 546f.
100. Ibid., p. 554.
101. Ibid., p. 555.
102. Matti Golan, *Secret Conversations*, p. 86.
103. Ibid.
104. Kissinger, *Years of Upheaval*, p. 569. It is doubtful that he took so benign a view at the time.
105. Ibid. p. 599, and Sadat, *In Search of Identity*, p. 266. Heikal, *Road to Ramadan*, p. 257, on the other hand, asserts that Sadat never suggested that the Soviets "should move their forces into the area. The only demand ever made or contemplated was that Russians and Americans should come to observe."
106. Kissinger, *Years of Upheaval*, p. 583.
107. Ibid., p. 584.
108. Ibid. It was a credible threat.
109. Sadat, *In Search of Identity*, p. 265.
110. "How Israel Got the Bomb," *Time*, April 12, 1976, p. 39.

111. Ibid.
112. This hypothesis gains substantial indirect support from Kissinger himself. In what otherwise is an exhaustive treatment of the "reasons" for the alert, Kissinger fails even to mention the facts—already revealed at the time he wrote—of Egyptian SCUDs, the detection of the shipment of Soviet nuclear materials, or Israeli nuclear weapons. See *Years of Upheaval*, pp. 575–91. If the alert was indeed to forestall deterioration of the conflict, then Washington's move was in no way the excessive overreaction it was charged.
113. Ibid., p. 597.
114. Ibid., pp. 588, 592.
115. Ibid., p. 608.
116. Ibid. (emphasis supplied).
117. Glassman, *Arms for the Arabs*, pp. 164–65.

Chapter Eight

1. See *New York Times*, January 19, 1974, for text.
2. Kissinger, *Years of Upheaval*, p. 747.
3. Ibid., p. 615.
4. Speech by Prime Minister Meir to the Knesset after the signing of the first disengagement agreement, as quoted in Gershon R. Kieval, *Party Politics in Israel and the Occupied Territories* (Westport, Conn.: Greenwood Press, 1983), p. 104.
5. Kissinger, *White House Years*, p. 1281.
6. Kissinger's memorandum for the president of December 19, 1973, makes these points explicitly. See *Years of Upheaval*, pp. 1249–50, n.5.
7. *New York Times*, January 19, 1974.
8. Kissinger, *Years of Upheaval*, p. 940–41.
9. Ibid., p. 1035.
10. Ibid.
11. Rabin, *Memoirs*, p. 122.
12. Golan, *Secret Conversations*, pp. 185–87.
13. Kieval, *Party Politics in Israel*, p. 109.
14. Golan, *Secret Conversations*, p. 218.
15. Ibid., pp. 217–18.
16. See Kissinger, *Years of Upheaval*, pp. 1253–54 for the text of the agreement and p. 1100 for the map.
17. Ibid., p. 1138.
18. Ibid., p. 1139.
19. Nadov Safron, *Israel, Embattled Ally* (Cambridge: Belknap Press of Harvard University, 1978) p. 535.
20. Kissinger, *Years of Upheaval*, p. 1139.
21. Ibid.
22. Golan, *Secret Conversations*, p. 218.
23. Ibid.

24. Kissinger, *Years of Upheaval*, p. 1139.
25. Ibid.
26. Ibid.
27. Rabin, *Memoirs*, pp. 240–41.
28. Kissinger, *Years of Upheaval*, p. 1141.
29. Golan, *Secret Conversations*, p. 218.
30. Kissinger, *Years of Upheaval*, p. 1141. The author defended his position in the following terms: "Simply to get Israel into a conference room with a group that had sworn its destruction and conducted a decade–long terrorist campaign against it would be a monumental assignment, consuming energy, emotion and enormous amounts of time during which all future progress would be frozen. I did not think it was achievable without demonstrating to Israel brutally and irrevocably its total dependence on American support. In my view, this would break Israel's back psychologically and destroy the essence of the state. . . . And even if my judgment was wrong and a psychologically undamaged Israel could be brought into the conference room with the PLO, it would be the beginning of a negotiating nightmare, not the end of it" (pp. 1138–39).
31. See the testimony of Joseph Sisco to the House Foreign Affairs Committee, cited in Golan, *Secret Conversations*, p. 219.
32. Ibid., p. 220.
33. *FBIS-MEA, Daily Report*, December 4, 1974, pp. N 1–4.
34. Any other interpretation must conclude that Rabin was either stupid or foolish, and he was neither of these, although he was outspoken and blunt. See Golan, *Secret Conversations*, p. 229.
35. *FBIS-MEA*, December 4, 1974.
36. Golan, *Secret Conversations*, pp. 229–31.
37. Ibid.
38. Lester A. Sobel, *Peace-Making in the Middle East* (New York: Facts on File, 1980), p. 82.
39. Ibid., p. 87.
40. Ibid.
41. Golan, *Secret Conversations*, p. 232.
42. Ibid., p. 233.
43. Sobel, *Peace-Making in the Middle East*, p. 83.
44. Ibid. (my emphasis).
45. Safron, *Israel, Embattled Ally*, p. 544. Golan, *Secret Conversations*, p. 235, curiously, omits substantive discussion of the terms of the proposed agreement.
46. Safron, *Israel, Embattled Ally*, p. 545.
47. Golan describes the "icy confrontation" between them, *Secret Conversations*, pp. 236ff. Rabin termed it "the most painful conversation we had ever had," *Memoirs*, p. 256.
48. Rabin personally accused Kissinger of "wording" the message, Golan, *Secret Conversations*, p. 237; Safron, *Israel, Embattled Ally*, p. 545, also strongly suggests it.
49. Rabin, *Memoirs*, p. 256.
50. Ibid., p. 255.
51. Safron, *Israel, Embattled Ally*, p. 546.

52. Ibid., p. 552.

53. Ibid., p. 550.

54. Sobel, *Peace-Making in the Middle East*, p. 66.

55. Safron, *Israel, Embattled Ally*, pp. 558–59.

56. See Ibid, pp. 554–57, for an extended discussion of the terms.

57. The initial wording of this clause, that "in case of involvement of a foreign power there would be active counter involvement by the United States," was weakened. The term "active counter involvement" was changed to "consultation." See Golan, *Secret Conversations*, pp. 248–49.

58. Cyrus Vance, *Hard Choices* (New York: Simon and Schuster, 1983), pp. 162–63.

59. It is, of course, not necessary to assume as the author does that Washington deliberately brought about the energy crisis to perceive United States use of it.

60. On the monetary situation, see Peter Ludlow, *The Making of the European Monetary System* (London: Butterworth Scientific, 1982), pp. 3f; on the energy question, see Werner J. Feld, "West European Foreign Policies Toward the Middle East: Responses to the Oil Crisis," in U.S. Congress, Joint Economic Committee, *The Political Economy of the Middle East: 1973–1978*, Washington, D.C., April 21, 1980, pp. 404–5.

61. Seymour, *OPEC, Instrument of Change*, p. 113.

62. These are Saudi Arabia, Kuwait, Iraq, Libya, Algeria, Egypt, Syria, Abu Dhabi, Bahrain, and Qatar.

63. Seymour, *OPEC, Instrument of Change*, pp. 117–18.

64. Blair, *Control of Oil*, pp. 275, 266–68.

65. Sampson, *Seven Sisters*, p. 257.

66. Seymour, *OPEC, Instrument of Change*, p. 124.

67. Ibid.

68. Especially in Europe; see, for example, the book by French economist Jean-Marie Chevalier, *The New Oil Stakes*, English edition (Middlesex: Penguin Books, 1975), p. 49.

69. See Kissinger, *Years of Upheaval*, pp. 888–89. Both Seymour, *OPEC, Instrument of Change*, p. 124, and Sampson, *Seven Sisters*, p. 258, describe the Saudi-Iranian split.

70. Kissinger, *Years of Upheaval*, p. 888.

71. See the informative essay by John Duke Anthony, "The Gulf States and Iraq," in *The Political Economy of the Middle East: 1973–1978*, pp. 224–29.

72. Kissinger, *Years of Upheaval*, pp. 871–95.

73. In all of the "participation" negotiations, it had been the strategy of the oil companies to bargain for long-term access to supply in return for transferring ownership of in-country operations. See MNC Report, pp. 135–40.

74. As late as 1968 Nigeria had produced a mere 141,000 barrels per day, but by 1970 was producing slightly over a million barrels per day. Daily production in 1971 was 1.5 million b/d and in 1972 reached 1.8 million b/d, see Seymour, *OPEC, Instrument of Change*, p. 275, and for annual production charts for all OPEC nations, pp. 267–79.

75. Ibid., pp. 278.

76. Gisselquist, *Oil Prices and Trade Deficits*, p. 93.

77. Kissinger, *Years of Upheaval*, p. 921.

78. Between 1974 and 1978 the average OPEC price for oil rose from $10.78 to $12.70, or an increase of $1.92 over the five-year period and an average increase of thirty-eight cents per year. By way of comparison, the price of Saudi Arabian Light crude between January 1, 1970 and October 4, 1973 rose from $1.39 to $3.01, an increase of $1.62 for the four-year period and an average yearly increase of forty cents. For the OPEC figures, see Seymour, *OPEC, Instrument of Change*, p. 177. When the effect of inflation is calculated, the real price of oil during the 1974–1978 period actually decreased.

79. Kissinger, *Years of Upheaval*, p. 903.

80. Ludlow, *The Making of the European Monetary System*, pp. 3–12.

81. Robert Lieber, *Oil and the Middle East War—Europe and the Energy Crisis* (Cambridge, Mass: Harvard University Press, 1976), p. 14.

82. Kissinger, *Years of Upheaval*, pp. 901–2.

83. This was the course on which Japan was determinedly embarked, but the problem was overwhelming. At this point in time 78 percent of Japan's oil came from the Middle East and 19 percent from Southeast Asia. Some 85 percent of Japan's oil was provided by non-Japanese, mostly American oil companies, which controlled roughly half of the nation's refining capacity. See Michael Morrow, "Oil: Catalyst for the Region," *Far Eastern Economic Review*, December 27, 1974, pp. 26–28.

84. Kissinger, *Years of Upheaval*, p. 905.

85. See Ed Shaffer, *The United States and the Control of World Oil* (New York: St. Martin's Press, 1983), pp. 176–79.

86. Seymour, *OPEC, Instrument of Change*, p. 131.

87. Ibid.

88. Ibid., pp. 295–96; Yamani interview in *Events*, January 14, 1977.

89. "Kissinger on Oil, Food and Trade," *Business Week*, January 13, 1975, p. 67.

90. Solomon, *International Monetary System*, p. 307.

91. For an insightful analysis of the ways in which the federal government kept domestic oil off the market by blocking access to lands in which major oil discoveries had occurred in the late sixties, in Alaska and the Santa Ynez unit off the California coast, see Milton R. Copulos, *Domestic Oil, The Hidden Solution* (Washington, D.C.: The Heritage Foundation, 1980).

92. Seymour, *OPEC, Instrument of Change*, pp. 133–34.

93. Shaffer, *Control of World Oil*, p. 182.

94. Ibid., pp. 183f. Even with higher oil prices, the United States undertook no substantial development of alternative energy sources.

95. "What we are witnessing today in the field of international economic relations—in the monetary field and now in the field of oil and raw material prices—is . . . a struggle for the world product," Helmut Schmidt, "The Struggle for the World Product," in William Bundy, ed., *The World Economic Crisis* (New York: W. W. Norton and Co., 1975), p. 110.

96. Gisselquist, *Oil Prices and Trade Deficits*, p. 95.

97. Richard J. Barnet, *The Alliance* (New York: Simon and Schuster, 1983), p. 335.

98. International Monetary Fund, *International Financial Statistics, Yearbook 1984*, Washington, D.C., 1985, p. 287. The appreciation rate was even, except for 1975: DM2.40 in 1974, DM2.62 in 1975, DM2.36 in 1976, DM2.10 in 1977, and DM1.82 in 1978.

99. For an excellent analysis of Bonn's domestic policy during the crisis, see the Joint Economic Committee staff study, *Monetary Policy, Selective Credit Policy, and Industrial Policy in France, Britain, West Germany, and Sweden*, June 26, 1981 (Washington, D.C.: Government Printing Office, 1981), pp. 131ff.
100. International Monetary Fund, *Direction of Trade Yearbook, 1979*, Washington, D.C., 1980, p. 131.
101. IMF, *International Financial Statistics Yearbook, 1984*, p. 287.
102. Ibid., p. 363.
103. C. Fred Bergsten, in "What to do about the U.S.-Japan Economic Conflict," *Foreign Affairs*, Summer 1982, p. 1066, supports the thesis of Japanese management of the yen/ dollar exchange rate, but argues incorrectly that the period 1976–1978 saw a "renewed *undervaluation* of the yen . . ." (my emphasis). Richard Cooper, under secretary for economic affairs, noted correctly that the "yen *increased* in value during this period." (my emphasis). See "Flexible Exchange Rates After 6 Years' Experience," a speech delivered before the World Affairs Council of Philadelphia, October 31, 1979. U.S. Department of State, *Current Policy*, no. 114 (Washington, D.C., November 1979), p. 2.
104. Trade figures are taken from IMF, *Direction of Trade, 1984*, p. 170.
105. "Flexible Exchange Rates After 6 Years' Experience" (my emphasis).

Chapter Nine

1. Selection of this particular course of action could hardly be explained by ignorance. As recently as July 1971, the Williams Commission, dealing with the broad question of United States international economic policy, made the congressional role in trade negotiations clear. "The U.S.Congress has the constitutional responsibility for regulating trade. It delegates the administration of this responsibility to the Executive, which has the constitutional responsibility for negotiations with foreign governments." John P. Hardt, "United States-Soviet Trade Policy," in U.S. Congress, Joint Economic Committee, *Issues in East-West Commercial Relations*, January 12, 1979 (Washington, D.C.: Government Printing Office, 1979), pp. 272–73.
2. See Paula Stern, *Water's Edge, Domestic Politics and the Making of American Foreign Policy* (Westport Conn.: Greenwood Press, 1979) for a detailed account of the legislative history of the Jackson-Vanick amendment, 1972–74, and its impact on American-Soviet economic relations.
3. For the commercial data, see Ronda A. Bresnick, "Chronology on East-West Relations," in *Issues in East-West Commercial Relations*, pp. 297–305.
4. Hardt, "United States-Soviet Trade Policy," p. 272.
5. For a brief but lucid description of what some have called the great grain robbery, see John P. Hardt and George D. Holliday, *U.S.-Soviet Commercial Relations: The Interplay of Economics, Technology Transfer, and Diplomacy*, House Committee on Foreign Affairs, June 10, 1973 (Washington, D.C.: Government Printing Office, 1973), pp. 66–69.
6. Hardt, "United States-Soviet Trade Policy," p. 273.

7. The text of the agreements can be found in Hardt and Holliday, *United States-Soviet Commercial Relations*, appendixes 2,3,4, pp. 83–99.

8. Soviet negotiators agreed to three unconditional payments of $48 million, the remainder to be paid after most-favored-nation status was granted.

9. See Bresnick, "Chronology on East-West Relations."

10. These are the views of, respectively, Stern, *Water's Edge*, p. 103 and Hardt, "United States-Soviet Trade Policy," pp. 273–74.

11. *Congressional Record*, June 19,1972, pp. S9599–9600.

12. In *Years of Upheaval*, p. 987, Kissinger says that Jackson ". . . did not want a compromise."

13. Stern, *Water's Edge*, p. 46. Incidentally, had the trade agreement been signed in June 1972, Jackson planned to restrict American-Soviet trade by conditioning it upon a lend-lease settlement, a much weaker strategem. See pp. 19–21.

14. Ibid., p. 42.

15. Ibid., pp. 60–61.

16. There is also the elementary point that if the United States-Soviet trade agreement were separated from the trade bill, even if the trade agreement were rejected the trade bill would allow trade and credits to be extended to other East bloc countries. A substantial portion of the technology and credit extended to Moscow's satellites undoubtedly would have found its way to the Soviet Union. In short, what would have been denied by closing the front door would have been given through the back door.

17. Stern, *Water's Edge*, p. 208–9.

18. Hardt, "United States-Soviet Trade Policy," p. 275 makes the same point in a different way, saying: "During 1972–1973 there were many opportunities for the Nixon administration to modify, withdraw or lobby for the new legislation working its way through Congress for decision in 1974, [but] no effective action was taken by the Executive." Hardt cites three occasions where action could have been taken: in February 1974 when the Jackson-Vanick amendment came up, the administration could have dropped the MFN section; when debate arose over the North Star and Yakutia projects, the Ex-Im Bank amendment could have been modified or dropped; finally, the administration could have taken the initiative in shaping export licensing policy but delayed taking action until it was too late.

19. Stern, *Water's Edge*, p. 117.

20. Kissinger, *Years of Upheaval*, p. 996.

21. Stern, *Water's Edge*, p. 115. It was no wonder that some in Congress were thoroughly confused, tending to echo the understandable but erroneous view of Representative Barber Conable: "The President and Mr. Kissinger may not have kept track of what was going on here. They did not realize that MFN was being opposed not just by the American Jewish community, but by a very impressive coalition" in Congress.

22. Ibid., p. 186.

23. Ibid., p. 49.

24. Ibid., p. 209.

25. Kissinger, *Years of Upheaval*, p. 252.

26. Ibid., pp. 992–97.

27. Stern, *Water's Edge*, p. 103.
28. Stern's evaluation is that "by limiting his contacts, Dobrynin also limited his understanding of the situation, since Kissinger obviously misapprehended the mood of Congress. This was particularly damaging to Soviet interests in 1973 when the threat of Jackson's amendment was vastly underestimated. In 1974, it may have contributed to Soviet miscalculations based on ignorance of developments of other events in Congress. This observation also applies to the Soviet misreading of the Export-Import Bank Bill, which enormously complicated the 1974 negotiations on the Jackson amendment." *Water's Edge*, p. 209.
29. For discussion of the basic stages of ICBM development, see chapter 1.
30. See "unilateral statement" number two of the Interim Agreement, which states: "If an agreement providing for more complete strategic offensive arms limitations were not achieved within five years, U.S. supreme interests could be jeopardized. Should that occur, it would constitute a basis for withdrawal from the ABM Treaty." For the agreement and accompanying protocols, agreed interpretations, common understandings, and unilateral statements, see Smith, *Doubletalk*, pp. 512f.
31. Kissinger, *Years of Upheaval*, p270.
32. Ibid.
33. Secretary of Defense Melvin R. Laird, in delivering his annual report to Congress, stated that "the Soviets may be preparing to deploy two new or modified ICBM systems." *Annual Defense Department Report, FY1973*, February 15, 1972 (Washington, D.C.: Government Printing Office, 1972), p. 39.
34. James R. Schlesinger, *Report of the Secretary of Defense, FY1976*, February 5, 1975, (Washington D.C.: Government Printing Office, 1975), pp. 11–12.
35. Garthoff, *Detente and Confrontation*, p. 328, n.24. Garthoff, a member of the negotiating team, acrimoniously notes that: "In fact, it was decided so hastily that only an incomplete proposal was approved . . . before Kissinger's departure. . . . This haste required the American delegation in Geneva, which was not fully informed, to withhold its presentation. It finally presented the position piecemeal on May 8, 11 and 15 — after Kissinger had raised the new proposal in Moscow."
36. Kissinger, *Years of Upheaval*, pp. 271, 1012.
37. See Ibid., pp. 1016–17.
38. Ibid., p. 271.
39. The SS-16 would be reconfigured and emerge as the intermediate-range SS-20, presenting as serious a threat to Europe as the new ICBMs did to the United States.
40. Ibid., p. 273.
41. Ibid., p. 1014.
42. While it was worth trying to ban MIRVs before Moscow began testing them, it became increasingly unrealistic to demand their proscription once Soviet testing was well under way. To insist upon a MIRV ban in the spring of 1974 was indeed "fairy-tale diplomacy."
43. Ibid., p. 1018.
44. Garthoff, *Detente and Confrontation*, pp. 417–19. Kissinger not so unaccountably omits mention of NSDM 242 as well as the decision it represented. See Kissinger, *Years of Upheaval*, pp. 1016–18.

45. Garthoff, *Detente and Confrontation*, pp. 418–19.

46. Kissinger, *Years of Upheaval*, p. 1018.

47. Ibid., p. 1019.

48. Garthoff, *Detente and Confrontation*, p. 420, believes that Dobrynin ". . . inadvertently gave a misleading signal on Soviet reactions to American SALT proposals," but it is doubtful that there was anything "inadvertent" about Dobrynin's action here.

49. Kissinger, *Years of Upheaval*, p. 1019.

50. Ibid., p. 1023.

51. Ibid., pp. 1023–24, 1153.

52. Ibid., pp. 1024–25.

53. Ibid., pp. 1153–54.

54. Ibid., p. 1022.

55. Ibid., p. 1025.

56. Ibid., p. 1026. The secretary termed the hostile reaction to his proposal "astonishing."

57. Paul Nitze made this exact point in a letter to the president at the same time. Ibid., p. 1155. Thomas Wolfe suggests that a "possible" internal debate was taking place in Moscow for and against detente and implies that Kissinger may have been attempting to influence it with his generous MIRV offer. If so, it had no discernible effect upon the Soviet negotiating position. See Thomas W. Wolfe, *The SALT Experience* (Cambridge, Mass.: Ballinger Books, 1979), pp. 166–68.

58. Kissinger, *Years of Upheaval*, pp. 1028, 1155.

59. Ibid., p. 1025; Nixon, *Memoirs*, p. 1035.

60. Nixon, *Memoirs*, p. 1032.

61. Ibid., p. 1035

62. Kissinger, *Years of Upheaval*, p. 1166. He adds in an evident attempt to evade responsibility, "In retrospect it is less clear to me than it seemed then, as I went along with the consensus, why protection of the missile fields would not have added to strategic stability especially after the MIRV threat emerged."

63. Ibid., p. 1175.

64. Ibid., pp. 1165–66.

65. Ibid., p. 1172.

66. Nixon, *Memoirs*, p. 1034. Brezhnev initially suggested Switzerland.

67. See chapter 5 above.

68. Kissinger, *Years of Upheaval*, p. 52.

69. Ibid., p. 55.

70. Ibid., p. 62.

71. Ibid., p. 57.

72. Ibid., p. 67.

73. Kissinger, *Years of Upheaval*, p. 302.

74. Ibid., p. 343 (my emphasis).

75. Snepp, *Decent Interval*. Despite the title, which suggests a pullout, the author's view is the opposite. Moreover, he confuses Nixon's strategy with Kissinger's. Snepp's view: "The essence of his [Kissinger's] 'postwar' strategy was equilibrium. A rough parity, economic and military, he felt, must be established between the

North and the South so that neither could impose a military solution on the other, and each would have an incentive to settle remaining differences peacefully. . . . This was the vision behind Kissinger's strategy: equilibrium leading to stalemate and finally to a live-and-let-live attitude on both sides." pp. 50–51.

76. Kissinger, *Years of Upheaval*, p. 70.
77. See Henry Bradsher, "China Policy Row Portends Political Trouble," *Washington Evening Star*, June 20, 1973.
78. *Mainichi Daily News*, January 17, 1973, p. 1.
79. For the Soviet reaction, see the front pages of the March 8, 9, and 10, 1973, editions of *Pravda*,
80. Kissinger, *Years of Upheaval*, p. 233.
81. Except for a session on the Middle East that followed late that same evening. See chapter 5.
82. Kissinger, *Years of Upheaval*, pp. 294–95.
83. See Thornton, *China: A Political History*, pp. 365, 488, n.8.
84. Ibid., p. 364.
85. Ibid., pp. 364–65.
86. See C.L. Sulzberger, "China Condemns USSR on Border Problems," *Asahi Evening News*, October 31, 1973, p. 2.
87. Thornton, *China: A Political History*, p. 369.
88. U.S. Army, Assistant Chief of Staff for Intelligence, *Chinese Amphibious Assault in the Paracel Archipelago*, No. SRD SR 44 72 (Washington, D.C.: Government Printing Office, 1974), p. 15.
89. See the early but useful account by Jay H. Long, "The Paracels Incident: Implications for Chinese Policy," *Asian Affairs*, April–March 1974, pp. 229–39.
90. Ibid.
91. Kissinger, *Years of Upheaval*, p. 343.
92. *International Herald Tribune*, July 11, 1975.
93. Kissinger, *Years of Upheaval*, p. 692.
94. Ibid.
95. Ibid., p. 698.
96. Ibid., pp. 678f.
97. U.S. Department of Commerce, Bureau of East-West Trade.
98. See Thornton, *China: Political History*, pp. 386–410.

Chapter Ten

1. See chapter 8.
2. The Vladivostok accord postulated equal but very high ceilings for both countries, 2,400 strategic launchers. Within that figure could be as many as 1,320 MIRVed launchers, but no more than 308 heavy MIRVed missiles. There were no limits on throwweight or on modernization of existing forces, but no new silos could be built. See the author's article, with William H. Lewis, "Arms Control and Heavy Missiles," *Naval War College Review*, January–February 1984, p. 99. For a fuller discussion, see Wolfe, *SALT Experience*, chapter 9.

3. See chapter 9 above.

4. Nor was Kissinger's Mideast policy faring well. United States–Israeli relations began to nosedive in the wake of Golda Meir's resignation on April 11, and attempts to reach a settlement on the Golan Heights seemed futile as Moscow and Syria announced a major arms deal on the sixteenth. See Chapter 8.

5. John A. Marcum, "Lessons of Angola," *Foreign Affairs* 54 (April 1976), p. 408.

6. Just prior to the coup he had published a book, *Portugal and the Future*, which was highly critical of Lisbon's colonial policy and offered federation as an alternative. See *New York Times*, March 16, 1974.

7. John A. Marcum, *The Angolan Revolution, Volume II: Exile Politics and Guerrilla Warfare (1962–1976)* (Cambridge: MIT Press, 1978), pp. 245–46.

8. One author, in a rough calculation of Soviet aid to the Third World, estimated that Soviet assistance to all of sub-Saharan Africa was less than $200 million for the *decade* 1965–1974, itself a cut of more than 50 percent over the previous decade. See David E. Albright, "Moscow's African Policy of the 1970s," in David E. Albright, ed., *Communism in Africa* (Bloomington: Indiana University Press, 1980), p. 42.

9. While all sources agree that Moscow had cut off aid to the MPLA prior to the Portuguese coup, the dates for aid suspension vary. Legum, in Colin Legum and Tony Hodges, *After Angola, The War over Southern Africa* (New York: Africana Publishing Company, 1976), p. 11, says that Moscow suspended aid to Neto in "1972 and 1973"; Charles K. Ebinger, in "External Intervention in Internal War: The Politics and Diplomacy of the Angolan Civil War," *Orbis*, Fall 1976, p. 688, says "in 1973"; and Marcum, in *Angolan Revolution*, quotes Legum in one place, p. 201, and in another cites interviews with State Department officials to offer "early 1974," following a visit to Luanda by Soviet agent Victor Louis, p. 221 and p. 413n.308. See also the interview by Neto in *Le Monde* (February 5, 1975) on the state of MPLA disarray in early 1974.

10. Mohamed A. El-Khawas and Barry Cohen, eds., *The Kissinger Study of Southern Africa* (Westport: Lawrence Hill and Company, 1976), p. 129.

11. Roger Morris, "The Proxy War in Angola: Pathology of a Blunder," *The New Republic*, January 31, 1976, p. 20. Arthur Jay Klinghoffer, *The Angolan War: A Study in Soviet Policy in the Third World* (Boulder: Westview Press, 1980), p. 82, also citing Morris, a former NSC staffer, asserts that Roberto was not entirely cut off but was reduced to an "intelligence source," receiving $10,000 per year from 1970.

12. *International Herald Tribune*, June 3, 1974. See also Marcum, *Angolan Revolution*, p. 245–46.

13. John Stockwell, *In Search of Enemies, A CIA Story* (New York: W.W. Norton and Co., 1978), p. 67. Stockwell notes that the funding was resumed "without 40 Committee approval." The Forty Committee was a subcommittee of the National Security Council, so named presumably because its membership consisted of four principals: Kissinger, CIA chief William Colby, JCS Chairman George S. Brown, and Deputy Secretary of Defense William Clements. The phrase "without 40 Committee approval" could only mean direct instructions from Kissinger to Colby bypassing the Forty Committee even though it was the official authorizing body for covert operations.

14. Roberto was married to Mobutu's sister-in-law.
15. Stockwell, *In Search of Enemies*, p. 67.
16. Ibid.
17. Marcum, *Angolan Revolution*, p. 246.
18. Stockwell, *In Search of Enemies*, p. 67.
19. Stockwell notes that "the Chinese had publicly announced their FNLA advisor program and we knew they were at Kinkuza, Zaire, but Roberto wouldn't talk to the CIA about them," ibid., p. 64. Later, Kissinger acknowledged that American involvement "was not coordinated with the Chinese. It was not discussed with the Chinese. It was done for our own reasons." See his news conference of December 23, 1975, U.S. Department of State *Bulletin*, no. 1908, January 19, 1976, p. 76.
20. It is doubtful that the Soviets were responding solely to Beijing's move, for although Chinese supplies arrived in early September, the announcement of the plan to build a 15,000-man FNLA army had been made the previous December, and advisers began arriving at the end of May. Thus, there was ample time for Moscow to have prepared a countermove, yet, as noted, through the first half of the year Moscow-MPLA relations were not the best as the Soviets explored alternatives to Neto, one of which was Chipenda.
21. It was only on April 15, 1981, that this information was released pursuant to successful suit by the ACLU against the Department of State. It reveals that Kissinger had agreed with Brezhnev that the proposed agreement "would exclude the Backfires," which "would be in a completely different category." For a fuller discussion of the issue, see Garthoff, *Detente and Confrontation*, p. 448.
22. Ibid.
23. Ibid., p. 446.
24. *New York Times*, August 11, 1974.
25. Marcum, *Angolan Revolution*, p. 246.
26. Ebinger, "External Intervention," pp. 686–87.
27. Marcum, *Angolan Revolution*, p. 255.
28. *FBIS-SU*, "Obstacles to Angolan Unity Will Be Swept Away," January 27, 1975.
29. According to Portuguese military estimates cited by Marcum, *Angolan Revolution*, p. 257, respective troop levels were: FNLA, 21,750; MPLA, 5,500; UNITA, 3,000; and Chipenda, 2,750.
30. Morris, "Proxy War," p. 21, noting that Kissinger's avid support for the FNLA was "rather to the surprise of agency officials whose recommendations for covert funding had been frequently shunted aside in the last half of 1974," makes clear that this was Kissinger's own closely held operation and that other members of the committee, except for Colby, as well as top "agency officials," were unaware of it.
31. See Gerald Bender, "Kissinger in Angola: Anatomy of Failure," in Rene Lemarchand, ed., *American Policy in Southern Africa* (Washington, D.C.: University Press of America, 1978), p. 77, who notes that "the combination of American and Chinese aid . . . was a clear signal to the Soviet Union that if they failed to escalate their support to the MPLA, Holden Roberto might possibly . . . crush the MPLA."

32. Victor Zorza, "Clues to Kissinger's Peking Failure," *Washington Post*, December 5, 1974, p. A27.

33. Kissinger, *Years of Upheaval*, p. 696.

34. The fact was that nothing would come of Beijing's trial balloon, but this could not be assumed at the time.

35. Morris, "Proxy War," p. 21. The reopening of the CIA station in Luanda in March also drew Moscow's attention, Stockwell, *In Search of Enemies*, p. 52.

36. Kenneth L. Adelman, "Report from Angola," *Foreign Affairs*, April 1975, p. 568.

37. Morris, "Proxy War," p. 21.

38. Bender, "Kissinger in Angola," pp. 80, 123.

39. Tony Hodges, "How the MPLA Won in Angola," in Legum and Hodges, *After Angola, The War over Southern Africa*, p. 50. Stockwell, *In Search of Enemies*, agreeing with Hodges account, concludes that with the Caxito massacre "the fate of Angola was . . . sealed in blood," p. 68.

40. Ebinger, "External Intervention," pp. 687–88, makes this argument, while failing to bring in Washington's funding decisions of 1974 and early 1975.

41. Stockwell, *In Search of Enemies*, p. 68.

42. See Jiri Valenta, "Soviet Decision-Making on the Intervention in Angola," in Albright, ed., *Communism in Africa*, p. 100.

43. Gabriel Garcia-Marquez, "Operation Carlota," *New Left Review*, February–April 1977, p. 124. Valenta, "Soviet Decision-Making," says 230 Cubans arrived, p. 101. Stockwell, *In Search of Enemies*, p. 170, says 260. William J. Durch, "The Cuban Military in Africa and the Middle East: From Algeria to Angola," Professional Paper No. 201, September 1977, Center for Naval Analysis, Arlington, Va., p. 42, says 230 Cubans arrived. Four training camps were established, at Henrique de Carvalho, Salazar, Benguela, and Cabinda.

44. Bender, "Kissinger in Angola," p. 107.

45. Marcum, *Angolan Revolution*, p. 265, citing Radio Lisbon of June 9 reporting on the visit of an MPLA delegation to Beijing.

46. The Chinese decision to disengage seems to have been a response to the Soviet arms buildup. Moreover, the decision to reverse policy appears to have been Deng's. As Zhou Enlai became progressively incapable of managing China's affairs, Deng Xiaoping's influence increased. By mid-1975 Deng was assuming day-to-day command of the premier's office, which would make the decision to disengage from Angola his. The evidence also strongly suggests that Mao opposed Deng's decision. See Thornton, *China: A Political History*, p. 377. Garthoff, *Detente and Confrontation*, pp. 514–15, asserts that the Chinese withdrew because they were "disillusioned by the very poor showing of the FNLA" and determined "not to be associated with the side collaborating with South Africa." The problem with this interpretation is that when the Chinese decided to withdraw, the FNLA had just lost the battlefield initiative, but it was not in any sense defeated. Indeed, the FNLA would mount a near-victorious drive in late October. Nor was there as yet any collaboration with South Africa. The probability of defeat and entanglement with Pretoria came sometime after the Chinese decision to withdraw. It seems highly unlikely that Beijing could have foretold either development in early June; therefore, neither factor seems likely to have been the reason for the decision to disengage.

47. Colin Legum, "Angola and the Horn of Africa," in Stephen S. Kaplan, *Diplomacy of Power, Soviet Armed Forces as a Political Instrument* (Washington: Brookings Institution, 1981), pp. 593–94.

48. The July 14 memorandum for the director of the CIA accompanying the Angola options paper stated explicitly that "large supplies of arms to Roberto and Savimbi would not guarantee [that] they could establish control of all Angola, but that assistance would permit them to achieve a military balance which would avoid a cheap Neto victory." Stockwell, *In Search of Enemies*, pp. 52–53.

49. Morris, "Proxy War," p. 22.

50. Ibid.

51. Nathaniel Davis, "The Angola Decision of 1975: A Personal Memoir," *Foreign Affairs*, Fall 1978, p. 111. Although it is unclear precisely when Davis was asked to chair the study, it had to be sometime in early June, shortly after the Forty Committee decided on it.

52. The Church Select Committee on Intelligence subsequently determined that Davis "never appeared to have actively engaged in covert efforts to subvert the elected government of Chile," Davis, "Angolan Decison," p. 109.

53. See Ibid., pp. 109–110.

54. Ibid, p. 112.

55. Stockwell, *In Search of Enemies*, p. 55.

56. Davis, "Angola Decision," pp. 113–14. Stockwell, *In Search of Enemies*, p. 54, incorrectly says the paper had been drafted on July 14. The executive summary which he quotes indicates that it had been drafted prior to July 9 when MPLA forces drove FNLA from the capital. The summary concluded that "Neto's forces appeared strong enough to take the Angolan capital. . . ."

57. Stockwell, *In Search of Enemies*, p. 54.

58. Davis, "Angola Decision," p. 113.

59. Ibid., p. 116.

60. Ibid.

61. Stockwell, *In Search of Enemies*, p. 55.

62. Davis, "Angola Decision," p. 116.

63. Ibid., p. 117. The ambassador resigned as soon as he learned of the decision to go forward with the plan.

64. Stockwell, *In Search of Enemies*, p. 55.

65. See ibid., pp. 72–78.

66. Morris, "Proxy War," pp. 22–23, in an otherwise valuable account, rather baldly attempts to shift responsibility for Angola away from his former chief, Kissinger, to the CIA by attributing the main part of the blame to "a government-wide system too prone to impulsive policies pursued for bureaucratic interests." His portrayal of Ambassador Davis as an incompetent, lone dissenter whose "advice was discredited with Kissinger and criticized by his own subordinates as lacking persuasive force," also suffers from a comparison with Davis' later account. Compare Davis.

67. Ebinger, "External Intervention," p. 689, could "hardly resist wondering whether the Chinese move was in any way coordinated with the U.S. covert-assistance program launched at the same time," but acknowledges that "there is no hard supportive evidence."

68. Stockwell, *In Search of Enemies*, pp. 58–59.
69. Ibid., pp. 162, 208.
70. Legum and Hodges, *After Angola*, pp. 36–37. Then–Defense Minister P. W. Botha dated South Africa's involvement in Angola from July 14, 1975, to January 23, 1976. Marcum, *Angolan Revolution*, p. 268, notes that both Chipenda and Savimbi had held substantive discussions with "South African officials" in May.
71. Ibid.
72. Stockwell, *In Search of Enemies*, p. 162.
73. The first public indication in the United States of any substantial foreign involvement came in a September 25, 1975, *New York Times* article by Leslie Gelb entitled "U.S., Soviet, China Reported Aiding Portugal, Angola."
74. Klinghoffer, *Angolan War*, p. 106, reasons that "the Soviet Union must have known that China was no longer supplying arms to Angolan movements and that it was not sending more military instructors. The actual threat from China was therefore not very great. . . . China could not have been a major factor in Soviet policy deliberations as it had basically withdrawn from the Angolan conflict."
75. For the general thrust of this campaign, see Radio Moscow, August 16, 1975, Tass reports of August 23 and 25, and *Pravda* and *Izvestia* of September 9.
76. Durch, "Cuban Military in Africa," p. 3, argues, on the contrary, that Cuba pursued policies in Africa in the sixties during the low point in Cuban-Soviet relations that were "essentially indistinguishable from its policies in the 1970's, a period of growing Cuban-Soviet cooperation."
77. See Durch, "Cuban Military in Africa," passim.
78. Ibid., pp. 43–45.
79. Garcia-Marquez, "Operation Carlota," p. 125.
80. Don Oberdorfer, "Cuban Intervention in Angola Intrigues World Capitals," *Washington Post*, February 18, 1976, p. A6.
81. Stockwell, *In Search of Enemies*, pp. 170, mentions no advisers. Marcum, *Angolan Revolution*, p. 273.
82. Michael Kaufman, "Angolans in Luanda Area Try to Regroup," *New York Times*, November 6, 1975, p. 37.
83. Stockwell, *In Search of Enemies*, p. 163–64.
84. Ibid., p. 164.
85. Legum, *After Angola*, p. 36, and Klinghoffer, *Angolan War*, p. 44.
86. Stockwell, *In Search of Enemies*, p. 170.
87. Ibid.
88. It must be emphasized that by Western standards none of the Angolan factions was skilled in the military arts, although the FNLA was generally considered to be the most warlike of the three.
89. Marcum, *Angolan Revolution*, p. 270.
90. South African Ministry of Defense press release, February 3, 1977, p. 3, as cited in Klinghoffer, *Angolan War*, p. 171.
91. Stockwell, *In Search of Enemies*, p. 165.
92. Michael Kaufman, "On Eve of Independence, Angola Faces More Strife," *New York Times*, November 10, 1975, p. 3.

93. Oleg Ignatyev, *Secret Weapon in Africa* (Moscow: Progress Publishers, 1977), p. 166. Ignatyev was assigned as a *Pravda* correspondent to Luanda during October and November 1975.

94. Ronda A. Bresnick and John P. Hardt, "Soviet Agriculture and the Grain Trade," in U.S. Congress, Joint Economic Committee, *Issues in East-West Commercial Relations* (Washington, D.C.: Government Printing Office, 1979), p. 237.

95. President Gerald Ford, speech to the American Farm Bureau Federation, January 5, 1976, Department of State *Bulletin*, no. 1909, January 20, 1976, p. 98.

96. Department of State *Bulletin*, no. 1901, December 1, 1975, p. 768.

97. Legum, "Angola and the Horn of Africa," p. 587. Kissinger repeatedly denied any "collusion" with South Africa and thus by definition any role in South African battlefield decisions. There appears to be little doubt, however, as CIA officials acknowledged, that the two countries "regularly" exchanged intelligence and that other channels of communication also existed. Indeed, both Defense Minister Botha and Prime Minister Forster asserted that the United States "requested" South African involvement, which is not to deny that Pretoria had its own reasons for taking action. See Klinghoffer, *Angolan War*, p. 44 and pp. 171–72, fn.22.

98. Garcia-Marquez, "Operation Carlota," p. 128.

99. Ibid.

100. Ibid. The *Brittannia*'s passenger capacity was about eighty, plus crew. Garcia-Marquez, p. 131, claims that when Washington arranged to deny refueling rights in Barbados and Guyana the Cuban government outfitted the *Brittannia* with four extra gas tanks strapped "to the aircraft cabin," which "made it possible to fly non-stop from Holguin to Brazzaville — albeit with thirty fewer passengers."

101. Stockwell, *In Search of Enemies*, pp. 213–14.

102. Ibid., p. 214.

103. Ibid., p. 217 and pp. 220–24. The last $7 million of the CIA contingency reserve was committed on November 27, partly for this effort.

104. Legum, "Angola and the Horn of Africa," p. 588, says November 17; Stockwell, *In Search of Enemies*, p. 215, November 14.

105. Klinghoffer, *Angolan War*, p. 44.

106. Garcia-Marquez, "Operation Carlota," p. 132. It would appear to be obvious that the conflict would have taken a different course had the northern pincer remained intact.

107. Ibid., p. 129.

108. U.S. Senate, Committee on Foreign Relations, Subcommittee on African Affairs, *Angola Hearings*, January 29, February 3, 4, and 6, 1976 (Washington, D.C.: Government Printing Office, 1976), p. 26. (Hereafter cited as Angola Hearings.) In his testimony, Kissinger stated: "I believe but will never be able to prove . . . that until the middle of December, the Soviet intervention was at the limit of what was sustainable by covert operations and that they would have to make in January the same decision I had already foreshadowed to the Church Committee; that is to say, whether they would put everything at risk by going into the sort of massive intervention that has now developed [or negotiate a settlement]."

109. Henry Kissinger, "Building an Enduring Foreign Policy," Department of State *Bulletin*, no. 1903, December 15,1975, p. 843. His words would ring with irony in early December when he himself revealed to the American public for the first time that the United States was deeply involved in Angola and thus fit this very description.

110. Ibid., p. 897.

111. Bernard Gwertzman, "Kissinger Puts Off His Visit to Soviet For Talks on Arms," *New York Times*, December 10, 1975, pp. 1, 12.

112. Stockwell, *In Search of Enemies*, p. 216. From Stockwell's viewpoint, these instructions reflected ". . . a thread of unreality, of wishful thinking. . . . The gap between Henry Kissinger's egotistical desire to win and the limits of his power in the real world became apparent."

113. David Binder, "Angola Reported Getting $50 Million in U.S. Arms," *New York Times*, December 12, 1975, p. 1.

114. David Binder, "Senate Schedules a Closed Session on Covert U.S. Role in Angola," *New York Times*, December 16, 1975, p. 2.

115. David Binder, "Administration and Legislators Differ Over Angola," *New York Times*, December 17, 1975, p. 4.

116. Ibid.

117. Angola Hearings, pp. 23–24.

118. *Congressional Quarterly Almanac–1975*, p. 873.

119. Seymour Hersh, "Early Angola Aid by U.S. Reported: Officials Say C.I.A. Received Approval to Give Funds Before Soviet Buildup," *New York Times*, December 19, 1975, p. 1.

120. David Binder, "Senate Votes to Cut Off Covert Aid for Angolans: Ford Predicts a 'Tragedy,'" *New York Times*, December 20, 1975, p. 1.

121. Bernard Gwertzman, "Kissinger Insists Stand on Angola Will Not Change," *New York Times*, December 24, 1975, p. 1.

122. Department of State *Bulletin*, no. 1908, January, 19, 1976, pp. 70–71.

123. Gulf Oil had suspended its drilling operations in Cabinda province in early November but was scheduled to pay royalties of $100 million and $102 million to the Luanda government on December 11 and January 15, respectively. To demonstrate his "firmness," yet provide "incentives for moderation," Kissinger prevailed upon Gulf to place $125 million into an escrow account on December 23, withholding the remainder until the political situation had been resolved. Stockwell, *In Search of Enemies*, p. 206.

124. Ibid., p. 76.

125. In his January testimony Kissinger, incredibly, attempted to place the blame on Congress for Soviet behavior. "Our diplomacy was effective so long as we maintained the leverage of a possible military balance. African determination to oppose Soviet and Cuban intervention was becoming more and more evident. On December 9, President Ford made a formal proposal to the Soviet Government through their Ambassador. Indeed, it appeared as if the Soviet Union had begun to take stock. They halted their airlift from December 9 until December 24. By mid-December we were hopeful that the OAU would provide a framework for eliminating the interference of outside powers by calling for an end to their intervention. At that point, the impact of our domestic debate

overwhelmed the possibilities of diplomacy. After the Senate vote to block any further aid to Angola, the Cubans more than doubled their forces and Soviet military aid was resumed on an even larger scale. The scope of Soviet-Cuban intervention increased drastically; the cooperativeness of Soviet diplomacy declined." Angola Hearings, p. 18.

126. Department of State *Bulletin*, no.1909, January 20, 1976, p. 98.
127. Ibid., pp. 101–2.
128. Jeremiah O'Leary, "Kissinger Expects Angola War's End Within a Month," *The Washington Star*, January 17, 1976, p. 1.
129. Department of State *Bulletin*, no. 1910, February 2, 1976, p. 128.
130. Klinghoffer, *Angolan War*, p. 91.
131. See Kissinger's news conference of February 12,1976, Department of State *Bulletin*, no. 1915, March 8, 1976, p. 285.

Index